S0-BQW-291

# LANGUAGE PROCESSING IN BILINGUALS:

## Psycholinguistic and Neuropsychological Perspectives

## NEUROPSYCHOLOGY AND NEUROLINGUISTICS

### Harry A. Whitaker, Series Editor

VAID:

Language Processing in Bilinguals:
Psycholinguistic and Neuropsychological
Perspectives

# LANGUAGE PROCESSING IN BILINGUALS:
# Psycholinguistic and Neuropsychological Perspectives


**Edited by**

JYOTSNA VAID
*The University of California, San Diego*



LEA LAWRENCE ERLBAUM ASSOCIATES, PUBLISHERS
1986 Hillsdale, New Jersey London

Lawrence Erlbaum Associates, Inc., Publishers
365 Broadway
Hillsdale, New Jersey 07642

**Library of Congress Cataloging-in-Publication Data**

Language processing in bilinguals.

(Neuropsychology and neurolinguistics)
Includes bibliographies and indexes.
1. Bilingualism. 2. Psycholinguistics. 3. Neurolinguistics. I. Vaid, Jyotsna. II. Series.
P115.L36 1986 404′.2 86-11541
ISBN 0-89859-674-2

Printed in the United States of America
10 9 8 7 6 5 4 3 2 1

# Contents

# Contributors

*The number in parentheses following each name refers to the page on which the author's contribution begins.*

**Martin Albert** (221), Aphasia Research Center, Veterans' Administration Medical Center, Boston, and Department of Neurology, Boston University

**Elizabeth A. Bates** (199), Department of Psychology and Center for Research in Language, University of California at San Diego.

**Prithika Chary** (183), Department of Neurology, Appollo Hospital, Madras.

**François Grosjean** (145), Department of Psychology, Northeastern University, Boston.

**Reiko Hasuike** (275), Department of Psychology, Princeton University

**Nancy Hatfield** (253), Experimental Education Unit, University of Washington, Seattle.

**Kirsten M. Hummel** (47), Department of Linguistics, McGill University, Montreal.

**Daisy Hung** (275), Department of Psychology, University of California, Riverside.

**Larry Juarez** (199), Department of Psychology, University of California at San Diego.

**Catherine Kettrick** (253), Department of Linguistics, University of Washington, Seattle.

**Kerry Kilborn** (199), Department of Psychology, University of California San Diego, La Jolla.

**Kim Kirsner** (21), Department of Psychology, University of Western Australia, Nedlands.

**Wallace E. Lambert** (65), Department of Psychology, McGill University, Montreal.

**Sandra Lozowick** (221), Aphasia Research Center, Veterans' Administration Medical Center, Boston.

**Edith Mägiste** (97), Department of Psychology, University of Uppsala.

**Miwa Nishimura** (123), Department of Linguistics, University of Pennsylvania, Philadelphia.

**Loraine Obler** (221), Department of Speech and Hearing Sciences, The Graduate School, City University of New York.

**Eta I. Schneiderman** (233), Department of Psychology, University of Ottawa.

**Norman Segalowitz** (3), Department of Psychology, Concordia University, Montreal.

**Carlos Soares** (145), Data General Corporation, Westboro, MA.

**Ovid Tzeng** (275), Department of Psychology, University of California at Riverside.

**Beverly B. Wulfeck** (199), Department of Psychology, University of California at San Diego.

# Foreword

For decades, bilingualism has resisted definition. There are about as many different characterizations of the phenomenon as there are books, articles, and dictionary entries on the subject. If bilingualism is defined as habitual, fluent, correct, and accent-free use of two languages, few individuals would qualify as bilinguals. A more viable approach may be to concede that people referred to as "bilingual" do not form a homogeneous population but are instead situated at different points on a multidimensional continuum that allows for differences in type as well as degree at each level of linguistic structure (phonetic, phonological, morphological, syntactic, lexical, semantic) and in each language skill (auditory, visual and gestural comprehension and production).

The psychological study of bilingualism encompasses a wide range of phenomena including the organization and representation of the grammar, the perception and production of language mixing, cerebral lateralization of language functions, and patterns of recovery of aphasic patients. In the present volume, Jyotsna Vaid has invited an international array of prominent and promising researchers in experimental psychology, linguistics, and neuropsychology to bring their expertise to bear on the critical issues that are raised by bilingual phenomena. For example, how do bilinguals manage to keep their languages separate while at other times switch effortlessly from one language to the other, even within a sentence? Do processes underlying reading differ across the two languages of the bilingual? What is the nature of the entries in the bilingual lexicon? Do bilinguals possess a single set of internal representations comparable to that in monolinguals or is the bilingual lexicon organized differentially by language? Is there a special role of the right cerebral hemisphere in language acquisition? What are the neuropsychological concomitants of signed versus spoken language processing, or of different forms of writing systems?

Each author in this volume works towards a solution to a puzzle that has many, many pieces. Each contribution sheds light from a different perspective and is a welcome step in the direction of a better understanding of a phenomenon as complex as bilingualism. As a state-of-the-art portrayal of critical issues surrounding language perception, production, organization, and representation in users of two or more languages, this collection provides an invaluable source of reflection for students and researchers in mainstream psycholinguistics, neurolinguistics, and clinical and experimental neuropsychology, as well those interested in bilingualism theory per se.

*Michel Paradis*
*McGill University*

# Preface

After having had a fairly marginal status in psychology for the better part of this century, the study of bilingual cognitive functioning has gradually come of age. Increased interest in bilingulism may reflect a growing recognition of the fact that, viewed globally, bi- or multilingualism is the rule rather than the exception (Grosjean, 1982).

Psycholinguistic and neuropsychological perspectives on bilingualism have developed more or less independently. Psycholinguistic approaches have their origin in studies conducted in the 1940s to 1960s on the relationship between bilingualism and intelligence or concept formation (Hakuta, 1986), in the debate over the existence of a switch mechanism, and in the literature on independent versus interdependent forms of bilingual language organization, and the influence of context of language acquisition on language functioning. Psycholinguistic research with bilinguals has in recent years shifted from these concerns to considerations of the nature of the bilingual lexicon, individual differences in cognitive functioning (see Djouider, 1986), visual word recognition, memory for bilingual discourse, and the acquisition (see Goodz, 1986), perception and production of mixed language.

Neuropsychological perspectives on bilingualism date back to early neurological writings about patterns of language impairment and recovery in bilingual or polyglot aphasics, and about the possibility of differential localization of language in the brain. These topics, together with studies of cerebral hemispheric specialization of language in brain-intact bilinguals, are still being studied in current research on the bilingual brain.

Since systematic, experimental investigations of both psycholinguistic and neuropsychological aspects of bilingualism are still fairly new, it may take some time before the two perspectives develop a common theoretical framework. Yet, as a few of the selections in the current volume indicate, some convergence is already taking place.

The aim of the present collection is to articulate current thinking about critical issues within the psychology of bilingualism, issues bearing on language perception, retention, organization, interaction, acquisition, and impairment in users of two or more languages. The contributors to this volume include psychologists, linguists and neurologists, all of whom share a longstanding interest in bilingualism, most having already published widely on the topic. Where recent texts (e.g., Grosjean, 1982) have introduced readers to the different facets of bilingualism, the present work is directed at those already somewhat acquainted with the field and interested in contributing to it or in reflecting on its contribution to their own focus of inquiry.

The thirteen chapters in this volume are organized into two sections, one focusing primarily on psycholinguistic issues, the other on neuropsychological approaches.

## Psycholinguistic Perspectives

This section begins with a chapter by Norman Segalowitz who sets out to account for slower second language reading in even highly skilled bilinguals. Reviewing a set of studies conducted in his laboratory, Segalowitz presents evidence for differences between the first and second language in the way automatic versus controlled processes, semantic activation, and phonological recoding operate during reading in skilled bilinguals.

Kim Kirsner in the next chapter examines lexical processing in bilinguals and monolinguals with a view to evaluating the impact of bilingualism on the delimitation of lexical entries. After reviewing studies on word frequency and repetition effects, attribute retention and semantic priming in a variety of language pairs, Kirsner concludes that bilingual lexical representation does not differ from that of monolinguals and that morphology, rather than language, defines the boundaries between lexical categories.

The next two chapters are concerned with the effectiveness of different input presentation conditions for retention of information in bilinguals. Kirsten Hummel begins with a review of the bilingual memory literature, which has essentially focused on single words presented out of context, and then reviews general studies of memory for discourse as a function of encoding context. She concludes with a novel finding that memory for prose is far superior under bilingual than unilingual presentation conditions.

In the chapter that follows, Wallace Lambert examines the effects on second language learning of different pairings of first and second language script and spoken dialogue. His findings, derived from an extensive set of experiments with French-English speakers, are unexpected and rich in their theoretical and pedagogical implications.

Issues of language learning are examined somewhat differently in the chapter by Edith Magiste, who summarizes her work on immigrant students in Germany and Sweden. Using response time measures on various elementary encoding and decoding language tasks, Magiste presents data on the influence of length of residence in the host country on the attainment of comparable levels of speeded performance in two languages, and discusses issues of language interference, automaticity, and optimal conditions for second and third language learning.

The psycholinguistics section concludes with two chapters that address the phenomenon of intrasentential code-switching. Miwa Nishimura examines the phenomenon from a theoretical perspective, focusing on the question of whether or not code-mixed sentences can be assigned a host language. Where previous studies of code-mixing have tended to use languages with a similar word order, Nishimura makes use of a Japanese-English corpus to argue the case for language assignment.

In the final chapter of this section, Grosjean and Soares present preliminary evidence from their ongoing research on the phonetic and prosodic accompaniments of code switched utterances, the on-line perception of code switches, and lexical access of code-switches versus language borrowings.

## Neuropsychological Perspectives

The first wave of research on neuropsychological aspects of bilingual language experience may be said to have ended with the publication of a comprehensive anthology of the largely European literature on polyglot aphasia (Paradis, 1983). Currently, several new studies on brain-injured and normal populations are at various stages of completion in different laboratories and it will be some time before their findings become ready for dissemination. In the selections for this portion of the book, I have avoided including reviews of the bilingual aphasia and lateralization literature, as a number of such reviews are already available (e.g., Albert & Obler, 1978; Vaid, 1983). I have opted instead to include preliminary reports from ongoing research projects and literature reviews of interesting sub-populations that have not yet received sufficient attention.

The first two chapters in this section are concerned with bilingual aphasia. Prithika Chary summarizes data from a larger project on the assessment of aphasia in multilingual speakers of Dravidian languages in South India. In her study of a group of bilingual aphasics, patients were randomly selected, thereby eliminating the danger of a sampling bias, a problem that has made much of the earlier aphasia literature suspect. A particularly interesting finding from her study is the high incidence of crossed aphasia in polyglots (similar to previous reports in the literature) but, unlike previous estimates, crossed aphasia in Chary's monolingual sample is also fairly high.

Beverly Wulfeck, Larry Juarez, Elizabeth Bates, and Kerry Kilborn use a sentence interpretation paradigm adapted from ongoing cross-linguistic research by Bates and Brian MacWhinney and present evidence from healthy and aphasic Spanish-English bilinguals for individual differences in modes of interpreting grammatically ambiguous sentences. They find that the performance of bilinguals on this task differs from that of their monolingual counterparts and reflects an amalgam of strategies from the two languages.

The next two chapters address changes in language and in lateralization as a function of language experience. Loraine Obler, Martin Albert and Sandra Lozowick compare the performance of healthy bilinguals and monolinguals in their 70s on a range of language and non-language tasks drawn from a larger project by Obler and Albert at the Boston V.A. Medical Center on language and dementia.

Looking at developmental issues from the other end of the lifespan, Eta Schneiderman integrates three bodies of literature—on child language, the role of the right hemisphere in language, and lateralization of language in proficient and non-proficient bilinguals—in an attempt to develop a coherent theoretical framework for the study of hemispheric specialization of language, whether a first or a second language.

The last two chapters of the book focus on lateralization of language in special populations—users of the Chinese writing system and of signed languages. Catherine Kettrick and Nancy Hatfield consider a population whose bilingualism has not generally been studied, or even acknowledged, despite its rather unique features. They review available clinical and experimental neuropsychological studies of deaf and hearing users of signed and spoken language.

In the final chapter, Reiko Hasuike, Ovid Tzeng, and Daisy Hung examine script-related differences in hemispheric specialization of written language, specifically, differences between kanji and kana processing. They conclude that, whatever differences there might be between the two, these need not be interpreted in terms of a differential reliance on the left and right hemispheres, respectively.

Whether presenting new data or evaluating existing evidence, the chapters in this volume were all written with a view to identifying relevant questions and suggesting viable directions for further approaches to these questions. It is hoped that a joint consideration of psycholinguistic and neuropsychological approaches will advance and refine our understanding of bilingual language functioning.

## REFERENCES

Albert, M. & Obler, L. (1978). *The bilingual brain*. New York: Academic Press.

Djouider, B. (1986). *Cognitive aspects of early vs. late onset of bilingualism: Inter-relationships of semantic interference, concept formation, and cognitive style*. Unpublished doctoral dissertation, School of Human Behavior, United States International University, San Diego.

Goodz, N. (1986, August). *Parental language to children in bilingual families: A model and some*

*data*. Paper presented at Third World Congress on Infant Psychiatry and Allied Disciplines, Stockholm.
Grosjean, F. (1982). *Life with two languages: An introduction to bilingualism*. Cambridge, MA: Harvard University Press.
Hakuta, K. (1986). *Mirror of language*. New York: Basic Books.
Paradis, M. (1983). *Readings on aphasia in bilinguals and polyglots*. Montreal: Didier.
Vaid, J. (1983). Bilingualism and brain lateralization. In S. Segalowitz (Ed.), *Language functions and brain organization*. New York: Academic Press.

# Acknowledgments

This project was supported in part by the John D. and Catherine T. MacArthur Foundation Transition Research Network at the Center for Research in Language, University of California, San Diego, and by National Institute of Health research grants to the Laboratory for Language and Cognitive Studies at the Salk Institute for Biological Studies, San Diego. I gratefully acknowledge Drs. Elizabeth Bates and Ursula Bellugi for allowing me the facilities and time needed to devote to this effort during the course of my research appointment at the University of California San Diego and the Salk Institute for Biological Studies.

I thank Harry A. Whitaker for taking an interest in publishing this book in his series and the contributors to this volume for their enthusiasm and cooperation. Helen Neville and David Corina of the Salk Institute for Biological Studies offered useful comments on specific chapters. Karen Hampton and Ann Cooreman of the University of California San Diego assisted me in checking references and in preparing the index. Sondra Guideman of Laurence Erlbaum Associates did a commendable job of copy-editing.

A number of colleagues have influenced my thinking about bilingualism over the course of the past decade: Wallace E. Lambert, Fred Genesee and Michel Paradis of McGill University, and Loraine Obler, Paul Kolers and François Grosjean, among others. I am indebted to them for their guidance and encouragement. Finally, I want to express my gratitude to Ramdas Menon for seeing me through this project from beginning to end.

# I

# PSYCHOLINGUISTIC PERSPECTIVES

# 1 Skilled Reading in the Second Language

Norman Segalowitz
*Concordia University, Montreal*

Can bilinguals read their second language as skilfully as they read their first? Often they do not, and there is much evidence that second language reading is generally slower, even in fluent bilinguals (as we shall see) and more difficult. A common explanation for this is that the reader lacks some of the basic linguistic knowledge necessary for skilled reading; the reader may not have a full and accurate command of the vocabulary and syntax of the language, the stylistic conventions of paragraph structure, or the cultural assumptions underlying the text (see e.g., Alderson & Urquhart, 1984, for discussion of these and related sources of second language reading difficulty). For example, Alderson (1984) offers two hypotheses about what is responsible for second language reading being weaker than first. One is that poor second language reading is due to the use of incorrect strategies, strategies different from those employed in native language reading. The other is that poor second language reading is due to insufficient knowledge of that language and the resulting inability to employ good first language strategies while reading it. Both these hypotheses focus on the bilingual's ability or inability to make use of linguistic knowledge while reading. A similar point has been made in some of the psychological literature in terms of the bilingual being less skilled in making use of redundancy in the second language to facilitate reading (Albert & Obler, 1978; Favreau, Komoda, & Segalowitz, 1980; Macnamara, 1970). While there is undoubtedly merit in attributing some first and second language reading differences to such sources, this chapter considers a different source of second language reading difficulty. It examines the idea that certain basic cognitive mechanisms underlying reading, not directly related to higher order syntactic, stylistic and rhetorical linguistic knowledge, function less efficiently when the bilingual is processing second as compared to first language material.

We examine two sets of studies we have recently completed that look at this issue in highly skilled or "fluent" bilinguals whose languages have relatively similar writing systems (English and French; for a discussion of the impact of different writing systems on reading, see Hung & Tzeng, 1981; Feldman & Turvey, 1983). By "fluent bilingual" is meant the person who has for all practical purposes rapid and accurate ability to use the vocabulary and syntax of a second language, at least when required to perform under normal speaking and listening conditions, and is also generally skilled at reading the second language. We are here considering people who can express most ideas equally well in each language, who demonstrate good mechanical fluency in the second language although they may possess a slight accent (we have no data on whether there are subtle differences in speaking rates) and whose reading rate when reading for general comprehension is within the normal range (say, about 200 words per minute or better) (see Favreau & Segalowitz, 1982, for details). Such individuals, while perhaps not comprising the majority of second language users, nevertheless represent a significant and growing number, including citizens of bilingual regions, many foreign students and scholars, diplomats, politicians, and workers in international agencies and companies. Although such people are characterized here as "fluent" bilinguals it cannot be suggested that they function like two monolinguals nor need they be so considered (see Grosjean & Soares, this volume). Most likely we can find subtle but important differences between first and second language reading when they are required to perform a speeded task, such as reading a long text within some time limit or making rapid judgments about written material. Such individuals are interesting from a theoretical point of view because they are both relatively fast and slow readers at the same time depending on the language being read. Their slow reading is not easily accounted for in terms of some general reading skill deficit (skills that would affect reading any language), nor in terms of some fundamental weakness in the second language such as unfamiliarity with vocabulary or syntax.

The question of when and why second language reading might differ from first language reading has practical interest (see, e.g., the papers in Alderson & Urquhart, 1984). For example, in the bilingual region in which our laboratory is found, there are hundreds of thousands of highly skilled bilinguals whose work requires them daily to read a great deal of text in both French and English. We have consistently found that the majority of fluent bilinguals who visit our laboratory read significantly more slowly in their second language compared to their first. Typically, the second language reading rate is of the order of 60–70% of the first language reading rate (Favreau & Segalowitz, 1982). This difference can place bilinguals at a considerable disadvantage with respect to their colleagues or coworkers of the other mother tongue by affecting their relative working efficiency and, consequently, their possibilities for advancement.

## INTERACTIVE PROCESSES

To begin, it will be useful to give a brief overview of current thinking regarding the nature of the reading process. In recent decades the focus of theories concerning the psychological mechanisms underlying native language reading has shifted from so-called bottom-up models and top-down models to models allowing for the dynamic interaction of processes at different levels of the system. Bottom-up models (e.g., Gough, 1972: LaBerge & Samuels, 1974) emphasize the one-way flow of information from low level perceptual analysing systems (e.g., mechanisms dealing with orthographic levels of the stimulus) to higher level semantic mechanisms (e.g., those dealing with lexical lookup and integration of textual material). Such models are generally now considered to be inadequate because they fail to account for a number of important phenomena studied by reading researchers (Rumelhart, 1977). For example, in one widely studied phenomenon known as the word superiority effect higher levels of processing (e.g., word recognition) affect lower levels of processing (e.g., letter identification) (Reicher, 1969; see Favreau et al., 1980, for a study of this in relation to first and second language reading differences in bilinguals). Similarly, various top-down models of reading (Goodman, 1976; Hochberg, 1970; Kolers, 1972; Levin & Kaplan, 1970: Neisser, 1967; Smith, 1973) that emphasize the direction of flow of information from higher levels to lower ones also have serious shortcomings (see McConkie & Rayner, 1976; Mitchell & Green, 1978; Rumelhart, 1977; Stanovich, 1980).

The general consensus among researchers appears to be that reading involves interactive processing. Information at one level may affect processes at a second level, regardless of which level is higher (Perfetti & Roth, 1981; Stanovich, 1980, 1981). This situation is illustrated in Fig. 1.1 which depicts in a general way the main levels of processing thought to underlie reading. (The figure conveys a rather simplified version of the interactive model insofar as few constraints on the interactions are made explicit; see e.g., Perfetti & McCutchen, 1982; Perfetti & Roth, 1981, for fuller discussions.) Three main levels are shown in the figure: a visual level concerned with the analysis of the printed stimulus, a lexical level concerned with word recognition, and a textual level concerned with integrating information across words to permit understanding of sentences, paragraphs, and stories. The figure also specifies two levels of phonological recoding, one prelexical between the visual and the lexical levels, and the other postlexical between the lexical and textual levels. The prelexical level reflects the possibility that visual information is converted into some form of phonological code (not necessarily subvocal speech, but possibly some abstract phonemic representation) as part of the process of recognizing the word (Lesgold & Perfetti, 1981; McCutchen & Perfetti, 1982). Perfetti and McCutchen (1982) propose that this happens automatically even though the speech based code so generated may not be directly involved in lexical access. The postlexical level

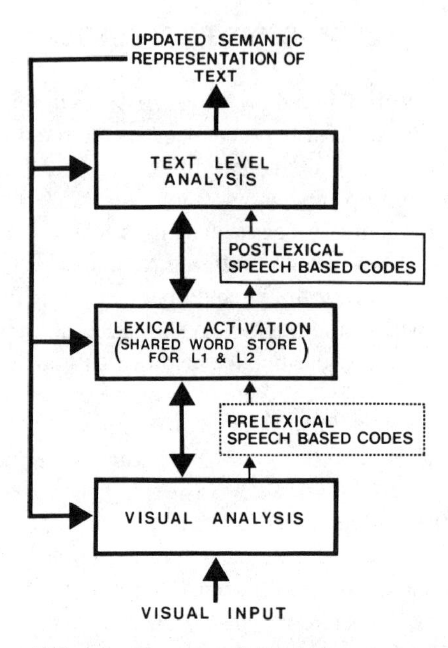


FIG. 1.1. Overview of the reading process.

reflects the possibility that already recognized words are recoded phonologically to facilitate holding them in memory (Barron, 1981) and thereby make them available to higher level linguistic processes (for syntactic parsing, propositional encoding, etc.). Finally, Fig. 1.1 also reflects the assumption that the lexical store for the two languages is common rather than separated (Caramazza & Brones, 1980; Nas, 1983; Albert & Obler, 1978; Segalowitz, 1977; Segalowitz & Lambert, 1969; but see also Hummel, this volume; Kirsner, Smith, Lockhart, King, & Jain, 1984; Scarborough, Gerard, & Cortese, 1984).

The studies reported here focus on just two aspects of reading as depicted in Fig. 1.1. One concerns whether there are first and second language differences in the degree to which a printed word automatically activates a meaning representation in the mental lexicon and differences in the extent and time course of that activation (see also Magiste, this volume). The second concerns the degree to which phonological codes are implicated in second language reading.

## AUTOMATIC AND CONTROLLED PROCESSES

The first issue we looked at concerns the degree to which word recognition with visual input is automatic. A complex activity such as reading is likely to involve many highly practised and automatized activities (LaBerge & Samuels, 1974) and skilled readers are thought to be better in automatic word recognition than unskilled readers (Stanovich, 1980). Automatic processing in reading research is often conceptualized in terms of the Posner and Snyder (1975) dual process model. They postulated the existence of two independent types of spreading activation. Automatic spreading activation is fast, does not use attentional resources and is not inhibitory. Controlled spreading activation, on the other hand, is slow, does use attentional resources and can be both facilitatory and inhibitory (see Schneider, Dumais, & Shiffrin, 1984, for a fuller discussion). Presumably, early in reading development, the processes of word recognition require effort and attention and only after extensive experience do they become automatized. Individual differences in reading skill may be partly due, therefore, to the degree to which this automatization has occurred. This suggestion is supported by the results of Stanovich and his colleagues (Stanovich, West, & Feeman, 1981; West & Stanovich, 1978) who report that younger readers are slower than older readers at word recognition and at the same time show greater effects of contextual information reflecting the operation of nonautomatic processes on word recognition. That is, their response times are more strongly influenced by contextual information that renders a target word expected or unexpected. The general conclusion from this work is that one important distinction between skilled and less skilled readers is the availability of fast automatic word recognition skills in the former.

## AUTOMATIC AND CONTROLLED PROCESSES IN BILINGUALS

Favreau and Segalowitz (1983) conducted a study concerned with the relationship between first and second language reading speeds and the use of automatic and controlled processing in a lexical decision task. Subjects were asked to judge if a string of letters formed a real word or not. The target string to be judged was preceded by another letter string, serving as a prime. Prime words were category names and the target words were category member names, and the influence of the prime on reaction times to the target was the main focus of the study. There were two principal manipulations of the relationship between the prime and the target. One concerned the semantic relationship between them and the other concerned the expectancy relationship between them. For example, sometimes the prime was semantically related to the target as in the case of the prime BIRD and the target ROBIN. Sometimes the prime was not semantically related to the target word as in the case of the prime FURNITURE and the target ROBIN. The other manipulation concerned the expectancy relationship between the prime and target. For example, subjects were instructed so as sometimes to expect to see a semantically related word (e.g., they were told that the word BIRD would be followed by the name of a particular bird) and sometimes to expect to see a semantically unrelated word (e.g., they were told that the word

FLOWER would be followed by the name of a fish). Finally, sometimes the nonword string OOOOO was employed as a neutral prime, a condition intended to provide baseline reaction time data for lexical decision without the influence of a semantic relationship between prime and target.

The experiment was patterned after the design used by Neely (1977). He found that when a prime was followed by an expected word then reaction time for lexical decision was faster compared to the neutral prime condition. Conversely, when a prime was followed by an unexpected word then reaction time for a lexical decision to the target was slower. This result was taken to reflect the subject's controlled preparation for expected words. Neely found that this facilitation and inhibition of reaction times occurred regardless of the semantic relation between them when the interval separating the prime and target was relatively long, for example, on the order of 1000 msec. When the interval was short, then there was only facilitation and only for semantically related words, regardless of whether they were expected or unexpected. This result was taken to reflect the subject's automatic activation of highly overlearned semantically associated words, a process that cannot be inhibited in the short interval available even when other words are expected. Neely interpreted these findings to show a dissociation between fast automatic processing of overlearned semantic relations between words and slower controlled processing based on expectancies.

In our study we used two groups of fluent English/French bilinguals: an "equal reading rate" group who read English and French equally fast and an "unequal reading rate group" who read their second language more slowly than their first. Half of each group had English as their mother tongue, and half French. Subjects were tested in separate blocks corresponding to the eight language (first language, second language) by expectancy (expected a related word, expected an unrelated word) by interval (long prime-target interval, short interval) combinations of factors discussed above.

The critical result came from the short interval condition. The equal reading rate group showed the same effects in both their first and second languages that Neely found, namely facilitation for targets that were semantically related and no inhibition for unrelated targets, regardless of expectation. The unequal reading rate group, on the other hand, showed these effects in the first language only. They showed no facilitation for related targets in the second language. In the long interval condition both groups showed the facilitation and inhibition effects presumed to reflect controlled processing similar to Neely (1977). Taken together, these results suggest that the unequal reading rate group was less able to process second language material automatically.

Stanovich found that slow readers appear to show increased effects of context on their word recognition times, a result predicted by his interactive/compensatory model of individual differences in (first language) reading. This model (Stanovich, 1980, 1981) is a variant of the interactive model discussed earlier. Stanovich argues for including in the interactive model the assumption that the component subskills of reading may operate in a compensatory fashion, that is, a process at one level can compensate for deficiencies of processes at another level. For example, deficiencies in word recognition should, according to this view, lead the reader to depend more on contextual information as an aid in word recognition. This follows from the distinction between automatic and controlled processes. If automatic activation is deficient, then there is time for processes under the subject's strategic control (those reflecting expectations) to exert their influence on recognition times. If automatic processes are fast and efficient, as they appear to be in skilled readers, then the slower strategically controlled processes do not have time to exert their influence. Thus although the skilled reader may be superior in using contextual information, a reader with poor word recognition skill may be more dependent upon it (Stanovich, West, & Feeman, 1981; Stanovich & West, 1979; West & Stanovich, 1978). As Stanovich points out, it is important to distinguish between skill in making use of contextual factors and in being more prone to rely on them.

From the perspective of the interactive-compensatory model, the reduced automaticity found in our experiment in the second language should lead to compensatory reliance on controlled processing, as reflected in increased effects of expectancies based on contextual information. That is, in the long interval condition for unexpected unrelated words, we might expect more inhibition in the second language than in the first. However, this did not obtain in our data. Instead of increased inhibition we found a significant result in the opposite direction: The inhibition for unexpected unrelated targets was smaller in the second language than in the first language for the unequal reading rate bilinguals. This might reflect a genuine absence of increased dependency on contextual information or it might reflect a ceiling effect (in the long interval condition the subjects had 1150 msec between the onset of the prime and the target, probably sufficient time for processes dependent on expectations to have exerted maximum influence). It would be worthwhile to clarify this in future research. If the reduced automaticity of word recognition does result in increased dependency on contextual information, then obviously the quality of that information becomes very important. Bilinguals who have a poor grasp of paragraph structure or the sense of certain syntactic structures will have poor quality contextual information to assist word recognition. Their increased reliance on context may thus result in yet slower reading rates and in reading marked by difficulties.

In a related series of experiments in our laboratory, Vasos (1983) further examined word recognition in bilinguals. Her experiments were not concerned with the issue of automaticity but with the speed with which a written word activates its underlying semantic representation and the extent or breadth of that activation. She used a paradigm adapted from Rosch (1975) in which a category name word-prime was found to facilitate judgments about pictures. In particular, Rosch found that reaction time to judge two different simultaneously presented pictured items (e.g., hat, coat) as belonging to the same category was faster if the pictures were preceded by the appropriate cateogry name (e.g., CLOTHING). Furthermore, she found that the effect of the word prime on judgments to pictures varied as a function of how prototypical the items in the pictures were of their category, facilitation being greatest for the most prototypical items.

Vasos used a similar paradigm with fluent and moderate bilinguals (English mother tongue; French second language) whose proficiency was assessed by their self ratings. The subject's task was to indicate whether a simultaneously presented pair of line drawings of items belonged to the same semantic category. On half the trials the items were from the same category, and on half the trials they were not. Further, when the items did come from the same category, half the time they were physically identical (i.e., the item was shown twice) and half the time they were different (but from the same category). Finally, same category items were either highly prototypical for their category or significantly less prototypical. The word prime came from a set of five familiar well-practised category names in English (CLOTHING, FURNITURE, TOOL, TOY, WEAPON) and their French equivalents and were used repeatedly in a mixed language design: One third of the primes were in English, one third in French, and one third of the time a neutral prime was used (the string "BZZZZ").

The most important results came from the condition in which different pictures from the same category were shown. Vasos found that, for fluent bilinguals, the appropriate category name facilitated judgments about pictures in both the first and second language conditions and equally for both levels of prototypicality of the items pictured. For the moderately fluent bilinguals she obtained similar results only for first language primes. With second language primes, there was only facilitation for the high prototypical items. Reaction times for the low prototypical items did not differ from the neutral prime trials with these same pictures. This result suggests that even very familiar and highly practised single words in a subject's second language may not activate as strong a representation as in the first in the sense that a more restricted semantic field was affected more by second language word primes than by first language word primes.

In another experiment Vasos (1983) had moderately fluent bilinguals judge whether a word correctly named the category of a pictured item. This experiment looked at the effect of one trial upon succeeding trials. For example, in a sequence of three trials the word-picture pairs might be (words are indicated in uppercase, pictures in lowercase):

CLOTHING
coat
WEAPON
couch
CLOTHING
hat

Thus, in this example the word CLOTHING is presented twice with a lag of 1, that is, with one intervening trial. Using the same category names and pictures as in the previously described experiment, Vasos constructed a series containing critical trials with lags of 0, 1, and 2. She was interested to see whether first and second language words exerted their effects over time in the same way. Two results from her data indicate that second language words exerted a weaker influence for these moderate bilinguals than did first language words. Facilitation was obtained for both languages in lag 0 conditions (i.e., no intervening trials). There were successively decreasing amounts of facilitation for lags 1 and 2 in the first language, but no facilitation in the second language. These results were obtained for both long (1650 msec) and short (200 msec) word-picture onset intervals (interval conditions were blocked). In addition, she found that while facilitation was greater for high than low prototypical items in both languages, there was an interaction effect indicating that the high–low prototypicality difference was greater in the second language than in the first. Thus, the benefit of activation by a recent presentation of a second language word was stronger for high prototypical items than for low. These results taken together suggest that for the moderate bilingual second language words do not produce activation effects extending over the same semantic domain nor for the same time duration as words in the first language.

In summary, the results of Favreau and Segalowitz (1983) and Vasos (1983) suggest that where the second language is weaker than the first language, there are corresponding deficiencies in the way single words activate meaning representations, even in highly skilled bilinguals. In Favreau and Segalowitz (1983) it was found that such activation was less automatic in the second language than in the first for those bilinguals who read more slowly in the second language. In Vasos (1983) it was found that semantic activation was less extensive and shorter in duration in the second language than in the first for moderately skilled bilinguals. These results are generally consistent with the finding in the monolingual reading literature that slower reading is associated with weaker skills in fast word recognition.

## PHONOLOGICAL RECODING IN BILINGUALS

The second main issue to be discussed concerns the degree to which bilinguals phonologically recode the visual input. The possibility of phonological recoding has been a central question for many years in reading research (McCusker, Hillinger, & Bias, 1981). Studies of skilled and less skilled readers have indicated that skilled readers are better able to phonologically encode (Barron, 1981). Other studies (e.g., Frederiksen & Kroll, 1976: Green & Shallice, 1976), however, have suggested that phonological recoding of visual input is not necessary for word recognition in English for adults. Some have demonstrated effects suggesting that readers may use phonological recoding in deciding the lexical status of an item if it is advantageous for them to do so, and not if it is disadvantageous given the conditions of the experiment (e.g., Davelaar, Coltheart, Besner, & Jonasson, 1978; McQuade, 1981). This has led to the general observation that phonological recoding is probably optional for readers of English (Henderson, 1982; Hung & Tzeng, 1981).

Perfetti (1984; see also Lesgold & Perfetti, 1981; Perfetti & McCutchen, 1982) proposes that visual perception of print normally automatically activates both word and phonemic codes consistent with the visual letter input. Support for this view can be found in the results of McCutchen and Perfetti (1982) (see also Humphreys, Evett, & Taylor, 1982). According to the interactive view put forward by Perfetti & McCutchen (1982), the automatically activated phonemic codes interact with the letter and word code activations, and can achieve a relatively high level of activation as a function of spelling regularity and other factors. Even so, such prelexical phonological codes may not be normally involved in lexical access if the reader is skilled and visual processing is fast. Less skilled readers will generally be poorer at generating phonemic codes or will do so more weakly (Barron, 1981). Thus the phonemic codes that are generated during the process of lexical access should exert less influence in the prelexical stages in the weaker second language than in the first. However, the role of the prelexically generated code may be not so much to aid lexical look-up but to provide a stable code for items in immediate memory, a code that would be more stable than a meaning-based code (Lesgold & Perfetti, 1981; Perfetti, 1984).

We report below one of a series of experiments conducted with Martine Hébert in our laboratory (Segalowitz & Hébert, 1985) concerning phonological recoding by monolinguals and bilinguals in English and French. Our interest was in whether reading rate differences between languages are associated with differential skills in using phonological codes. We considered two possible outcomes. One is that those bilinguals who are relatively more skilled in their second language will demonstrate more phonological coding effects than will less skilled readers. This follows from the general finding in the literature regarding reading ability and phonological coding skills (Barron, 1981). This could be because the better one's reading skill the more automatic the activation (as in Favreau & Segalowitz, 1983). It could also be that the slower second language readers will have less spare capacity for higher level processing (cf. Dornic, 1980) and so other processes requiring attention will interfere with speech-based codes in memory (Perfetti & McCutchen, 1982). The other possible outcome is that the less skilled readers will be more dependent (yet possibly less effective) on phonological codes in the second language than are either skilled bilingual readers in that language or than they themselves are in their first language. They may adopt a strategy of relying on refreshing items in immediate memory because their higher level linguistic processes that operate on the contents of immediate memory are themselves slower. We chose the sentence verification and lexical decision tasks to investigate these questions in bilinguals. These tasks are now described briefly in turn below.

*Sentence verification.* In the sentence verification task, subjects had to decide whether a string of words formed a meaningful sentence (cf. Baron, 1973). Sets of four critical words were composed to be inserted into sentence frames. One word was a homophone (e.g., FLARE) and one a control word (e.g., FLAME). A third member of the set was semantically incorrect for its sentence frame but was phonologically congruent with a word that could fit in that position in the sentence. The fourth was a homophone control word for the third member that was phonologically incongruent with any word that could fit into the sentence frame in that position. Below are sample English and French sentences to illustrate each of the four types just described:

1. Meaningful/Homophone:
   They detected the flare coming out of the woods.
   *Les enfants aiment jouer dans la boue.*
2. Meaningful/Control:
   They detected the flame coming out of the woods.
   *Les enfants aiment jouer dans la neige.*
3. Meaningless/Congruent:
   They detected the flair coming out of the woods.
   *Les enfants aiment jouer dans la bout.*
4. Meaningless/Incongruent:
   They detected the stare coming out of the woods.
   *Les enfants aiment jouer dans la toux.*

Subjects were English-French bilinguals (mother tongue English). As in the Favreau and Segalowitz (1983) study half the group read their two languages at about the same rate (equal reading rate group) and half read their second language significantly more slowly (unequal reading rate group).

The first set of results to be discussed concerned the meaningless congruent and incongruent sentence conditions. Both groups made significantly more errors across languages on congruent sentences than on incongruent sentences. There was also evidence of differential group effects in the second language. In particular, the reaction time data revealed a three way interaction (subjects analysis only; this restricts our confidence in generalizing to other language items; Clark, 1973) indicating that the unequal reading rate bilinguals were slower in their second language on congruent sentences than on incongruent sentences while the equal reading rate bilinguals were not. Thus both groups showed phonological effects when an incorrect word appeared in the sentence, regardless of language, since both groups made more errors if the incorrect word sounded like a correct one. In addition, however, the unequal reading rate subjects were relatively slower with such congruent items in their second language compared to their first. This result is consistent with the idea that higher level processes operating on the phonologically coded congruent words in memory were themselves less efficient in that language. That is, the difficulty may lie not in generating the phonological code itself, but in using information after it has been so recoded.

The second set of results concerns the meaningful homophone and control sentence conditions. Here, evidence of phonological effects in the second language appeared only in the unequal reading rate group's error data. In particular, a three way interaction revealed that the unequal reading rate group made significantly more errors on homophone sentences in their second language than on control sentences while the equal reading rate group did not. Both groups showed homophone error effects in their first language but similar effects in reaction time were not obtained. Thus only the unequal reading rate bilinguals appear to show second language phonological effects and they did so in their error data.

These data suggest that in the second language, the unequal reading rate bilinguals were sensitive to the phonological properties of words both when the sentences were meaningful and meaningless. The equal reading rate bilinguals, on the other hand, showed second language phonological effects (in errors) only when the sentences were meaningless. It is tempting to conclude from this that the unequal reading rate bilinguals were thus more dependent on phonological coding since they used it in more situations. The problem, however, is that they showed phonological effects in their first language too, yet they were significantly faster in reading it than the equal reading rate subjects (378 vs. 322 words per minute). In other words, they were showing significant phonological effects both in their fast and slow languages. We cannot, therefore, conclude that the unequal reading rate bilinguals were more dependent on phonological codes in their second language just because it was slower. Rather, the results seem to indicate that they were generally dependent on phonological coding, regardless of language, but they were less effective with it in the second language.

The equal reading rate bilinguals presented a somewhat different picture. They did not show phonological effects in their second language when the sentence was meaningful but did in their first. This result is difficult to interpret but it may be related to language specific factors. French is very much more regular in spelling-to-sound correspondences. It is characterized by a many-to-one mapping pattern with very few exceptions. For example, the strings __OIT, __OIX, __OIS, and __OIE are always pronounced the same way as in TOIT, VOIX, POIS and FOIE and only in this way. English on the other hand has a many-to-many mapping pattern. For example, the strings __OUR, and __OOR, can both be pronounced the same way as in YOUR and MOOR but they can also be pronounced differently as in HOUR and DOOR. This mapping difference may result in overall faster and more accurate speech-based codes in French than in English. (See Feldman & Turvey, 1983, for discussion of Serbo-Croatian which exhibits a one-to-one mapping within each of its two alphabets.)

*Lexical decision.* In the lexical decision task subjects had to decide whether a string of letters formed a real word. Some of the strings used were nonwords but sounded like words when pronounced (e.g., the pseudohomophone CROKE). Performance in rejecting this as a nonword has sometimes been found to be worse than in rejecting pronounceable nonwords that do not sound like real words (e.g., DROKE) (Coltheart, Davelaar, Jonasson, & Besner, 1977). It has also been found that sometimes performance in accepting strings that are homophones (e.g., WEAK) as real words is also worse than performance with nonhomophonic control words (Davelaar et al., 1978). However, these results have been found to depend critically on certain conditions of the experiment. The pseudohomophone effect obtains only when a relatively small proportion of the nonwords used are pseudohomophones (McQuade, 1981). Taft (1982) further showed that the pseudohomophone effect disappeared when pseudohomophones and control nonwords were carefully matched for degree of visual similarity to real words. A homophone effect is found only for the less frequent member of the homophone set (e.g., WEAK instead of WEEK) (Davelaar et al., 1978).

Our study took these considerations into account in the generation of the stimulus materials. English and French stimulus lists were developed, each consisting of homophones (e.g., WEAK), control words (e.g., BEEF), pseudohomophones (e.g., CROKE) and control nonwords (e.g., DROKE). None of the strings in one language list were valid words in the other language, and the homophones used were the lowest frequency member of a homophone set. Homophones and control words were matched on number of letters, consonant-vowel structure and frequency of occurence. Pseudohomophones and control nonwords were matched to real words on visual similarity.

In this task there was no evidence of differential phonological effects as a function of language or reading skill. Both groups showed a general pseudohomophone effect across both languages, that is, they made significantly more errors and were slower with pseudohomophones than with control nonwords. (A two-way interaction in the subjects analysis of the reaction time data indicated that the pseudohomophone effect was greater in the *first* language than in the second.) There was also a significant homophone effect in reaction times across groups and languages (subjects analysis only). Thus, the lexical decision data suggest that both groups of subjects were equally strong in generating speech based codes, and that they did so in both their languages, at least for nonwords.

The overall results of this study on phonological coding indicate that the fluent bilinguals studied here did not make differential use of phonological codes. This was true even when second language reading was slower as in the case of the unequal reading rate subjects. These unequal reading rate subjects were, however, slower in one condition and made more errors in another. The pattern of results is consistent with the idea that higher level processes utilizing phonological codes, rather than those generating them, did not function as effectively in these bilinguals as in the equal reading rate bilinguals. These differential effects obtained only in the sentence verification task, which further supports the idea that they are probably due to processes operating on immediate memory.

## GENERAL DISCUSSION

The data reviewed here demonstrate that even in highly skilled bilinguals there may be first and second language differences in the way basic underlying cognitive processes function during reading. In particular, we found that reduced automaticity of word recognition was associated with slowed second language reading in otherwise fluent bilinguals. In addition, moderately skilled bilinguals provided evidence that single words in the second language will activate semantic representations less deeply and do so for a shorter duration than do the translation equivalents in the native language. Finally, there was evidence that the relatively slower second language reading of some fluent bilinguals is associated with deficient use of phonologically coded information in memory. Together these data suggest that the way the basic processing apparatus functions, as distinct from the strategic use made of linguistic knowledge, may be a factor responsible for the relatively slow second language reading of many bilinguals.

These results may have important implications regarding training to improve a bilingual's second language reading efficiency. It would be interesting to know, for example, how much reading speed might improve just from training that increased automaticity of word recognition compared to training in specific linguistic knowledge for more effective use of "reading strategies." The fluent bilingual is already a relatively skilled reader in the first language and has a very high level of knowledge of the second. The reading speed problem may, therefore, lie principally in the efficiency with which lower levels of the cognitive apparatus provide information to higher levels, and not necessarily in the unavailability or faulty application of linguistic knowledge. As suggested by Macnamara (1970) and Albert and Obler (1978), slowed reading prevents the reader from thinking about what has been read. This probably prevents even skilled bilinguals from making maximum use of contextual knowledge.

## ACKNOWLEDGMENTS

The author gratefully acknowledges the constructive comments of Elizabeth Gatbonton, Melvin Komoda, Martine Hebert and Cathy Poulsen during earlier stages of the writing of this chapter. The research described here was supported by a grant from the Quebec Ministry of Education FCAC EQ-1163.

## REFERENCES

Albert, M., & Obler, L. (1978). *The bilingual brain. Neuropsychological and neurolinguistic aspects of bilingualism.* New York: Academic Press.

Alderson, J.C. (1984). Reading in a foreign language: A reading problem or a language problem? In J.C. Alderson, & A.H. Urquhart (Eds.), *Reading in a foreign language.* London: Longman.

Alderson, J.C., & Urquhart, A.H. (Eds.). (1984). *Reading in a foreign language.* London: Longman.

Baron, J. (1973). Phonemic stage not necessary for reading. *Quarterly Journal of Experimental Psychology, 25,* 241–246.

Barron, R.N. (1981). Reading skill and reading strategies. In A. Lesgold & C. Perfetti (Eds.), *Interactive processes in reading.* Hillsdale, NJ: Lawrence Erlbaum Associates.

Caramazza, A., & Brones, I. (1980). Semantic classification by bilinguals. *Canadian Journal of Psychology, 34,* 77–81.

Clark, H. (1973). The language-as-a-fixed-effect fallacy: A critique of language statistics in psychological research. *Journal of Verbal Learning and Verbal Behavior, 12,* 335–359.

Coltheart, M., Davelaar, E., Jonasson, J., & Besner, D. (1977). In S. Dornic (Ed.), *Attention and performance VI.* New York: Academic Press.

Davelaar, E., Coltheart, M., Besner, D., & Jonasson, J.T. (1978). Phonological recoding and lexical access. *Memory & Cognition, 6,* 391–402.

Dornic, S. (1980). Language dominance, spare capacity and perceived effect in bilinguals. *Ergonomics, 23,* 369–377.

Favreau, M., Komoda, M., & Segalowitz, N. (1980). Second language reading: Implications of the word superiority effect in skilled bilinguals. *Canadian Journal of Psychology, 4,* 370–381.

Favreau, M., & Segalowitz, N. (1982). Second language reading in fluent bilinguals. *Applied Psycholinguistics, 3,* 329–341.

Favreau, M., & Segalowitz, N. (1983). Automatic and controlled processes in reading a second language. *Memory & Cognition, 11,* 565–574.

Feldman, L., & Turvey, M. (1983). Word recognition in Serbo-Croatian is phonologically analytical. *Journal of Experimental Psychology: Human Memory & Learning, 9,* 288–298.

Frederiksen, J.R., & Kroll, J.F. (1976). Spelling and sound: Approaches to the internal lexicon. *Journal of Experimental Psychology: Human Perception and Performance, 2,* 361–379.

Goodman, K.S. (1976). Reading: A psycholinguistic guessing game. In H. Singer & R. Ruddell (Eds.), *Theoretical models and processes of reading* (2nd edition). Newark, DE: International Reading Association.

Gough, P. (1972). One second of reading. In J.F. Kavanaugh & I.G. Mattingly (Eds.), *Language by ear and eye.* Cambridge, MA: MIT Press.

Green, D., & Shallice, T. (1976). Direct visual access in reading for meaning. *Memory & Cognition, 4,* 753–758.

Henderson, L. (1982). *Orthography and word recognition in reading.* London: Academic Press.

Hochberg, J. (1970). Components of literacy: Speculation and exploratory research. In H. Levin & J. Williams (Eds.), *Basic studies in reading.* New York: Basic Books.

Humphreys, G.W., Evett, L.J., & Taylor, D.E. (1982). Automatic phonological priming in visual word recognition. *Memory & Cognition, 10,* 576–590.

Hung, D.L., & Tzeng, O. (1981). Orthographic variations and visual information processing. *Psychological Bulletin, 90,* 377–414.

Kirsner, K., Smith, M., Lockhart, R., King, M., & Jain, M. (1984). The bilingual lexicon: Language-specific units in an integrated network. *Journal of Verbal Learning and Verbal Behavior, 23,* 519–539.

Kolers, P. (1972). Experiments in reading. *Scientific American, 227,* 84–91.

LaBerge, D., & Samuels, S.J. (1974). Toward a theory of automatic information processing in reading. *Cognitive Psychology, 6,* 293–323.

Lesgold, A., & Perfetti, C. (1981). Interactive processes in reading: Where do we stand? In A. Lesgold & C. Perfetti (Eds.), *Interactive processes in reading*. Hillsdale, NJ: Lawrence Erlbaum Associates.

Levin, H., & Kaplan, E. (1970). Grammatical structure and reading. In H. Levin & J. Williams (Eds.), *Basic studies in reading*. New York: Basic Books.

Macnamara, J. (1970). Comparative studies of reading and problem-solving in two languages. *TESOL Quarterly, 4,* 107–116.

McConkie, G., & Raynor, K. (1976). Identifying the span of the effective stimulus in reading: Literature review and theories of reading. In H. Singer & R. Ruddell (Eds.), *Theoretical models and processes of reading* (2nd edition). Newark, DE: International Reading Association.

McCusker, L.X., Hillinger, M.L., & Bias, R.G. (1981). Phonological recoding and reading. *Psychological Bulletin, 89,* 217–245.

McCutchen, D., & Perfetti, C.A. (1982). The visual tongue-twister effect: Phonological activation in silent reading. *Journal of Verbal Learning and Verbal Behavior, 21,* 672–687.

McQuade, D. (1981). Variable reliance on phonological information and visual word recognition. *Language and Speech, 24,* 99–109.

Mitchell, D., & Green, D. (1978). The effects of context and content on immediate processing in reading. *Quarterly Journal of Experimental Psychology, 30,* 609–636.

Nas, G. (1983). Visual word recognition in bilinguals: Evidence for a cooperation between visual and sound based codes during access to a common lexical store. *Journal of Verbal Learning and Verbal Behavior, 22,* 526–534.

Neely, J. (1977). Semantic priming and retrieval from lexical memory: Roles of the inhibitionless spreading activation and limited-capacity attention. *Journal of Experimental Psychology: General, 106,* 226–254.

Neisser, U. (1967). *Cognitive psychology*. New York: Appleton-Century Crofts.

Perfetti, C.A. (1984). Individual differences in reading abilities. In National Academy of Science & Chinese Academy of Sciences, *Issues in Cognition,* Washington, D.C.: American Psychological Association, 137–161.

Perfetti, C.A., & McCutchen D. (1982). Speech processes in reading. In N. Lass (Ed.), *Advances in speech and language VII*. New York: Academic Press.

Perfetti, C.A., & Roth, S.F. (1981). Some of the interactive processes in reading and their role in reading skill. In A. Lesgold & C. Perfetti (Eds.), *Interactive processes in reading*. Hillsdale, NJ: Lawrence Erlbaum Associates.

Posner, M., & Snyder, C. (1975). Attention and cognitive control. In R.C. Solso (Eds.), *Information processing and cognition: The Loyola Symposium*. Hillsdale, NJ: Lawrence Erlbaum Associates.

Reicher, G. (1969). Perceptual recognition as a function of meaningfulness of stimulus material. *Journal of Experimental Psychology, 81,* 274–280.

Rosch, E. (1975). Cognitive representations of cognitive categories. *Journal of Experimental Psychology: General, 104,* 192–233.

Rumelhart, D. (1977). Toward an interactive model of reading. In S. Dornic (Ed.), *Attention and performance VI*. Hillsdale, NJ: Lawrence Erlbaum Associates.

Scarborough, D.L., Gerard, L., & Cortese, C. (1984). Independence of lexical access in bilingual word recognition. *Journal of Verbal Learning and Verbal Behavior, 23,* 84–99.

Schneider, W., Dumais, S.T., & Shiffrin, R.M. (1984). Automatic and control processing and attention. In R. Parasuraman & D. Davies (Eds.), *Varieties of attention*. New York: Academic Press.

Segalowitz, N. (1977). Psychological perspectives on bilingual education. In B. Spolsky & R. Cooper (Eds.), *Frontiers in bilingual education*. Rowley, MA: Newbury House.

Segalowitz, N., & Hebert, M. (1985). *Phonological recoding in English and French by monolinguals and bilinguals*. Unpublished manuscript, Concordia University, Montreal.

Segalowitz, N., & Lambert, W. (1969). Semantic generalization in bilinguals. *Journal of Verbal Learning and Verbal Behavior, 8,* 559–566.

Smith, F. (1973). *Psycholinguistics and reading.* New York: Holt, Rinehart & Winston.

Stanovich, K. (1980). Toward an interactive-compensatory model of individual differences in the development of reading fluency. *Reading Research Quarterly, 16,* 32–71.

Stanovich K. (1981). Attentional and automatic context effects in reading. In A. Lesgold & C. Perfetti (Eds.), *Interactive processes in reading.* Hillsdale, NJ: Lawrence Erlbaum Associates.

Stanovich, K., & West, R. (1979). Mechanisms of sentence context effects in reading: Automatic activation and conscious attention. *Memory & Cognition, 7,* 77–85.

Stanovich, K., West, R., & Feeman, D. (1981). A longitudinal study of sentence context effects in second-grade children: tests of an interactive compensatory model. *Journal of Experimental Child Psychology, 32,* 185–199.

Taft, M. (1982). An alternative to grapheme-phoneme conversion rules? *Memory & Cognition, 10,* 465–474.

Vasos, H. (1983). *Semantic processing in bilinguals.* Unpublished doctoral dissertation, Concordia University, Montreal.

West, R., & Stanovich, K. (1978). Automatic contextual facilitation in readers of three ages. *Child Development, 49,* 717–727.

# 2 Lexical Function: Is a Bilingual Account Necessary?

Kim Kirsner
*University of Western Australia*

This chapter is concerned with the impact of bilingualism on lexical function. Our approach to the issue has been guided by the proposition that most or all of the processes encountered in bilingualism have a monolingual parallel. If this proposition is correct, it means that the onus is on the investigator to demonstrate that a particular effect is unique to bilingualism, and so requires a specifically bilingual explanation. An additional implication of this stance is that primary consideration must be given to *general* models of cognitive function, thereby effecting both economy of explanation, and isolation of phenomena unique to bilingualism.

Lexical function could be moderated by bilingual experience in a number of ways. One possibility is that language operates as a criterial feature, defining either the boundary between lexical systems, or the boundaries between lexical units. If language defines the boundary between lexical systems, two general predictions may be made. First, lexical delimitation will be governed by lingual as opposed to morphological considerations. Thus, words that are morphologically related but lingually distinct (e.g., CATEGORY and CATEGORIA) should be represented independently. Second, words that are semantically or associatively related but lingually distinct (e.g., BREAD and BUERRE) should behave as if they belong to independent lexical systems. A second possibility is that language defines the boundaries between lexical units or categories, but not systems. In this case, only the first of the above predictions is applicable. Semantically or associatively related words will behave as if they belong to a single, integrated lexical network. But morphological relationships will still be overridden by language differences. A third possibility is that lexical representation is indifferent to bilingual experience, in which case morphological or semantic (or associative) principles will moderate interlingual as well as intralingual function.

Research into the impact of bilingualism on lexical function necessarily involves consideration of two behavioral domains, involving individual and linguistic variation respectively. Under the individual heading, the order in which the two languages are acquired, the amount of practice in each language and, possibly, individual differences in the strategies invoked during first and second language acquisition may influence lexical function in the adult bilingual. As an illustration of the way in which experience might influence lexical representation in particular, consider the problem of delimitation (Henderson, 1984). How are boundaries between lexical or perceptual categories established? One possibility is that the boundaries are determined solely by orthographic features, in which case the operation of a simple parsing rule may be sufficient to ensure that CATEGORY and CATEGORIA access the same lexical representation. A second possibility is that pronounciation contributes to delimitation, even for print, in which event the acquired pronunciation of the second language form may be crucial. For example, if the stem of CATEGORY is pronounced as it would be for CATEGORIA by a native Spanish speaker learning English, recognition of CATEGORY and CATEGORIA may involve access to the same representation because the stems do not differ on any feature. But if the modal English pronounciation is attained, distinct representations may be formed. In this chapter, however, only passing consideration is given to the impact of individual differences in ability, experience, and cognitive style. The chapter is concerned with the impact of linguistic variation on lexical representation.

In developing a theory to account for the full range of cognitive and bilingual phenomena, major consideration must be given to the mechanisms of discourse comprehension (Hummel, this volume), to the way in which knowledge is accessed and used during discourse comprehension (Sanford & Garrod, 1981), and to the way in which the knowledge base is modified by an understanding of new events. However, the arguments set out in this chapter have been guided by a more limited ambition, concerning lexical representation. The assumptions underlying this restriction are that information is available to the individual listener or reader via a number of channels; that *one* of these channels involves the categorization of verbal information into codes which correspond to the functional or linguistic units of the language concerned; and that these codes constitute one source of evidence during discourse comprehension. An understanding of these lexical processes is *necessary* for a complete communication model, but it is not assumed that this source of information is *sufficient* for this purpose.

## MODELS AND METAPHORS

Monolingual benchmarks for the consideration of bilingual phenomena generally take one of two forms. In empirical terms, the issue is whether or not a particular interlingual effect has an intralingual parallel. For example, is there an intralingual parallel to the way in which the frequency of occurrence of a word in one language influences performance on its cognate in another language (Caramazza & Brones, 1979)? Our review of the lexical evidence is governed by considerations of this type. In theoretical terms, the issue is not straightforward. Although a general model of lexical function would provide a most appropriate point of departure, owing to the state of flux in the area there is no modal model.

The state of flux in theoretical accounts of lexical function may be characterized as a contest between two research areas and their associated paradigms. Questions about *item occurrence* (e.g., Has CATEGORIA appeared in this chapter?) and *attribute retention* or *memory for surface form* (e.g., Was CATEGORIA presented in lower case or capital letters?) are typical of memory research, whereas *lexical decision* (e.g., is CATEGORIA a genuine English or Spanish word?) and *word identification* under stimulus-limited conditions are traditional language comprehension tasks. Until recently these paradigms have been associated with domain-referenced theories. Thus, item occurrence and attribute retention tasks have been used to develop and test theories about instance-based memory systems (e.g., Murdock, 1974), whereas lexical decision and word identification have been used to develop and test theories about a-historical or abstract recognition systems (e.g., Henderson, 1984; Morton, 1969). Recently, however, this distinction has broken down, and there is now strong evidence of covariation in the effect of selected variables on performance in tasks from the two domains (Brown, Sharma, & Kirsner, 1984; Cristoffanini, Kirsner, & Milech, in press; Downie, Milech, & Kirsner, in press; Jacoby, 1983a, 1983b: Kirsner & Dunn, 1985; Oliphant, 1984).

In an elegant analysis of this problem, Jacoby and Brooks (1984) have set out the theoretical issues which must be resolved. Specifically, they organize the problem in terms of the contrast between "nonanalytic" (episodic) and "analytic" (abstract) approaches to lexical function. According to Jacoby and Brooks (1984), analytic models of word recognition depend on access to stable and abstract cognitive structures, where access involves a measure of analysis or decomposition so that some portion of the stimulus array, a morpheme for example, can be matched against a corresponding and abstract representation. By definition, the representational units in such a system are instance-dependent. Two models of this type have influenced much recent research into word recognition processes. According to Morton's (1969, 1979) account, the word recognition units (logogens) can operate in parallel on stimulus information; frequency and repetition effects reflect criterial differences between units, and morphology determines the boundaries between units. According to Forster (1976), information about meaning and other word characteristics is stored in a master file directory which is accessed via a serial search through an orthographically defined and frequency ordered bin. Here, too, frequency and repetition effects can be explained (by reference to stack status) and morphological and orthographic effects have their impact through constraints on the search set.

In nonanalytic models, on the other hand, the major assumption is that recognition is achieved via access to an instance-based memory system and that it, like performance on Old/New judgments and attribute retention, is unstable and subject to context effects. A further distinguishing property of nonanalytic models involves the procedures or means by which information is acquired. According to Jacoby and Brooks (1984) this procedural information is detachable. If task demands emphasize surface qualities, procedural information may be preserved as a part of the record of the episode, but under other circumstances procedural information may be neglected, and therefore "lost." According to Kolers, however, (Kolers, 1978, 1979; Kolers & Roediger, 1984) the distinction between procedures and data, an essential property of the computational metaphor, is false; people remember what they do, and memory therefore consists of a record of the procedures invoked to solve problems.

In a recent paper, Kirsner and Dunn (1985) developed an account that specifically links lexical function and memory for surface form. The central features in this account are as follows. First, a perceptual record is created automatically as a result of the perceptual processing of a stimulus through a series of levels of abstraction. Second, the perceptual record is instrumental in determining the pattern of repetition effects in perceptual categorization tasks, through either reengagement of the original processes or access to a product of those processes. Third, the perceptual record also influences performance in attribute retention tasks, although in this case increasing intersection between the encoding and test records will impair rather than facilitate performance. Thus, if the encoding stimulus is PANADERIA and the test stimulus is BAKERY (its translation), process intersection will be low, and memory for surface form will be reliable. In contrast, if the encoding and test stimuli are CATEGORY and CATEGORIA, respectively, process intersection will be high, discrimination will be difficult, and memory for surface form will be correspondingly poor. Additional issues concerning attribute retention under recall conditions (where it may be assumed that form judgments depend on record generation), and Old/New judgments (where record access may be more important than the relationship between the encoding and test records) are not considered here.

The evidence set out in the section on frequency and repetition transfer establishes the extent to which translations (used here to refer exclusively to morphologically unrelated translations) and cognates (used here to refer to morphologically related translations) are represented on a language-specific basis. In addition, the notion of a perceptual record is exploited to establish the comparative status of translations and cognates; one implication of our analysis being that morphology rather than language is the critical variable where lexical representation is concerned.

The issue under consideration in this section concerns the language specificity of those units or processes which underlie word recognition and classification. The methodology and the results summarized here are based on the proposition that language-specificity is revealed by the patterns of transfer effects present between cognates and translations. Where a language-independent unit or process is involved, transfer will be complete, but where language-specific units or processes are involved, transfer will be absent. In the remainder of this section the relevant transfer data are organized and interpreted, and a number of additional problems concerning the relationship between repetition and frequency, the form of the transfer function in repetition tasks, and the character of the lexical data base are addressed.

## FREQUENCY EFFECTS

Conjoint consideration of frequency and repetition effects rests on the assumption that the two tasks reflect the operation of a common mechanism. Where word frequency is concerned, the argument is that the boundaries of a functional unit are defined by the range of inflections, derivations, cognates, and translations which contribute to the effective frequency status of a particular word. Thus, if it is assumed that word recognition involves access to an abstract representation of the stem morpheme for each word in a person's vocabulary, and that this is restricted to, for example, regular inflections and derivations, it follows that the effective frequency for a word such as CLING will be influenced by the frequency of occurrence of CLING, CLINGS, and CLINGING, but not by the frequency of occurrence of CLUNG. In principle, this analysis can be implemented by assessing the effect of a range of intralingual and interlingual forms on performance, but no systematic work of this kind has yet been published. The available work suggests however that: (a) the frequency of occurrence of the translation of a word does not influence performance when that word is morphemically unrelated, and (b) frequency of occurrence does influence performance when the translation is morphemically related.

In a post hoc analysis of lexical decision latency for New words, Cristoffanini et al. (in press) compared reaction time for two sets of low frequency English words, where the sets were defined by the frequency of occurrence of their Spanish translations (Juilland & Chang-Rodriguez, 1964). The high and low frequency sets had Spanish word frequency counts of 14 and 0 per million, respectively; the English word frequency count being 2 in each case. The mean reaction times were 804 and 811 msecs for the high and low frequency sets respectively, and this difference was not significant. The conclusion that translations are represented independently is also supported by the results of a frequency encoding study conducted by Marshall and Carareo-Ramos (1984). They manipulated the frequency of occurrence of English and Spanish translations under either pure or mixed language conditions, and found that reaction time on a subsequent frequency judgment task was longer under mixed language conditions, as if separate registers were involved.

The outcome is quite different where a morphological relationship exists. Reaction time for a word in one language is sensitive to the frequency of occurrence of its cognate in a second language. Caramazza and Brones (1979), for example, tested Spanish-English bilinguals on orthographically identical cognates (e.g., GENERAL) and found that the reaction time for these words was context-independent. When they were presented in a set of Spanish words, mean reaction time was equal to that observed for a set of noncognates of equal frequency. However, when the cognates were presented in a set of English words, their mean reaction time was unchanged even though reaction time was much longer for the relevant control words. Cristoffanini et al. (in press) found a qualitatively similar effect in a group of balanced bilinguals, and extended the effect to nonidentical cognates (e.g., PUBLICIDAD/PUBLICITY), thereby excluding the possibility that Caramazza and Brones' (1979) result simply reflects direct access to a single, lexemically defined entry. In their study Cristoffanini et al. (in press) compared sets of words where the English word frequency count was the same in each case (4 per million) but the Spanish frequency counts were quite different. For example, DONATION and DECADENCE have the same English frequency counts (2 per million) but the corresponding frequency counts for their Spanish cognates are 0 for DONATIO and 18 for DECADENCIA. The results were clear. The high frequency sets enjoyed a reaction time advantage in each of four types of cognates, namely, orthographically identical cognates, regular cognates of the CION/TION type, regular cognates of the DAD/TY type, and irregular cognates such as CALUMNY/CALUMNIA and ITINERARIO/ITINERARY.

In summary, whereas performance on word judgment tasks is influenced by the frequency of occurrence of cognates, this does not apply to translations, an outcome which implies that only the latter are organized on a language-specific basis. The material discussed in the next section involves the monolingual parallels to translations and cognates; that is, synonyms, and inflections and derivations.

Synonyms probably offer fertile ground for comparative research. They certainly share with translations a number of problems regarding definition, transitivity, and type and similarity of meaning (Herrman, 1978). No frequency transfer data appear to have been published for synonyms.

The monolingual data demonstrate clearly that frequency transfer does occur among morphologically related words, although the precise boundary conditions have not been established. Both the cluster frequency of a word (e.g., the sum of the frequency counts for KICK, KICKING, KICKS, etc.,) and its particular form frequency (i.e., the frequency count for KICK) influence performance in a lexical decision task (Bradley, 1979; Taft, 1979). The lack of clarity in regard to the criterial features governing delimitation is clearly demonstrated in a contrast between the monolingual and bilingual data for words with the /TION/ suffix.

Although Bradley found frequency transfer for words ending in /NESS/, /MENT/, and /ER/, she found no such transfer for words ending in /TION/. This outcome is inconsistent with the frequency transfer results reported by Cristoffanini et al. (in press), and with the monolingual and bilingual repetition data summarized below (Cristoffanini et al., in press; Downie et al., in press). Furthermore, as all of these studies used frequency counts based on just one source, the suggestion by Taft (Taft, in press) that Bradley's (1979) results reflect inherent limitations in the data base appears to be unjustified.

To summarize, there is no suggestion of frequency transfer where translations are concerned, but it is present for both cognates and intralingual derivations. The presence of frequency transfer between cognates is open to a number of interpretations apart from shared representation. One possibility is that the words or their stems are represented independently, but that presentation of a cognate activates each unit. Another possibility is that bilinguals are biased or trained toward the use of cognates during second language acquisition or use (Banta, 1981), thereby giving such words an inflated frequency count relative to their frequency of occurrence in monolingual experience. Repetition transfer is probably free from the second of these problems, and the next section examines the relevant bilingual and monolingual data.

## REPETITION EFFECTS

The next set of data to be reviewed involve repetition priming, procedure that is generally (although not universally) regarded as an experimental analogue of word frequency analysis. In outline, the paradigm involves preliminary presentation of words in one of two languages, say English and French, followed by a test phase during which some words are repeated in the same language, some words are repeated in the alternative language, as translations, and some New words (words not presented previously in the experiment) are presented for identification or classification. When words are repeated in the same language in a lexical decision task, reaction time is shorter for the Old or repeated words than it is for New words (Forbach, Stanners, & Hochhaus, 1974; Kirsner & Smith, 1974). The critical question concerns the presence or absence of transfer in the translation conditions. Specifically, does exposure to /FROMAGE/ improve performance on /CHEESE/? If transfer is absent it may be inferred that distinct representations are involved, but if transfer is present, it follows that a common representation or process is involved.

Historically, the use of just one alternative surface form (modality for example) has encouraged an "all or none" approach to the issue, and more subtle possibilities involving, for example, a transfer continuum, have received little consideration. In a recent review of the relevant material, Kirsner and Dunn

(1985) suggested that repetition data should be treated in relative terms. Thus, an index of relative priming (RP) may be calculated by the following formula:

RP = (alternative form — control)/(same form — control)

thereby providing a statistic which permits direct comparisons between, first, data obtained under stimulus identification and classification conditions and, second, tasks where the dependent variable is expressed in reaction time, accuracy, or threshold terms.

Bilingual repetition data are available for three types of words; translations where the words are morphologically unrelated (e.g., /FROMAGE/ and /CHEESE/), translations where the words are morphologically related and presented in the same script (e.g., /OBSERVACION/ and /OBSERVATION/), and translations where the words are morphophonemically related but presented in lingually marked scripts.

Table 2.1 is a summary of the bilingual repetition data. In each case, consideration was restricted to studies involving retention intervals of 10 min or more, and in which incidental retention learning conditions applied. Where necessary, the results are averaged over word frequency (see below), but information about the direction of transfer is preserved. Thus the RP value for the transfer from French to English is calculated by expressing the absolute priming value observed when a word is encoded in French and tested in English as a fraction of the absolute priming value when a word is encoded and tested in English.

For the six lexical decision experiments involving translations, the outcome is unambiguous; the RP values range from −.20 to +.18, with a mean of .01 (s = .09, n = 6). The result therefore complements the frequency analysis summarized above, there being no suggestion at this level that there is any transfer between morphologically unrelated translations. As it may be argued that lexical decision is a shallow test relative to, for example, semantic classification (e.g., Is /FROMAGE/ a living or man-made object?), results from two experiments of this type are also included. Here, too, no statistically significant interlingual transfer was recorded, and the RP values are consistent with this conclusion (see Kirsner, Smith, Lockhart, King, & Jain, 1984, Experiment 3, and Harvey, 1981, in Table 1).

The closest monolingual parallel to translations involves synonyms, but the only relevant data, published by Cofer and Shepp (1957), used short intervals and introduced the possibility of expectancy by using the ascending method of limits. When semantically or associatively related pairs of words are tested (see below), the bilingual as well as the monolingual data demonstrate that the relevant priming effects are transient, surviving either one or two intervening items, and this material is therefore examined separately.

Contact between translations may occur in several ways. The experiments involving semantic classification rather than lexical decision were based on the assumption that this may be achieved by accessing supralingual and semantically

TABLE 2.1

Summary of Results and Relative Priming (RP) Values for Repetition Experiments Involving Language Manipulation

| Study | Exp. | Language Combination and Type of Word | Notes | Repetition Treatment NW | AL | SL | RP |
|---|---|---|---|---|---|---|---|
| Kirsner et al. (1980) | | Hindi → English trans. | (a,c) | | -22 | 109 | -.20 |
| | | English → Hindi trans. | (a,c) | | 23 | 125 | .18 |
| Scarborough et al. (1984) | 1 | Spanish → English trans. | (a,c) | | -4 | 72 | -.06 |
| Kirsner et al. (1984) | 1 | French → English trans. | (a) | 636 | 640 | 609 | -.16 |
| | | English → French trans. | (a) | 656 | 647 | 596 | .15 |
| Cristoffanini et al. (in press) | 1 | Spanish → English: | | | | | |
| | | identical cognates | (a) | 799 | 745 | 733 | .82 |
| | | regular cognates (TION) | (a) | 921 | 815 | 813 | .98 |
| | | regular cognates (TY) | (a) | 866 | 796 | 783 | .84 |
| | | irregular cognates | (a) | 858 | 792 | 769 | .74 |
| | | translations | (a) | 908 | 906 | 811 | .02 |
| Kirsner et al. (1984) | 3 | French → English trans. | (b) | 847 | 834 | 797 | .26 |
| | | English → French trans. | (b) | 981 | 967 | 902 | .18 |
| Harvey (1981) | | Italian → English: | | | | | |
| | | trans: same task | (b,d) | 823 | 828 | 743 | -.06 |
| | | trans: related task | (b,e) | 753 | 751 | 693 | .03 |
| | | trans: different task | (b,f) | 808 | 813 | 759 | -.10 |
| Brown et al. (1984) | 1 | Urdu → Hindi | (a) | 1269 | 1209 | 1182 | .69 |
| | | Hindi → Urdu | (a) | 1101 | 977 | 964 | .91 |
| Hatta & Ogawa (1983) | | Katakana → Hiragana | (a,c) | | 50 | 108 | .46 |
| | | Hiragana → Katakana | (a,c) | | 59 | 117 | .50 |

Notes: RP = relative priming, NW = new words, AL = alternative language, SL = same language, a = lexical decision (msec), b = semantic classification (msec), c = difference values (msec) as reported in cited study, d = living/nonliving during the study and test phases, e = animal/nonanimal and living/nonliving during the study and test phases respectively, f = big/small and living/nonliving during the study and test phases respectively.

defined units. Although evidence consistent with the proposition is available under immediate testing conditions (see section on semantic priming below), the results discussed earlier indicate that the underlying mechanism is qualitatively different from those which sustain frequency and repetition transfer. If supralingual units exist, their content, boundaries, and persistence characteristics are quite different from those which apply to lexical representation.

Another way in which contact may be achieved between lexical representation involves the use of elective processes, directed specifically at translation. If the perceptual record resulting from these generative processes is similar to that which results from stimulus processing, and there is much evidence that generation is functionally similar to perception (Shepard, 1978), repetition priming should be achieved. Kirsner et al. (1984, Experiment 2) tested this hypothesis by asking their subjects to name the first letter and specify the number of letters in translations, and they found RP values approaching unity under all except the lowest of four word frequency conditions.

The results of the experiments summarized above suggest that elective translation has a boundary, in word frequency terms, below which translation is either too slow or "expensive." A closely related question concerns the possibility that there is an upper boundary, above which translation or "cross-talk" between representations occurs spontaneously. We have reexamined the repetition transfer data to evaluate this proposition.

Figure 2.1 summarizes the relationship between word frequency and repetition. RP values are shown either as single points, where word frequency was not manipulated in the experiment concerned, or as a function when a number of word frequency levels were tested and reported. Although the outcome must be treated with caution in the absence of planned experimentation, the results are consistent with the proposal that some spontaneous translation occurs at high frequency levels (above 100 occurrences per million, for example).

The idea that cross-talk influences repetition priming is not new. Kirsner and Smith (1974) invoked the concept to explain variation in the levels of intermodality priming. However, comparison between the forms of the word frequency-RP relationships for modality and language suggest that it is the latter where transfer increases as a function of increasing word frequency, which reflects cross-talk. The word frequency-RP relationship for modality presumably reflects representational processes. In this context, it is interesting to note that Old/New judgments show a similar sensitivity to frequency, particularly under intermodality conditions (Gregg, 1976; Lee, Tzeng, Garro, & Hung, 1978).

In summary, the repetition transfer data indicate that representation is language-specific for translations. It is possible that this does not apply to high frequency words (> 100/million), but even here it seems likely that transfer reflects elective operations rather than common representation.

The results summarized in Table 2.1 show that translations and cognates behave in quite different ways. Whereas transfer is absent altogether for moder-

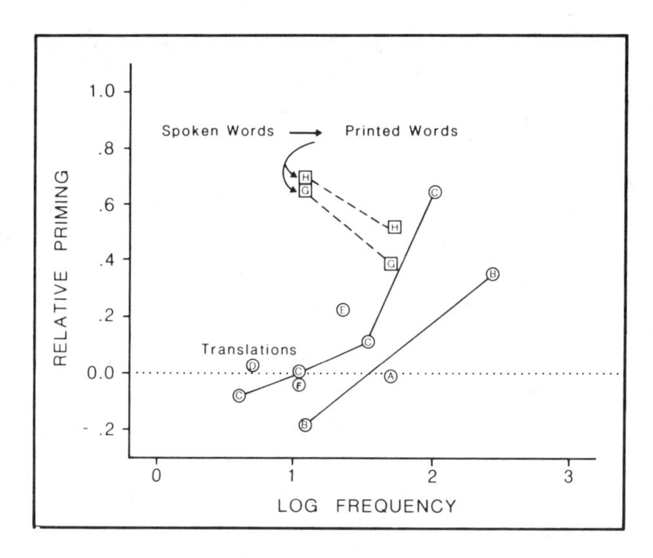


FIG. 2.1. Relationship between relative priming and word frequency (log). (A) Kirsner et al., 1980; (B) Scarborough et al., 1984; (C) Kirsner et al., 1984, Experiment 1; (D) Cristoffanini et al., in press (E) Kirsner et al., 1984, Experiment 3; (F) Harvey, 1981; (G) Kirsner et al., 1983, Experiments 4–6; (H) Kirsner et al., 1983, Experiments 7/8.

ate and low frequency translations, the RP values for cognates range from .74 to .98 in the experiment reported by Cristoffanini et al. (in press). The results are therefore broadly consistent with the proposition that morphology influences or governs the boundaries between word recognition units or processes. Where words have the same or similar structure, presentation of either one will affect performance when its cognates is presented, even though it is in another language.

The monolingual data for morphological priming may be used to establish a range within which cognate priming values should fall if they are subject to the same morphological considerations. In a series of experiments conducted by Stanners, Neiser, Hernon, and Hall (1979) comparisons involving inflection-to-base and derivation-to-base priming were made where the chosen treatments varied systematically in regard to the amount of variation in their stem morphemes. For example, Stanners et al. (1979) included several types of inflections where the stem morpheme was unchanged between the priming and test presentations (e.g., BURNS → BURN), several types of derivations with what they refer to as "lesser variations in the stem morpheme" (e.g., HANG—HUNG), and several types of variations with "greater variations in the stem morpheme" (e.g., DESTRUCTION—DESTROY). For our purposes, the most interesting aspect of their data is that when the RP values are calculated, the means for the three treatment types are .99 (s = .09, n = 3), .60 (s = .02, n = 3), and .33

(s = .06, n = 3), respectively. If it is assumed that morphological influence is restricted to the graphic domain, and that language is irrelevant, it follows that the RP values for cognates should approach 1.0. If phonemic influence is also present, lesser values may be observed. However, if language is critical, the RP values for cognates should approach zero, as they do for translations.

Another way to establish a standard for cognates involves consideration of word classes with the same suffixes (e.g., /PRODUCION/, /PRODUCTION/ and /PRODUCT/). No direct tests of this type have been reported, but indirect comparison is possible. Downie et al. (in press) used a different test procedure from that adopted by Cristoffanini et al. (in press), but the results are complementary. In the former study, word recognition rather than lexical decision was used, and parameter estimation by sequential testing (Pentland, 1980) was implemented to ensure that individual performance levels were at or near threshold levels. Despite these procedural differences, the RP values observed for derivation-to-base priming for /ITY/ and /ION/ words are similar to those reported by Cristoffanini et al. (in press). The actual values for the /NATIVIDAD → NATIVITY/ and /CAPTIVITY →CAPTIVE/ word sets were .84 and .66, respectively. The corresponding values for the /PRODUCION → PRODUCTION/ and /PRODUCTION → PRODUCT/ word sets were .98 and .77. The results therefore show that the cost of these form variations is small, and comparable under intralingual and interlingual conditions.

To summarize, the repetition transfer results for cognates complement the frequency transfer data, providing further support for the proposition that cognates access a common representation. The RP analyses also suggest that repetition transfer is, if anything, greater for cognates than it is for comparable monolingual combinations. We return to the relationship between language and morphology in the next section.

The third word class for which transfer data are available concerns morphophonemically identical cognates which differ in script. One case of particular interest occurs in North India where a substantial part of the dominant spoken language includes words that are common to Hindi and Urdu, although each language has unique words as well. In their written forms, therefore, the Hindi and Urdu scripts are commonly used to depict words with the same phonetic structure and meaning. See Fig. 2.2 for an illustration of the Hindi and Urdu renditions of the Hindustani word for ''water,'' namely, /pani/. The question in this case is whether or not script influences or determines the boundary conditions for lexical representation or whether, like case (Scarborough, Cortese, & Scarborough, 1977) and handwriting (Morton, 1979), it produces little or no cost in RP terms. As shown in Table 2.1, the RP values for Hindi and Urdu are similar to those observed for morphologically related translations when there is no script change. Thus, it may be inferred that morphophonemic similarity is a sufficient basis for transfer; orthographic similarity may be sufficient but it is not necessary.

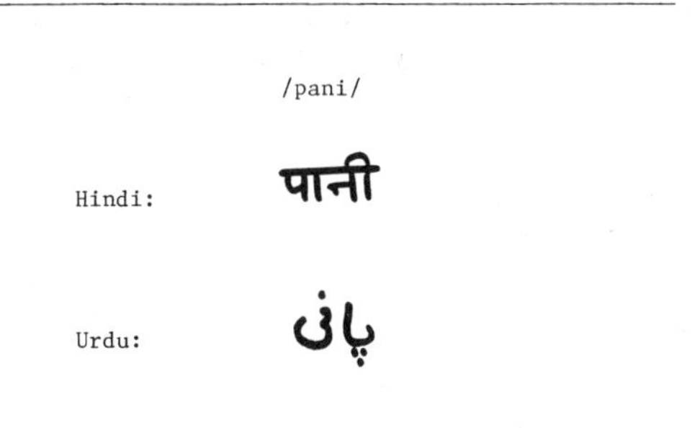


FIG. 2.2. The Hindustani word /*pani*/ written in the Hindi (*Devanagari*) and Urdu (Arabic) script.

An RP analysis of Brown, Sharma, and Kirsner's (1984) results suggests that, as is the case for semantic priming (see Segalowitz, this volume; Kirsner et al., 1984, Experiment 4), the balance of lingual skills can influence lexical function. In the present case, the subjects had received their initial and major educational experience in Urdu, a fact which is evident in the New word data; the mean reaction-time values being 1101 and 1265 msecs for the Urdu and Hindi items respectively. However, the outcome of direct interest is that RP is much greater under Hindi →Urdu than Urdu→Hindi conditions, suggesting that reference was made to information about script during encoding, but only when the presented stimulus was in the non-preferred script.

One further study by Hatta and Ogawa (1983) merits consideration. Hatta and Ogawa used native Japanese words, and these were presented to subjects in either Hiragana or Katakana in the first part of the experiment, and then tested in either the same script or the alternative script in the second part of the experiment. New words were included in each script, and a lexical decision task was used. In RP terms, their result (RP = .48) falls mid-way between the results observed for morphologically unrelated translations and morphologically identical translations which involve a script difference (i.e., Hindi-Urdu).

Interpretation of transfer patterns between Hiragana and Katakana is complex, however. In terms of their physical properties, the relationship between the Japanese scripts parallels that which applies to Hindi and Urdu. The syllabaries depict the same set of sounds, and they can be used to depict a common set of spoken words. However, their relationship is quite different in other respects. Although Hindi and Urdu constitute distinct languages, with their own literary traditions and, to some extent, their own vocabularies, there are no prescriptive rules governing the relationship between script and vocabulary; Hindi and Urdu words may be used to depict words of Arabic, Sanskrit, or English origin, although social convention may indicate a preference under certain circumstances. Where the Japanese scripts are concerned, however, usage is prescribed; Hiragana and Katakana must be used to depict Japanese and foreign loan words respectively. Considered overall, the fact that words depicted in Hiragana and Katakana yield RP values of .48 could reflect: (a) a facilitatory influence from their shared morphophonemic structure, (b) interference which may be attributed to the fact that the interscriptal test structure violates rules governing the presentation of Japanese and foreign words, or (c) elective processes associated with the presence of some very high frequency words in their experiment (the mean for the set of translations given by the authors is approximately 101/million).

In summary, despite the fact that words depicted in Hindi and Urdu differ radically in their physical form and direction-of-reading (Hindi is read from left-to-right, Urdu from right-to-left), the observed RP values were similar to those which can be calculated for handwriting (.73, Morton, 1979) and case (.95+, Scarborough, Cortese, & Scarborough, 1977) variations. The major implication of this result is that the dimension which determines RP values is *not* a simple product of physical similarity. The feature which the interscript and intrascript variations appear to share is that there is a one-to-one mapping between the character sets in each case. Thus, with some minor exceptions, a regular mapping rule may be used to substitute a representation based on elements from one class with a corresponding representation from the alternative class.

## ATTRIBUTE RETENTION

The results discussed in this section complement those reported in the section on frequency and repetition transfer effects. Despite the fact that the data sets are drawn from the perceptual and memory domains, respectively, they support the same conclusions. Translations are represented on a language-specific basis, but this is restricted to morphologically unrelated translations and the effect may therefore reflect their morphological independence rather than their lingual status.

There are several reasons for using data from memory as well as perceptual tasks to test ideas about lexical function. One theoretical position set out in the introduction is that perceptual categorization as well as memory depend on access to an instance-based memory system, the implication for our purposes being that if the same processes are involved in each case, memory data may be used to test ideas about lexical function as well as vice versa. The particular proposition under scrutiny is that those variations in surface form which yield a RP gradient from 0.0 to 1.0 should influence performance on explicit memory tests as well.

The precise way in which variations in surface form will influence performance on explicit memory tasks may depend on the effect of the task on retrieval. If it is a simple Old/New decision task, then increasing similarity may facilitate performance, as demonstrated for letter matching at short interstimulus intervals (Kirsner & Sang, 1979, Experiment 1). But if the task involves an explicit form match, then increasing similarity may impair performance (Kirsner & Sang, 1979, Experiment 2). In the present case consideration will be restricted to memory for surface form because: (a) the relevant effects may be obtained under recall as well as recognition conditions, thereby countering the claim that they simply reflect judgments about perceptual fluency (Jacoby, 1983a), and (b) the data clearly support the proposition that variations in surface form influence memory in systematic ways, whereas the Old/New data are equivocal in this respect.

The final justification for this use of memory as well as perceptual data in this chapter on lexical function is that the perceptual system can, regardless of its actual mode of operation, be viewed as a filter. Repetition priming examines changes in the status of elements in the filter. Memory for surface form examines encoded products of the filter's operations, the assumption being that if the filter defines linguistic units, the product will—in the absence of intentional or schematic processes—reflect the boundaries and operating characteristics of the perceptual categories embodied in the filter.

In a now classic study involving morphologically unrelated translations, Kintsch (1970) used a continuous presentation procedure in which subjects made either Old/New or Same/Different decisions. In the former case, the subject's task was to ignore language, and respond "old" if a word or its translation had been presented before, and "new" if it had not been presented before in either language. In the latter case, subjects were required to answer "same" whenever a word was repeated in the same language, and "different" in all other cases. Kintsch (1970) found that a language change produced a small cost on the accuracy of Old/New decisions, and that memory for language of presentation was very reliable, at approximately 89% correct. The fact that the stimuli were presented in a continuous sequence, with Old/New or attribute retention decisions being made on each trial meant, however, that intentional learning was possible, even though there were no explicit instructions to this end. The difficulty with intentional learning is that it permits or even encourages a range of extra-lexical processes. If a subject is expecting to be tested for language of presentation (or modality or voice for that matter), a variety of elaborative or imaginal processes can be invoked to aid performance, and this runs counter to an analysis of purely lexical function.

In fact, when consideration is restricted to performance obtained under incidental learning conditions, the data indicate that there is little if any effect of intentionality on this attribute. Experiments reported by Saegert, Hamayan, and Ahmar (1975), Rose and Carroll (1974), Winograd, Cohen, and Barresi (1976), Brown et al. (1984), MacLeod (1976), and Cristoffanini et al. (in preparation) tested memory for language of presentation under incidental learning conditions, and the accuracy values for their studies range from 80% correct (Cristoffanini et al., in press, Experiment 2) to 95% correct (MacLeod, 1976, Experiment 2), with a mean of 87%. Similarly, in a direct comparison between incidental and intentional learning conditions, Kirsner and Dunn (1985) found a small and statistically unreliable advantage for intentional learning conditions. Assuming, then, that there is no benefit from intentionality it may be suggested that, where translations are concerned, language and word information are integral. Languages may represent alternative ways of communicating ideas, but the words are language-specific; strictly speaking, they do not constitute alternative surface forms at all.

The proposition that repetition priming and attribute retention involve access to either the same perceptual record or to the product of a shared encoding process leads to the prediction that memory for language of presentation will be poor when cognates are tested. Assuming that morphology alone governs lexical function, cognates should behave like structurally similar inflections and derivations. The words in each cognate pair will invoke a similar set of processes during encoding, and it will be correspondingly difficult to discriminate between them, and therefore language of presentation, during testing. In addition to their analysis of repetition effects, Cristoffanini et al. (in press) examined memory for language of presentation using translations. The results were clear. Memory for language of presentation was reliable when unrelated translations were tested but barely above chance for the three testable cognate conditions (memory for language of presentation cannot of course be tested under visual conditions when the 'translations' are orthographically identical). The range of values (in percentage correct) for the cognate conditions was 57.9 to 63.1, and these values all lie within the range set by reference to the only available monolingual evidence. The monolingual study conducted by Downie et al. (in press) was virtually identical to that conducted by Cristoffanini et al. (in press), the main difference being that in the latter case four derivational conditions were selected on the basis of phonological and stress variation. The range of values in the Downie et al. (in press) study was 56.0 to 64.0.

In summary, then, memory for form of presentation is unreliable when cognates are concerned, and the observed performance level is similar to that observed for qualitatively comparable (intra-lingual) derivations.

## REPETITION PRIMING AND ATTRIBUTE RETENTION

The relationship between repetition priming and attribute retention is set out in Fig 2.3. Figure 2.3a shows a meta-analysis of the relevant data. Each condition for a particular attribute is determined by the mean of the RP (x axis) or attribute retention (y axis) values for the set of available studies. The RP values are based on the following experiments; translations: Kirsner, Brown, Abrol, Chaddha, and Sharma (1980), Scarborough, Gerard, and Cortese (1984, Experiment 1), Kirsner et al. (1984, Experiments 1 and 3), Cristoffanini et al. (in press, Experiment 1), and Harvey (1981); transfer from speech to print: Kirsner and Smith

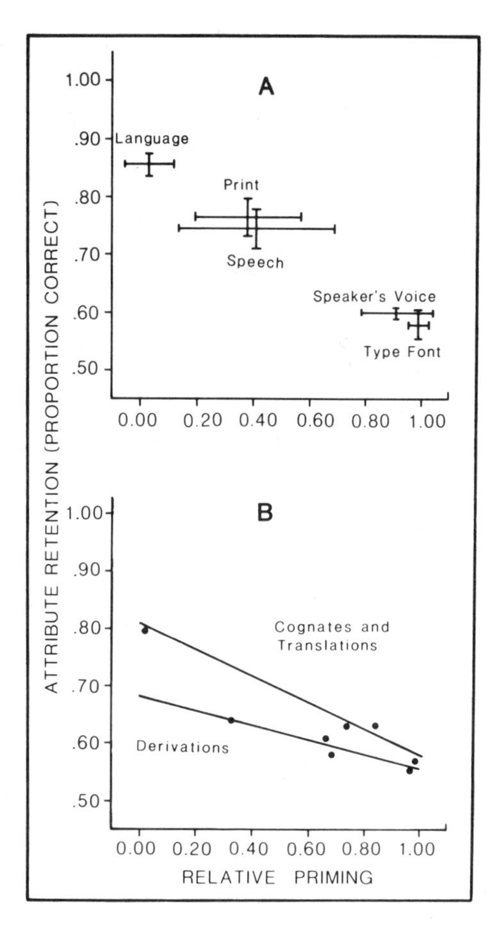


FIG. 2.3. Attribute retention (proportion correct) as a function of relative priming for (A) A meta-analysis of the results from experiments which have tested different attributes, and (B) Within-attribute comparisons from experiments involving derivations (Downie et al., in press) and cognates (Cristoffanini et al., in press).

(1974), Kirsner, Milech, and Standen (1983, Experiments 1–6 and 7/8), Monsell (in press, Experiment 5), Clarke and Morton (1983, Experiments 2 and 3), and Jacoby and Dallas (1981, Experiment 6); transfer from print to speech: Kirsner and Smith (1974), Monsell (in press, Experiment 6), Jackson and Morton (1984), and Standen and Kirsner (in preparation); transfer between upper and lower case print: Scarborough et al. (1977), Standen and Kirsner (in preparation); and male and female speakers: Jackson and Morton (1984), and Standen and Kirsner (in preparation). The attribute retention values are based on the following experiments; translations: see attribute retention section above; memory for modality following auditory presentation: Lehman (1982, Experiments 1

& 2), Siple, Fischer, and Bellugi (1977), Hintzman, Block, and Inskeep (1972), and Bray and Batchelder (1972); memory for modality following visual presentation: (as for memory for modality following auditory presentation); case: Light and Berger (1974), Hintzman et al. (1972), and Brown et al. (1984); and speaker's voice: Hintzman et al. (1972). The selection criteria were that: (a) the data were collected under incidental learning conditions, a constraint which eliminates experiments involving a sequence of interleaved Old and New trials, and (b) the encoding and test procedures involved presentation of isolated words, a constraint which excludes thematic (Fisher & Cuervo, 1983) and sentential effects (Geiselman & Belleza, 1976).

The results summarized in Fig. 2.3a demonstrate clearly that there *is* a relationship between repetition priming and attribute retention. However, caution is required because the correlation ($r = .99$, $df = 4$) follows averaging over experiments, items, subjects, and, possibly, processes. The nature of the relationship might be quite different at the intraindividual level, the crucial question where process modeling is concerned (Brown & Kirsner, 1980).

From the point of view of bilingual function, the major implication of the analysis is in the support which it provides for the relative position of translations. The results show that two completely independent procedures identify language as an "end-point" in so far as lexical function is concerned; the amount of processing overlap between morphologically unrelated translations is low, so low in fact that there is no transfer in repetition tasks, and subjects experience no difficulty in identifying language of presentation in a memory task. The results also suggest that there is considerable processing overlap where modality is concerned, and virtually complete processing overlap for the intramodality manipulations, involving case and speaker's voice in this example. McCormack (1976, 1977) described a variety of effects which demonstrated that language, like modality, orthography, position, and other attributes, should be thought of as an "attribute of memory," in Underwood's (1969) terminology. The present results clearly demonstrate the relative power of this attribute.

Figure 2.3b shows that the relationship between repetition priming and attribute retention is obtained when the analysis involves a number of levels of one attribute, rather than a range of attributes. In this case we have plotted the repetition priming and attribute retention data from the transfer and cognate conditions in the two experiments reported by Cristoffanini et al. (in preparation), and an equivalent set of data from the study involving derivations (Downie et al., in press). The results demonstrate that the relationship holds across a number of levels of a given attribute, in this case morphological derivation. The data are consistent with the general view that morphology rather than language is critical, but they also suggest that, where memory for surface form is concerned, language makes a unique contribution. This additional contribution is manifest in the difference between the intercepts and the slopes of the functions from the two studies. The relationship per se is stable but, for a given level of repetition priming, memory for surface form is more reliable when there is a language difference as well as a morphological difference. Whether or not this language effect would survive systematic control of subject, syntactic, and semantic status is unclear.

The following section on semantic priming suggests that there is a sharp division between the long-term consequences of word processing—as discussed in this and the previous sections—and the temporary patterns of activation which accompany discourse comprehension. In the latter case, accessibility is dominated by functional considerations: if information is semantically related to the current topic it is temporarily activated, and the facilitatory effects of this are modality-independent and language-independent.

## SEMANTIC PRIMING

Thus far, we have examined lexical function with selective reference to the behavior of isolated words as distinct from sets of words or sentences, and we have ignored theoretical questions concerning the role of semantic networks and extensive meaning. Each of these issues will be addressed in this final section.

Where individual words are concerned, the gist of our argument is that representation is language-specific, but only as an artifact of morphological independence. When this constraint is relaxed, as it is with cognates, the results suggest that language is not a critical factor, and this conclusion must hold for individual units and for the lexicon as a whole. One corollary of the proposition that there are no language-specific lexical systems is that *semantic priming* should also be language-independent. That is, if there is a single, language-independent lexicon, it follows that effects which purportedly reflect relationships between lexical entries should occur under interlingual as well as intralingual conditions. They do. The classic though unpublished experiment of this type was conducted by Meyer and Ruddy (1974). They presented English/German bilinguals with pairs of genuine or false words in one or both languages, where each genuine pair consisted of two English words, two German words, or one word from each language. Meyer and Ruddy (1974) found that relative to performance when subjects were presented with a semantically unrelated pair of English and German words, reaction time was shorter when either: (a) the words were semantically related, or (b) the words were in the same language. Furthermore, these effects were additive. Kirsner et al. (1984, Experiment 4) confirmed Meyer and Ruddy (1974) main finding regarding the presence of interlingual priming under mixed language conditions, and demonstrated that the cost of mixing languages is eliminated when different scripts (English and Hindi in this case) are used.

In establishing a formal account of semantic priming and its significance for bilingualism, it is necessary to contrast the effects with those observed in repetition priming. Whereas repetition priming is sensitive to attribute variations involving language (see above), modality (spoken and written language) and mode (picture and word), semantic priming is either absolutely or relatively insensitive to these manipulations. Provided that subjects are equally competent in each language or symbol system, the fact and possibly the magnitude of semantic priming are unaffected by changes in language (Meyer and Ruddy 1974; Kirsner et al., 1984, Experiment 4), modality (Swinney, Onifer, Prather, & Hirshkowitz, 1979), and mode (Vanderwart, 1984). A second line of evidence supports the claim that repetition priming may be observed for hours or days (Scarborough et al., 1977; Jacoby & Dallas, 1981), but that semantic priming is eliminated by the presence of one or two intervening items (Gough, Alford, & Holley-Wilcox, 1981; Dannenbring & Briand, 1982; Henderson, Wallis, & Knight, 1984). Semantic priming effects involving translations are no exception to this rule (Kirsner et al., 1984, Experiment 5).

The usual interpretation placed on semantic priming is that it reflects activation or proximity in a semantic network (e.g., Schvaneveldt & Meyer, 1973), and this proposition has been extended to the bilingual case (Meyer et al., 1974; Kirsner et al., 1984). The special assumption which must be made in the bilingual case is that words are organized according to their semantic or associative status (cf. Lupker, 1984) without formal regard to language.

Semantic priming effects may be interpreted without reference to semantic networks, however. Johnson-Laird and his associates (Johnson-Laird, 1981; Johnson-Laird, Heerman, & Chaffin, 1984) have developed an account of discourse comprehension which involves the notion of a "mental model." According to Johnson-Laird, discourse is first translated into a mental code which provides a direct linguistic representation of the message, including its lexical content. A second stage then uses the linguistic representation and other information to form a mental model of the described state of affairs. To this basic account can be added the assumption that an established mental model can moderate the linguistic processing system, rather in the fashion of the interpretation process in schema theories of memory (Alba & Hasher, 1983). This being the case, instantiation of, for example, CUTLERY following presentation of the word KNIFE will facilitate recognition of words which share the same referent. FORK is an obvious example of such a word. One final point is that as mental models are, by definition, coded in a perceptual or conceptual as distinct from linguistic form, it follows that they are independent of language of presentation, although this does not preclude a lingual or sociolingual influence on the character of a particular model.

In some respects, this account provides an interesting parallel to that developed by Brown (1979) and Perecman (1984) to account for a range of symptoms observed in polyglot aphasia. The most interesting of these for our purposes is spontaneous translation, which may be observed when a polyglot has a receptive deficit in one language and an expressive deficit in another language. Perecman explains the condition by referring to a pre-linguistic system, arguing that spontaneous translation reflects direct access to this abstract and non-linguistic domain. The feature which Johnson-Laird's (1981) and Perecman's (1984) accounts share is that they both draw a sharp line between lingual and nonlingual function, and imbue the latter with a central role in comprehension.

## CONCLUDING REMARKS

The primary aim of this chapter was to identify the impact of bilingualism on lexical function. The results which we have summarized appear to support the following conclusions. First, considered in isolation the bilingual results suggest that translations but not cognates are represented on a language-specific basis. However, when the bilingual data are given a monolingual context involving synonyms (for which little data are available) and inflections and derivations, the results suggest that morphology rather than language determines the boundaries between lexical categories. Second, when the relationships between pairs of words are considered, the results suggest that contact between lexical representations involves access to a language-independent medium, although the character of this medium is unclear.

The foregoing requires some qualifications. If the lexicon is not language-specific, and if comprehension involves access to a language-independent domain, how can bilinguals restrict themselves to a single language? Clearly, computation involving syntactic and phonological rules will play an important role. But it may also be necessary to posit the functional co-existence of a variety of lexical structures, one of which sustains language-specific access. Contextual selection of this type does not set bilinguals apart in processing or representational terms, however. Essentially the same proposition is firmly embedded in theories of discourse comprehension. Whether the knowledge base is artificial or natural, temporary partitioning of the system is an essential prerequisite for efficient comprehension (Sanford & Garrod, 1981).

Our analysis of bilingualism has implications for general cognitive function. The data summarized here are consistent with the proposition that there is a division between input and central processes. The material described in the frequency transfer, repetition transfer, and attribute retention sections indicates that lexical representations can be defined in terms of the encoding operations which are brought to bear on the stimulus input, but the effects in question are abolished when word relationships can be exploited.

Considered together, the perceptual categorization and attribute retention data reveal a systematic ordering in the effects of encoding operations that is not governed by either physical similarity or morphological complexity alone. The ordering is evident when comparisons are made across a range of attributes, such as language, modality, case, and speaker's voice, and also when they involve a number of levels from a single attribute, as is the case for cognates and derivations. In a first approximation to the nature of the dimension underlying these systematic effects, it is suggested that the critical feature involves the complexity of the mapping relationship between the representations concerned. At one extreme there is no mapping relationship, just an arbitrary association. Translations and synonyms which mean the "same" thing but share no morphology belong in this category. At the other extreme the mapping rules are regular and computationally simple, and surprisingly large variations in visual form can be ignored. Between these extremes there are a number of examples where a mapping relationship exists, but it is a complex one involving differences between the representation of spoken and written language and different lexical forms.

## SUMMARY

The evidence presented in this chapter is consistent with the following conclusions. First, lexical representation in bilinguals is governed by morphology rather than language. Second, lexical representations may be defined in terms of the operations brought to bear on the stimulus input. Third, the mapping relationships between alternative forms of representation may provide the basis for a unified theory of perceptual categorization and memory.

## ACKNOWLEDGMENTS

Grateful acknowledgment is made to Heather Brown, John Dunn and Colin Macleod for their assistance in the preparation of this chapter, and to the Australian Research Grants Scheme for financial support.

## REFERENCES

Alba, J. W., & Hasher, L. (1983). Is memory schematic? *Psychological Bulletin, 93,* 203–231.

Banta, F.G. (1981). Teaching German vocabulary: The use of English cognates and common loan words. *Modern Language Journal, 65,* 129–136.

Bradley, D. (1979). Lexical representation of derivational relations. In M. Aranoff & M.L. Kean (Eds.), *Juncture.* Cambridge, MA: MIT Press.

Bray, N.W., & Batchelder, W.H. (1972). Effects of instructions and retention interval on memory of presentation mode. *Journal of Verbal Learning and Verbal Behavior, 11,* 367–374.

Brown, J.W. (1979). Language representation in the mind. In H.D. Steklis & M. Raleigh (Eds.), *The neurobiology of social communication in primates.* New York: Academic Press.

Brown, H.L., & Kirsner, K. (1980). A within subjects analysis of the relationship between memory span and processing rate in short-term memory. *Cognitive Psychology, 12,* 177–187.

Brown, H.L., Sharma, N.K., & Kirsner, K. (1984). The role of script and phonology in lexical representation. *Quarterly Journal of Experimental Psychology, 36A,* 491–505.

Caramazza, A., & Brones, I. (1979). Lexical access in bilinguals. *Bulletin of the Psychonomic Society, 13,* 212–214.

Clarke, R., & Morton, J. (1983). Cross-modality facilitation in tachistoscopic word recognition. *Quarterly Journal of Experimental Psychology, 35A*, 79–96.

Cofer, C.N., & Shepp, B.E. (1957). Verbal context and perceptual recognition time. *Perceptual and Motor Skills, 7*, 215–218.

Cristoffanini, P., Kirsner, K., & Milech, D. (in press). Bilingual lexical representation: The status of cognates. *Quarterly Journal of Experimental Psychology.*

Dannenbring, G.L., & Briand, K. (1982). Semantic priming and the word repetition effect in a lexical decision task. *Canadian Journal of Psychology, 36*, 435–444.

Downie, R., Milech, D., & Kirsner, K. (in press). Unit definition in the mental lexicon. *Australian Journal of Psychology.*

Fisher, R.P., & Cuervo, A. (1983). Memory for physical features of discourse as a function of their relevance. *Journal of Experimental Psychology: Learning, Memory and Cognition, 9*(1), 130–158.

Forbach, G.B., Stanners, R.F., & Hochhaus, L. (1974). Repetition and practice effects in a lexical decision task. *Memory & Cognition, 2*, 337–339.

Forster, K.I. (1976). Accessing the mental lexicon. In R.J. Wales & E. Walker (Eds.), *New approaches to language mechanisms.* Amsterdam: North-Holland.

Geiselman, R.E., & Bellezza, F.S. (1976). Long-term memory for speaker's voice and source location. *Memory & Cognition, 4*(5), 483–489.

Gough, P.B., Alford, J.A., & Holley-Wilcox, P. (1981). Word and contexts. In O.J.L. Tzeng & H. Singer (Eds.), *Perception of print: Reading research in experimental psychology.* Hillsdale, NJ: Lawrence Erlbaum Associates.

Gregg, V. (1976). Word frequency, recognition and recall. In J. Brown (Ed.), *Recall and recognition.* London: John Wiley.

Harvey, R. (1981). *The structure of semantic representation in bilinguals.* Unpublished honors thesis. University of Western Australia.

Hatta, T., & Ogawa, T. (1983). Hiragana and Katakana in Japanese orthography and lexical representation. *Language Sciences, 5*(2), 185–186.

Henderson, L. (1984). Writing systems and reading processes. In L. Henderson (Ed.), *Orthographies and reading.* Hillsdale, NJ: Lawrence Erlbaum Associates.

Henderson, L., Wallis, J., & Knight, D. (1984). Morphemic structure and lexical access. In H. Bouma & D. Bouhuis (Eds.), *Attention and performance X.* Hillsdale, NJ: Lawrence Erlbaum Associates.

Herrmann, D.J. (1978). An old problem for the new psychosemantics: Synonymity. *Psychological Bulletin, 85*(3), 490–512.

Hintzmann, D.L., Block, R.A., & Inskeep, N.R. (1972). Memory for mode of input. *Journal of Verbal Learning and Verbal Behavior, 11*, 741–749.

Jackson, A., & Morton, J. (1984). Facilitation in auditory word recognition. *Memory & Cognition, 12*(6), 568–574.

Jacoby, L.L. (1983a). Perceptual enhancement: Persistent effects of an experience. *Journal of Experimental Psychology: Learning, Memory and Cognition, 9*(1), 21–38.

Jacoby, L.L. (1983b). Remembering the data: Analyzing interactive processes in reading. *Journal of Verbal Learning and Verbal Behavior, 22*, 485–508.

Jacoby, L.L., & Brooks, L.R. (1984). Nonanalytic cognition: Memory, perception and concept learning. In G.H. Bower (Ed.),*The psychology of learning and motivation: Advances in research and theory, Vol. 18.* New York: Academic Press.

Jacoby, L.L., & Dallas, M. (1981). On the relationship between autobiographical memory and perceptual learning. *Journal of Experimental Psychology: Learning, Memory and Cognition, 110*, 306–340.

Johnson-Laird, P.N. (1981). Comprehension as the construction of mental models. *Philosophical Transactions of London Bulletin, 295*, 353–374.

Johnson-Laird, P.N., Herrman, D.J., & Chaffin, R. (1984). Only connections: A critique of semantic networks. *Psychological Bulletin, 96*(2), 292–315.

Juilland, A., & Chang-Rodriguez, E. (1964). *The Romance languages and their structures: Frequency dictionary of Spanish words.* The Hague: Mouton.

Kintsch, W. (1970). Recognition memory in bilingual subjects. *Journal of Verbal Learning and Verbal Behavior, 9,* 405–409.

Kirsner, K., Brown, H.L., Abrol, S., Chaddha, N.N., & Sharma, N.K. (1980). Bilingualism and lexical representation. *Quarterly Journal of Experimental Psychology, 4,* 585–594.

Kirsner, K., & Dunn, J.C. (1985). The perceptual record: A common factor in repetition priming and attribute retention. In M.I. Posner & O.S.M. Marin (Eds.), *Mechanisms of attention: Attention and performance XI.* Hillsdale, NJ: Lawrence Erlbaum Associates.

Kirsner, K., Milech, D., & Standen, P. (1983). Common and modality-specific coding in the mental lexicon. *Memory & Cognition, 11*(6), 621–630.

Kirsner, K., & Sang, D.L. (1979). Visual persistence and code selection in short-term memory for letters. *Journal of Experimental Psychology: Human Perception and Performance, 5*(2), 260–276.

Kirsner, K., & Smith, M.C. (1974). Modality effects in word identification. *Memory & Cognition, 2,* 637–640.

Kirsner, K., Smith, M.C., Lockhart, R.L.S., King, M-L., & Jain, M. (1984). The bilingual lexicon: Language-specific effects in an integrated network. *Journal of Verbal Learning and Verbal Behavior, 23,* 519–539.

Kolers, P.A. (1978). On the representations of experience. In D. Gerver & W. Snaiko (Eds.), *Language interpretation and communication.* New York: Plenum.

Kolers, P.A. (1979). Reading and knowing. *Canadian Journal of Psychology, 33,*(2), 106–117.

Kolers, P.A., & Roediger, H.L. (1984). Procedures of mind. *Journal of Verbal Learning and Verbal Behavior, 23,* 425–449.

Lee, A.J., Tzeng, O.J.L., Garro, L.C., & Hung, D.L. (1978). Sensory modality and the word frequency effect. *Memory & Cognition, 6*(3), 306–311.

Lehman, E.B. (1982). Memory for modality: Evidence for an automatic process. *Memory & Cognition, 10,* 554–564.

Light, L.L., & Berger, D.E. (1974). Memory for modality: Within-modality discrimination is not automatic. *Journal of Experimental Psychology, 103*(5), 854–860.

Lupker, S. (1984). Semantic priming without association: A second look. *Journal of Verbal Learning and Verbal Behavior, 23,* 709–733.

MacLeod, C.M. (1976). Bilingual episodic memory: Acquisition and forgetting. *Journal of Verbal Learning and Verbal Behavior, 15,* 347–364.

McCormack, P.D. (1976). Language as an attribute of memory. *Canadian Journal of Psychology, 30*(4), 238–248.

McCormack, P.D. (1977). Bilingual linguistic memory: The independence-interdependence issue revisited. In P. Hornby (Ed.), *Bilingualism: Psychological, social, and educational implications.* New York: Academic Press.

Marshall, P.H., & Carareo-Ramos, L.E. (1984). Bilingual frequency encoding. *Journal of Psycholinguistic Research, 13,*(4), 295–306.

Meyer, D.E., & Ruddy, M.G. (1974, April). Bilingual word recognition: Organization and retrieval of alternative lexical codes. Paper presented at the Eastern Psychological Association annual meeting, Philadelphia.

Monsell, S. (in press). Repetition and the lexicon. In A.W. Ellis (Ed.), *Progress in the psychology of language, Vol. 1.* Hillsdale, NJ: Lawrence Erlbaum Associates.

Morton, J. (1969). Interaction of information in word recognition. *Psychological Review, 76,* 165–178.

Morton, J. (1979). Facilitation in word recognition: Experiments causing change in the logogen model, In P.A. Kolers, M.E. Wrolstad, & H. Bouma (Eds.), *Processing of visible language*. New York: Plenum.

Murdock, B.B. (1974). *Human memory: Theory and data*. Hillsdale, NJ: Lawrence Erlbaum Associates.

Oliphant, G.W. (1984). Repetition and recency effects in word recognition. *Australian Journal of Psychology, 35*(3), 393–403.

Pentland, A. (1980). Maximum likelihood estimation: The best PEST. *Perception and Psychophysics, 28*(4), 377–379.

Perecman, E. (1984). Spontaneous translation and language mixing in polyglot aphasia. *Brain and Language, 23*, 43–63.

Rose, R.G., & Carroll, J.F. (1974). Free recall of a mixed language list. *Bulletin of the Psychonomic Society, 3*(4), 267–268.

Saegert, J., Hamayan, E., & Ahmar, H. (1975). Memory for language of input in polyglots. *Journal of Experimental Psychology: Human Learning and Memory, 1*(5), 607–613.

Sanford, A.J., & Garrod, S.C. (1981). *Understanding written language*. Chichester: Wiley.

Scarborough, D.L., Cortese, C., & Scarborough, H.S. (1977). Frequency and repetition effects in lexical memory. *Journal of Experimental Psychology: Human Perception and Performance, 3*, 1–17.

Scarborough, D.L., Gerard, L., & Cortese, C. (1984). Independence of lexical access in bilingual word recognition. *Journal of Verbal Learning and Verbal Behavior, 23*, 84–99.

Schvaneveldt, R.W., & Meyer, D.E. (1973). Retrieval and comparison processes in semantic memory. In S. Kornblum (Ed.), *Attention and performance IV*. New York: Academic Press.

Shepard, R. (1978, February). The mental image. *American Psychologist*, 125–137.

Siple, P., Fischer, S.D., & Bellugi, U. (1977). Memory for nonsemantic attributes of American sign language signs and English words. *Journal of Verbal Learning and Verbal Behavior, 16*, 561–564.

Standen, P., & Kirsner, K. (in preparation). *Modality and morphological effects in word indentification*. University of Western Australia.

Stanners, R.F., Neiser, J.J., Hernon, W.P., & Hall, R. (1979). Memory representation for morphologically related words. *Journal of Verbal Learning and Verbal Behavior, 18*, 399–412.

Swinney, D.A., Onifer, W., Prather, P., & Hirshkowitz, M. (1979). Semantic facilitation across sensory modalities in the processing of individual words and sentences. *Memory & Cognition, 7*(3), 159–165.

Taft, M. (1979). Recognition of affixed words and the word frequency effect. *Memory & Cognition, 7*(4), 263–272.

Taft, M. (in press). The decoding of words in lexical access: A review of the morphographic approach. In D. Besner, T.G. Walker & G.E. McKinnon (Eds.), *Reading research: Advances in theory and practice, Vol. V*. New York: Academic Press.

Underwood, B.J. (1969). Attributes of memory. *Psychological Review, 76*, 559–573.

Vanderwart, M. (1984). Priming by pictures in lexical decision. *Journal of Verbal Learning and Verbal Behavior, 23*, 67–83.

Winograd, E., Cohen, C., & Barresi, J. (1976). Memory for concrete and abstract words in bilingual speakers. *Memory & Cognition, 4*(3), 323–329.

# 3 Memory for Bilingual Prose

Kirsten M. Hummel
*McGill University*

Bilingualism has been investigated from several different perspectives. Psycholinguistic studies of bilingualism have focused on bilingual memory. One clear advantage of investigating memory in bilinguals is that it is possible to study memory for information encoded and transmitted in two linguistically distinct channels. A study of the interaction between language and memory allows one to examine whether the distinct surface structures which characterize two languages have significant effects on cognitive processes such as retention.

Memory is a particularly interesting avenue of research since human cognitive development is largely dependent on access through memory to previously acquired experiences and information. The close association between memory and learning can be demonstrated by the fact that retention tests constitute virtually the only method developed to determine degree or extent of learning. As Cermak (1972) notes, "In a very real sense, what is meant by 'learning' is really 'remembering' " (p. 4).

Much of the research in bilingual memory has tended to parallel traditional verbal learning research paradigms by focusing on aspects of lexical decision and free recall of word lists. Such tasks have given rise to divergent results as well as to conflicting interpretations of these results.

The present chapter first points out certain drawbacks of studies in the bilingual memory literature and goes on to suggest that bilingual memory be studied using contextualized materials. This suggestion is followed by a discussion of current issues in verbal memory research. A theoretical framework for the study of memory for prose in bilinguals is then developed, and an hypothesis concerning the relative effectiveness of a bilingual versus unilingual transmission of information is formulated. Two experiments are then presented which test this hypothesis.

## Bilingual Lexical Memory

The types of experimental paradigms that have been used to study lexical memory in bilinguals include recall of word lists (e.g., Champagnol, 1973; Dalrymple-Alford & Aamiry, 1969; Glanzer & Duarte, 1971; Kolers, 1965, 1966, 1968; Lambert, Ignatow, & Krauthamer, 1968; Nott & Lambert, 1968; Tulving & Colotla, 1970), semantic differential (e.g., Lambert, Havelka, & Crosby, 1958) and association tasks (e.g., Kolers, 1963; Macnamara, 1967; Taylor, 1971, 1976), and proactive and retroactive interference tasks (e.g., Goggin & Wickens, 1971; Lopez, Hicks, & Young, 1974; Young & Navar, 1968). Such paradigms have been and still are designed to identify the nature of the bilingual lexicon (see also Kirsner, this volume). However, it is not unusual to find these studies addressing the issue of bilingual language organization in a more general sense, in terms of the processing of information transmitted by two languages.

One perspective on bilingual language organization that has emerged from these studies is that lexical items in the bilingual's two languages are organized in a common storage system or that there is one underlying representation for each word and its translation equivalent. This view has been variously termed the interdependent, or single store view of bilingual lexical organization. Alternatively, it has been argued that a more accurate characterization of bilingual lexical organization is in terms of separate, distinct systems for the lexical items of each language; that is, a separate lexical representation is believed to be accessed via each language. This view is known as the independent or separate store view of bilingual lexical memory.

*Free Recall Tasks.* One task that has commonly been used to investigate the independence/interdependence issue involves free recall of word lists. Kolers (1965) found that bilinguals recalled an approximately equivalent number of words from a unilingual list as from a mixed language word list. His results were confirmed by Nott and Lambert (1968) and by Lambert et al. (1968). Two additional free recall studies (Lopez & Young, 1974; Liepmann & Saegert, 1974) also support this interdependence view of lexical organization in bilinguals. However, other studies have supported a separate store view. Tulving and Colotla (1970) found that memory for items progressively deteriorated from unilingual to trilingual visually presented word lists. Their interpretation of this finding was that semantic information is less easily accessed when encoded in two more languages. Champagnol (1973) similarly found that free recall for unilingual list items was superior to that for bilingual list items. These results argue for a separate systems view of bilingual lexical storage.

An alternative explanation for poorer recall from bilingual than unilingual lists was proposed by Liepmann and Saegert (1974; see also McCormack, 1977). They suggested that there is a single lexical store but that the recall decrement is due to an increased memory load associated with language "tags" which serve to differentiate the two languages. Thus, they consider language to be an attribute of memory in a mixed language recall task. However, still other studies suggest that language tags are more or less effortlessly encoded (e.g., Lambert et al., 1968; Rose, Rose, King, & Perez, 1975).

*Interference Tasks.* In a proactive interference task, Goggin and Wickens (1971) found that recall deteriorated due to interference from successive lists of words except when the semantic category of the words was changed; such a change resulted in a release from interference. An almost equivalent release from interference was found when the language of the stimuli was changed across trials. According to Goggin and Wickens (1971), these results favor the view that the two languages of bilinguals are psychologically distinct.

*Verbal and Pictorial Coding.* Paivio and Lambert (1981) outlined a dual coding view of underlying representation in the bilingual. The dual coding hypothesis was originally formulated to account for the different effects that verbal material and imagery (pictorial stimuli) have on memory. This hypothesis proposes that an imagery system, representing knowledge of the world, exists distinct from a verbal system. An extension of the dual coding hypothesis has been invoked to characterize the bilingual's two verbal systems (Paivio & Desrochers, 1980). The two systems are suggested as being functionally independent of each other as well as of the image system. At the same time, the verbal systems are thought to be interconnected via representations corresponding to translation equivalents.

Support for this view of bilingual memory comes from a study by Paivio and Lambert (1981) involving incidental memory for words differing in encoding conditions. Retention was found to be greatest for words that had been sketched; words that had been translated were in turn better remembered than words that had been copied (Paivio & Lambert, 1981). However, in a follow-up study using a similar paradigm, no significant difference in level of recall was found for words whose translations had been generated and those whose synonyms had been generated (Vaid, 1982). Thus, it is unclear whether an independence view or a levels-of-processing view (discussed in the next section) provides a better account for these findings.

## Limitations of Lexical Studies of Bilingual Memory

Although tasks involving single words are convenient in that they provide material that can be easily manipulated for experimental purposes, these tasks nevertheless have a number of limitations. For one thing, in recalling words, the subject is essentially remembering the event surrounding a particular word's occurrence; the word itself already exists in the subject's long-term memory (cf. Kintsch, 1970). Thus, memory in most free recall tasks refers almost exclusively to episodic memory, i.e., memory for an episode or an event, as opposed to semantic memory, i.e., one's long-term conceptual and linguistic knowledge of the world.

One could conceivably remember the occurrence of particular words in one or the other language, regardless of one's expertise in the languages being used, merely on the basis of memory for each item's form, e.g., its sound and/or spelling (see Tulving, 1983), for word recognition or recall, or even lexical decision, need not entail semantic processing (see Snodgrass, 1984).

Furthermore, where semantic processing does occur in lexical studies of memory, one cannot be certain that subjects have made the same semantic interpretation since even commonly occurring lexical items are polysemous (e.g., "table," "letter"). In such cases, only a syntactic or pragmatic context could constrain the range of possible interpretations and enable the selection of a particular meaning which would be consistent across the subject population.

It is suggested, in short, that attempts to determine whether memory in bilinguals involves a common, or interdependent, system of representation underlying both languages, or relatively separate, independent systems, one for each language, cannot be conclusively argued when the principal experimental stimulus is the lexical item, divorced from a grammatical context. The issue of common or separate codes can more productively be addressed through experimental paradigms which ensure that semantic processing has occurred. Even when it can be determined that lexical experiments do access the semantic level, the artificiality of a learning situation where lexical items are isolated from a grammatical context limits the generality of the results. As Tulving (1983) points out: "The essence of any natural language . . . does not consist of the lexical units but the syntactic, semantic and pragmatic rules of operation" (p. 70).

## MEMORY FOR WORDS IN CONTEXT

In this section, some of the major issues in current verbal memory research are raised to provide a framework within which to hypothesize about the effects on memory of information transmitted bilingually. A study of memory for information conveyed through two languages should contribute to our knowledge of linguistic performance by revealing the effects (or lack of effects) specific surface structures have on memory.

The notion of encoding is central to any discussion of verbal memory. The encoding of verbal information refers to the transformation of the to-be-remembered linguistic structures into a form which is compatible with the cognitive structures that process the information.

## Levels-of-Processing Framework

The levels-of-processing theory of memory (Craik & Lockhart, 1972) suggests that the nature and durability of memory traces are determined by the level at which a stimulus is processed. Semantic encoding is considered to be at a deep level of processing, while structural and perceptual aspects of stimuli are thought to be encoded at a more shallow level. The levels-of-processing framework maintains that the stimulus is analyzed progressively from the shallow, structural aspects to the deep, semantic aspects, and that the resulting memory traces reflect those analyses, the deeper traces being more durable.

In its original formulation, this theory could not account for evidence that, aside from the level of processing, distinctiveness of stimulus material leads to important differences in recall as well (e.g., Morris, Bransford, & Franks, 1977; Stein, 1978). Recent work using the levels-of-processing framework has therefore emphasized interaction among different levels of analysis (e.g., Cermak & Craik, 1979) rather than positing a fixed, linear processing order. Thus, "depth of processing" has been taken more broadly to reflect processing effort rather than solely as a measure of semantic processing.

Nevertheless, it is well established that semantic information is more resistant to forgetting. Some researchers have suggested that the better retention of semantic information is due to the more elaborate and distinctive memory traces resulting from the deeper processing (e.g., Eysenck, 1979). Jacoby and Craik (1979) argue that elaboration of the stimulus leads to a more distinctive encoding which in turn facilitates retrieval of the specified encoding (see also Craik & Jacoby, 1979). Elaboration is thought to entail a change in encoding which is largely quantitative. Thus, an elaborated trace is characterized by additional information which allows the formation of an increased number of interconnections. The greater retention in semantic encoding is thus attributed to the greater scope this level provides.

Jacoby and Craik clarify the relationship between elaboration and depth of processing by arguing that deeper, more meaningful structures are more highly articulated and hence allow more possibilities for reconstructive retrieval. However, they caution against making a strict dichotomy between perceptual and semantic aspects of stimuli. Although perceptual aspects are generally not well remembered, in certain cases the surface features of a stimulus can become particularly meaningful due to the construction of a cognitive structure which allows distinct stimuli to be differentiated. This issue is discussed in a subsequent section with reference to the different surface features associated with two languages.

The argument of Jacoby and Craik is thus that a combination of depth of processing and degree of elaboration produces the distinctiveness of the encoding. It is important to note that the authors stress the relativity of the notion of distinctiveness; a given stimulus is distinctive only in relation to other encodings.

## Attributes of Memory

A number of researchers in the domain of verbal memory (e.g., Herriot, 1974; Underwood, 1969; Wickens, 1970) conceive of memory as a process of accessing a number of encoded attributes or features associated with the stimulus material. Memory is considered to be multiply encoded, involving both perceptual and semantic attributes. An attribute is defined as any formal or conceptual property of a linguistic unit that distinguishes it from another unit.

Baddeley (1976) offers the notion of encoded features as an explanation for the durability of semantic encodings in memory. He suggests that their strength lies in their multidimensionality; that is, semantic encoding will include verbal associates and perceptual and cognitive dimensions of the semantic information. The multidimensional coding allows for greater discriminative capacity, and redundant coding. Baddeley (1976) suggests that "the greater the number and range of encoded features, the greater the probability that one of these will be accessed, hence allowing the item to be retrieved" (p. 357).

## Encoding Variability

It has been suggested that information encoded with a greater number and variety of features or attributes is more easily accessed than information encoded with a more limited number and range of features (e.g., Bevan, Dukes, & Avant, 1966; Herriot, 1974).

In an early study of the effects of encoding variability (Bevan et al., 1966), materials which included pictures representing easily identifiable objects, as well as verbal stimuli (nouns) were presented to subjects. In one condition, the same object or noun was shown twice, while in another condition two different specimens of each object or noun with two different modifiers were presented (e.g., a red apple and a green apple; or for the verbal stimuli, "rainy weather" and "sunny weather"). The results clearly indicated that a variation in presentation enhanced memory for the concept. Particularly interesting was the fact that this advantage increased with the passage of time. Bevan et al. (1966) suggest that the increased number of cues provided by two nonidentical stimuli representing one global concept provides greater facility of access to that concept. The better recall is therefore attributed to the greater number of attributes characterizing a varied presentation, and, it can be noted, is compatible with Baddeley's position concerning the greater effectiveness of multidimensional encoding.

Similar results were found in a related experiment where letter sequences rather than word or pictorial stimuli were employed (Ellis, Parente, & Walker, 1974): varied input facilitated recall. Other studies indicate that variation in time and place of encoding also results in better retrieval. For example, Melton (1970) found that if an item is repeated in a list it is recalled better when there is more spacing between the occurrences of the item. The performance superiority can be explained by the distinctiveness resulting from the greater difference in encoding contexts at longer repetition intervals as predicted by the encoding variability principle.

*Encoding Variability in Bilingual Studies.* According to Landry (1978), bilingual repetitions should have effects similar to those found in studies of encoding variability. Due to their different linguistic and cultural origins, bilingual repetitions often have different connotations. Landry suggests that these connotations be viewed as different attributes of memory.

Landry also invokes the notion of encoding variability to account for results by Leopold (1949) that a bilingual presentation induces subjects to pay more attention to the meaning conveyed by sentences appearing in two languages. Landry (1978) carried out a study requiring the identification of changes in the meaning of isolated sentences; the study revealed better performance in the condition where sentences were presented in two languages than when sentences undergoing the changes appeared in one language only. Landry attributed the better recall for sentences in two languages to subjects' greater attention to meaning when exposed to two different linguistic forms.

## Memory for Mental Operations

According to Kolers (1973, 1975a, 1975b, 1979) what is stored in memory is not merely a collection of attributes or features of the stimulus but also the mental operations performed when acquiring the stimulus information. Kolers and Ostry (1974) conducted a series of experiments where subjects were exposed to sentences in familiar or unfamiliar typography. They found better retention for the sentences written in the unfamiliar typography. These results indicate that formal features of sentences are remarkably well preserved in memory. Kolers interprets his findings to indicate that subjects may remember the sentences by remembering the operations performed to acquire or encode the words. The greater the number of operations the subject has to perform to acquire a sentence, as when unfamiliar graphemes characterize a sentence, the greater the number of events available as aids to recognition. According to Kolers, then, the analytic activities or cognitive operations that characterize initial acquisition play a significant role in subsequent recognition and recall. Moreover, where more operations are applied, more of the stimulus is acquired. Thus, sentences requiring extensive analysis should be recognized better than sentences requiring less analysis.

Other researchers have supported Kolers' hypothesis that the procedures and operations may be stored as part of the cognitive structure. Siple, Fischer, and Bellugi (1977), who presented deaf subjects with signs and English words, reported that the retention of information about language and modality may be explained by these characteristics being byproducts of such stored operations. Siple et al. (1977) point out that this kind of interpretation does away with the need to posit attribute tags or separate sensory images for the retention of language and modality information.

It is important to note that the memory for operations hypothesis is not incompatible with the attributes of memory hypothesis; indeed, the two theories are essentially complementary. Memory can be conceived as a complex, dynamic process which preserves static components (both perceptual and semantic) of the stimulus material. It is equally capable of preserving the cognitive operations used in analyzing and acquiring stimulus material.

## FORM VERSUS CONTENT IN MEMORY

Related to the foregoing issues in verbal memory research is an issue that has generated considerable debate, namely, the respective roles of surface features and components of meaning in memory. The distinction between memory for form and memory for semantic content may have important implications for studies of bilingual memory.

As mentioned earlier, a major drawback of the bilingual lexical memory studies has been that their very design has contributed to an undue emphasis being placed on surface form features. For example, the requirement for verbatim recall of words necessarily induces a greater attention to form and perhaps less so to semantic content.

The distinction between memory for form and memory for semantic content becomes particularly crucial when generalizations are made beyond the laboratory to memory for verbal material occurring in more natural contexts. The form versus content distinction is thus particularly central to the issue of bilingual memory for discourse. Using a bilingual paradigm to investigate this distinction should prove to be especially revealing since one can examine the interaction between semantic information and the linguistically distinct structures used to convey the same information. It affords the powerful advantages of allowing the manipulation of surface structures while leaving the semantic content essentially unchanged.

### Evidence from Studies with Unilinguals

A number of studies with unilinguals have specifically investigated the roles of surface and semantic features and have yielded contradictory results. Some studies report that surface features have little effect on retention (e.g., Fillenbaum, 1973; Sachs, 1967, 1974; Wanner, 1974), while others suggest that aspects of the surface structure may play a relatively active role in the retention process (e.g., Ehrlich, Kail, & Segui, 1977; Hayes-Roth & Thorndyke, 1979; Hunt & Elliott, 1980).

For example, in Fillenbaum's (1973) study, subjects were given a long list of sentences followed by a set of four alternative sentences as a recognition test for the sentences originally presented. Fillenbaum noted that subjects were much more likely to choose as the original sentence one whose meaning was similar to that of the actual original sentence, although with some changes in form, than one with a similar form but whose meaning differed.

Sachs (1967, 1974) examined memory for grammatical features of text passages. Subjects were presented with passages where sentences were occasionally repeated, undergoing either syntactic or semantic changes, and had to decide whether the repeated sentences had indeed been changed in any way. The results indicated that recognition memory for syntactic features when tested after a delay was very poor, while little semantic information was lost over the same interval. Jarvella (1971) showed that subjects only retained in its verbatim form the immediately preceding phrase when presented with continuous discourse. Also, they were only able to retain the form when this preceding phrase was part of the sentence which was interrupted. Jarvella interpreted these results as evidence that subjects encode discourse in terms of its meaning, retaining the exact form of words only of the sentence currently being processed.

Studies such as the preceding suggest that individuals encode a text in terms of its meaning and do not retain its surface features. On the other hand, under certain conditions, information about surface form can be retained over substantial intervals, particularly when subjects are aware that they will be tested on surface aspects of the stimulus material.

Ehrlich, Kail, and Segui (1977) distinguish between two views of encoding: (a) a unidimensional view, according to which only information about the meaning of the message is stored, and (b) a multidimensional conception of coding, according to which information about various dimensions—semantic, syntactic, lexical—is stored in memory. In an experiment involving immediate and long-term memory for text, Ehrlich et al. (1977) found that (a) the syntactic format used to convey a given content does not affect retention in short-term memory but does affect it in long-term memory; (b) information about linguistic format is stored and is still available after a long delay; and (c) subjects tend to integrate elementary information given in the text into global, semantic units. These findings lend support to a multidimensional view of memory coding.

Hunt and Elliott (1980) found significant retention for nonsemantic information (orthography) even following semantic orienting tasks. The findings of Kolers (1975b; Kolers & Ostry, 1974), mentioned earlier, namely, that sentences requiring extensive graphemic analysis were remembered better than those requiring analysis only at the semantic level, are also pertinent here. Taken together, these findings suggest that semantic processing cannot be considered as necessarily resulting in better retention than nonsemantic processing, but, rather, that any feature of verbal material (graphemic, syntactic, etymological, etc.) can be selected as a level of analysis with strong effects on retention. The suggestion here is that surface features of verbal material can have significant effects on retention depending on the manner in which information is acquired and the subsequent testing contexts.

## RETENTION FOR PROSE PRESENTED BILINGUALLY

The preceding review provides a theoretical framework for a study of memory for bilingual prose. The issue may be formulated in terms of the following question: what are the effects on retention when information is conveyed via two languages as compared to a unilingual transmission of information? Two possibilities may be considered: (1) that language is merely a transparent code, having few or no effects on memory, or (2) that the encoding of information in two languages significantly affects memory for that information, in which case the question becomes whether the effect is one of inhibition or facilitation of information retrieval.

*Bilingual versus Unilingual Transmission of Information: An Hypothesis.* It may be hypothesized that a bilingual transmission of information will result in a superior level of retention compared to a unilingual transmission.

Theoretical support for the positive effect of a bilingual presentation is provided by the various verbal memory hypotheses discussed in the previous section. The notions of elaboration and distinctiveness, for example, can be invoked to support this hypothesis. An elaborated trace is characterized by additional information which allows the formation of an increased number of interconnections. Moreover, an elaborated trace contributes to producing a more distinctive encoding which should be more resistant to interference, and therefore more memorable. The suggestion here is that a bilingual transmission of information can be characterized as providing a more elaborated and thus more distinctive set of traces which facilitates later retrieval from memory.

When the same information is presented via two languages there are more structural features associated with the transmission of information than in a unilingual transmission. The bilingual transmission constitutes a quantitative change in encoding by virtue of the dual set of structures which characterize two languages. These structural differences occur across all linguistic levels of analysis, from the level of the physical stimulus (graphemic or acoustic forms), to the phonological, morphological, syntactic, and lexico-semantic levels.

The notion of elaboration can further be illustrated with reference to lexico-semantic features in the context of bilingualism. A word and its translation equivalent are often characterized by semantic fields which do not precisely overlap due to both cultural and linguistic factors. Thus, a lexical item in one language often does not include identical semantic components in the closest equivalent item in another language. Mental representations are organized differently across languages, with different aspects of an experience being picked out for inclusion in a given language's unit of expression. Clark and Clark (1977) observe that a given language does not have propositions available for referring to all possible aspects of experience and therefore verbalizability varies from one language to another.

Thus, denotation may differ to some extent between certain lexical items of one language and their translations; contextual aids are normally enlisted to achieve equivalence in translation of connected discourse. The bilingual transmission is therefore characterized by greater elaboration with regard to denotation. Just as denotation may vary, even more so might the connotations for equivalent items. The corresponding lexical item in a second language, i.e., the translation equivalent, will rarely have the same set of connotations or evoke the same associations.

Given these differences, one can predict that the elaboration resulting from evocation of related concepts would be quantitatively greater in a bilingual situation than in a unilingual situation.

As mentioned earlier, distinctiveness can be considered to be closely related to elaboration, since the additional information added to a memory trace allows greater possibilities for that information to be distinctive in contrast to the available information. If distinctiveness is indeed a significant factor in memory, as many studies indicate, then one can suggest, by extension, that a bilingual transmission of information, being structurally more distinctive than a corresponding unilingual transmission of the same information, should significantly enhance retention.

The notion of encoding variability provides further basis for predicting greater retention for bilingual transmission of information. Encoding variability predicts that information encoded via a greater number and variety of attributes will be more memorable and resistant to interference than information encoded in only one way, or with a smaller number of attributes. Encoding verbal material via two distinct sets of linguistic structures, as in the bilingual case, is considered here to constitute a variable encoding. Given results from other studies (e.g., Bevan et al., 1966; Melton, 1970) which reveal high retention with a variable encoding, one would predict the bilingual presentation to reflect a similar performance advantage.

Also contributing support to a prediction of a bilingual performance advantage are the studies by Kolers and colleagues, discussed earlier, which suggest that the mental operations carried out during the acquisition of verbal material are stored in memory. The operations performed when information is accessed through one language will rarely match in degree of ease or complexity those performed when information is accessed through a second language (see also Magiste, this volume). Just as in monolinguals certain grammatical or lexical structures may be less familiar to an individual than others (as in the case of register differences), so might differences exist in the analytic operations necessary to encode information in two different languages. The degree to which these analytic operations differ between two languages will, of course, depend on the individual's degree of proficiency or familiarity with each language. However, it is likely that, for most bilinguals, one of the languages will be dominant, at least in certain spheres of language activity (see Grosjean, this volume). Therefore, more cognitive operations may be necessary to access information from the language that is weaker in certain domains. The difference in the amount of cognitive processing necessary to encode information from the two languages would render the bilingual presentation more distinctive than a corresponding unilingual presentation.

For all these reasons, it is suggested that a bilingual presentation of information offers a greater possibility than a unilingual presentation for a memorable encoding.

Let us turn now to the two experiments conducted by the author to test the above hypothesis; a more detailed account of these experiments is available elsewhere (see Hummel, 1986).

*Hummel (1986) Study.* The study consisted of two experiments designed to test the hypothesis that the greater number and variety of cues characterizing a bilingual presentation enable better information retrieval than that possible in a corresponding unilingual presentation of verbal material. The experiments involved recall of information from a prose passage that was followed either by passages in the same language that slightly differed in their meaning (and were thereby interfering) or by translations of these passages.

## EXPERIMENT 1

### *Retroactive Interference as a Function of Unilingual or Bilingual Presentation of Prose*

In this experiment, subjects were tested for recall of an initial passage in the face of interference generated by subsequent passages, which referred to slightly differing events. These latter passages were presented in either the same or different language as that of the initial passage.

## METHOD

*Subjects.* Subjects were 40 French/English bilingual college students with French as their first language. They had scored within native speaker norms on a vocabulary and reading comprehension subtest of the Test of English as a Foreign Language (TOEFL, 1980). Bilinguals were randomly subdivided into four groups, where one group received all the test passages in French, another received all the passages in English, a third group received two passages in French followed by two in English, and the fourth group received two passages in English, followed by two in French.

*Procedure.* The paradigm used was adapted from a retroactive interference method of Bower (1974), in which subjects were to read a short passage which described events that had occurred on a particular, fictitious island. This passage was followed by three other passages which also referred to events on an island, but the details of the events and the names of the island were changed. Following each passage, subjects were given a set of questions on the content of the passage. After the final passage had been presented, subjects were tested again on the contents of the first passage. Thus, they were required to remember details from an earlier passage in the face of interference generated across subsequent passages.

## RESULTS

As no significant differences were found between the two unilingual conditions (where all passages were either in French or in English), nor between the two bilingual conditions (where the passages were either in French followed by English, or vice versa), the scores were combined to allow for an overall comparison of the unilingual versus the bilingual condition.

An analysis of variance performed on the data revealed a strong main effect of Condition, $F(1,38) = 7.71$, $p < .01$. See Table 3.1. That is, subjects in the bilingual condition remembered significantly more information from the tested passage following the interfering passages in the other language than did subjects in the unilingual condition.

TABLE 3.1
Mean Percentage Errors in Initial Passage Comprehension in Experiment 1

| Condition | Mean Percent Errors | | | |
|---|---|---|---|---|
| Unilingual | 28.8 | (F4) | 31.7 | (E4) |
| Bilingual | 13.9 | (F2/E2) | 16.1 | (E2/F2) |

Note:
F4: all four passages in French
E4: all four passages in English
F2/E2: two passages in French, followed by two in English
E2/F2: two passages in English, followed by two in French

## EXPERIMENT 2

### *Memory for a Passage Repeated in the Same Language or in Translation*

In this experiment, the question of interest was the effects on memory of reading a passage that was either repeated in the same language or in translated form.

## METHOD

*Subjects.* As in the first experiment, all subjects were native French-speaking bilinguals who scored within native speaker norms in English on the TOEFL reading skills test. There were a total of 48 bilinguals. Subjects were randomly assigned to the following four experimental conditions: (1) the test passages were read twice in French; (2) the test passages were read twice in English; (3) the passage was first read in French and then in English, and (4) the passage was read first in English, followed by a reading in French.

*Procedure.* Subjects were to read a short text either twice in the same language or once in each of their two languages. The text described fictitious though plausible events that occurred during a natural disaster in a small village. Between each reading, subjects read an interfering text which contained details similar to those in the original passage. They were instructed to pay close attention to the second reading of the passage. Following a distractor test, they

TABLE 3.2
Mean Percentage Errors in Comprehension of Repeated Passage in Experiment 2

| Condition | Mean Percent Errors | | | |
|---|---|---|---|---|
| Unilingual | 32.1 | (F/F) | 29.6 | (E/E) |
| Bilingual | 20.0 | (F/E) | 21.4 | (E/F) |

Note:

F/F: Passage read twice in French
E/E: Passage read twice in English
F/E: Passage read first in French, followed by English
E/F: Passage read first in English, followed by French

were given a list of questions (in the language of the first presentation of the passage) pertaining to the repeated passage.

## RESULTS

As in Experiment 1, no significant differences were found between the two unilingual conditions nor between the two bilingual conditions; the scores from each of these were therefore combined to allow for a comparison of the overall unilingual versus bilingual presentation. Table 3.2 provides a summary of the mean percent errors in recall of the repeated passage.

An analysis of variance revealed a strong main effect of Condition, $F(1,46) = 8.01$, $p < .01$, indicating that the bilingual presentation resulted in higher retention than did the unilingual presentation.

## DISCUSSION AND CONCLUSION

The findings from these two experiments suggest that the greater number and variety of cues (structural, semantic, and operational) characterizing a bilingual presentation of prose enable better information retrieval than that possible in a corresponding unilingual condition. As such, the present findings do not concur with those from previous studies (e.g., Champagnol, 1973; Tulving & Colotla, 1970), in which isolated words had been used.

The present findings also support a separate systems or independence view of bilingual organization. If the underlying representations of the two languages were not to some extent separate, one would not have obtained a significant difference in performance as a function of whether information was conveyed via one language or two.

The significant reduction of interference under conditions of bilingual presentation may be attributed to the discriminability of material on a number of levels involving linguistic form and meaning, as well as to the cognitive operations involved in acquiring information via two languages. However, the extent to which this enhanced access may be attributed to the physical features of the stimulus, to semantic features or to the cognitive operations associated with the acquisition of information via two languages cannot be determined on the basis of the experiments reported here. One can nevertheless speculate that the enhanced access exhibited in the bilingual condition is due to an interaction between the various linguistic levels (e.g., orthographic, phonological, syntactic, semantic) that characterize connected discourse, and the cognitive operations involved in accessing these levels, an interaction that in studies employing lexical items in isolation is generally (but see Kirsner, this volume) not revealed.

## ACKNOWLEDGMENTS

This research was conducted in partial fulfillment of the requirements for the Ph.D. in linguistics, at McGill University. Portions of this research were reported at the International Congress of Linguists held in Tokyo in 1982, and at the Association Internationale de Linguistique Appliquée, held in Brussels in 1984.

## REFERENCES

Baddeley, A. D. (1976). *The psychology of memory.* New York: Basic Books.

Bevan, W., Dukes, W., & Avant, L. (1966). The effects of variation in specific stimuli on memory for their superordinates. *American Journal of Psychology, 79,* 250–257.

Bower, G. (1974). Selective facilitation and interference in retention of prose. *Journal of Educational Psychology, 66*(1), 1–8.

Cermak, L. S. (1972). *Human memory: Research and theory.* New York: Ronald Press.

Cermak, L. S., & Craik, F. I. M. (Eds.). (1979). *Levels of processing in human memory.* Hillsdale, NJ: Lawrence Erlbaum Associates.

Champagnol, R. (1973). Organisation sémantique et linguistique dans le rappel libre bilingue. *Année Psychologique, 73,* 115–134.

Clark, H. H., & Clark, E. (1977). *Psychology and language.* New York: Harcourt, Brace and Jovanovitch.

Craik, F. I. M., & Jacoby, L. (1979). Elaboration and distinctiveness in episodic memory. In L.G. Nilsson (Ed.), *Perspectives on memory research* (pp. 145–166). Hillsdale, NJ: Lawrence Erlbaum Associates.

Craik, F. I. M., & Lockhart, R. (1972). Levels of processing: A framework for memory research. *Journal of Verbal Learning and Verbal Behavior, 11,* 671–681.

Dalrymple-Alford, E., & Aamiry, A. (1969). Language and category clustering in bilingual free recall. *Journal of Language Learning and Language Behavior, 8,* 762–768.

Ehrlich, M. E., Kail, M., & Segui, J. (1977). The role of syntactic format in prose memory. *International Journal of Psycholinguistics, 4–2,* 83–92.

Ellis, H. C., Parente, F. J., & Walker, C. W. (1974). Coding input versus repetition in human memory. *Journal of Experimental Psychology, 102,* 284–290.

Eysenck, M. W. (1979). Depth, elaboration, and distinctiveness. In L. S. Craik & F. I. M. Cermak (Eds.), *Levels of processing in human memory* (pp. 89–118). Hillsdale, NJ: Lawrence Erlbaum Associates.

Fillenbaum, S. (1973). *Syntactic factors in memory?* The Hague: Mouton.

Glanzer, M., & Duarte, A. (1971). Repetition between and within languages in free recall. *Journal of Verbal Learning and Verbal Behavior, 10,* 625–630.

Goggin, J., & Wickens, D. (1971). Proactive interference and language change in short-term memory. *Journal of Verbal Learning and Verbal Behavior, 10,* 453–458.

Hayes-Roth, B., & Thorndyke, P. W. (1979). Integration of knowledge from text. *Journal of Verbal Learning and Verbal Behavior, 18,* 99–102.

Herriot, P. (1974). *Attributes of memory.* London: Methuen.

Hummel, K. M. (1986). *Bilingual memory: The effect of two languages on retention of prose.* Unpublished doctoral dissertation, McGill University.
Hunt, R. R., & Elliott, J. M. (1980). The role of nonsemantic information in memory: Orthographic distinctiveness effects in retention. *Journal of Experimental Psychology: General, 109,* 49–74.
Jacoby, L. L., & Craik, F. I. M. (1979). Effects of elaboration of processing at encoding and retrieval: Trace distinctiveness and recovery of initial context. In L. S. Cermak & F. I. M. Craik (Eds.), *Levels of processing in human memory* (pp. 1–21). Hillsdale, NJ: Lawrence Erlbaum Associates.
Jarvella, R. M. (1971). Syntactic processing and connected speech. *Journal of Verbal Learning and Verbal Behavior, 10,* 409–416.
Kintsch, W. (1970). Models for free recall and recognition. In D. A. Norman (Ed.), *Models of human memory* (pp. 331–373). New York: Academic Press.
Kintsch, W. (1977). *Memory and cognition.* New York: Wiley.
Kolers, P. A. (1963). Interlingual word associations. *Journal of Verbal Learning and Verbal Behavior, 2,* 291–300.
Kolers, P. A. (1965). Bilingualism and bicodalism. *Language and Speech, 8,* 122–126.
Kolers, P. A. (1966). Interlingual facilitation of short-term memory. *Journal of Verbal Learning and Verbal Behavior, 5,* 314–319.
Kolers, P. A. (1968). Bilingualism and information processing. *Scientific American,* 78–86.
Kolers, P. A. (1973). Remembering operations. *Memory and Cognition, 1,* 347–355.
Kolers, P. A. (1975a). Memorial consequences of automatized encoding. *Journal of Experimental Psychology: Human Learning and Memory, 1,* 689–701.
Kolers, P. A. (1975b). Specificity of operations in speech recognition. *Cognitive Psychology, 7,* 284–306.
Kolers, P. A. (1979). A pattern-analyzing basis of recognition. In L. S. Cermak & F. I. M. Craik (Eds.), *Levels of processing in human memory* (pp. 363–384). Hillsdale, NJ: Lawrence Erlbaum Associates.
Kolers, P. A. & Ostry, D. J. (1974). Time course of loss of information regarding pattern analyzing operations. *Journal of Verbal Learning and Verbal Behavior, 13,* 599–612.
Lambert, W. E., Havelka, J., & Crosby, C. (1958). The influence of language acquisition contexts on bilingualism. *Journal of Abnormal and Social Psychology, 56,* 239–244.
Lambert, W. E., Ignatow, M., & Krauthamer, M. (1968). Bilingual organization in free recall. *Journal of Verbal Learning and Verbal Behavior, 7,* 207–214.
Landry, R. (1978). Le bilinguisme; Le facteur répétition. *Canadian Modern Language Review, 34,* 548–576.
Leopold, W. (1949). *Speech development of a bilingual child* (vol. 3). Evanston, IL: Northwestern University Press.
Liepmann, D., & Saegert, J. (1974). Language tagging in bilingual free recall. *Journal of Experimental Psychology, 103,* 1137–1141.
Lopez, M., & Young, R. K. (1974). The linguistic interdependence of bilinguals. *Journal of Experimental Psychology, 102,* 981–983.
Lopez, M., Hicks, R., & Young, R. (1974). Retroactive inhibition in a bilingual A-B, A-B′ paradigm. *Journal of Experimental Psychology, 103,* 85–90.
Macnamara, J. (1967). The linguistic independence of bilinguals. *Journal of Verbal Learning and Verbal Behavior, 6,* 729–736.
McCormack, P. (1977). Bilingual linguistic memory: The independent-interdependent issue revisited. In P. A. Hornby (Ed.), *Bilingualism* (pp. 57–66). New York: Academic Press.
Melton, A. W. (1970). The situation with respect to spacing of repetitions and memory. *Journal of Verbal Learning and Verbal Behavior, 9,* 596–606.

Morris, C. D., Bransford, J. D., & Franks, J. J. (1977). Levels of processing versus transfer appropriate processing. *Journal of Verbal Learning and Verbal Behavior, 16,* 519–533.

Nott, C., & Lambert, W. (1968). Free recall of bilinguals. *Journal of Verbal Learning and Verbal Behavior, 7,* 1065–1071.

Paivio, A., & Desrochers, A. (1980). A dual-coding approach to bilingual memory. *Canadian Journal of Psychology, 34,* 390–401.

Paivio, A., & Lambert, W. (1981). Dual coding and bilingual memory. *Journal of Verbal Learning and Verbal Behavior, 20,* 532–539.

Rose, R. G., Rose, P. R., King, N., & Perez, A. (1975). Bilingual memory for related and unrelated sentences. *Journal of Experimental Psychology: Human Learning and Memory, 1,* 599–606.

Sachs, J. (1967). Recognition memory for syntactic and semantic aspects of connected discourse. *Perception and Psychophysics, 2,* 437–444.

Sachs, J. (1974). Memory in reading and listening to discourse. *Memory and Cognition, 2,* 95–100.

Siple, P., Fischer, S. D., & Bellugi, U. (1977). Memory for nonsemantic attributes of American Sign Language signs and English words. *Journal of Verbal Learning and Verbal Behavior, 16,* 561–574.

Snodgrass, G. (1984). Concepts and their surface representations. *Journal of Verbal Learning and Verbal Behavior, 23,* 3–22.

Stein, B. S. (1978). Depth of processing reexamined: the effects of the precision of encoding and test appropriateness. *Journal of Verbal Learning and Verbal Behavior, 17,* 165–174.

Taylor, I. (1971). How are words from two languages organized in bilinguals' memory? *Canadian Journal of Psychology, 25,* 228–240.

Taylor, I. (1976). Similarity between French and English words: A factor to be considered in bilingual language behavior. *Journal of Psycholinguistic Research, 5,* 85–96.

*Test of English as a Foreign Language.* (1980). Princeton, NJ: Educational Testing Service.

Tulving, E. (1983). *Elements of episodic memory.* Oxford: Oxford University Press.

Tulving, E., & Colotla, V. (1970). Free recall of bilingual lists. *Cognitive Psychology, 1,* 86–98.

Underwood, B. J. (1969). Attributes of memory. *Psychological Review, 76,* 559–573.

Vaid, J. (1982). *Bilingualism and dual coding: A re-examination.* Unpublished manuscript, University of California, San Diego.

Wanner, E. (1974). *On remembering, forgetting and understanding sentences.* The Hague: Mouton.

Wickens, D. (1970). Encoding categories of words: An empirical approach to meaning. *Psychological Review, 77,* 1–15.

Young, R., & Navar, M. (1968). Retroactive inhibition with bilinguals. *Journal of Experimental Psychology, 77,* 109–115.

# 4 Pairing First- and Second-Language Speech and Writing in Ways that Aid Language Acquisition

Wallace E. Lambert
*McGill University*

The studies reported here started with questions we, as psychologists, asked ourselves about how the media might be better used in the teaching and learning of foreign or second languages. For instance, we wondered why certain people are bothered by the presence of subtitles when viewing foreign films. Necessary as subtitles seem to be for the majority, they nontheless force viewers to return to the script of their native language (L1) to pick up the story line, thereby reducing the foreign flavor of the film and reminding them of their inadequacies in the second language (L2). Some viewers, in fact, are perturbed enough to hold a hand in the line of view in order to block out the L1 script so that they can "try themselves out" in the L2. For similar reasons, many viewers are bothered by a foreign film with dubbed L1 dialogue because they are deprived of the original version. Much depends, of course, on one's competence in L2: The novice in L2 would be lost without the subtitling or dubbing; it is those who are relatively experienced with L2 who are perturbed. These observations started us thinking about possible modifications. In the second place, many people at relatively advanced stages in L2 experience have great trouble following the recordings of vocalists in L2, much more than is typically encountered with L1 music. To catch the message of the lyrics they are often forced (perhaps with much personal profit in the long run) to play and replay a record. However, when the actual script of the lyrics is provided, the listener is amazed at how easily the words of the songs are "pulled apart." We argue later than the interplay between spoken dialogue and script can be advantageous both ways—that once the words are isolated through the script they can be profitably mapped onto the dialogue and vice versa. Third, many of us have had the experience of a guided tour in a foreign setting where the tour guide (or electronic substitute for the guide) runs through a descriptive message in various languages. Once tourists pick up the message in their base language, they are often surprised at how well they can then pick out words and phrases in one or more of the supposedly long forgotten L2. We argue that the words and phrases would not have been recognized if the story line had not first been grasped through L1.

From these common personal experiences, coupled with a general interest in methods for teaching and learning foreign languages, we were prompted to think about ways in which films, TV, and radio might be used to substitute for or supplement more conventional teaching/learning methods. For instance, immigrants often claim that they have learned their new L2 mainly through TV. Whether this is true or not, some estimates have it that, on the average, 4 or more hours per day are spent watching television in the United States and Canada, and thus, TV could be an enormously valuable teaching/learning resource not only for immigrants but also for inadequately educated and minimally literate English-speaking Americans. However, TV restricts the viewer to one mode of verbal input, spoken language. Could script be effectively added? In what language should the script be presented for the non-L1 speaker or for the minimally literate L1 speaker? What would be the best choice of language for the spoken dialogue for the non-L1 speaker if dialogue were to be paired with script?

To illustrate the approach to be suggested here, consider a recent innovation in the Metropolitan Opera House in Manhattan where a large screen provides English subtitles—what we call Standard Subtitling—for operas in progress. This makes good sense to the casual onlooker who might otherwise be lost searching for the story line. But we would argue that serious opera buffs, even those who are essentially monolingual in English, realize that the flavor of an Italian opera is erased by standard subtitles because they immediately transform the story into colloquial English. Perhaps they would be more appreciative of subtitles in Italian, especially if they have studied and thought about different productions of the opera and its text and music. In fact, Italian subtitles when coordinated with Italian singing—an example of what we will call Bimodal L2 Input—might snap the whole story into place, keep its cultural background, and aid in learning Italian, all at the same time. If learning Italian were a major interest, then one might worry about standard subtitling because it erases the Italian feature of the communication, whereas Bimodal L2 Input or what we will call Reversed Subtitling could become effective alternatives, the choice depending on the listener's level of skill in Italian and/or interest in learning the language. This procedure, in fact, might prompt opera singers to take some lessons on enunciation and diction from Ella Fitzgerald or Frank Sinatra, especially when they have to sing in what is for them a foreign language.

We designed the present set of studies with hunches more than hypotheses in mind. Thus, we wondered whether the Bimodal L2 Input would promote *deeper* processing, as reflected in better memory, than the Standard Subtitling condition and whether there would be differences as a function of degree of second language experience. The results have helped us answer these questions and others we had not anticipated. For instance, it turns out that certain presentation conditions using particular combinations of script and spoken dialogue are much more promising for the development or maintenance of foreign language skills than is the conventional "Standard Subtitling." One combination in particular stands out as extremely promising in its implications for both formal and informal modes of education.

Although the emphasis in these studies appears to be mainly applied, the questions we asked were derived from interests and reading in various current research domains, for instance, the ongoing debate about "depth of processing"; current interpretations of the process of reading; the differences and similarities in first and second language learning; and the possible ways spoken language and silent reading might interact. These more theoretical notions are introduced in the discussion sections to follow.

## STUDY 1: AN EMPIRICAL TEST OF VARIOUS INPUT COMBINATIONS[1]

*Subjects.* The subjects were grade 5 and 6 pupils from eight public elementary schools in the greater Montreal area, 199 in grade 5 (average age 10.9 years), and 171 in grade 6 (11.9 years). The schools varied in social class makeup, from solidly middle class neighborhoods to working class districts. Small groups of 10 to 12 students from a designated class were assigned at random to one of 9 input presentation conditions.

The salient feature of the pupils included was their language experiences. All had English as the only home language but all had attended French "immersion" programs from kindergarten on. "Immersion" is an educational program wherein some language (in this instance, French) other than the home language is used as the only medium of instruction, by monolingual (French) teachers, for grades K, 1 and 2. Home language instruction in the form of an English Language Arts course starts at grade 3 and English is also used as a separate language of instruction progressively more each year so that by grades 5 to 7, approximately 60% of instruction is conducted via the home language and 40% via the second language (see Lambert & Tucker, 1972; Swain, 1974; and Genesee, 1978–79).

Language background questionnaires permitted us to identify and eliminate from consideration any pupil who had any other language than English as the home language or any pupil with exceptional or regular exposure to French outside of school. Pupils also made subjective evaluations of their proficiency in French and English. In general, they described themselves as slightly more English dominant than French in writing, reading, and understanding and some-

---

[1]The original report is presented in Lambert, Boehler, & Sidoti, 1981.

what more English dominant for speaking. Interestingly, there were no significant grade level differences in these self ratings.

*Materials.* Audio tapes of radio programs were prepared in French and English along with videotapes of the typed word-for-word transcriptions of the audio messages. This permitted us to present various combinations of spoken dialogue and/or printed script in either the first language (L1) or second language (L2) or in mixtures of L1–L2, according to the input conditions to be described. The nine original passages were recorded from The Canadian Broadcasting Corporation's French language radio programs; they included a newscast, a radio drama, and a call-in program. These passages, in fact, make up an auditory comprehension test (Test de Comprehension Auditive, Level B, 1979), designed and standardized for grade 6 English speaking pupils who had participated in a French immersion program from kindergarten on. We can illustrate the level of difficulty of the passages with the radio drama: Subjects listened to a 3–4 minute story performed by professional actors and then answered questions, written in French, about the plot, for example, why the heroine was so emotionally upset:

a. il y avait eu un holdup de la diligence dans laquelle elle voyageait (there was a holdup of the stagecoach in which she was travelling);
b. celui qui l'attendait n'était pas son père (the one waiting for her was not her father);
c. Victor Corbeil venait de tuer son père (Victor Corbeil had just killed her father);
d. l'homme qui devait la recontrer était mort (the man who was to meet her was dead).

Translated English versions of the same passages were prepared for the present study with the help of professional translators and technicians who copied the background sounds of the original as closely as possible while English speaking actors copied the style and emphasis of the French version. In addition, exact word-for-word written scripts of the spoken dialogues were prepared in English and French, permitting us to construct various presentation conditions. French and English versions of the posttests of comprehension were developed as well.

*Presentation Conditions.* Of the nine presentation conditions constructed for our purposes, five called for French posttests of comprehension, and four for English posttests.

Condition 1—is called Bi-modal L2 Input and is symbolized as F,F/F, indicating that the dialogue, the script and the posttesting are all in French.

Condition 2—L2 Dialogue Only, F,–/F; dialogue in French, no script, and posttesting in French.

Condition 3—L2 Script Only, –F/F; no dialogue, script in French, posttesting in French.

Condition 4—Standard Subtitling, F,E/F; indicating that, as in foreign films, the dialogue is in L2 and the script a translation of the dialogue into L1. Here we tested in L2.

Condition 5—Reverse Subtitling-L2, E,F/F; indicating that the dialogue is in the listener's L1 and the script in L2, with L2 posttesting.

Condition 6—Bimodal L1 Input, E,E/E; where dialogue, script and posttesting are all in L1.

Condition 7—L1 Dialogue Only, E,–/E; dialogue in English, no script, posttesting in English.

Condition 8—L1 Script Only, –E/E; no dialogue, English script and English posttesting.

Condition 9—Reverse Subtitling-L1, E,F/E; the match for condition 5 except that the testing is in L1.

*Testing.* The French and English versions of the comprehension posttests had a common format: Testing was partly oral, partly written; subjects heard a tape-recorded voice ask a question and they then selected the correct answer among multiple-choice alternatives given them in a booklet. The part-audio/part-visual feature of the testing was meant to minimize the effects of testing format on type of message presentation, since some of the presentation conditions emphasized spoken dialogue, some written script and some both dialogue and script. A second means of minimizing the effect of testing format was to rely on comprehension questions that called for an understanding of the message rather than a memory for certain words or phrases, whether originally presented in the form of dialogue or script. For example, in the illustration given above, subjects had to infer that the heroine was upset; the input passages did not explicitly state that Victor Corbeil had just killed her father. However, one of our supplemental tests, that for accuracy of spelling, would certainly be biased toward a script form of input; subjects would only get clues on how to spell words through script input.

*Supplemental Test.* In addition to the test of overall comprehension, we introduced three separate tests of memory for passage details in the French posttests: a test of *contextual meaning* of selected terms; a test of *accuracy of spelling* of selected French words, and a test of *memory for the form of phrasing* used in the passages. An example of a contextual meaning test item is: Dans ce passage, ''exécution'' veut dire (In this passage, ''execution'' means): (a) exécution d'un criminel (the execution of a criminal); (b) exécution d'un morceau de musique (the execution of a piece of music); (c) exécution d'un ordre (execution of an order); (d) exécution d'une idée (execution of an idea). For spelling: Choisissez le mot qui a une faute d'orthographe (Choose the word which has a spelling error): (a) advertis, (b) extrêmement, (c) projet, (d) routière. For phrasing form: Choisissez la structure qui a été utilisée dans le texte (Choose the structure actually used in the text): (a) à cause de la tempête; (b) en raison de la tempête.

*Procedure.* Each subgroup of subjects first completed language background questionnaires. Then the purpose of the study was explained, namely, that they were to listen to audio presentations of a series of passages and/or read video scripts of the same passages, and that they would be asked questions to test their comprehension of the information relayed. According to the presentation condition they were assigned to, they knew in advance which language (English or French) would be used for the dialogues and/or scripts and for the testing. They also were taken through a practice trial. In the conditions involving both dialogue and script, the importance of attending to both was stressed. The instructions were recorded. Extra time was given between passages for the French testing of contextual meaning, spelling, and phrase form.

Tapes were played on a 3650 AV playback unit connected to a TV monitor with a 24 inch screen. In preparing the tapes, the transcripts of the passages had been typeset using 16 point bold Helvetica and then filmed by panning a CEI #280 TV camera over them at a rate equal to the speed of the spoken dialogue passages so that the dialogues and scripts were synchronized. Filming was arranged to allow 2.5 lines of script to be seen at a time, moving up the screen and then disappearing. During the presentations, subjects were seated so as to see and/or hear the material presented without obstructions.

## RESULTS AND DISCUSSION

### Comprehension

A 9 (conditions) × 2 (grade level) × 2 (male, female) least squares ANOVA was applied, using the SPSS "classical" approach. Multiple group comparisons were tested using the Newman-Keuls procedure with an .05 alpha level.

*Main Effects.* On the comprehension test measure, there were two significant main effects, one for conditions, $F(8,334) = 25.82$, $p < .001$, and one for grade, $F(4,175) = 36.75$, $p < .001$. For the condition main effect, follow-up analyses showed statistically reliable subset differences in mean performance as diagramed below (from best to poorest): Members of a bracketed subset are not significantly different from one another.

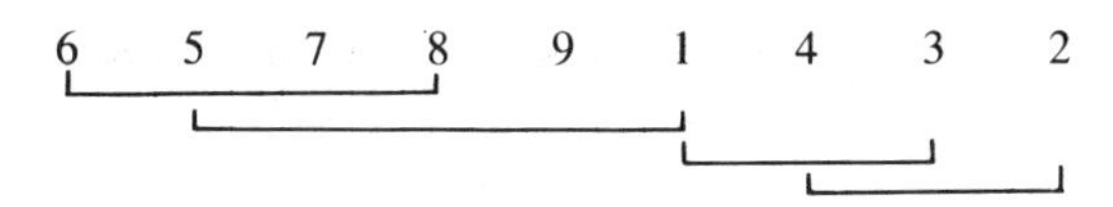


Thus, comprehension scores were generally higher for those conditions that provided L1 (English) information in at least one channel, with Bimodal L1 Input (i.e., dialogue and script both in English, condition 6) being highest of all but not reliably different from single mode English input conditions (7 and 8, see Fig. 4.1). The Stardand Subtitling (condition 4), which provides French dialogue and English script in preparation for a comprehension test in French, facilitated comprehension little; it did not differ significantly from conditions 2 or 3 where L2 input is presented in one channel or the other. Bimodal L2 Input (condition 1) was not better than L2 Script Only (condition 3) but it did prove to

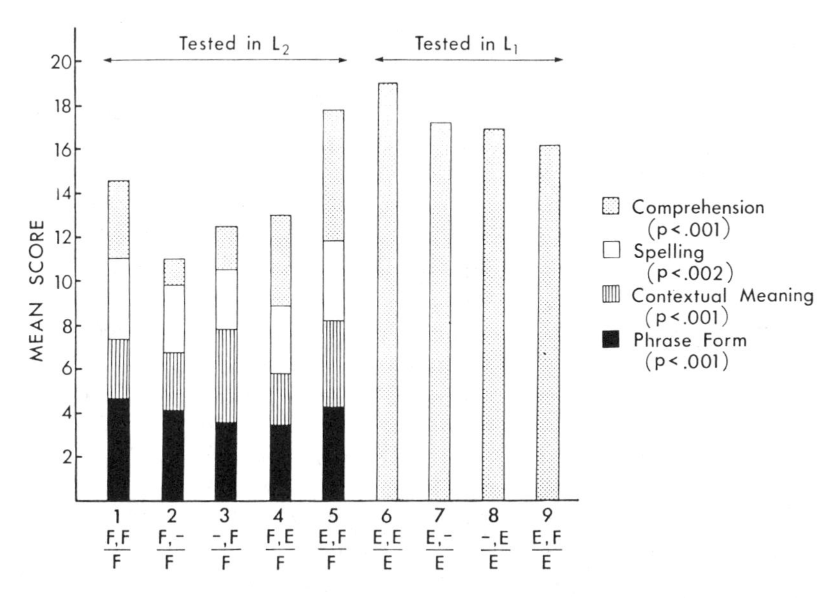


FIG. 4.1. Condition differences in test scores, total sample grade 5 and 6 students.

CONDITIONS

*Explanation of labels:*

Testing conducted in French
1. F,F/F Bi-modal Input-L2
2. F,−/F L2 Dialogue Only
3. −,F/F L2 Script Only
4. F,E/F Standard Subtitling
5. E,F/F Reversed Subtitling-L2

Testing conducted in English
6. E,E/E Bi-modal Input-L1
7. E,−/E L1 Dialogue Only
8. −,E/E L1 Script Only
9. E,F/E Reversed Subtitling-L1

be more advantageous than L2 Dialogue Only (condition 2) and at the same level as the Reversed Subtitling L1 (condition 9).

The second most favorable condition (which we had not anticipated in our research planning) turned out to be condition 5, Reversed Subtitling L2, in which English dialogue is paired with French script and the comprehension test is administered in French. Note that it was not significantly different from the Bimodal L1 Input (condition 6), the one condition which favors English most because it has dialogue and script in English, followed by an English comprehension test. Thus, Reversed Subtitling L2 is the only condition involving French input and French testing that ranks among the most beneficial for overall comprehension. It is in fact as beneficial as the Bimodal L1 format and generally more beneficial than either the English dialogue only or the English script only formats (conditions 7 and 8) which also involve English testing.

Our interpretation for the surprisingly good performance of subjects under condition 5 is that the basic message or story line is presented in the subjects' dominant language (English) through the more transient auditory channel. Subjects are accordingly able to follow the audio message relatively effortlessly, with time available to match the story line with the French script, giving them the opportunity to review for themselves the L2 format of the message ("Oh, yes, that's the way it's put in French") or to discover the L2 format ("So that's the way it's put in French"). Reviewing or discovering the L2 format would of course prime subjects for the French testing to follow and give them an opportunity to grasp more of the details of the L2 message. These details are required not only for the comprehension tests but also for the tests of contextual meaning, spelling, and phrase form.

From another perspective, one can argue that the Reversed Subtitling L2 stands out as particularly effective because it very closely approximates ideal reading conditions for a monolingual reader. Current theories of reading suggest that efficient readers know what to look for in a passage. They are said to enter the passage with a set to confirm or verify their guesses as to what is in the passage (see Cziko, 1978). This phenomenon is referred to as "analysis by synthesis" (Neisser, 1967), "a psycholinguistic guessing game" (Goodman, 1967), "a constructive process" (Ryan & Semmel, 1969) or "a sampling from the printed page" (Smith, 1971). We might add that a very similar process likely holds for listening comprehension as well as reading, and it might be a general cognitive approach to information processing. The main point is that our condition 5 supplies the processor with the message's meaning via L1 auditory input and permits him or her to then read the corresponding L2 message for its goodness of fit. Standard Subtitling (where subtitles are in English and the dialogue is in French) is less helpful than the Reversed Subtitling L2 condition because in the former, the French story line—even for subjects as functionally bilingual as ours—is likely not processed automatically. The concentration needed to capture the meaning of the message in French is offset by the more automatic tendency to process the corresponding English script. This would very likely wash out the French feature of the message input, and detract from the subjects' readiness to process effectively the subsequent French test of comprehension. Some such preparedness factor seems necessary to explain why condition 5 was a more efficient input condition than condition 9 which is identical to 5 except for the language of testing.[2]

## Contextual Meaning

There is a statistically significant condition effect for the contextual meaning scores $F(4,175) = 6.69$, $p, < .001$. The Newman-Keuls analysis ranks the conditions, from best scores to poorest, in subsets as follows:

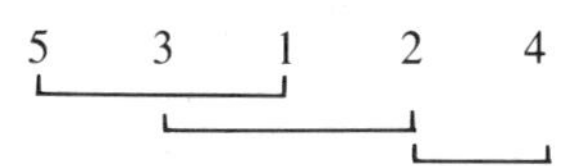


This means that the mode of presentation of information in L2 differentially affects the grasping of contextual meaning (see Fig. 4.1). The best processing takes place in the Reversed Subtitling L2 condition (5), while the poorest processing occurs in conditions 4 and 2, Standard Subtitling and L2 Dialogue Only. Thus, French dialogue alone (2) and French dialogue with English script (4) are of relatively little benefit in grasping L2 contextual meaning. In contrast, those presentation conditions that provide script in L2 (conditions 5, 3, 1) apparently establish a deeper base for the type of semantic processing and storage called for in this subtest. The Reversed Subtitling L2 condition stands out here again, adding weight to our argument about its potential value in various forms of comprehension. The results show that subjects found it particularly easy to extract semantic information in L2 when presented with an easily decipherable story line through L1 dialogue which is accompanied by L2 script. The Standard Subtitling condition is less beneficial, we believe, because the important visual channel is filled with potentially interfering information in L1, the wrong language for cases where the posttesting is to be conducted in L2. Our hunch is that the interference would come from a too-deep involvement with the L1 script which would tend to wipe out the L2 dialogue component.

---

[2]A significant interaction of grade and sex appeared for the comprehension tests. It did not affect the major outcomes described here. The complete analysis can be found in Lambert et al., 1981, pp. 141–143.

## Spelling

For spelling accuracy, there was a significant condition effect ($F(4,175) = 4.41$, $p, < .002$) and the Newman-Keuls analysis isolated the following subsets:

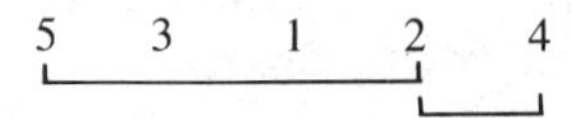


This pattern of scores is essentially the same as that for comprehension and contextual meaning, namely that Reversed Subtitling L2 along with L2 Script Only and Bi-modal L2 Input (conditions 5, 3, and 1) provide better means for processing the details of spelling than do Normal Subtitling or L2 Dialogue Only (conditions 2 and 4). The arguments already offered for the value of conditions 5 and 1 and the drawbacks of condition 4 hold for spelling as they did for comprehension and contextual meaning. However, in this case there is the additional fact that students bring with them different levels of proficiency in spelling in L2, depending upon their experience. This is evident in the significant grade level difference in spelling [$F(1,175) = 23.87$, $p < .001$], indicating that grade 6 pupils are clearly stronger than grade 5 pupils in L2 spelling. Nonetheless, particular presentation conditions help or hamper performance in spite of these more stable competence levels associated with grade level.

There was a significant condition by grade interaction for spelling, $F(4,175) = 4.04$, $p < .004$. When analyzed, it shows that the grade 6 advantage is evident only in conditions where no French script is provided; thus, grade 5 and 6 students differ significantly ($p < .01$ level) only for conditions 4 and 2. This means that grade 5 students suffer in spelling when no French script is provided in the input whereas grade 6 students are not only better at L2 spelling but are also less dependent on the L2 script input.

## Phrase Form

Memory for the form of phrasing used in the L2 scenarios differed according to the presentation conditions, $F(4,175) = 4.95$, $p < .001$, with the following subsets of mean scores:

1 5 2 4 3

Thus, the Bimodal L2 Input condition (1) is the most beneficial for remembering the exact form of phrasing in L2; in condition 1, subjects could both see and hear the L2 sentence composition. But because conditions 5 and 2 are not reliably different from 1, Reversed Subtitling L2 is again a relatively helpful input condition. By contrast, Standard Subtitling (4) is a relatively hampering input condition. It is interesting that L2 Dialogue Only (condition 2) is more helpful for phrase memory than is L2 Script Only (3), suggesting that visual input in L2 is not as helpful for this form of processing as it is for comprehension, contextual meaning and spelling.

## SUMMARY AND CONCLUSIONS

The purpose of this study was to explore ways in which second or foreign language learning might be improved through novel uses of L1 and L2 scripts and dialogues in the media, especially TV, films, radio, and books. In the study, we made systematic variations in the languages used for the spoken dialogue and/or the written script of messages (programmed radio materials from L1 and L2 broadcasts) as these were presented through an audio-visual playback unit. Subjects were tested in L1 and L2 for their overall comprehension of the input messages, their grasp of contextual meaning of concepts used in the L2 messages, their memory for the form of phrasing used in L2, and their accuracy in spelling in L2. The subjects were grade 5 and 6 native English-speaking students in public elementary schools who had followed French immersion programs from Kindergarten on. They had thus developed a degree of functional bilingualism that would probably be equivalent, albeit at a lower age level, to that of English language college students in North America majoring in French.

Subjects' efficiency of processing messages presented in "Standard Subtitling" condition, when posttesting was conducted in L2, is relatively poor, suggesting to us that the Standard Subtitling procedure is an unpromising mode of strengthening or improving skills in L2. This finding is important precisely because Standard Subtitling is essentially the only model now popularly used in the media, suggesting to us that innovative changes are called for in order to exploit the educational possibilities of modern forms of the common media.

Some potentially valuable directions for change are seen in the results for alternative forms of message input that were included in our study. One is the "Reversed Subtitling L2" condition wherein the message dialogue comes through L1 and the script through L2, with testing again conducted in L2. Its relative effectiveness was particularly good, making its potential extremely interesting. In fact, the Reversed Subtitling L2 format is generally as good as the "Bimodal L1 Input" condition in which dialogue, script and posttesting are all presented in L1, the linguistically most direct and clear form possible for native speakers of L1. Furthermore, the Reversed Subtitling L2 format fits nicely with current theories of information processing which stress the "top-down" nature of efficient information processing in reading and, we would argue, comprehension in general (see Cziko, 1978). These theories draw on research that shows that effective reading entails a set on the part of the reader to enter a written text with hypotheses as to what is to come and what should be looked for, rather than focusing on written or phonemic subunits of words that can be built in order to ultimately arrive at contextual meaning (the "bottom-up" alternative). Thus, the Reversed Subtitling L2 format provides subjects with a linguistically uncomplicated story line in the form of L1 dialogue that is processed rapidly and automatically, leaving the processor free to explore the L2 script with an active hypothesis-testing set. Subjects are thus given an opportunity to map the auditorily processed L1 dialogue onto the L2 script or, stated otherwise, to attend to and rehearse the L2 written transformation of the already-comprehended underlying story line. The advantages of the Reversed Subtitling L2 format were seen in tests of comprehension, contextual meaning, phrasing form, and spelling. The potential of this input format is exciting because it could assist even the novice in L2 as he/she starts to develop listening and reading skills, and the benefits might well accumulate with practice and exposure.

With subjects more advanced in L2 skills, as ours were in this study, the incorporation of Reversed Subtitling as a learning/studying device would certainly be valuable, but other results suggest that those with more advanced experience in L2 would profit even more from a gradual shift to a Bi-modal L2 format wherein dialogue and script are both presented in L2. For our subjects, the "Bi-modal L2 Input" condition was more effective than Standard Subtitling; and although less effective than Reversed Subtitling L2, it is promising as a learning/studying device because it provides subjects with the opportunity to map L2 dialogue directly onto L2 script, with the interplay of script and dialogue possibly working both ways—visual analysis of L2 material enriching auditory processing in L2 and vice versa. Experimental testing of its accumulated effects are now called for. For this purpose, one need not rely exclusively on complicated audio-visual machinery; one could more simply exploit the use of foreign language "talking books" wherein tape recorded readings and text material are both presented in L2.

## STUDY II: TESTING EFFECTS OVER TIME[3]

The second study focused more closely on the more promising input procedures noted in the first study. In particular we wanted to determine if the initial advantage of listening to L1 dialogue while reading L2 script (i.e., Reversed Subtitling) would hold up over time, and if the Bimodal L2 input procedure would gain effectiveness through usage. Accordingly, the present study ran for an 11-week period. As a comparison or control procedure, we included a matched group of pupils who simply read the input passages in French, referred to here as the "L2 script-only" condition. This we considered a strong control

[3]A full report is given in Holobow, Lambert, & Sayegh, 1984.

condition because subjects have no competing input to contend with and they profit from the quiet feature of silent reading.

## METHOD

### Subjects

The full set of subjects were 77 grade 5 pupils (36 males and 41 females) and 59 grade 6 pupils (31 males and 28 females) from eight classrooms in two elementary schools in the English language public school system of greater Montreal. Their ages ranged from 10 years, 5 months to 11 years, 9 months. All subjects had middle-class backgrounds. They also had participated in a French "immersion" program starting in kindergarten (see Lambert & Tucker, 1972). We included in the study only those children who had English as a mother tongue and who were not exposed in any consistent way to French outside of the school situation.

Administrators and teachers assured us that the various schools involved were basically similar in terms of social class makeup and educational performance. However, pretest results indicated fairly strong classroom and school differences. As a consequence, the analyses to follow were based on subsets of pupils who had been matched for scores on pretests of their achievement levels in L2.

### Presentation Conditions

Within each grade level, classes were randomly assigned to one of three input presentation conditions: (1) a *Reversed Subtitling* condition, in which pupils listened to dialogue in L1 (English) while reading scripts of the same information in L2 (French); (2) a *Bi-modal L2 Input* condition, in which pupils listened to dialogues in French while reading scripts of the same information, also in French; or (3) an *L2 Script Only* condition, in which no dialogues were available; pupils simply read the French versions of the scripts.

### Test Materials

A group test of French-language achievement was administered to all subjects as the grounds for matching groups. This was a French version of Form A of the Peabody Picture Vocabulary Test devised by Dunn (1959). A single word is pronounced by an examiner and subjects choose the one picture out of four projected on a large screen before them that best represents the meaning of the word heard. Items 70 through 149 were administered, meaning that a score represented the number correct out of a possible total of 80.

### Training Session Tests

In collaboration with the teachers, a series of 20 different grade-appropriate French stories (10 for each grade) were selected from various books and readers, other than text books. The stories did not represent a progression of difficulty, but were rather a random selection of passages unfamiliar to the pupils. An exact and polished English translation of each story was made for use in the Reversed Subtitling condition. Each story was judged to be slightly above the actual level of the children, containing some vocabulary that would be novel. Accordingly, they were presented with a list of the new words and their English glosses at the start of each session.

Tests were developed for each story, with questions designed to test for *comprehension* of the passage, *contextual meaning* of certain of the terms used, and memory for the exact *form of phrasing* as described earlier.

### Procedure

All subjects first completed a language background questionnaire and then completed the pretest. Training sessions started the following week and continued over a 10-week period, one session per week.

A fluently bilingual experimenter was present for all sessions. Pupils had face-down in front of them a typed copy of the story and a test sheet. After discussing the list of new French words that would be encountered, the story was then presented. Children in the control condition were instructed to read the story through carefully and then to turn it over and answer the test questions provided on a separate sheet. For the Reversed Subtitling and Bimodal L2 Input conditions, the passage was read out loud in the appropriate language, while the children followed the written script. The importance of paying close attention to both script and dialogue was stressed. The test questions were then presented. Each session lasted approximately 30 minutes.

## RESULTS AND DISCUSSION

In order to minimize possible classroom, school, and teaching differences, subgroups were formed through pretest matching. This necessarily reduced sample sizes, and in order to keep subgroups reasonably large, we pooled grade 5 and grade 6 scores. The test used for equating the groups was the French version of the Peabody Picture Vocabulary Test (FPPV). There was a total of 69 subjects used, 23 in each of the three conditions. The mean score for each group (condition) on the FPPV pretest was 35.22, with scores ranging between 25 and 42 (out of a possible maximum of 80). The 11 males in each group had a mean score of 35.18 and the 12 females a mean score of 35.25.

Because grade 5 and 6 pupils received a different series of stories, the 10 test scores for each grade level were transformed into standard score format. (The standard scores were further transformed through multiplying them by 15 and adding 50 in order to eliminate negative numbers.)

Ten separate 3 (conditions) × 2 (sex) analyses of variance were computed, one analysis for each week's total test score. Further analyses of variance were done on the combined scores over the 10 week period for each test component (phrase form, contextual meaning, comprehension and for a "ten-week total" score). These scores were also transformed into standard score format before being analyzed. For condition comparisons, one-tailed *a priori* t-tests, using the appropriate error terms, were applied throughout, with an .05 alpha level. Such a priori tests were justified on the basis of predictions that were generated by our previous research; namely, that pupils in the Reversed Subtitling condition would receive higher scores than those in the Bimodal L2 Input condition, who in turn would perform better than pupils in the L2 Script-Only condition. Figure 4.2 shows the mean scores for each week of treatment. There were significant condition main effects on five of the ten treatment tests ($p < .01$ or $< .05$), and on three other tests, condition effects approached significance ($p < .07$ or

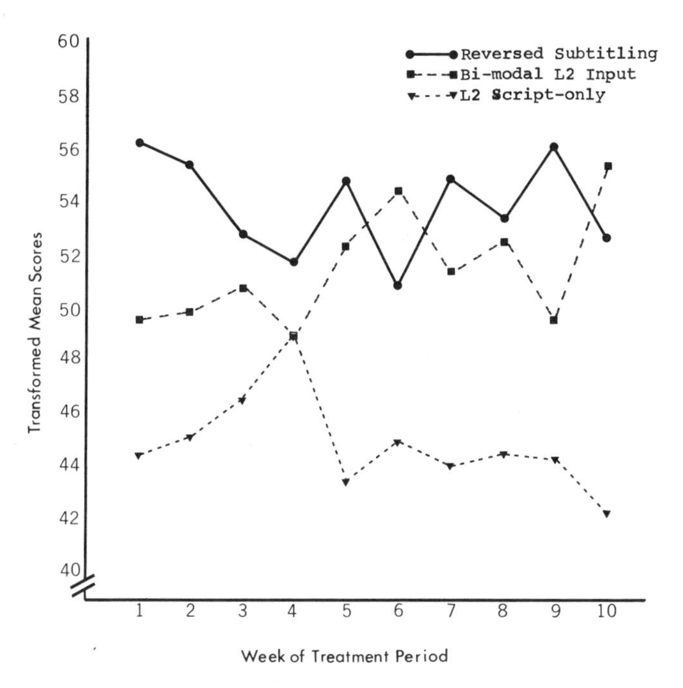


FIG. 4.2. Comparisons of mean total test scores per condition for groups matched on French picture vocabulary test.

< .08). When conditions were compared, the Reversed Subtitling condition was significantly higher than the L2 Script-Only condition on six treatment tests, and on four treatment tests the Bimodal L2 Input condition was significantly higher than the Control condition (see Table 4.1). However, there were no significant differences between the Reversed Subtitling and the Bimodal Input conditions.

In general, the pattern that held for each week of the testing period, except the last, was consistent with our predictions. Even though condition differences were not significant in every instance, the Reversed Subtitling scores were generally higher than the Bimodal L2 Input scores which in turn were higher than the Control condition scores.

*Time Trends.* Interestingly, for the final week of treatment, the highest scores were obtained by pupils in the Bimodal L2 input condition, followed by those in the Reversed Subtitling condition, with both groups scoring higher than those in the Control condition. This outcome raised the possibility that, with a longer period of practice, the most effective mode of improving second language

TABLE 4.1
Transformed Mean Score Comparisons: Groups Matched on French Vocabulary Test

| | Condition | | | | |
|---|---|---|---|---|---|
| Weekly Test | Reversed Subtitling | Bi-Modal L2 Input | L2 Script Only | $F^a$ Ratio | p |
| 1 | 56.17 | 49.57 | 44.43 | 3.96 (2,66) | .02 |
| 2 | 55.26 | 49.87 | 45.09 | 2.75 (2,66) | .07 |
| 3 | 52.70 | 50.87 | 46.57 | 1.03 (2,66) | .36 |
| 4 | 51.83 | 49.00 | 49.04 | 0.27 (2,66) | .77 |
| 5 | 54.74 | 52.30 | 43.30 | 4.11 (2,66) | .02 |
| 6 | 50.70 | 54.39 | 44.91 | 2.54 (2,66) | .08 |
| 7 | 54.78 | 51.35 | 44.00 | 3.41 (2,66) | .04 |
| 8 | 53.22 | 52.48 | 44.43 | 2.60 (2,66) | .08 |
| 9 | 56.04 | 49.65 | 44.26 | 3.99 (2,66) | .02 |
| 10 | 52.61 | 55.22 | 42.17 | 5.59 (2,66) | .01 |

Note: Means connected by a horizontal line differ significantly ($p < .05$) according to a $t$-test.

[a] Degrees of freedom for each $F$-ratio are indicated within parentheses.

skills might well be one based on the Bi-modal L2 Input format, at least for those who already have a good command of a second language, as was the case for our immersion students. To examine this possibility more closely, we performed three trend-line analyses (one for each condition), plotting the transformed mean scores for each week against a weekly time increment. The resulting correlation coefficients were tested for significance.

In the Reversed Subtitling condition, the correlation between mean scores and time was $-.19$ (df $= 8$, $p$ is not significant), indicating that the effects of this condition did not change over time, but held fairly constant, with only a slight downward trend. The correlation in the Bimodal L2 Input condition was $+.58$ ($t = 1.998$, df $= 8$, $p < .05$), indicating a significant increase in scores over the 10 week treatment period. Had the experiment continued over an even longer time period, it is likely that scores in this condition would have surpassed those of the Reversed Subtitling condition. The mean scores for the L2 Script-Only condition plotted against time yielded a correlation of $-.49$ ($t = 1.607$, df $= 8$, $p < .10$), indicating that pupils tended to perform poorer as time went on.

Our speculation is that the Bimodal L2 Input condition provides subjects with the best opportunity of mapping L2 dialogue directly onto L2 script. Presumably the combination of the visual and audio inputs enriches and deepens the processing of the incoming information. Our results indicate that the effectiveness of this and the Reversed Subtitling condition hold up over the long term, making both promising devices for learning a second or foreign language or using that language for learning content material. The Bimodal L2 Input condition, however, may only be appropriate for those with relatively advanced L2 skills.

Two other effects emerged from the analyses. The first was a main effect of sex on the fifth test [$F(1,63) = 6.21$, $p$, $< .05$] wherein females scored significantly higher than males. The second was an interaction effect of condition with sex which occurred on test six [$F(2,63) = 3.62$, $p$, $< .05$], and in this case females scored higher than males, except in the Control condition. Since no other sex factors were found, we viewed these effects as isolated events only.

*Subcomponent Analyses.* The transformed mean scores for the subcomponents of the tests are presented in Table 4.2. Memory for the *form of phrasing* used in the input stories did not differ according to the presentation conditions [$F(2,63) = 1.55$, $p$ is not significant]. However, the mean scores place the groups in the following order: the Bimodal L2 Input condition ranked first, the Reversed Subtitling second, and the L2 Script-Only third. We had predicted that receiving both inputs in the same language would best entrench the exact wording used in the passages.

For the *contextual meaning* scores, there was a statistically significant condition effect [$F(2,63) = 3.16$, $p < .05$], indicating that the scores for the Reversed Subtitling and the Bimodal L2 input conditions were both significantly higher than those of the Control condition.

TABLE 4.2
Transformed Mean Score Comparisons: Groups Matched on French Vocabulary Test

| | Mean Scores for Conditions | | | F Ratios | | |
|---|---|---|---|---|---|---|
| Component | Reversed Subtitling | Bimodal L2 Input | L2 Script Only | Condition[a] | Sex | Condition x Sex |
| Phrase Form | 48.26 | 54.43 | 47.26 | 1.55 (2,63) | 0.21 (1,63) | 0.64 (2,63) |
| Contextual Meaning | 54.35 | 51.30 | 44.43 | 3.16* (2,63) | 3.81 (1.63) | 3.42* (2,63) |
| | Male Female | Male Female | Male Female | | | |
| | 53.36 55.25 | 41.64 60.17 | 45.00 43.92 | | | |
| Comprehension | 57.65 | 50.43 | 41.96 | 7.53*** (2,63) | 0.69 (1,63) | 0.44 (2,63) |
| 10-Week Total | 55.87 | 51.43 | 42.70 | 5.24** (2,63) | 1.03 (1,63) | 0.82 (2,63) |

Note: Means connected by a horizontal line differ significantly ($p < .05$) according to a $t$-test (one-tailed).

[a]Degrees of freedom for each $F$ ratio are indicated within parentheses.

$^{*}p < .05$; $^{**}p < .01$; $^{***}p < .001$

A significant condition effect was found for the *comprehension* measure [$F(2,63) = 7.53$, $p < .001$]. Each condition differed significantly from each other and in the manner predicted. As anticipated, the Reversed Subtitling condition proved to be the most effective aid to L2 comprehension. Our speculation is that, when verbal information is presented through the L1 auditory channel, subjects are thereby better able to concentrate on the written L2 form of the same information and, in a sense, better decipher it, perhaps because the L1 story line is more accessible, making it easier to hold the overall meaning of the passage and discrete words therein, and to match L1 forms of the message with their L2 counterparts, as discussed earlier.

The Bimodal L2 Input condition, although less effective than Reversed Subtitling, was nonetheless more effective than the L2 Script-Only condition. We interpret this to mean that presenting a verbal passage through both auditory and visual modes helps to "solidify" or "root" the message, in the sense that visual analysis of L2 material may enrich L2 auditory processing, and vice versa. Of course, for the Bimodal L2 condition to have this solidifying effect, subjects must have attained sufficient skill in L2 to enable them to arrive at meanings through that language.

The *ten-week total* measure represented each subject's total score for all 10 tests, with subcomponents combined. The analysis of variance revealed a significant condition effect [$F(2,63) = 5.24$, $p < .01$]. Actually, pupils in both the Reversed Subtitling and Bimodal L2 Input conditions scored significantly higher than those in the L2 Script-Only condition. The mean score for the Reversed Subtitling condition was higher than that of the Bimodal L2 Input condition (again, in line with expectations), but the difference was not statistically significant.

## DISCUSSION

Several features of the second study merit comment. First, as with the first study, we were again impressed with the effectiveness of the Reversed Subtitling procedure which showed itself not only in tests of L2 comprehension, but in tests of L2 contextual meaning as well. Its effectiveness also held up over the 10-week treatment period. Second, this study provided support for our expectations that the Bimodal L2 Input condition might gain in effectiveness with extended practice. For those who already have some training in or knowledge of a particular L2, the improvement in L2 comprehension associated with Bimodal L2 Input is noteworthy, making it a practical alternative mode of strengthening and improving L2 skills, along with or in alternation with Reversed Subtitling. Third, this study also enhances our confidence in the reliability of the phenomena under discussion. The main findings of the first study were replicated here, even with the introduction of a strong control condition (silent reading in L2) that might well have minimized between-condition effects. However, this study has clear limits. We cannot generalize the findings to debutantes in second or foreign language study. For example, the Bimodal L2 Input procedure obviously requires a certain level of skill in L2, and to test its generalizability, studies are needed with pupils who have more conventional levels of skill in L2, e.g., levels one usually finds in French-as-a-second-language programs. This issue is examined in our third study.

Nonetheless, our first two studies, taken as a set, have potentially important implications of three different sorts, (a) very practical implications for utilizing television and radio more effectively in second and foreign language education; (b) more theoretical implications for interpreting how verbal information might be processed through auditory and/or visual channels; and (c) pedagogical implications for modifying teaching approaches so as to capitalize on the apparently beneficial features of Reversed Subtitling and/or Bimodal L2 Input procedures.

*Practical Suggestions.* Many new ideas for the pedagogical use of television and radio come to mind. In the North American context, one possibility would be to add English script to educational television programs that normally have English dialogue only. For those with English as their only language but who are poor readers, poor spellers or illiterate in English, this simple addition could become a valuable aid over time, not only for improving literacy and reading abilities, but also for enhancing and enriching listeners' general comprehension of verbal information presented in L1. Such a coordination of English script and English dialogue would also provide a pure example of Bimodal L2 Input for those with some other language than English as their L1. As they develop their skills in English as a second language, we would expect them, on the basis of the results of Study II, to profit from the addition of L2 script and improve their L2 skills as a function of their experience with the Bimodal L2 procedure.

A second step would be to provide television programming in Spanish and other minority languages in the USA, comparable to the separate French and English programs available in Canada, and in each instance coordinate the script of the minority language with the corresponding minority language dialogue. Thus, Spanish speakers could be enriched with programs that have spoken Spanish and Spanish subtitling. This possibility could, of course, be extended to any number of minority languages in the United States or Canada. Such an extension would simultaneously provide the Bimodal L2 Input procedure for those English speaking listeners whose L2 (e.g., Spanish) was advanced enough to profit from the double L2 input.

A third phase of the same plan would provide opportunities for the use of the Reversed Subtitling option by having some English language programs subtitled in languages other than English (for example Spanish or Arabic in the USA) and by having some Spanish, Arabic (or whatever) programs subtitled in English. Program viewers would be informed of the purpose of the mixed-language format and that they would profit most by choosing the combination in which the script appeared in their L2. Thus, native speakers of Spanish would be induced to choose programs with Spanish dialogue and coordinated English script, whereas native speakers of English would choose programs with English dialogue and coordinated Spanish (Arabic, or whatever) script. In this fashion, with a minimum of language learning formalities, bilingualism might be fostered for some, and brought to fruition or maintained for others.

In less developed areas of the world, it is financially unrealistic to consider television as a possible aid to education, whereas with transistorization, radio has become a dependable educational adjunct that can reach the most isolated areas of any nation (see Futagami, 1981). Suggestions for strengthening education and literacy in less developed areas have to emphasize radio's potential (see Lambert & Sidoti, 1981). For instance, audio input in the form of radio programs of readings could be coordinated with script versions in textbooks and school readers. For adults not in school settings, stories and daily events taken from newspapers could be read by radio broadcasters at appropriate speeds so as to provide a useful Bimodal L1 Input for those with little formal education. In other words they would be taught how to follow the newspaper text while hearing the same materials read over radio. Similarly, languages of wider access could be taught in schools and in adult education programs in less developed areas through Reversed Subtitling and Bimodal L2 Input procedures.

*Theoretical Implications.* With respect to the processing of verbal information, these two studies have found that single channel L2 inputs (either auditory or visual) are less effective for L2 comprehension and memory than are certain two-channel input combinations, in particular Reversed Subtitling (with script in L2 and dialogue in L1) and Bimodal L2 input (with both script and dialogue in L2). However, not all bimodal (or bilingual) inputs are effective, since standard subtitling (with dialogue in L2 and script in L1) is relatively very ineffective. With the exception of standard subtitling, bimodal inputs generally strengthen or enhance the verbal message, suggesting that the double modal input may be processed more *deeply* because attention can alternate from the auditory to the visual format or be directed along parallel visual and auditory routes simultaneously. Rather than being a distraction, the double modal input appears to enhance comprehension better than simply processing script through silent reading. Perhaps reading itself would be improved if readers were encouraged to read aloud so as to provide themselves with an auditory accompaniment.

Because the two most effective input procedures for L2 comprehension and memory are Reversed Subtitling and Bimodal L2 Input, we see their potential residing in the fact that the script format in both cases is in L2. This suggests that the message is better retained if occasions are provided to map the auditory message onto L2 script. The mapping would be easy with the reception of the auditory message in the more powerful L1 format, but when L2 skills are advanced, the L2 auditory message seems to be as easily mapped as the L1, and the L2 mapping appears to improve with practice.

It is also clear that L2 script is much more powerful than L2 dialogue in enhancing message comprehension and meaning, suggesting that input introduced visually leaves a longer and perhaps deeper impression of the message than does the apparently more ephemeral impression aroused by auditory inputs.

*Pedagogical Implications.* Finally, these studies suggest new ways of teaching that might incorporate certain features of the Reversed Subtitling and Bimodal L2 Input procedures. For instance, judging from the results of both studies, it would apparently be beneficial in L2 instruction to have the more advanced pupils follow the script of L2 text materials while the teacher reads the same materials aloud to them in L2. (Because they do not have native-like command of L2, beginners might be discouraged from reading aloud in L2 until their production skills are advanced.) Similarly, taped material could be played in L2 while pupils follow the texts of the same material written in L2. For those less advanced in L2 skills, the Reversed Subtitling results indicate that they would profit from opportunities to actively map L1 dialogues onto L2 script. This could be accomplished through L1 to L2 literal translations placed side by side, as found in a "trot" or "pony," the quasi-legal translations of Latin classics we used to consult regularly when learning Latin. Or the pupil could first read aloud a passage in L1 and then immediately follow the L2 script version of the same passage. Ultimately, we are led to the potential value of *la dictée* as the method *par excellence* for developing L2 skills, because pupils in that case hear the message spoken by a native L2 speaker and are required to supply the L2 script on their own. The active searching required makes *la dictée* an excellent example of the Bimodal L2 Input procedure, and if it were to become routinized, pupils would learn to carefully code and store for future reference the all-important L2 script materials encountered in second and foreign language courses. It might be best to have students redo *la dictée* one or more times after they had made all necessary corrections on the first trial.

## STUDY III: TESTING STUDENTS WITH ORDINARY FRENCH-AS-A-SECOND-LANGUAGE EXPERIENCE[4]

Since the first two studies were conducted with subjects who had immersion experience in a second language, the present experiment tests the generalizability of the conclusions reached so far by considering a more typical pool of subjects, namely, Anglophone students in conventional English-language school programs whose introduction to French as an L2 is limited to a single course for a limited

[4]A full report is given in Lambert & Holobow, 1984.

time per day, and taught through a French-as-a-second language approach. The purpose of this experiment therefore was to determine (a) how beginners of second or foreign language study would react to various combinations of L1 and L2 dialogue and script, and (b) how their modes of processing information through L1 and L2 would compare with those who are acquiring L2 through immersion experiences.

## METHOD AND PROCEDURE

### Subjects

The subjects were 84 grade 7 pupils (47 males and 37 females) from five classrooms in three high schools of the English-language public school system of greater Montreal. They had all followed a conventional English-language school curriculum from Kindergarten through grade 7 which included approximately 45 minutes per day of French-as-a-second-language (FSL) instruction from grades 1 through 7. All those included in the study had English as their mother tongue and home language, and were not exposed in any consistent way to French outside of the school situation.

### Pretests

Because in our previous research pretest results indicated fairly strong classroom and school differences, the analyses to follow were based on subsets of pupils who had been matched for scores on a pretest of achievement in L2. For this purpose, a French version of the Peabody Picture Vocabulary Test (Dunn, 1959) was administered.

### Presentation Conditions

The five classrooms were randomly assigned to one of the five input presentation conditions described below. (1) *Reversed Subtitling*: students listened to spoken dialogues of various passages that were presented in L1 (English) while reading printed scripts of the same passages presented in L2 (French). (2) *Bimodal L2 Input*: students listened to spoken dialogues in L2 (French) while reading the same material in script form, also presented in L2. (3) *L2 Script Only*: no spoken dialogues presented; students simply read L2 (French) scripts. (4) *Standard Subtitling*: students listened to dialogues in L2 (French) while reading coordinated scripts in L1 (English). (5) *L1 Script Only*: no dialogues presented; students simply read L1 (English) scripts.

The first four conditions had been used with Immersion students in Study I, and the first three in Study II. Note that condition 3 is a simple reading-in-L2 control for conditions 1 and 2. The only new condition is 5, L1 Script Only, which was included as a control for Standard Subtitling, to determine whether the addition of French (L2) dialogue along with English (L1) script helps or hinders performance of English-speaking subjects on a French posttest.

### Condition Tests

Audio tapes were prepared in French and English as were video tapes of the typed word-for-word transcriptions of the audio messages using the same passages as were described in Study I.

The French audio tapes actually form an interesting listening comprehension test (Test de Compréhension Auditive, Level B, 1979) prepared by the Ontario Institute for Studies in Education. This full test became our *comprehension* measure. Other questions were developed to test *contextual meaning* of certain terms used, *spelling*, and memory for the exact *form of phrasing* used in the passages. All questions were presented in written or spoken French, as described in Study I. In general, subjects heard a taped voice ask a particular question and they had to select the correct answer among written alternatives presented in a separate booklet.

## RESULTS AND DISCUSSION

### Comparison of FSL and Immersion Students

The subjects in the present study are a more representative sample of second language learners than the Immersion students used in Studies I and II, in that they followed a conventional English language curriculum with a FSL (French-as-a-second-language) component only. The FSL students were necessarily older than the Immersion students tested earlier because the listening comprehension test we used had been standardized with non-Immersion students at the grade 7 level or above.

What is interesting to us are the differences between the FSL and the Immersion groups in modes of processing L1 and L2 input information, as is evident by comparisons in Figs. 4.1 and 4.3. These contrasts, we presume, are attributable to differences in degrees of competence in French as the L2.

First, most of the input conditions that are helpful for FSL students are a hindrance for the Immersion students, and vice versa. This is apparent for the Bimodal L2 Input, the L2 Script Only and the Standard Subtitling conditions. In particular, the FSL subjects get very little information from Bimodal L2 Input or from L2 Script Only, suggesting that they are not competent enough in L2 to process L2 information either visually or auditorily. In comparison, the Immersion subjects profit a good deal from L2 information, regardless of the mode of presentation, the contrast being most striking in the Bimodal L2 Input condition.

Second, the FSL subjects profit a good deal from the Standard Subtitling condition, suggesting that subjects at this level of competence rely mainly on L1 script to maintain the storyline and ignore as much as possible the accompanying L2 dialogue. In sharp contrast, Immersion subjects appear to be hampered in their processing of L2 information when it is presented via the Standard Subtitling format (see Fig. 4.1). The performance of the FSL group on the L1 Script Only control condition (which is identical to Standard Subtitling except for the omission of the L2 dialogue) also indicates that subjects with this level of achievement in L2 tend to seek out and rely on L1 input and avoid if possible or make minimal use of L2 (see Fig. 4.3). When later tested through L2 for comprehension, they apparently translate in and out of the information previously stored through their L1.

Third, the Reversed Subtitling condition is an exception to the trends just mentioned because on L2 posttests, both FSL and Immersion subjects profit most

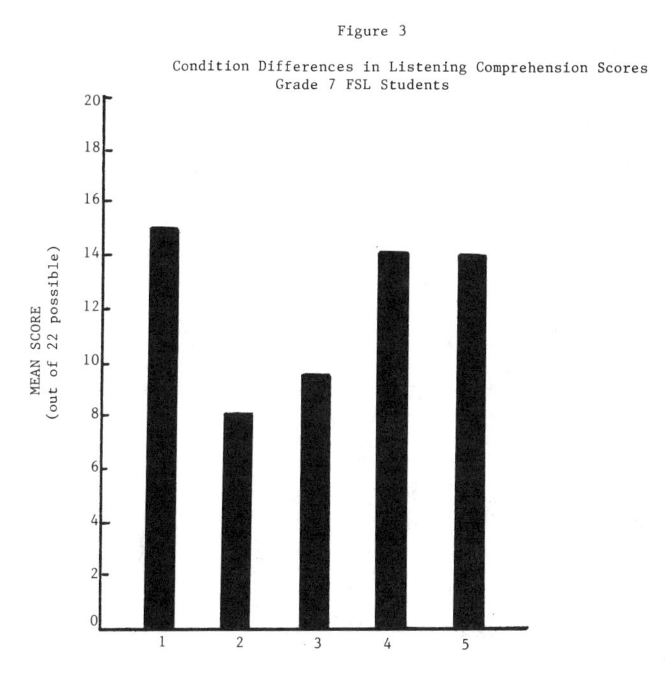


FIG. 4.3. Condition differences in listening comprehension scores, Grade 7 FSL students.

*CONDITIONS*

1. Reversed Subtitling (English dialogue, French script)
2. Bimodal L2 Input (French dialogue, French script)
3. L2 Script Only (No dialogue, French script)
4. Normal Subtitling (French dialogue, English script)
5. L1 Script Only (No dialogue, English script)

when the input information arrives in the form of L1 dialogue coupled with L2 script. The advantages of Reversed Subtitling were found to be substantial and statistically significant for the Immersion subjects in Studies I and II, and are also marginally significant in the analyses of the performance of FSL students that follow. Thus, it is possible that beginning students may be able to map the L1 storyline picked up through the spoken dialogue of Reversed Subtitling onto the accompanying L2 script, thereby enhancing cross-language correspondences which could help on L2 tests of comprehension, contextual meaning, etc. Furthermore, since Immersion students not only profited consistently from Reversed Subtitling but also tended to improve their processing in L2 through training (see Study II), it is also possible that FSL students could similarly learn to capitalize on L2 inputs through training in Reversed Subtitling or Bimodal L2 Input procedures.

## FSL Subjects' Strategies for Processing L1 and L2

The focus in this section is on FSL students exclusively and on their modes of reacting to monolingual and/or bilingual input. Separate one-way (five conditions) analyses of variance were performed for all components of the post-testing (listening comprehension, contextual meaning, phrase form, spelling) we well as for overall composite scores. The basic data are presented in Table 4.3. Since preliminary analyses showed that the factor sex was not significant either as a main effect or as an interactor, it was eliminated from subsequent analyses.

## Listening Comprehension

The mean scores for listening comprehension are given in row "a" of Table 4.3. The overall test was highly significant, [$F(4,71) = 14.53$, $p < .001$], and the Newman-Keuls test showed statistically reliable subset differences in mean performance as follows:

1 4 5 | 3 2

The analyses revealed two contrasting levels of performance: Conditions 1, 4, and 5 (Reversed Subtitling, L1 Script Only, and Standard Subtitling) produced significantly higher mean scores than did conditions 3 and 2 (L2 Script Only and Bimodal L2 Input). Apparently, input conditions that present messages in L2 script along with L2 dialogue or in L2 Script Only are of little value to our FSL students. This means that messages not presented in L1, either in script or dialogue form, are not grasped by FSL students. This is evident in the relatively poor comprehension scores for conditions 2 and 3, those that utilize L2 only. In fact, the FSL students are helped significantly more in their L2 comprehension if

TABLE 4.3

Performance Scores for FSL Subjects: Input Condition Comparisons

| Test | Reversed Subtitling (n = 19) | Bimodal L2 Input (n = 17) | L2 Script Only (n = 15) | Standard Subtitling (n = 15) | L1 Script Only (n = 18) | df | F |
|---|---|---|---|---|---|---|---|
| Pretest: | | | | | | | |
| French Peabody Picture Vocabulary (Max. score, 80) | 39.32 | 37.24 | 40.33 | 38.80 | 36.22 | (4,79) | 1.03 |
| Posttests: | | | | | | | |
| a) Listening Comprehension (Max. score, 22) | 14.65 | 8.08 | 9.07 | 14.07 | 14.00 | (4,71) | 14.53*** |
| b) Contextual Meaning (Max. score, 18) | 7.35 | 4.77 | 5.43 | 6.00 | 6.00 | (4,71) | 3.94** |
| c) Phrase Form (Max. score, 18) | 7.06 | 8.92 | 8.93 | 8.47 | 7.12 | (4,71) | 2.62* |
| d) Spelling (Max. score, 18) | 8.71 | 7.08 | 6.21 | 6.20 | 7.65 | (4,71) | 2.23 |
| Composite Score: | | | | | | | |
| Components a-d (Total possible, 76) | 37.76 | 28.85 | 29.64 | 34.73 | 34.88 | (4,71) | 5.27*** |

$^{*}p < .05$; $^{**}p < .01$; $^{***}p < .001$

the input comes in the form of L1 Script Only (condition 5). In this case they can grasp the message and then by some form of internal translation, answer questions about the message posed in L2. They can also profit from bilingual input in the form of Standard or Reversed Subtitling (conditions 4 and 1), that is, with L2 in either dialogue or script form, as long as L1 is presented simultaneously. It may be that the FSL students simply process L1 information only, ignoring L2 in both conditions 4 and 1. However, there may be more for them to gain from Reversed Subtitling since Immersion students, with more extensive experience in L2 were hampered by Standard Subtitling whereas they profited greatly from Reversed Subtitling. With further study in L2 or with training in the use of Reversed Subtitling, we might expect a similar pattern to emerge for FSL students. Because Reversed Subtitling does pull away from Standard Subtitling in the composite score, to be discussed below, it is likely that the FSL subjects are already able to map the storyline, picked up easily through the L1 dialogue, onto the continually flowing L2 script. The Reversed Subtitling procedure provides opportunities for this to happen.

## Contextual Meaning

Very similar results emerged for the test of L2 contextual meaning (row "b" in Table 4.3), [$F(4,71) = 3.94$, $p < .01$]. The mean scores form the following progression:

1 4 5    3 2
(1, 4, 5 underlined together; 3, 2 underlined together)

In this case, condition 1 (Reversed Subtitling) is the most helpful input procedure, even more so than Standard Subtitling and L2 Script Only, (conditions 4 and 5), both of which provide L1 script. This suggests that FSL subjects are able to pick up clues to the meaning of concepts in L2 because of the Reversed Subtitling. How this is done is less clear. Our guess is that in coordinating the L1 storyline with the L2 script, the underlying meanings generated in L1 are transferred to the L2 concepts.

## Phrase Form

The picture changes for the test of phrase form—a test of memory for the exact wording of the L2 version of the input message (see row "c" in Table 4.3). In this case, the overall $F$-ratio is significant [$F(4,71) = 2.62$, $p < .05$], but the multigroup comparisons are not. The ordering of the means is nonetheless suggestive. The highest scores are for conditions 2 and 3 (Bimodal L2 Input and L2 Script Only), while the lowest scores are for conditions 1 and 5 (Reversed Subtitling and L1 Script Only). This represents a full reversal in the sense that those input conditions that were most and least helpful for tests of L2 comprehension and contextual meaning become, respectively, the least and most helpful for remembering L2 phrase form. In one sense this is a reasonable outcome: Subjects in conditions 2 and 3 who heard and saw or simply saw L2 versions of the passages would be expected to have better recollection of the actual phrasing than would those who did not have L2 input. The puzzle is why Reversed Subtitling, which also provides L2 script, produces at the same time the lowest mean score for phrase form and the highest scores for comprehension and contextual meaning. Our explanation of these results, provisional as it must be, is that the FSL students, as demonstrated earlier, get little or no meaning from L2 input that does not have some L1 accompaniment, but as suggested here, they apparently can grasp and retain superficial features of unaccompanied L2 input, such as form of phrasing. In contrast, the same subjects when presented material through Reversed Subtitling seem to miss the more superficial, structural features, such as phrase form, perhaps because that procedure directs attention more to meanings, i.e., the meaning of the L1 storyline that has to be related to the L2 script. Although tentative only, these possibilities are worth further experimental study, particularly because the FSL students differ from the Immersion students. The latter, for example, are able to use Reversed Subtitling to their advantage for phrase form as well as comprehension and contextual meaning, as mentioned in Study I.

## Spelling in L2

The mean scores on the test of L2 spelling are given in row "d" of Table 4.3. The $F$-ratio for condition effects is not significant $[F(4,71) = 2.23, p < .05]$ nor are any of the multiple group comparisons. Thus, our samples of FSL students show no differential help or hindrance from one input condition or another in terms of their memory for the exact spelling of French words in the input messages. Here again the FSL subjects differ from the Immersion subjects whose L2 spelling scores were clearly related to the type of input condition.

## Composite Scores

Overall performance scores for all four of the component tests were calculated by simply summing the separate scores given in rows "a" through "d". These composite mean scores are listed in the bottom row of Table 4.3. They differ significantly $[F(4,71) = 5.27, p < .001]$, and the multiple group comparisons form the following sets:

1 5 4 3 2

(1 5 4 underlined as one set; 5 4 3 2 underlined as another set)

## CONCLUSION

These more general indices of performance in L2 permit us to draw a number of conclusions:

First, for our sample of FSL subjects, the least helpful input conditions were Bimodal L2 Input and L2 Script Only (conditions 2 and 3). This means that beginners in the study of L2 apparently have difficulty gleaning and holding information presented exclusively through L2. Thus, if the input message is presented in L2 script form only or in a combination of L2 dialogue and script (e.g., hearing a phrase like: "J'ai dix-sept ans" while seeing the same phrase in script form *J'ai dix-sept ans*), FSL subjects have a great deal of difficulty on L2 tests of comprehension or conceptual meaning. Under these same input conditions, however, they perform relatively better on a test of phrase form, suggesting that they do grasp superficial structural features of L2 input rather than the deeper, semantic aspects of the input information, arriving exclusively via L2.

Second, FSL students find the Standard Subtitling input procedure (condition 4) particularly helpful for L2 posttests, but since they perform essentially the same under the L1 Script Only condition as they do under Standard Subtitling, it is very likely that students at this level of skill in L2 rely, perhaps exclusively, on the L1 script accompaniment found in Standard Subtitling. We even argue that Standard Subtitling encourages this dependence on L1 by permitting the listener-viewer to bypass the L2 dialogue, thereby bypassing the opportunity to begin processing through L2.

Third, the input procedure that shows most promise, even for students at the beginning stages of L2 study, is Reversed Subtitling (condition 1), which tended to produce somewhat higher scores than Standard Subtitling (condition 4) on the overall composite and the contextual meaning measures. Although only marginally better than conditions 4 and 5, the procedure of combining L1 dialogue and L2 script does appear to aid L2 comprehension as well as contextual meaning for the beginning student of L2. We believe that this is so because Reversed Subtitling provides a convenient structure for relating a message picked up through the more comfortable L1 storyline to the continuously present L2 script. In other words, even the beginning student is able to take L1 dialogues, (e.g., "I'm seventeen!") and link them and their meanings to L2 scripts (e.g., *J'ai dix-sept ans!*) as though an important mental connection is established, much like what happens when one discovers that *"that's the way they put it in French."* Not only does Reversed Subtitling appear to prompt mapping from L1 to L2, but it also establishes a relationship that could well become habitual and increasingly more valuable for L2 processing over time. We suggest this because the results of Study II showed that after a training period, immersion students showed an improvement in L2 processing and a decrease in reliance on L1 input information.

Fourth, with these experiments we have uncovered important differences in the styles of processing materials presented in L1 and L2 by comparing beginners and more advanced students of L2. It is clear that beginners have great difficulty with material presented exclusively through L2; they are much more comfortable with Standard Subtitling because it permits them to bypass L2 processing completely. Advanced students of L2, in contrast, are hampered by Standard Subtitling, and profit appreciably from L2 input presented in either the Reversed Subtitling or Bimodal L2 formats. What is encouraging in the present study is the suggestion that Reversed Subtitling is potentially valuable also for less advanced students of L2.

This study also adds new information about the ways incipient bilinguals process in their first and second languages, and this brings our research in line with current work on dual access processing models (as described for example by McCusker, Hillinger, & Bias, 1981), and with theoretical attempts to explain how readers extract meaning both from visually mediated information as well as from phonologically recoded information. The bilingual complication may enrich these theoretical developments.

Finally, this series of studies throws a new light on L2 teaching methods, old and new, suggesting that methods could be developed or redeveloped so as to capitalize on the attractive features of Reversed Subtitling and Bimodal L2 Input. As mentioned earlier, the potential value of *la dictée* (where the teacher reads aloud a passage in L2 and pupils attempt to write what they hear) may be worth careful reexamination as a teaching procedure because it is an excellent example of what we call Bimodal L2 processing, one that can be utilized at all stages of L2 study.

## ACKNOWLEDGMENT

This study was supported in part by grants from the Social Sciences and Humanities Research Council, Ottawa, Ontario to Professor Wallace E. Lambert and Professor Fred Genesee.

The research reported here was conducted jointly by the author, Naomi Holobow, Inga Boehler, Nellie Sidoti, and Lilian Sayegh.

## REFERENCES

Cziko, G. A. (1978). Differences in first- and second-language reading: The use of syntactic, semantic and discourse constraints. *The Canadian Modern Language Review, 34*, 473–489.

Dunn, L. M. (1959). *Peabody Picture Vocabulary Test*. Nashville, TN: American Guidance Service.

Futagami, S. (Ed.). (1981, October). *The educational use of mass media.* World Bank Staff Working Paper No. 491. Washington, DC: The World Bank.

Genesee, F. (1978–1979). Scholastic effects of French immersion: An overview after ten years. *Interchange, 9,* 20–29.

Goodman, K. S. (1967). Reading: A psycholinguistic guessing game. *Journal of the Reading Specialist, 6,* 126–135.

Holobow, N., Lambert, W. E., & Sayegh, L. (1984). Pairing script and dialogue: Combinations that show promise for second or foreign language acquisition. *Language Learning, 34,* 59–76.

Lambert, W. E., Boehler, I., & Sidoti, N. (1981). Choosing the languages of subtitles and spoken dialogues for media presentations: Implications for second language education. *Applied Psycholinguistics, 2,* 133–148.

Lambert, W. E., & Holobow, N. (1984). Combinations of printed script and spoken dialogues that show promise for beginning students of a foreign language. *Canadian Journal of Behavioral Science, 16,* 1–11.

Lambert, W. E., & Sidoti, N. (1981, October). Choosing instructional languages for educational radio broadcasts in less developed countries. In S. Futagami (Ed.), *The educational use of mass media.* World Bank Staff Working Paper Number 491. Washington, DC: The World Bank.

Lambert, W. E., & Tucker, G. R. (1972). *Bilingual education of children. The St. Lambert experiment.* Rowley, MA: Newbury House.

McCusker, L. X., Hillinger, M. L., & Bias, R. G. (1981). Phonological recoding and reading. *Psychological Bulletin, 89,*(2), 217–245.

Neisser, U. (1967). *Cognitive psychology.* New York: Appleton-Century-Crofts.

Ryan, E. B., & Semmel, M. I. (1969). Reading as a constructive language process. *Reading Research Quarterly, 5,* 59–83.

Smith, F. (1971). *Understanding reading.* New York: Holt, Rinehart and Winston.

Swain, M. (1974). French immersion programs across Canada. *The Canadian Modern Language Review, 31,* 117–128.

Test de Compréhension Auditive, Niveau B. (1979). The Ontario Institute in Education, Toronto.

# 5 Selected Issues in Second and Third Language Learning

Edith Mägiste
*University of Uppsala*

This chapter is concerned with a form of bilingualism that can be found among young immigrants in Germany and Sweden who go to schools which offer bilingual education. The chapter covers a variety of issues such as the optimal age for second-language learning, the relationship between automaticity and interference, the role of language proficiency in determining the direction of interference between languages, and certain strategies in learning a third language. For the most part, the research reviewed here examines language processing in bilinguals as measured by speeded performance on simple encoding and decoding tasks such as color, picture, or number naming.

## DEVELOPMENT OF EQUIVALENT LEVELS OF SPEEDED LANGUAGE PERFORMANCE

The increasing language heterogeneity of populations in modern societies precipitated by migration raises a question of great importance for many people: How long does it take to attain a comparable level of performance in two languages?

An excellent opportunity to follow various aspects of the second-language acquisition process is provided by the German School in Stockholm. This is a private school where instruction is in German and Swedish at both elementary and high school levels, with German being the dominant classroom language. The students are taught Swedish history, political science, and the Swedish language in Swedish by Swedish teachers. Other topics are taught by German teachers and include German history, German, mathematics, physics, chemistry, two or three foreign languages, gymnastics, and music. Each grade includes students who range widely in their residence times in Sweden, from some days after arrival from Germany up to several years or birth in Sweden, so that various degrees of bilingual proficiency can be found. For all subjects, German is the first language, spoken at home, at least during the initial years of residence in Sweden. Swedish is acquired outside the home in a natural milieu and in school. An optimal level of language performance can be expected in these young students who have the possibility of acquiring two languages both in informal environments and in formal teaching situations. All subjects started learning Swedish upon coming to Sweden, so that residence in Sweden is certainly an important variable bearing on the issue of optimal level of language performance.

## Method

*Subjects.* Subjects were 163 students in the age range 13–18 years, divided into eight groups according to their length of residence in Sweden, which ranged from 6 months to 16 years. The number of subjects in the groups was different with a variation between 8 and 39 subjects. The mean age in each group was around 14 years with the exception of group 8, who had a mean age of 16 years. A Swedish monolingual control group of 20 subjects (mean age = 16 years) was also included.

*Tasks.* By using a cross-sectional approach covering a period of 16 years, Mägiste (1979a) examined developmental changes in the following encoding and decoding tasks in German and Swedish: (1) naming 75 pictures of common objects (this is a shortened version of Ervin's (1961) language dominance test which in its original version consists of 120 stimuli); (2) naming 20 two-digit numbers; (3) reading aloud 20 nouns, ranging from four to seven letters in length, and (4) performing 16 comprehension tasks which place demands on attention and elementary language skill, for example, "Mark the third letter from the left." Subjects were instructed to perform each of these tasks as quickly as possible first in one language and then in the other. The order of languages and tasks was counterbalanced across subjects.

## Results

Figure 5.1 shows the response times for naming pictured objects and two-digit numbers in German and Swedish. During the first 5 years of residence in Sweden, object naming latencies in Swedish decrease rapidly, while those in German increase. After 6 years of residence, equivalence is achieved for speed of naming

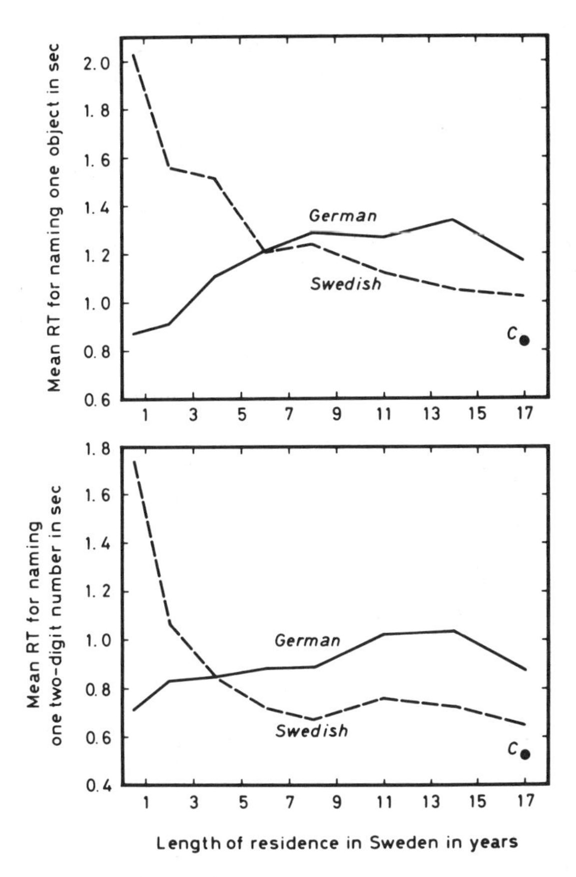


FIG. 5.1. Development of response times for production tasks as a function of length of residence in Sweden. The upper half of the figure shows the mean response time for naming objects, the lower half, for naming two-digit numbers. C = Swedish monolingual control group.

pictures in each language. This stage is so short as to almost coincide with the point where response times in Swedish become shorter than those in German. For naming two-digit numbers, the point of equivalent response times in the two languages is reached after about 4 years of stay in Sweden, after which performance in the two languages stabilizes up to 14 years of residence.

The point marked C in Fig. 5.1 represents the mean performance of the Swedish monolingual control group. In naming pictures, Swedish monolinguals have response times nearly identical to those of the German group in German at the beginning of their residence in Sweden. However, for naming numbers, the Swedish group responds significantly faster than the bilingual group, suggesting language differences in the order of reading two-digit numbers, which is from left to right in Swedish and from right to left in German. After 16 years of residence in Sweden, the bilingual group needs significantly more time to perform the two naming tasks in either language than the Swedish monolinguals need in their one language.

Figure 5.2 shows the development of response times for word reading and sentence comprehension tasks in both languages. To read words with comparable speed in the two languages takes about 4 years. Compared to object and number naming, performance on this task is less consistent. However, the Swedish control group reads Swedish words significantly faster than the bilingual group does in Swedish after 16 years in Sweden. Moreover, the German subjects who just arrived from Germany read German words significantly faster than the bilingual group does in German after living 10 years in Sweden.

The lower half of Fig. 5.2 shows the development of solving simple comprehension tasks. The curves are essentially similar to those for naming pictured objects. The shifting point occurs somewhat earlier, after 5 years in Sweden.

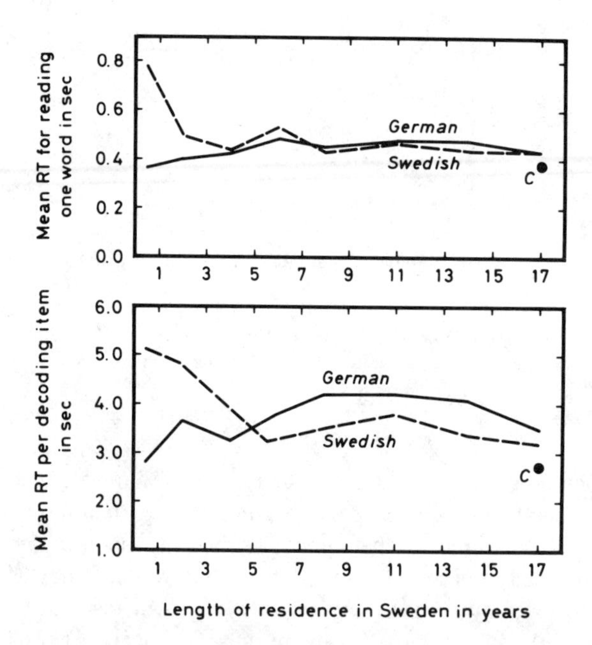


FIG. 5.2. Development of response times for comprehension tasks as a function of residence time in Sweden. The upper half of the figure shows the mean response time for reading words, the lower half, for comprehension of sentences. C = Swedish monolingual control group.

Thus, depending on the task, language equivalence in adolescents as measured by a reaction time technique may be achieved as early as 3 years or as late as 6 years.

## OPTIMAL AGE OF SECOND-LANGUAGE LEARNING

A controversial question in connection with foreign and second-language learning has been and still is the time at which it is most appropriate to start this instruction. There are three main views: According to the optimal age hypothesis, young children possess an innate facility for language learning. The view that languages can be learned best at the age of four through eight has been advanced by Chomsky (1959) and Donoghue (1965), who give putative neurological and psychological reasons for why young children should have a pronounced language acquisition facility. Children's superior imitative ability has frequently been noted (see Delaunay, 1977; Hill, 1978; Patkowski, 1980; Schmidt-Schönbein, 1980; Wilkins, 1972). These researchers also point out that young children are usually spontaneous and uninhibited and therefore easily adopt a new mode of linguistic behavior, while older children tend to be more conscious and self-critical. Lenneberg (1967) extends the optimal age hypothesis by postulating the existence of a critical period for language acquisition that ceases at the onset of puberty.

Scovel (1969, 1978) maintains that the optimal period should be limited to phonological learning. This view is in line with Fathman (1975), who compared pronunciation, morphology and grammar in immigrants over the age range 6–15 years and found significantly better pronunciation in the younger group, whereas older immigrants performed better in morphology and grammar. Similar results were obtained by Oyama (1976, 1978) with Italian immigrants and by Seliger, Krashen, and Ladefoged (1975) with Jewish immigrants to the United States.

The existence of a single optimal age for second-language learning is denied by Jakobovits (1970) and Stern and Weinrib (1977) who claim that every age has its advantages and disadvantages with regard to the learning of foreign languages. It has been argued that older individuals have an advantage as compared to small children primarily due to their more developed intellectual capacity (Burstall, 1975; Cook, 1978; Cummins, 1980; Ekstrand, 1979; Ervin-Tripp, 1974; Macnamara, 1973; McLaughlin, 1977; West, 1959). The optimal age hypothesis has also been criticized for its lack of empirical data.

In view of the relative absence of experimental data, a study was undertaken to compare the results from naming tasks with high school students (Mägiste, 1979a) with data from elementary school students (Mägiste, 1984a). By using these simple language tasks, it is possible to avoid some of the methodological problems associated with translation or with comparing students from different age groups.

## Method

*Subjects.* Seventy-seven high school students in the age range 13–18 years (mean = 14 years) and 74 elementary students aged 6–11 years (mean = 8 years) participated in the experiment. The students were divided into five groups according to their length of residence in Sweden. All subjects were taken from the German School in Stockholm and, for all of them, German was the first language.

*Tasks.* These were the same as those described earlier, including picture and number naming.

## Results

Figure 5.3 shows the mean response times for naming pictured objects in German and Swedish. The developmental changes in German and Swedish languages are very similar in both groups of students. With increasing length of residence in Sweden, the response times in German become longer, whereas those in Swedish become shorter. After about 4 years in Sweden, the elementary school students have reached a point of language balance in that task. The high school students reach this point 2 years later, i.e., after 6 years of residence in

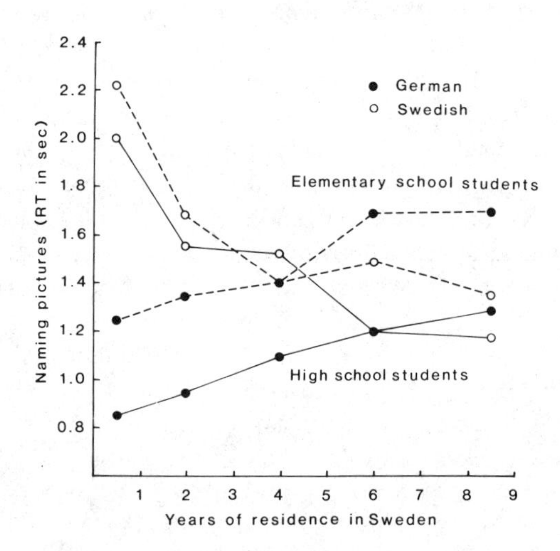


FIG. 5.3. Development of response times for naming pictured objects in German and Swedish as a function of age and residence time in Sweden.

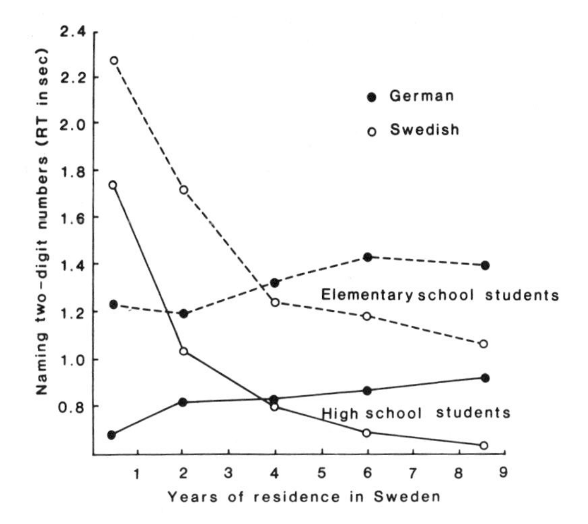


FIG. 5.4. Development of response times for naming two-digit numbers in German and Swedish as a function of age and residence time in Sweden.

Sweden. After this point of language balance, response times in German continue to increase for both groups of students. Response times in Swedish become clearly faster despite the fact that German is the dominant classroom language.

A corresponding development occurs in naming two-digit numbers in German and Swedish, as can be seen in Fig. 5.4. A highly significant main effect of student category indicates that this task is much more difficult and time-consuming for the elementary students than for the high school students. Despite the fact that the elementary school students need about twice as much time to perform this task as the high school students, both groups of students reach the point of language balance after about 3 to 4 years of residence in Sweden. In keeping with the results for the picture naming tasks, this is only a short transition point, after which Swedish, the subjects' second language, becomes the better language. The clear tendency for faster response times in naming Swedish numbers may be attributable, as previously discussed, to the fact that Swedish numbers are processed from left to right, which is less time-consuming than processing German two-digit numbers from right to left with an additional "und" between the digits.

In summary, this study shows that elementary school students in the age range 6–11 years took relatively less time than high school students to acquire an elementary vocabulary in the second language. This advantage for the younger students disappears when the task becomes more difficult, as indicated here by two-digit number naming. However, it is remarkable that the elementary school students achieved the point of language balance at the same time as the high school students despite the fact that this task was much more difficult for the younger students, as indicated by their longer response times. A further increase in task difficulty would presumably give high school students a still greater advantage over elementary school students. The latter have an advantage only as long as the task corresponds to their mental age.

The significantly longer response time in both groups of students as one effect of their increasing bilingual proficiency is an interesting outcome of this study. This effect has previously been observed by Durga (1978), Ervin (1961), Gutiérrez-Marsh and Hipple-Maki (1976), Kovac (1965, 1967, 1969), and Mägiste (1979b, 1980, 1982) and has been attributed either to a lower level of fluency and/or to interference between languages.

## AUTOMATICITY AND INTERFERENCE

The prolonged times for naming verbal stimuli found in bilingual students are of course group effects. There are great individual differences, with some bilingual and even trilingual subjects who respond faster than monolinguals. Nevertheless, considered as a group, bilingualism seems to set an upper limit on these tasks. This finding is further illustrated in Fig. 5.5, which represents a sample of 40 English-German high school students from the John F. Kennedy School in West-Berlin, which was founded in 1960 as a public German/American Community School. At present the school has 1400 students from preschool to high school level preparing the students for the American High School Diploma after grade

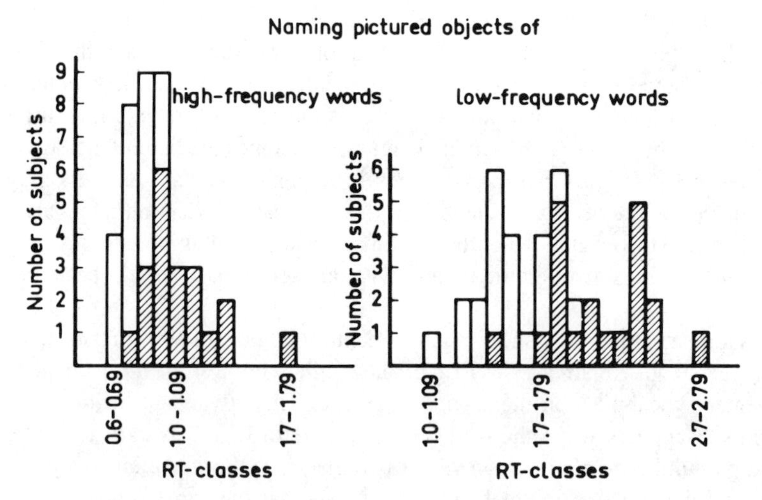


FIG. 5.5. Distribution of 40 bilingual subjects (20 English-German balanced, 20 English dominant) on response time for naming pictures in English (□ = dominant subjects, ▨ = balanced subjects).

12 and/or the German Abitur after grade 13 while conforming to the established educational standards of the USA and Germany. The language of the classroom is 50% English and 50% German. Half the teaching staff and half the students are American, the other half German.

Twenty subjects with English as their clearly dominant language are compared to 20 English-German balanced bilinguals in response times for naming 40 pictured objects of high-frequency words like "cat" (from Ervin's language dominance test) and 40 low-frequency words representing compound nouns like "vacuum cleaner." All subjects in the balanced group had learned both languages before puberty and had a native language proficiency in them. On 5-point scales they rated their skills as equally good in English and German in terms of speaking, reading, writing, and understanding. In the dominant group, English is handled with the competence of the native speaker, while German, the weaker language, is not.

As can be seen in Fig. 5.5, there is more overlap on the high-frequency than on the low-frequency words for subjects from the two groups, which is also indicated by significant group × task interaction effects. For both word types in English the English-German balanced group responded significantly more slowly when compared to the English dominant group. Similar results were obtained for a German-Swedish balanced group of 20 subjects from the German School in Stockholm when compared to German for a German dominant group. The balanced group responded on the average significantly more slowly in either language than the dominant group in their better language.

If a lower level of automaticity accounts for these results this would mean that the typical bilingual who has been dealing with two languages since infancy only exceptionally achieves the same high degree of automaticity as someone who has been concentrating mainly on one language. If, for example, an English-German bilingual subject is instructed to name the picture of a cat as quickly as possible in German, the word *Katze* might be less practiced, less overlearned than this word is for a monolingual subject. The picture could also automatically activate the associated information with *Katze*—cat—in the long-term store and place it in the short-term store. In that case, interference is involved; the activation of a competing response will result in reduced retrievability which might impair performance.

Since it was not clear if and to what extent both mechanisms actually were involved, an attempt was made to separate automaticity from interference by selecting proficient and nonproficient bilinguals with equivalent response time scores on a shortened version of Ervin's language dominance test (Mägiste, 1982b). There were 40 balanced bilinguals and 40 subjects with one clearly dominant language. The tasks involved recall and recognition of word lists. It was hypothesized that any group differences in recall and recognition should be due to interference effects, since the groups had identical scores in naming speed, i.e., they had the same degree of automaticity.

The results indicated significantly poorer recall (but not recognition) among balanced bilinguals when compared to the dominant language of non-fluent bilinguals. These results are difficult to interpret, because one can think of two types of automaticity: one which is highly dependent upon practice and thereby subject to interference, and the other relatively independent of practice, and related to a more general speed factor which may be congenitally determined. Practice may then only be a by-product rather than a source of automaticity. Certainly, extensive practice will improve performance, but performance will also vary with the inherent skill or speed of the performer. It seems important to distinguish between these two types of automaticity since automaticity, when reflecting a more general speed factor, may very well be identical with the absence of interference.

The isolation of this general mental speed factor is relatively easy and has been successfully achieved by the matching procedure in the present study. However, this general mental speed factor does not exclude the possibility that balanced bilinguals continue to suffer from a lower level of automaticity in recall despite equivalent response time scores. To isolate automaticity from interference in bilingual processing seems exceedingly demanding methodologically, since automacity is one indicator of interference. There is a strong relation between automaticity and interference, both determined by training. Training increases automaticity and diminishes interference. In any practical situation, it could be argued that automaticty and interference refer to the same thing. In particular, from the point of view of Anderson and Bower (1973) the speed of encoding and of name retrieval should vary for reasons identical with those responsible for interference effects.

## THE DIRECTION OF INTERFERENCE: FROM THE DOMINANT TO THE WEAKER LANGUAGE

Interference phenomena have for the most part interested researchers in applied linguistics and language teaching. According to many linguistic investigations, the direction of interference generally occurs from the dominant language to the nondominant one. Even among second-language learners as young as 5-years-of-age, it is possible to tell from a sample of recently acquired English whether their first language was French, Spanish, Cantonese, or German (Fillmore, 1976). That is, given a possibility of choosing between two types of output, the element with the strongest internally or externally motivated association is most likely to be retrieved. This seems to be a basic principle that is not restricted to natural interference in linguistic behavior. It can be found for example in motor behavior, when one gesture is substituted for another more accustomed one.

The purpose of this study was to follow the developmental changes in intra- and interlingual interference to find out whether there are parallels between interference in the natural context and experimentally induced interference. Experimentally induced interference was measured by Stroop tasks in the visual modality and by dichotic translation tasks in the auditory modality (Mägiste, 1984b).

In the Stroop color-word task, the time it takes to name a series of ink colors in which semantically incongruent color words are printed is compared with the time it takes to name colored patches or Xs in a control condition. The bilingual form of the test presents the color words in one language, with the instruction that the ink colors are to be named in the bilingual's other language. For example, a German/English bilingual subject may be asked to respond with *blau* to the word "red" printed in blue ink. The Stroop effect, that is, slower responses to incongruent than to congruent word-ink combinations, is a well-documented phenomenon. The bilingual Stroop test allows comparison of the pattern of interference that occurs when stimulus and response are in the same language, versus when the response is in the other language than that of the color-word stimuli.

If experimentally induced interference as measured by Stroop and similar tasks follows the observed pattern in natural contexts, interference should be strongly related to language proficiency. However, in several studies of experimental interference this is not clearly evident; interference in these studies seems to be mainly determined by stimulus characteristics. When there was little resemblance between color names in the two languages, response times were longer for the intralingual condition, that is, when the language in which subjects were required to respond was the same as that in which the color names were written, relative to interlingual conditions when different languages were used in the two cases. However, when color names in the two languages resembled each other, intra- and interlingual response times were equivalent. These interference patterns were evident among English dominant as well as French/English, Hungarian/English, and German/English balanced bilinguals (Preston & Lambert, 1969). Dyer (1971) obtained similar results from Spanish/English bilinguals, and Kiyak (1982) with English/Turkish bilinguals.

One way to ascertain whether the differential pattern of intra- and interlingual interference in the Stroop test is mainly stimulus-dependent or determined by language proficiency is to study how Stroop interference patterns change in immigrant students who first use L1 exclusively, then become bilingual, and ultimately use L2 more than L1.

## STROOP INTERFERENCE

### Method

*Subjects.* Seventy-four German-Swedish bilingual students in the age range 14–19 years participated. The students were divided into five groups, according to their residence in Sweden which varied between 0.5 years up to 16 years.

*Procedure.* Subjects were tested on the Stroop color-word task, using 300 items, 150 items in each language including a control condition of simple naming of color patches and two interference conditions (intra- versus interlingual). To study a greater range of stimuli than that afforded by the color-word Stroop, a picture-word version of the Stroop test was also given. This consisted of 120 stimuli including control and interference conditions in both languages. Whereas color words in German and Swedish are very similar, names of pictured objects are not.

## Results

*Stroop Color-Word Interference.* Figure 5.6 shows the mean response times on the Stroop color tasks for the five groups who varied in their second language experience. It will be seen from the left half of the figure that German students with a short residence in Sweden display more interference from the German color words than from the Swedish. Intralingual interference then decreases such that, after about 3 years in Sweden, intra- and interlingual interference are equivalent. After this time, interlingual interference exceeds intralingual interference to a varying extent over a period of about 13 years.

When Swedish is the response language, as will be seen from the right half of Fig. 5.6, it is the interlingual condition—again German color words—that leads to most interference early on. Somewhere after about 6 years there is a shift to greater intralingual interference. Swedish has now become the more dominant language, and the differential pattern between intra- and interlingual interference resembles that when German is the dominant language after a short residence in Sweden (see the first points in the left panel of Fig. 5.6).

*Picture-Word Interference.* The development of response times for the picture-word tasks in both languages is shown in Fig. 5.7. The developmental patterns in this task are similar to those in the color-word tasks. Words in the dominant language produce greater interference than words in the weaker language. As can be seen in the left panel of Fig. 5.7, intralingual interference dominates initially when German is the dominant language. After about 10 years in Sweden, there is a shift so that interlingual interference predominates, becoming clearly greater than intralingual interference after 16 years.

With Swedish as the language of response (right panel of Fig. 5.7), greater interlingual interference can be observed in subjects who maintain a clear dominance for German during their initial years in Sweden. With increased length of residence in Sweden, the subjects become more proficient in Swedish, which results in less marked differences between intra- and interlingual interference. However, after 16 years in Sweden, interference from Swedish words is clearly stronger than interference from German words.

There is a varying time at which interlingual interference exceeds intralingual or vice versa, depending on the language of response. Characteristics of the

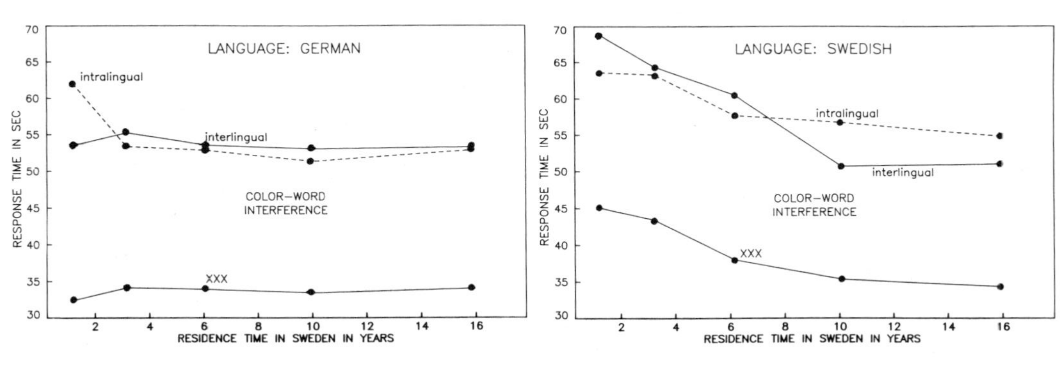


FIG. 5.6. Development of intra- and interlingual interference in Stroop color-word tasks as a function of residence in Sweden (German is response language in the left panel, Swedish in the right panel).

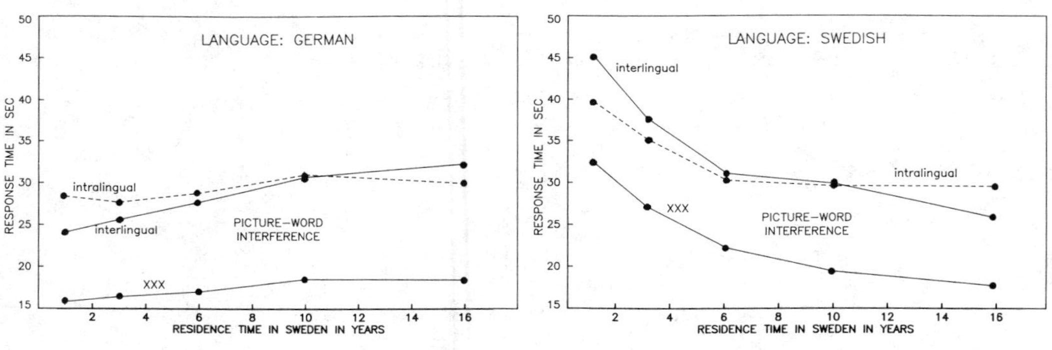


FIG. 5.7. Development of intra- and interlingual interference in picture-word interference tasks as a function of residence in Sweden (German is the response language in left panel; Swedish, in right panel).

stimuli are of importance in determining the shifting point: This point is achieved earlier for naming the few colors whose names resemble each other in Swedish and German than for naming pictures whose names lack any resemblance in the two languages. However, the present results suggest that the main determinant of the differential pattern between intra- and interlingual interference is not stimulus similarity of translation equivalents. What seems to be more important is the degree of proficiency in the respective language. Clear dominance in one language—as is the case for subjects in German on arrival in Sweden and for subjects in Swedish after 16 years in Sweden—leads to greatest differences between inter- and intralingual interference.

## DICHOTIC TRANSLATION

To see whether or not similar patterns of interference are present in the auditory modality, a dichotic translation task was administered.

### Method

*Subjects.* Forty German/Swedish bilingual subjects participated; 20 German dominant subjects with a short residence stay in Sweden and 20 Swedish dominant subjects, all born in Sweden.

*Procedure.* The task involved translation of concrete and abstract sentences from German into Swedish. Sentences were presented to the right ear via earphones. For half the trials, the left ear carried Swedish sentences, and for the remainder, German sentences. In the control condition German sentences were presented to the right ear for translation into Swedish and no distractor sentences were presented to the left ear.

### Results

Figure 5.8 shows the mean percentage of error for translation of concrete and abstract sentences into Swedish. The top panel presents the results of the German dominant group with little experience in Swedish. This group committed significantly more errors in all conditions than the Swedish dominant group who had more experience in both languages (bottom panel). Most importantly, subjects in the two groups were differentially affected by the language of the interfering channel as also indicated by significant interaction effects of language × interference condition. For both types of sentences, the German dominant subjects made more errors when the interfering channel was also German, whereas the Swedish dominant subjects committed slightly more errors when Swedish was on the irrelevant channel.

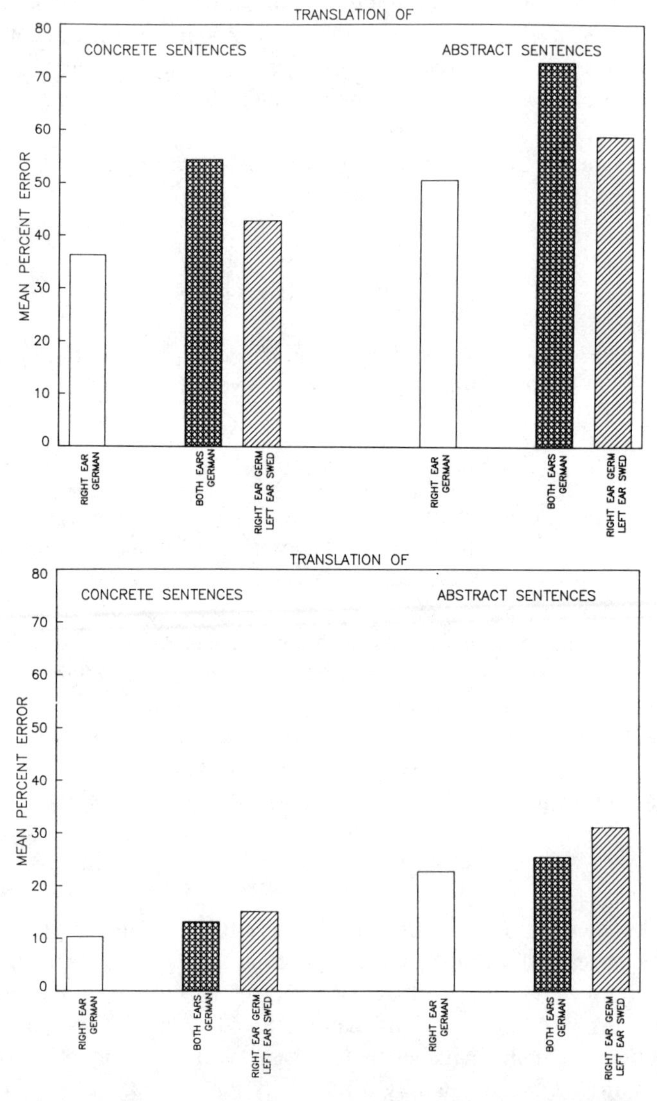


FIG. 5.8. Mean percentage of error in dichotic translation as a function of language dominance (Data for the German-dominant group are presented in the top panel; those for the Swedish-dominant group are shown in the bottom panel).

In conclusion, the evidence across modalities suggests that the differential pattern of intra- and interlingual interference is mainly determined by language dominance. It is the degree of language experience that determines whether equivalent or different amounts of interference will be obtained between languages in a Stroop-like task. Physical characteristics of the stimuli and task are of some importance in determining the level of interference, since the more demanding the task, the longer it takes to achieve about equal proficiency in it in both languages. Language balance, it is predicted, will result in equivalent amounts of intra- and interlingual interference.

## LEARNING A THIRD LANGUAGE

Is learning a third language easier for bilingual immigrant students than learning a second language is for monolingual students? This question is discussed in the present section in connection with current results from Germany and Sweden.

In a nation-wide investigation by Balke-Aurell and Lindblad (1982), Grade 8 immigrant students in Sweden were compared with Swedish students on their performance in English. The study, initiated by the Swedish National Board of Education, was based on results from a standardized test in English, which consists of four parts: word comprehension, reading comprehension, listening comprehension, and grammar. Other information included parental educational background, time of immigration, the students' proficiency in Swedish and in the first or home language, and the language used by the student and his/her parents at home. A total of 2,736 immigrant students participated. They were considered to be representative of immigrant students following the regular English curriculum in Grade 8.

### Best in English: Immigrant Students with a "Passive" Home Language

Generally, the test results and grades in English for the immigrant students did not differ from those of the Swedish student population as a whole. It is only when different groups are analyzed separately that interesting differences emerge.

Almost half of the participating immigrant students had Finnish as their first language. These students had on average lower test results than other immigrant students. This result applied at all levels of parental educational background, being most pronounced at the lower levels. A non-Indo-European language like Finnish, which linguistically differs markedly from Germanic languages, considerably augments the problems in learning English.

The rest of the students were divided into two groups: those who always spoke Swedish at home, but knew their first or home language passively, and those who actively used their first language at home daily.

Table 5.1 presents the mean results on the standardized English tests for Swedish and immigrant students taking the general and the advanced course in English. The data indicate that immigrant students with a passive knowledge of their home language had the best results on average in both the general and the advanced course in English. They performed clearly better than immigrant students who use their home language actively and slightly better than Swedish monolingual students. There is strong evidence here for transfer of skills from the first and second language to English which is in line with Lambert and Macnamara's (1969) findings from French immersion programs; Students with English as their native language, but without any formal training in English, made progress in English because much transfer occurred from French to English.

## Studies of Immigrant Students with Active Use of Two or More Languages

Three experimental studies have examined immigrant students who actively use two or more languages daily.

In West Germany, Jung (1981) compared the acquisition of English grammar by 28 bilingual immigrant students and 28 German monolingual students from Grade 5 in the comprehensive school. The two groups were matched in their socioeconomic status, school, teacher, and teaching method. Jung found that the order of acquisition was the same for both groups, although somewhat later in the bilingual group. The mean difference between the groups was 7%.

Jung's results were confirmed by Mägiste (1979a) in a study of simple decoding and encoding processes. Trilingual high school students were compared to German monolingual, Swedish monolingual, and German/Swedish bilingual students (24 in each group). Subjects' mean age was 15 years, and for the bi- and trilingual groups the mean time of residence in Sweden was 5 years. The trilingual group was somewhat heterogeneous, for, besides German and Swedish, the subjects used 11 different languages as a necessary daily medium of interac-

TABLE 5.1

Mean Results on Standardized English Tests for Swedish and Immigrant Students (Excluding Finnish- and English-Speaking Students)

| Group | English | | | |
|---|---|---|---|---|
| | General Course | | Advanced Course | |
| | No. of Ss. | Score | No. of Ss. | Score |
| Immigrants | | | | |
| Active home language | 280 | 97.4 | 910 | 100.1 |
| Passive home language | 141 | 103.4 | 586 | 105.5 |
| Swedish | 13622 | 99.8 | 43540 | 102.5 |

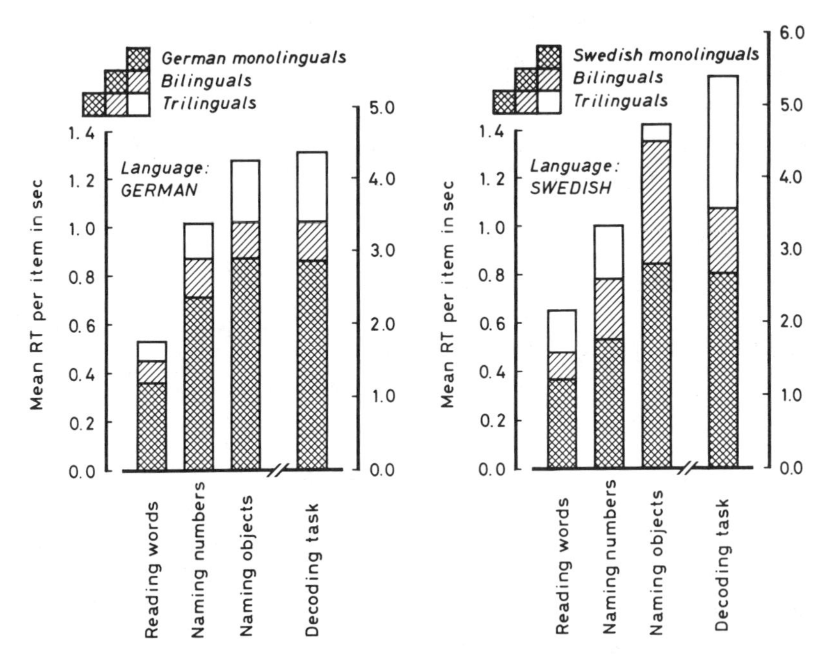


FIG. 5.9. Mean response times for different verbal tasks in German and Swedish as a function of language systems with trilingual subjects showing the longest response times.

tion. Figure 5.9 shows the mean response times on the different tasks for the monolingual and multilingual groups. With increasing number of language systems, response times for the different verbal tasks increase in both German and Swedish.

To see whether interference patterns as measured by Stroop tasks were related to intelligence, bilingual and trilingual subjects (Mägiste, 1984c) were tested with Raven's Progressive Matrices, a nonverbal intelligence test. Seventy-four German/Swedish bilingual high school students and a group of 15 trilingual students participated. Besides German and Swedish, the trilingual subjects had a third language which in most cases was the language at home, but not necessarily the best language. Table 5.2 presents the correlations between response times in the different Stroop tasks and Raven's Progressive Matrices when residence time in Sweden is partialled out. For the bilingual group, most of the correlations are around zero; only three out of a possible 12 correlations reach significance. For the trilingual group, the results in German are similar: All correlations are around zero. In Swedish, however, five out of a possible six correlations are clearly significant. It is interesting to note that the tasks which are obviously easy to perform in one's first or second language become rather demanding in one's third language. Swedish is, for most of the trilingual subjects, the third language, as also indicated in Table 5.3 by the longer response times for all Swedish com-

TABLE 5.2
Partial Correlations Between Response Times in Stroop Tasks and Raven's Progressive Matrices with Length of Residence Held Constant

| Group | German | | Swedish | | Naming | |
|---|---|---|---|---|---|---|
| | Color Words | Picture Words | Color Words | Picture Words | Color of Xs | Pictures with Xs |
| Bilinguals (N=74) | | | | | | |
| German response | -0.18 | 0.07 | -0.26** | 0.04 | -0.20* | 0.03 |
| Swedish response | -0.20* | -0.07 | -0.06 | 0.10 | -0.16 | -0.15 |
| Trilinguals (N=15) | | | | | | |
| German response | -0.01 | 0.15 | -0.09 | -0.03 | 0.05 | -0.14 |
| Swedish response | -0.49* | -0.34 | -0.54** | -0.50* | -0.53** | -0.59** |

$^{*}p < .05$, $^{**}p < .025$

pared to German tasks. With an increasing number of language systems, the response times the for different Stroop tasks increase under otherwise equal background conditions. Matched on the basis of age, length of residence in Sweden, and results on Raven's Progressive Matrices, trilingual subjects needed more time to perform the tasks in their second and third language than bilingual subjects did in their first and second language, as can be seen in Table 5.3.

In conclusion, the present findings reveal a new and interesting effect: passive bilingualism seems to facilitate learning a third language, while active bilingualism might delay it. This pattern was evident with different types of tests. It is somewhat contrary to a common notion in the literature, that people who become bilingual at an early stage will later have greater facility in picking up a third language (e.g., Albert & Obler, 1978). This may certainly be the case at certain metalinguistic levels, but not automatically at this very elementary level of language learning. Instead, strategy seems to play a major role. It appears that the potential for interference increases with the number of languages a student knows. A language that is known only passively does not give rise to interference

TABLE 5.3
Mean Response Times (in Seconds) for Bilingual and Trilingual Subjects in Stroop Tasks as a Function of Language Systems

| Group | German | | Swedish | | Naming | |
|---|---|---|---|---|---|---|
| | Color Words | Picture Words | Color Words | Picture Words | Color of Xs | Pictures with Xs |
| Bilinguals (N=15) | | | | | | |
| German response | 54.1 | 28.7 | 52.7 | 27.0 | 33.4 | 15.6 |
| Swedish response | 62.8 | 34.5 | 60.0 | 32.6 | 38.9 | 24.1 |
| Trilinguals (N=15) | | | | | | |
| German response | 61.4 | 31.6 | 57.9 | 31.6 | 35.9 | 20.1 |
| Swedish response | 62.4 | 37.0 | 63.3 | 37.3 | 42.1 | 27.3 |

in the same sense. On the contrary, passive command of a language means that the student has acquired the technique of learning another language, which obviously improves the learning of additional languages. By mainly concentrating on one language and knowing the other latently, a student chooses a strategy that maximizes positive transfer effects. When immigrant students periodically refuse to use their first language, this is mostly interpreted as a need to conform with the language of the majority, sometimes in connection with feelings of shame for their first language. According to the present results, their refusal might also be a way of intuitively expressing their effort to function most efficiently.

Another important factor in learning a language is the similarity between the mother tongue and the language to be learned. In related languages the learner is able to recognize and understand familiar concepts, which facilitates learning, at least at initial and intermediate stages. The findings are consistent with a study from Finland by Ringbom (1981), who compared different types of errors in Finnish-speaking and Swedish-speaking Finns when learning English. He found fewer errors in Swedish-speaking Finns; not surprisingly, there were more positive transfer effects from Swedish than from Finnish.

## GENERAL DISCUSSION

Achieving proficiency in a new language is a slow process even under optimal conditions with systematic training in two languages through both formal teaching and informal contacts. As indicated by response time measures on various elementary language tasks, it takes a somewhat shorter time for proficiency in the decoding processes of the second language to develop than that needed for the development of proficiency in the encoding processes.

If the language task is suited to the students' cognitive capability, elementary school students will generally acquire that task with greater ease than high school students due to their greater spontaneity, flexibility, and imitative ability. With increasing age, language learners may become more conscious and reserved, and their readiness to make contacts and to imitate other people may decrease considerably. These essentially social factors may make the acquisition of foreign languages more difficult for older as compared to younger learners.

An interesting observation concerns the shorter response times in Swedish—despite predominantly German schooling—for both elementary and high school students after some years of residence in Sweden. This illustrates the strong influence of the residence country's language, which cannot be outweighed either by another language spoken at home or at school. Similar results were obtained by Haugen (1977) and Smolicz (1983) with young immigrants to the United States and Australia. English soon became the better language despite another home language and another language of instruction used in school.

The longer response times to verbal stimuli found in multilingual subjects provide evidence for the general phenomenon of competition which might occur whenever there are more response alternatives. The very fact of having available more than one response to the same stimulus may lead to slower reactions unless the two response systems are hermetically isolated from each other. This is a very common finding even in simple situations involving decision-making and becomes perhaps most evident in athletic competition where specialization guarantees best (fastest) results. The sportsman who goes in for one branch may win by tenths or hundredths of a second like the monolingual for whom the processing of information between input and output can be thought of as a straightforward procedure. The athlete concentrating on several branches as well as the multilingual may face a rather different task here because of a larger set of response alternatives.

The results obtained in the laboratory setting cannot automatically be extended to everyday language behavior but are confined to very specific experimental tasks which may or may not be generalizable to bilinguals' efficiency of performance in normal, day-to-day communicative interactions and problem solving. In normal language behavior, speed is not a relevant parameter; no one expects people to respond as fast as possible in daily communication. Moreover, even if there might be some situations where slower response times may be a disadvantage, there are compensatory advantages of knowing several languages.

For example, apart from obvious practical advantages of being able to communicate in a much wider range of environments, some recent studies suggest that bilingualism confers an advantage on tasks involving metalinguistic awareness (Cummins, 1978), or separating word sounds from word meaning (Ianco-Worrall, 1972), in generating synonyms (Mägiste, 1979b), in sensitivity to communicative needs (Genesee, Tucker, & Lambert, 1975), and in perceiving new sounds (Cohen, Tucker, & Lambert, 1967). Carringer (1974) and Lambert (1973) found a greater flexibility and originality in creativity tests on the part of bilinguals as compared to monolinguals; others have similarly discussed creativity in association with bilingualism (see Macnamara, 1970) and Ruke-Dravina (1971, 1976).

In light of these findings, slightly longer response latencies for bilinguals on naming tasks would seem to be of minor importance. As an experimental technique, the measurement of speed of response on tasks tapping elementary cognitive operations provides a sensitive index of degree of bilingualism, and relates to other measures of language dominance. Lasonen and Toukomaa (1978), for example, followed language development in Finnish-Swedish immigrant students by using conventional standardized tests and obtained results similar to those of Mägiste (1979a).

Which aspects can be expected to show language interference and which not? Obviously, it turns out to depend on the task and the level of language processing as to whether bilinguals will experience interference. Use of related versus semantically unrelated material also appears to influence the results; for example, the significant differences in recall found between balanced and dominant bilinguals (Mägiste, 1982b) were all found when unrelated word lists were used. If categorized word lists are used the difference between the two groups diminishes. According to fact-retrieval studies, the more facts a person learns about a concept, the longer it takes the person to retrieve any of those facts. However, as Smith, Adams, and Schorr (1978) have shown, when the facts are integrated in some way, the retrieval process involves a focused memory search which ignores irrelevant information. Smith et al. refer to this as the paradox of interference.

Similarly, Tulving and Colotla (1970) found that memory for single, unrelated lexical items progressively deteriorated from unilingual to trilingual word lists. In contrast, Hummel (this volume) found that bilingual text was better recalled than unilingual text due to the greater distinctiveness and elaboration that characterizes connected discourse, which is absent when isolated lexical items from the two languages are used.

When interference does occur between the bilingual's two languages, it generally occurs in a particular direction, from the dominant language to the nondominant one, as indicated by color-word and picture-word Stroop results (Mägiste, 1984b) and in translation of dichotically presented sentences from the two languages. This developmental perspective on the direction of interference can explain previous contradictory results (e.g., Ehri & Ryan, 1980; Kiyak, 1982) and reveals parallels between interference in the natural context and experimentally induced interference.

## REFERENCES


Albert, M. L., & Obler, L. K. (1978). *The bilingual brain*. New York: Academic Press.

Anderson, J. R., & Bower, G. H. (1973). *Human associative memory*. Washington, DC: Winston.

Balke-Aurell, G. & Lindblad, T. (1982). Immigrant students and their languages. Report No. 23, Dept. of Educational Research, University of Gothenburg, Sweden.

Burstall, C. (1975). Factors affecting foreign-language learning: A consideration of some recent research findings. *Language Teaching & Linguistics, 8*, 5–25.

Carringer, D. (1974). Creative thinking ability of Mexican youth: the relationship of bilingualism. *Journal of Cross Cultural Psychology, 5*, 492–504.

Chomsky, N. (1959). Review of B. F. Skinner's "Verbal Behavior". *Language, 35*, 26–58.

Cohen, S. P., Tucker, G. R., & Lambert, W. E. (1967). The comparative skills of monolinguals and bilinguals in perceiving phoneme sequences. *Language & Speech, 10*, 159–168.

Cook, V. J. (1978). Second-language learning: A psycholinguistic perspective. *Language Teaching & Linguistics, 11*, 73–89.

Cummins, J. (1978). Bilingualism and the development of metalinguistic awareness. *Journal of Cross Cultural Psychology, 9*, 131–149.

Cummins, J. (1980). The cross-lingual dimensions of language profiency: Implications for bilingual education and the optimal age issue. *TESOL Quarterly, 14*, 175–187.

Delaunay, A. (1977). Vers un monde bilingue. *Cahiers Pedagogiques, 153,* 7–11.

Donoghue, M. R. (1965). A rationale for FLES. *French Review, 38,* 523–529.

Durga, R. (1978). Bilingualism and interlingual interference. *Journal of Cross Cultural Psychology, 9,* 401–415.

Dyer, F. N. (1971). Color-naming interference in monolinguals and bilinguals. *Journal of Verbal Learning and Verbal Behavior, 19,* 297–302.

Ehri, L. C., & Ryan, E. B. (1980). Performance of bilinguals in a picture-word interference task. *Journal of Psycholinguistic Research, 9,* 285–302.

Ekstrand, L. H. (1979). Early bilingualism: Theories and facts. *Reprints and miniprints,* Malmö School of Education, No. 305.

Ervin, S. M. (1961). Learning and recall in bilinguals. *American Journal of Psychology, 74,* 446–451.

Ervin-Tripp, S. M. (1974). Is second-language learning like first? *TESOL Quarterly, 8,* 111–127.

Fathman, A. (1975). The relationship between age and second language productive ability. *Language Learning, 25,* 245–266.

Fillmore, L. (1976). The second time around: Cognitive and social strategies in second language acquisition. (Doctoral dissertation, University of Stanford, 1976). *Dissertation Abstracts International, 37,* 6443A.

Genesee, F., Tucker, G. R., & Lambert, W. E. (1975). Communication skills of bilingual children. *Child Development, 46,* 1010–1014.

Gutiérrez-Marsh, L., & Hipple-Maki, R. (1976). Efficiency of arithmetic operations in bilinguals as a function of language. *Memory & Cognition, 4,* 459–464.

Haugen, E. (1977). Norm and deviation in bilingual communities. In P. A. Hornby (Ed.), *Bilingualism* (pp. 91–102). New York: Academic Press.

Hill, L. A. (1978). Learning a language at the tertiary level through a reading approach. *English Language Teaching Journal, 32,* 318–322.

Hummel, K. M. (1986). Memory for prose in bilinguals. In J. Vaid (Ed.). *Language processing in bilinguals: Psycholinguistic and neuropsychological perspectives.*

Ianco-Worrall, A. D. (1972). Bilingualism and cognitive development. *Child Development, 43,* 1390–1400.

Jakobovits, L. A. (1970). *Foreign language learning.* Rowley, MA: Newbury House Publishers.

Jung, U. O. (1981). Englisch als Fremdsprache für Kinder mit Deutsch als Zweitsprache. *Grazer Linguistische Studien, 14,* 83–97.

Kiyak, H. A. (1982). Interlingual interference in naming color words. *Journal of Cross Cultural Psychology, 13,* 125–135.

Kovac, D. (1965). On psychological problems of commanding more languages by an individual. *Studia Psychologica, 7,* 158–159.

Kovac, D. (1967). Psychological aspects of multilingualism. *Pszichologiai Tamulmanyok, 10,* 51–58.

Kovac, D. (1969). Command of several languages as a psychological problem. *Studies of Psychological Problems, 11,* 249–258.

Lambert, W. E. (1973). Cognitive and attitudinal consequences of bilingual schooling. *Journal of Educational Psychology, 65,* 141–159.

Lambert, W. E., & Macnamara, J. (1969). Some cognitive consequences of following a first-grade curriculum in a second language. *Journal of Educational Psychology, 60,* 86–96.

Lasonen, K., & Toukomaa, P. (1978). Linguistic development and school achievement among Finnish immigrant children in mother tongue classes in Sweden. *Research Report No. 70,* Department of Education, University of Jyväskylä, Finland.

Lenneberg, E. H. (1967). *Biological foundations of language.* New York: Wiley.

Macnamara, J. (1970). Bilingualism and thought. *Monograph Series of Language and Linguistics, 23,* 25–45.

Macnamara, J. (1973). Nurseries, streets and classrooms: Some comparisons and deductions. *Modern Language Journal, 57,* 250–254.

Mägiste, E. (1979a). The competing language systems of the multilingual: A developmental study of decoding and encoding processes. *Journal of Verbal Learning and Verbal Behavior, 18,* 79–89.

Mägiste, E. (1979b). Recall of concrete and abstract sentences in bilinguals. *Scandinavian Journal of Psychology, 20,* 179–185.

Mägiste, E. (1980). Memory for numbers in monolinguals and bilinguals. *Acta Psychologica, 46,* 63–68.

Mägiste, E. (1982a). The importance of language strategy in simple arithmetic. *Educational Psychology, 2,* 159–166.

Mägiste, E. (1982b). Automaticity and interference in bilinguals. *Psychological Research, 44,* 29–43.

Mägiste, E. (1984a). Further evidence for the optimal age hypothesis in second-language learning. *Delaware Symposium on Language Studies VI,* Newark.

Mägiste, E. (1984b). Stroop tasks and dichotic translation: The development of interference patterns in bilinguals. *Journal of Experimental Psychology: Learning, Memory, and Cognition, 10,* 304–315.

Mägiste, E. (1984c). Learning a third language. *Journal of Multilingual and Multicultural Development, 5,* 415–421.

McLaughlin, B. (1977). Second-language learning in children. *Psychological Bulletin, 84,* 438–459.

Oyama, S. (1976). A sensitive period for the acquisition of a nonnative phonological system. *Journal of Psycholinguistic Research, 5,* 261–283.

Oyama, S. (1978). The sensitive period and comprehension of speech. *Working Papers on Bilingualism* No. 16, 1–17.

Patkowski, M. S. (1980). The sensitive period for the acquisition of syntax in a second language. *Language Learning, 30,* 449–472.

Preston, M. S., & Lambert, W. E. (1969). Interlingual interference in a bilingual version of the Stroop color-word task. *Journal of Verbal Learning and Verbal Behavior, 8,* 295–301.

Ringbom, H. (1981). The influence of other languages on the vocabulary of foreign language learners. In *Proceedings from the 6th International Congress of Applied Linguistics,* 9–14 August. Lund, Sweden.

Ruke-Dravina, V. (1971). Word associations in monolingual and multilingual individuals. *Linguistics, 74,* 66–84.

Ruke-Dravina, V. (1976). *The ability of Swedish-Latvian bilingual teenagers to describe events.* Paper presented at the Symposium on Child Speech. Belgrade, Yugoslavia.

Schmidt-Schönbein, G. (1980). Evaluation of the teaching of English to German children of preschool age. *English Language Teaching Journal, 34,* 173–178.

Scovel, T. (1969). Foreign accents, language acquisition, and cerebral dominance. *Language Learning, 19,* 245–253.

Scovel, T. (1978). *The recognition of foreign accents in English and its implications for psycholinguistic theories of language acquisition.* Paper presented at the 5th International Conference of Applied Linguistics. Montreal, Canada.

Seliger, H. W., Krashen, S. D., & Ladefoged, P. (1975). Maturational constraints in the acquisition of second language accent. *Language Sciences, 36,* 20–22.

Smith, E. E., Adams, N., & Schorr, D. (1978). Fact retrieval and the paradox of interference. *Cognitive Psychology, 10,* 438–464.

Smolicz, J. J. (1983). Modification and maintenance: Language among school-children of Italian background in South Australia. *Journal of Multilingual and Multicultural Development, 4,* 313–337.

Stern, H. H., & Weinrib, A. (1977). Foreign languages for younger children: Trends and assessment. *Language Teaching & Linguistics, 10,* 5–25.

Tulving, E., & Colotla, V. (1970). Free recall in trilingual lists. *Cognitive Psychology, 1,* 86–98.

West, M. (1959). At what age should language study begin? *English Language Teaching, 14,* 21–26.

Wilkins, D. A. (1972). *Linguistics in language teaching.* Cambridge: MA: MIT Press.

# 6 Intrasentential Code-Switching: The Case of Language Assignment

Miwa Nishimura
*University of Pennsylvania*

In communities where two or more languages are in contact, alternate use of these languages in a single situation often arises. The alternation is rapid and occurs even within a sentence. This phenomenon was recognized by Weinreich (1953) in his well-known work which may be said to have approached the study of language contact in a comprehensive manner for the first time. However, Weinreich considered constant language switching to be an exceptional case, noting that "an ideal bilingual switches from one language to the other according to appropriate changes in the speech situation (interlocutor, topic, etc.), but not in an unchanged speech situation, and certainly not within a single sentence" (p. 73). This view was also prevalent among other researchers in language, including Ferguson (1964), Ervin-Tripp (1964) and Fishman (1965), who all attempted to describe the contextual factors that would elicit language switching in bilinguals. Ervin-Tripp (1964), for instance, demonstrated how topic influences bilinguals' lexical choice as well as syntactic performance. Fishman (1965) classified human activities into *domains* (employment, family, education, religion, etc.) and attempted to correlate these domains with language choice in multilingual communities.

In more recent works, however, it has been acknowledged that switching takes place so often even within a sentence that not all switching can be attributed to contextual features and that it may be more appropriate to view language alternation in terms of the norm of the community (Gal, 1978; Gumperz, 1976; Poplack, 1978, 1979; G. Sankoff, 1971). It is now generally agreed that alternate use of two or more languages is in fact an appropriate speech mode in some bilingual communities. Gumperz (1976) referred to this as "conversational code-switching," distinguishing it from "situational code-switching" in which a given language is associated with a particular situation.

Functional and communicative aspects of code-switching have been extensively examined. Gillian Sankoff (1971) notes that the village entrepreneur in New Guinea code-switches constantly between Tok Pisin and Buang in village meetings so that he can be in touch with all segments of the audience that he is addressing. Poplack (1978), examining the speech of a Puerto Rican in New York City, argues that code-switching is a way of showing group solidarity among individuals with a common ethnic background. Gumperz (1976) and Gal (1978) considered communicative effects that code-switching achieves in conversations. According to Gal (1978), in a Hungarian/German bilingual community in Austria, switches to German from Hungarian are "used to strengthen, command and to assert expertise and authoritativeness on an issue or about a technical speciality" (p. 236). Moreover, far from reflecting a lack of control over either language, intrasentential code-switching has been found to be more prevalent in bilinguals who are proficient in both languages (Poplack, 1979). Thus, it is generally agreed now that code-switching is not a random phenomenon.

## Formal Studies of Intrasentential Code-Switching

With the recognition of the prevalence of nonrandom intrasentential code-switching among fluent members of bilingual communities, linguists are now seeking to formalize the syntactic contexts under which language mixing is possible. Various constraints governing switches within sentences have been put forth. While earlier studies simply listed syntactic categories or sites at which switches were or were not possible (Gumperz, 1976; Pfaff, 1979; Poplack, 1978, 1979; Timm, 1975), more recent studies have proposed constraints on intrasentential code-switching using various theoretical frameworks (Doron, 1981; Joshi, 1985; Muysken, di Sciullo, & Singh, 1981; Sankoff & Poplack, 1980; Sridhar & Sridhar, 1980; Woolford, 1980, 1983).

A recurring theme in these recent studies is whether or not it is necessary to assign any one language to code-switched sentences. Sankoff and Poplack (1980), who worked with two typologically very similar languages (Spanish and English), denied the necessity of assigning a language to code-switched sentences, especially for discourse in which language switching occurs several times, as in the following speech sample (Sankoff & Poplack, 1980, p. 25):

> There was a guy, you know, que [that] he se monto [got up]. He started playing with congas, you know, and se monto y empezo a brincar [got up and started to jump] and all that shit. (P.R.) (1)

For such stretches of discourse which involve frequent switching, Sankoff and Poplack (1980) argue that bilinguals, in uttering sentences, may use constituents of one language at one point and those of another at another point, as long as the order of these constituents is shared by the two languages. They call this the "equivalence constraint"; Figure 6.1 illustrates permissible code-switching points, according to this constraint. Woolford (1980, 1983), who proposed an alternate approach to Sankoff and Poplack's formulation (1980), also does not see the necessity of assigning language to code-switched sentences. Working with Spanish/English data as well, she views code-switched sentences as resulting from a mixture of phrase structure rules extracted from the two languages. She argues that phrase structure rules of the two languages can be freely mixed in the construction of the tree structures of code-switched sentences.

In contrast to Sankoff and Poplack (1980) and Woolford (1980, 1983), Sridhar and Sridhar (1980) assume that there is a basic language to bilingual discourse and propose the terminology *guest* and *host* languages to describe code-switched utterances. They argue, giving examples from Kannada and English, that intrasentential code-switching is a case where guest elements, which have their own internal structure, occur in the sentence of the host language obeying the placement rules of the host language.

Joshi (1985) holds a similar position with regard to language assignment. He claims that all his examples of Marathi/English code-switched sentences must be assigned Marathi as the host language (or the matrix language, Joshi, 1985) to the extent that Marathi is the dominant language in the community from which his examples were taken. Joshi then attempted to derive his code-switched sentences from Marathi sentence structure by establishing rules of switching. His rules include an "asymmetry constraint," according to which switching may take place only in one direction, from the matrix language to the embedded (or guest) language. Joshi further argues that so-called closed class items cannot be switched, whereas open class items can. Doron (1981), working with a Hebrew-English sample, essentially adopts Joshi's framework, except that she further claims that the first occurring major constituent determines the language of the code-switched sentence.

| | I | : | seen | : | everything | : | 'cause | I | : | didn't | take | : | anything |
|---|---|---|---|---|---|---|---|---|---|---|---|---|---|
| A. Eng. | I | : | seen | : | everything | : | 'cause | I | : | didn't | take | : | anything |
| | ↓ | : | ↓ | : | ↓ | : | ↓ | ↓ | : | ╳ | ↓ | : | ↓ |
| B. Sp. | Yo | : | vi | : | todo | : | porque | yo | : | no | cogi | : | nada. |
| C. CS | I | | seen | | everything | | 'cause | I | | no | cogí | | na'. |

*Note.* Switching would be possible at any syntactic sites marked by dotted lines, since the relative order of constituents at these sites is common in Spanish and English. The actual performance of the speaker is represented in C.

FIG. 6.1. Permissible code-switching points within the framework of Sankoff and Poplack (1980).

## The Present Study

The above approaches towards formalizing the rules governing intrasentential code-switching fall into two groups: One group maintains that assignment of language to code-switched sentences is not necessary, while the other regards it as necessary. The former approach is based on data from languages (Spanish and English) which share the same word order at many points and which occur in a bicultural milieu. In contrast, the approach emphasizing language assignment is based on data from languages with differing word order (Marathi and English; Kannada and English) in a perhaps less bicultural setting.

The present study was undertaken to explore further the issue of language assignment of code-switched sentences by considering a bilingual group that has not so far received much study, namely, second generation Japanese in North America. Japanese word order is subject-object-verb, which is opposite from that of English, a subject-verb-object language. Another feature of Japanese immigrants is that Japanese and English are used more or less interchangeably among members of the community. A study of Japanese/English code-switching might therefore provide interesting insights into the general issue of formal constraints on code-switching, and the specific question of language assignment of code-switched sentences. The present study attempted to determine whether (a) Japanese/English code-switched sentences can be assigned to one language, and (b) whether the same one language is assigned to all code-switched sentences, or whether a particular language is assigned at one time and another, at another time.

## Japanese Sentence Structure

A brief review of Japanese sentence structure is in order. In Japanese, all cases are marked by postpositional particles (not suffixes) represented by P. Thus, the surface structure of Japanese sentences with the nominative case and the accusative, for instance, can be described as in (2).

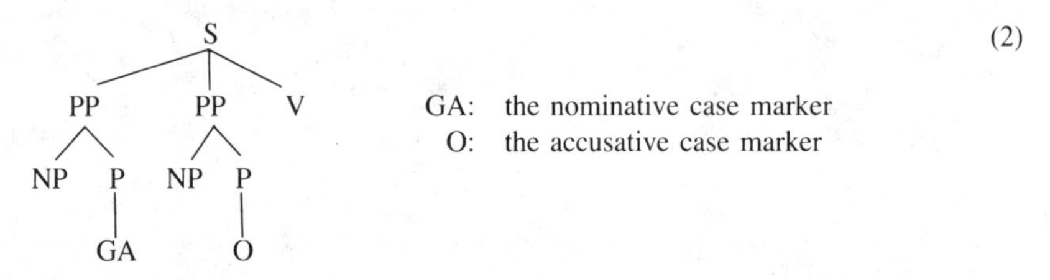


Some Japanese case markers such as O (the accusative marker), NI and E (both are directional) are deletable. Deletion of GA (the nominative) is controversial (Kuno, 1973; Martin, 1975). Furthermore, the nominative, accusative and dative NP are deletable together with the case-marking particles when recoverable from the context.

## METHOD

### Subjects

Subjects were all Niseis (second generation) in the age range of 50 to 60 years, whose parents had come to North America around the turn of the century. They had a high level of competence in both languages, and had learned Japanese at home from their parents (with the exception of one subject who had spent a number of years in Japan as a child). All subjects were educated and worked in a predominantly English speaking-environment. Code-switching appeared to be a normal part of the subjects' daily interactions with other members of the bilingual community.

### Procedure

Speech samples totalling approximately 4 hours were tape-recorded in two geographically distinct communities of Japanese/English bilinguals, one in Toronto and the other in San Francisco. The samples included both interviews (with the author) and natural speech. The interviews were designed to include at least two bilingual community members so that code-switching between them could be elicited, for it is a common observation that bilinguals do not usually code-switch with people outside their community.

The tape-recorded speech was transcribed into written Japanese and English. Sentences containing both Japanese and English elements were extracted for further linguistic analysis. Of these, any place names or individual names were excluded from the analysis.

Each simple sentence, embedded clause and conjoined clause, was considered as a separate sentence. When two clauses, dependent and independent, are conjoined from two languages, it is an interesting problem whether it is possible to assign one language to the highest sentence node. Even so, each clause has an internal sentence structure of its language. Thus, when such a clause contains a language switching, it should be analyzed within the sentence structure of that language, independently from the language of the higher sentence. For this reason, each clause was considered as one sentence for the analysis.

## RESULTS

The first question of interest was whether switching takes place between two constituents whose relative order is not shared by the two languages. Sankoff and Poplack (1980) argued that language assignment of code-switched sentences is impossible and inappropriate, partly because switches take place between constituents whose order is shared by the two languages. From this it follows that language assignment may be possible if switches take place between constituents whose order is not shared by the two languages, as in the case of Japanese and English.

In fact, when one surveys the corpus, one finds a large number of sentences in which switching took place between two constituents whose order is not shared by the two languages. Observe the sentence given below:

Only small prizes MORATTA NE. (MN) (3)
verb(past)
get

"(We) got only small prizes, you know."

In (3), an English object noun phrase (NP) is followed by a Japanese verb. In English, preposed object NPs are possible in topicalization, or the so-called *Yiddish movement* (Prince, 1981). However, such an order is marked in English and occurs mainly in the spoken language. In Japanese, this order is the natural order. Also, the absence of the subject NP referring to *we* would be normal in Japanese. Thus, one could assign Japanese to sentence (3).

The derivation of sentence (3) is illustrated below.

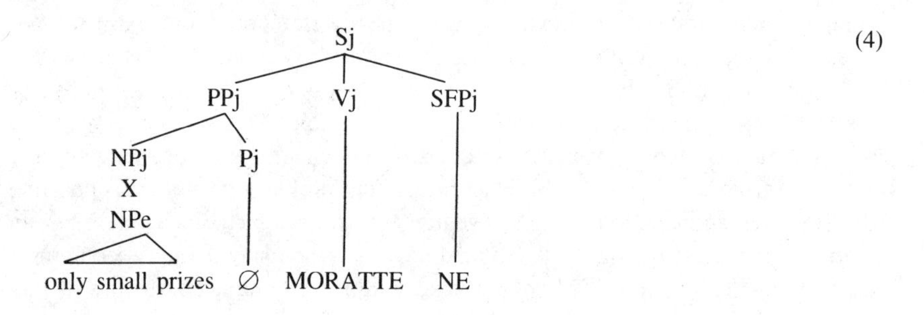


In (4), the symbol 'x' represents a language switch. The convention is borrowed from Joshi (1985). Moreover, the subscript 'j' stands for Japanese and 'e' stands for English.

From the above observation, the following working hypothesis may be proposed:

When switching takes place between constituents whose relative order is possible only in one language, that language is the language of the sentence.

## Sentences Assigned to Japanese or English on the Basis of Their Constituent Order

The following sentences would be assigned as Japanese sentences judging from their constituent order:

SOREKARA, his wife NI YATTARA, . . . (MN) (5)
ADV P V (conditional)
in addition dative give
"In addition, if (we) give (it) to his wife, . . ."

Right in the center grow—SHITARA,[1] (MN) (6)
helping-verb (conditional)
"If (they) grow (it) right in the center of (it), . . ."

In (5), an English NP "his wife" occurs with a Japanese postpositional particle "NI," the dative case marker. The English dative marker would precede the NP. Thus, it would be only explicable if we derive this PP, "his wife NI," from Japanese, as shown below:

(7)

PPj
NPj Pj
X
NPe
his wife NI

The overall sentence can be derived as follows:

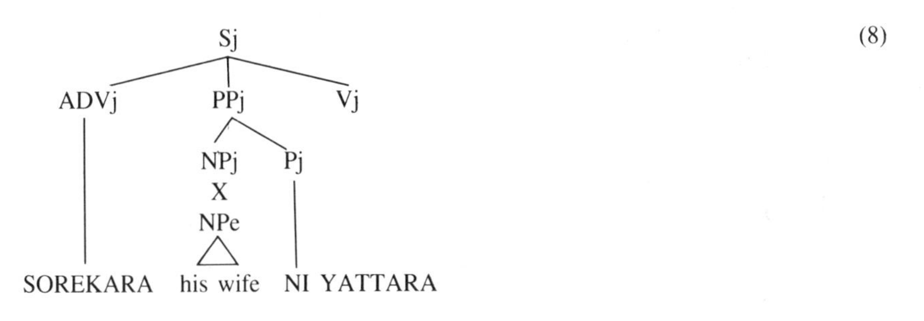


[1] "SHITARA" is the conditional form of a Japanese helping verb "SURU." In ordinary Japanese, this helping verb combines with nouns, mostly of Chinese origin, and creates new verbs meaning "to do what the noun refers to." Our informants use this verb with English verbs as in this sentence "grow-SHITARA." Joshi (1985) reports that Marathi has a similar verb and it is used with an English verb.

In (6), an English PP occurs with a Japanese verb. Judging from the discourse context, this PP could not be a thematic PP in English; that is, it cannot be preposed to the beginning of the sentence in English. The order of a nonthematic PP followed by a V belongs to Japanese; thus, Japanese would be assigned to this sentence. Additional evidence to support this analysis is that if (6) were English, it would not start with "right in the center" but with "if," since it is a conditional clause. The derivation of this sentence is illustrated below.

It should by now be clear that, in all the above sentences, although an English constituent is followed by a Japanese constituent, that does not mean that there is a change of system from English to Japanese, from left to right. It was demonstrated that these sentences must be derived from the Japanese sentence structure by switching certain constituents, NP and PP, into English.

However, in the converse case, that is, where English is assigned, the assignment of English on the basis of constituent order alone cannot be argued for, since constituent order is flexible in Japanese. Although Japanese is a verb-final language, other constituents could occur postverbally as "afterthoughts" (Kuno, 1973; Martin, 1975), especially in colloquial speech. Thus, English cannot automatically be assigned to sentences represented by (10) and (11).

I slept with her basement DE. (VY) (10)
P
location
"I slept with her in the basement."

What do you call it NIHONGO DE? (GN) (11)
noun P
Japanese instrumental
"What do you call it in Japanese?"

In these sentences, a Japanese PP occurs after an English VP. There is a possibility that these Japanese PPs occurred as afterthoughts. If so, it would appear that a switch of system has taken place from English to Japanese. However, one can assign English to both sentences, for we may recall that sentence (6) was assigned a Japanese sentence whose locative PP was switched to English. Sentence (10) is in fact the converse case of (6); (10) has an English locative PP switched to a Japanese locative PP. If we adopt this position, we can now say that (11) is also an English sentence. The derivation trees for these two sentences are given below.

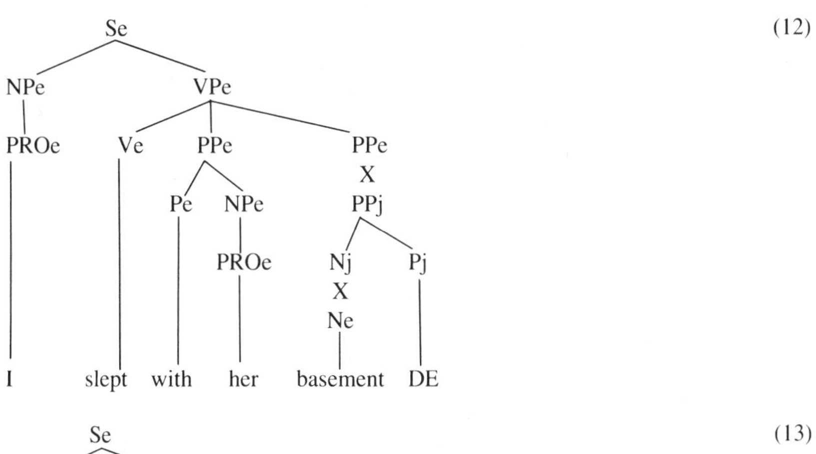


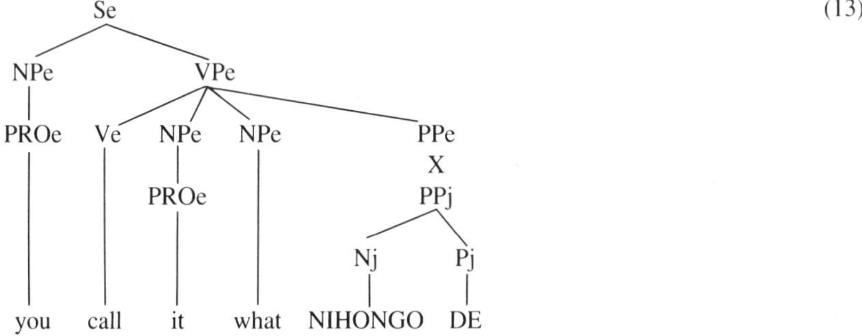


The position of the copula relative to a nominal, an adjectival and a PP is opposite in the two languages, as shown in the figures below.

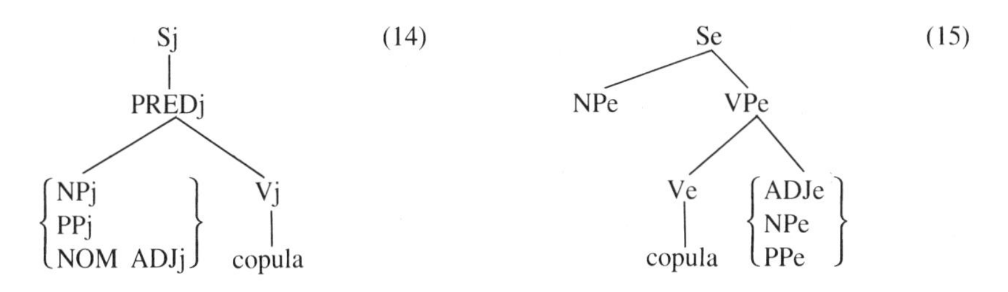

Thus, when the copula of one language takes a constituent of the other language, the necessity of language assignment becomes obvious. Observe (16) and (17) for this:

Under sixteen DATTARA, (VY) (16)
copula (conditional)
"If (your child) is under sixteen,"

The ones we've seen are BIMBOO NA KODOMO. (MN) (17)
poor children
"The one's we've seen are poor children."

The derivation trees for these sentences are given below:

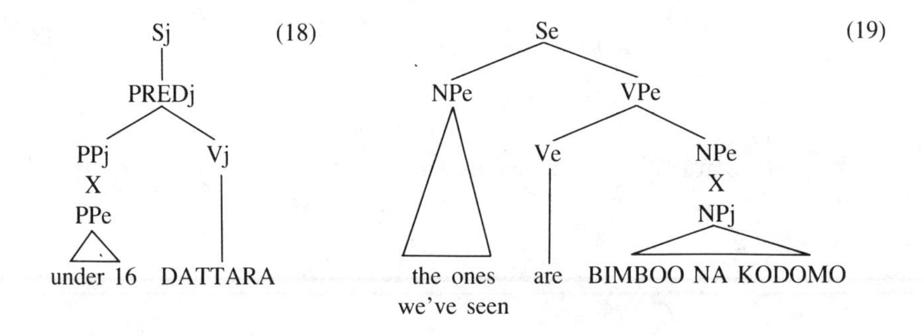


With the concept of constituent order in mind, observe the following:

MANNAKA NI they're growing. (GN) (20)
middle in
"They're growing in the middle."

ASOKO she goes. (HH) (21)
that place
"She goes over there."

KAERI NI WA border DE we got stopped, eh? (22)
return on topic marker on (VY)
"On the way home, we got stopped on the border."

At first glance, it looks as though sentences (20) to (22) are English sentences whose preposed PP's (the directional "NI" or "E" is deleted in (21)) are switched to Japanese. Notice that the first PP in (22), "KAERI NI WA," is thematic; our present concern is with the second PP, "border DE." When we examine the discourse context, we can discern that these PPs would not be preposed in normal English; that is, they are not thematic. Notice that the constituent order of these three sentences would be a normal one in Japanese. For this reason, I propose that these are Japanese sentences whose predicates are switched to English. In this analysis, the English "sentences" in the above sentences, "they're growing," "she goes" and "we got stopped," are not complete sentences but are used as equivalents of the Japanese predicates, all inflected verbs, "HAETEIRU," "IKU" and "TOMERARETA," respectively. For the present purpose, let us call these English sentences semisentences. The derivation trees for (23) to (25) are given below:

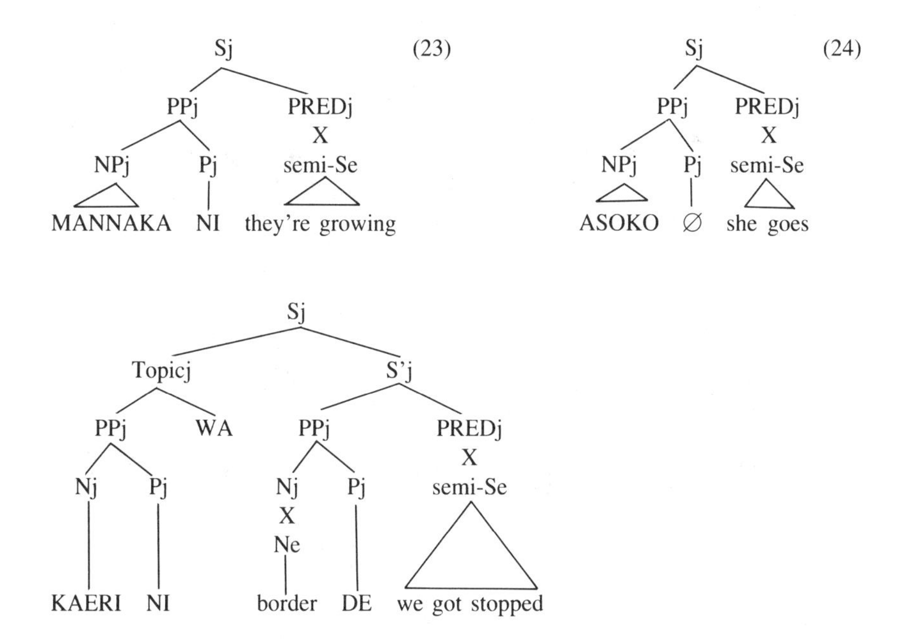


## Use of Discourse-Related Elements Across Languages

A question arises here: What happens to language assignment when a switch takes place between constituents whose order is shared by the two languages? Possible constituent orders common in Japanese and English are the following:

$$S \rightarrow \left\{ \begin{matrix} \text{CONJ} \\ \text{ADV} \end{matrix} \right\} S$$

$$S \rightarrow \text{Subject} \quad \text{Predicate}$$

In fact, switches take place between these constituents in my data. Let us look first at conjunctions and adverbs. Observe the following:

DAKEDO I don't like New York. (SS) (26)
conunction
but

'Cause WAKANNAI DESHO. (MN) (27)
"'Cause you don't know."

Anyway, ATAMA GA FURUI YO. (HH) (28)
adv
"Anyway, (they) are old-fashioned."

Since the constituent order at the switch site in these sentences is shared by the two languages, our current approach cannot account for these cases. In (26) and (27), a conjunction of one language is used with a sentence of another language. This is a frequent type of switch in others' data (Pfaff, 1979; Poplack, 1979) as well. Previous researchers report that conjunctions and related items are rather loosely connected with the rest of the sentence. Some conjunctions and adverbs occur in monolingual English speech without serving a syntactic function; Stubbs (1984) calls these "pragmatic connectors," whose function is mainly to connect clauses in sequence in a discourse context. It is plausible that they serve a discourse function in code-mixed speech as well. Examples of these words in the present corpus include the English words "because," "but," "so," "anyway," "and then," "and," "first of all," and the Japanese "SOSHITE," "DAKEDO," "DEMO," and their contracted forms. Sentences (26) to (28) can accordingly be given the following structures:

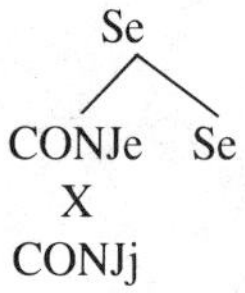

Se (29) 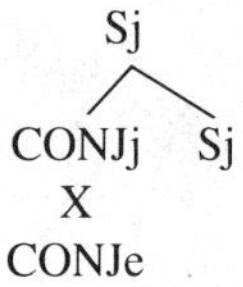
CONJe Se
X
CONJj

Sj (30) 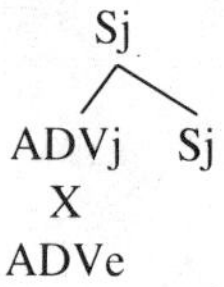
CONJj Sj
X
CONJe

Sj (31)
ADVj Sj
X
ADVe

To account for the insertion of conjunctions and adverbs from one language into a sentence from another language, we appealed to the pragmatic function of such words. Sentences (32) to (33) may be analyzed within the same framework.

The idea is bound to change NE. (MN) (32)

He is in Japan YO. (YV) (33)

In sentences (32) and (33), English sentences are followed by Japanese sentence-final particles. Judging from the constituent order of (32) and (33), Japanese would be assigned to these sentences:

```
  ?Sj                                   (34)
  /  \
Sj   sentence-final particle
X
Se
```

Alternatively, one might say that these sentences can be derived from English by switching tags, as in the following:

```
  ?Se                                   (35)
  /  \
Se   TAGe
      X
     sentence-final particle
```

However, although Japanese sentence-final particles are similar to the English tag, "you know," there are many more Japanese sentence-final particles and their meanings are more diverse. "NE," for instance, roughly corresponds to "don't you think?", and "YO" means "I'm telling you." Thus, to derive these sentences from English as described in (35) may not be justifiable. Probably the most natural way to explain sentences like (32) and (33) is that Japanese sentence-final particles are useful additions to English sentences.

## Switches Between the Subject and the Predicate

Let us now look at cases where switches take place between the subject and the predicate. First, observe the following:

KODOMOTACHI liked it. (SS) (36)
noun
children
"Children liked it."

HAKUJIN NO HEITAI-SAN didn't like NIHONJIN or (37)
noun noun nou
white soldier Japanese
something. (KN)
"(The) white soldier didn't like Japanese or something."

USHIRO NO KAO WA looks like Japanese. (MN) (38)
face topic
marker
"The face (of a man) in the background looks like Japanese."

Camp-SEIKATSU GA made him rough. (MN) (39)
life nom.
"(That) camp-life made him rough."

First, notice that the Japanese NP in (36) and (37) is not marked by any postpositional particle, whereas in (38) and (39), it is marked by "WA" and "GA" respectively. In this context, recall that the English nominative case is marked by word order, not a case-marker. This might explain the absence of a Japanese postpositional particle in (36) and (37). I suggest that, for our bilingual informants, a Japanese NP without a particle is equivalent to an English subject NP. Likewise, a Japanese NP without a particle is equivalent to an English object NP. If we accept this, we can assign English to (36) and (37) and derive them as below:

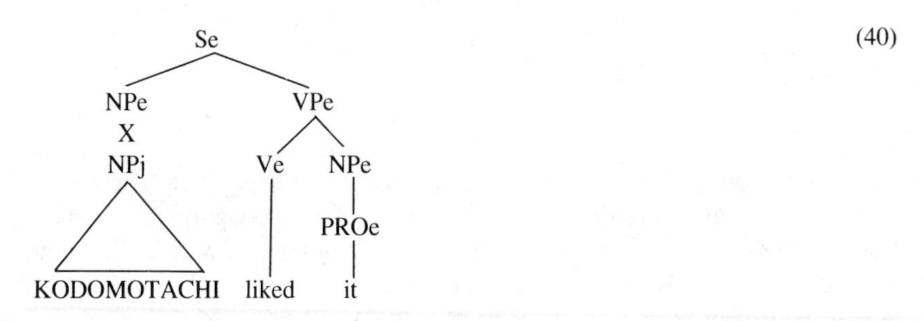


(40)

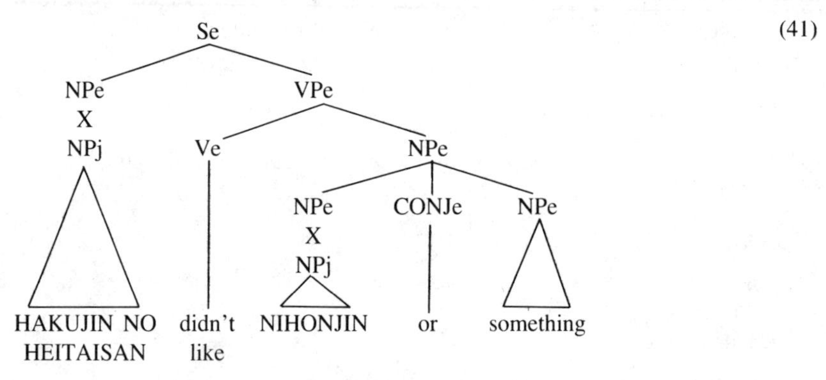


(41)

Regarding (38) and (39), the presence of "WA" and "GA" makes it unjustifiable for us to derive them from the English sentence structure by switching the subject NP to Japanese. At this point, observe the following:

She-WA took her a month to come home YO. (MN) (42)
topic
marker
"Talking about her, it took her a month to come home, you know."

(38) and (42) have an identical structure: NP followed by ''WA'' occurring with an English VP. In (42), since ''she'' could not be the grammatical subject of ''took her a month to come home,'' I propose that the dummy subject pronoun was dropped and that ''she-WA'' is a Japanese topic. Our informants often say ''me-WA'' to refer to themselves; then, it is possible that they say ''she-WA'' analogously to refer to the feminine third person. (38) and (42) were uttered by the same speaker; it is possible to argue for the pronoun deletion for (38) as well. This enables us to say that (38) also consists of a Japanese topic and an English sentence. The following structure can be given to this sentence:

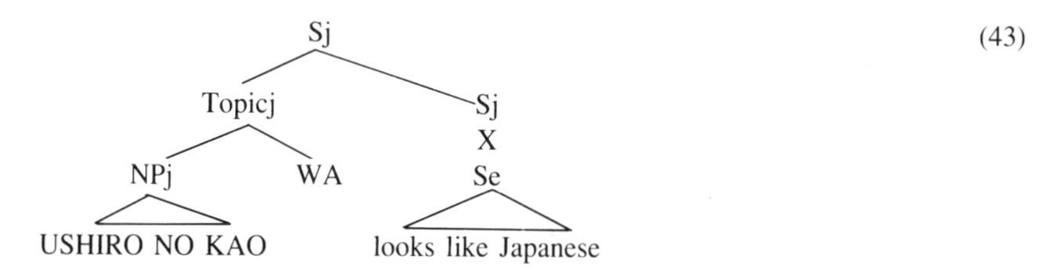


(43)

With regard to (39), 'GA' is the subject marker. The following structure can be given:

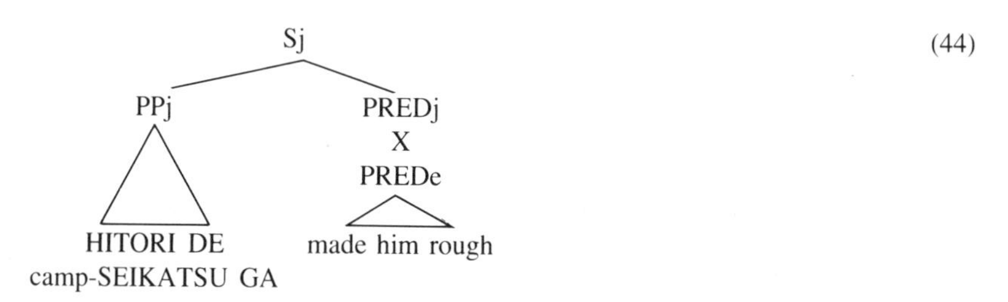


(44)

Observe the following reverse cases in which an English NP occurs with a Japanese verb:

All that fish GA NARANDEN NO YO. (SS) (45)
nom.verb
lie
''All that fish is lying (there), you know.''

She KARITA. (MN) (46)
verb (past)
borrow
''She borrowed (it).''

He never MORATTA from anybody. (MN) (47)
verb (past)
get
''He never got (it) from anybody.''

An English NP in (45) is followed by "GA," the nominative case marker. Derivation of this sentence is shown below.

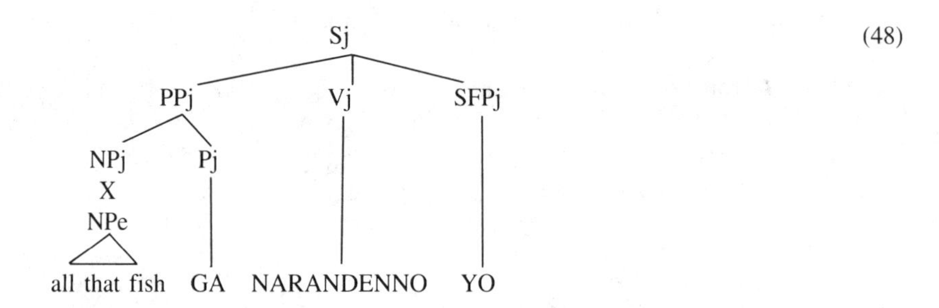


Japanese is assigned to (45).

However, English would be assigned to (46) and (47). In (46) and (47), the subject NP is not marked by a Japanese preposition. This enables us to say that the subject of these sentences is English NP. Then, I propose the following structure for these sentences:

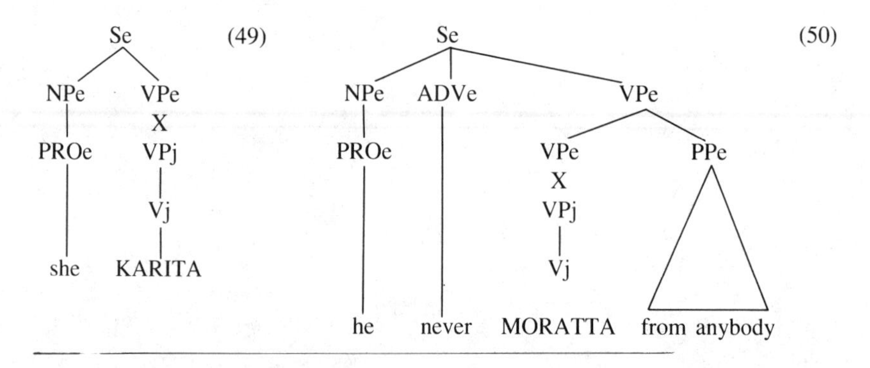


The absence of the object NP in these sentences might look problematic. However, it is normal in Japanese to drop the object NP when it is recoverable from the context. Thus, this can be taken care of by establishing a switch of VP from English to Japanese as shown in (49) and (50). Further evidence to assign English to the above sentences is this: Japanese negation must be marked on the verb. Notice that in (47), it is not; rather, negation is expressed by the English adverb "never." We can say that the occurrence of the past tense of a Japanese verb without negation marking in a negative sentence is due to the fact it is used in place of an English VP as shown above. Also, in (46), the Japanese verb "KARITA" is not followed by a sentence-final particle. In MN's speech, as in ordinary Japanese speech, many Japanese sentences end with some kind of sentence-final particles. This further supports my analysis here.

## Portmanteau Sentences

There is a group of sentences to which one language cannot be assigned in the Japanese/English data. They are typically sentences which consist of an English sentence and a Japanese sentence both of which are combined with a shared element in between. Observe the following:

You pull this much TSUKAU DESHO. (MN) (51)
V (non-past)
use

You should see his KARADA KIMOCHI WARUI N DA. (52)
N N ADJ (MN)
body appearance awful-is

In (51), an English sentence, "you pull this much," is combined with a Japanese sentence, "this much TSUKAU DESHO," "(you) will use this much." In (52), "you should see his KARADA (= body)" is combined with "KARADA KIMICHI WARUI N DA," "(his) body's appearance is awful." This phenomenon seems to be possible because the final element of an English sentence (whether it is a switched element or English) can serve as the initial element of a Japanese sentence.

Sentences involving the same mechanism are found in the speech of monolingual English speakers as shown below:

That's the only thing he does is fight. (53)
(from Kroch: personal communication)

In (53), the two sentences, "That's the only thing he does" and "the only thing he does is fight," are combined with a shared element, "the only thing he does." Thus, one might say that the sentence type represented by (50) and (51) is not specific to the Japanese/English code-switching mode.

The frequency of this type of sentence, however, seems greater in the code-switching data than in monolingual usage; this may be a byproduct of the mirror-image correspondence in many constituent orders in Japanese and English, as Smith (1978) has pointed out (see Table 6.1 for some examples of this mirror-image order). From my corpus, the typical utterance of this type involves an expression in English which is repeated or rephrased in Japanese. The following are examples:

We bought about two pounds GURAI KATTEKITA NO. (SS) (54)
about bought

Let's become KECHI NI NAROO. (VY) (55)
tight become

TABLE 6.1
Some Mirror-Image Constituent Orderings in English and Japanese

| English | Japanese |
|---|---|
| VO | OV |
| V Complement | Complement V |
| there V NP | NP V |
| P NP | NP P |
| COMP S | S particle |

There's children IRU YO. (MN) (56)
V (existential)

Look at the things she buys for Sean NI. (VY) (57)
for

She got told that next three months KA NAN KA WA (58)
or so
you can't buy anything TTE. (VY)
P
quotative
''She got told that for the next three months or so, you can't buy anything.''

In the above examples, underlined words are shared elements and those with broken lines underneath are equivalents from the two languages. In (54), an English SVO is combined with a Japanese OV with a common O. In (55), ''Let's become KECHI'' is combined with its Japanese equivalent ''KECHI NI NAROO''; a complement is a shared element. In (56), an English existential sentence is combined with its Japanese equivalent. In (57), an English PP is combined with a Japanese PP. In (58), an English embedded clause preceded by COMP is combined with its Japanese equivalent.

It is noteworthy that there were no cases where the sentence began in Japanese and was combined with an English sentence with a shared element. Since Japanese is a verb-final language, one wonders if Japanese verbs could serve as the initial elements of English sentences. There were no such cases found in the present corpus. Moreover, these Japanese verbs would have to be the nonpast form followed by no other elements as sentence-final particles for such forms would correspond to imperatives of English verbs. Japanese forms in the nonpast form followed by any other elements are rare. Perhaps for this reason, no cases were present where a Japanese sentence is combined with an English sentence with a shared element.

It should be obvious, then, that mirror-image sentences cannot be assigned one language. Rather, these sentences all involve a switch of system, typically from English to Japanese.

## DISCUSSION

In this paper, I have demonstrated that one language must be assigned to each Japanese/English code-switched sentence, and that the language may be Japanese in some cases and English in others. This conclusion was argued as follows: cases were presented which could not be accounted for unless one language was assigned. These were cases where switchings take place between constituents whose order is possible only in one language. For the cases where this argument does not apply, I first appealed to discourse functions of certain syntactic items (conjunctions, adverbs, and sentence-final particles). I argued that, since these items are used for pragmatic rather than syntactic reasons, they should not pose any problem to language assignment even when the constituent order at the switch site is shared by the two languages. For the cases where switches occur between the subject and the predicate, language assignment was argued by appealing to several syntactic facts of the two languages including the case-marking system, the negation system and the concept of topic.

We have seen that each Japanese/English code-switched sentence possesses the sentence structure of one language, whether Japanese or English. We have also seen that each sentence can be derived from the sentence structure of one language by switching certain constituents into the other language at some level of the derivation process excluding Japanese sentence-final particles. Thus, intrasentential code-switching is not a phenomenon that proceeds from left to right in a linear order at the point where two constituents from the two languages occur one after the other.

The findings from the Japanese/English data are similar to the Kanada/English data of Sridhar and Sridhar (1980) and the Marathi/English data of Joshi (1985) who have also argued for the necessity of assigning a language to code-switched sentences. However, the present findings differ from theirs in that evidence was found for assignment to either of the two languages involved. Sridhar and Sridhar (1980) and Joshi (1985) claim that language assignment must proceed in a particular direction only. It is possible that the bidirectional switching characterizing the Japanese/English data and the unidirectional switching of Indian communities reflect differences in the speech habits of the communities.

This paper has demonstrated, on the basis of linguistic argumentation, that language can be assigned to intrasentential code-switching. This claim may have interesting repercussions for how code-switched sentences are produced and perceived. One issue which could be explored is to pinpoint the stage at which language assignment may occur in sentence production; presumably it must occur at a fairly early stage in sentence planning. One may further examine whether language assignment is necessary for comprehension—i.e., from the listener's perspective. Does language assignment facilitate sentence processing? Processing implications of different types of code-switched structures may also be studied; for example, do portmanteau sentences take longer to be understood than other code-mixed constructions? A more general issue has to do with the implications of the claim that language assignment is necessary for theories of the nature of the bilingual lexicon (see Kirsner, Hummel, this volume). It is hoped that psycholinguistic research begins to address these and related questions in the area of language switching in fluent bilinguals.

## ACKNOWLEDGMENT

An earlier version of this paper was presented at the 1st Annual Conference on Japanese and Korean Linguistics, Harvard University, May 6–8, 1983. I would like to thank Gillian Sankoff, Susumu Kuno, William Labov and Anthony Kroch for their comments which helped to shape this paper. I also thank Jyotsna Vaid for editorial help. However, all errors are strictly mine.

## REFERENCES

Doron, E. (1981). On formal models of code-switching. Unpublished paper, University of Texas, Austin.

Ervin-Tripp, S. M. (1964). An analysis of the interaction of language, topic and listener. In J. Fishman (Ed.), *Readings in the sociology of language*. The Hague: Mouton, 192–211.

Ferguson, C. A. (1964). Diglossia. In D. Hymes (Ed.), *Language in culture and society*. New York: Harper & Row.

Fishman, J. (1965). Who speaks what language to whom and when? *La Linguistique 2*, 67–88.

Gal, S. (1978). Variation and change in patterns of speaking: Language shifts in Austria. In D. Sankoff (Ed.), *Linguistic variation*. New York: Academic Press.

Gumperz, J. (1976). The sociolinguistic significance of conversational code-switching. *Working Papers of the Language Behavior Research Laboratory, #46*. Berkeley: University of California.

Joshi, A. K. (1985). Processing of sentences with intrasentential code-switching. In D. Dowty, L. Kartunnen, & A. Zwicky (Eds.), *Natural language processing: Psychological, computational and theoretical perspectives*. Cambridge: Cambridge University Press.

Kuno, S. (1973). *The structure of the Japanese language*. Cambridge, MA: MIT Press.

Martin, S. (1975). *Reference grammar of Japanese*. New Haven: Yale University Press.

Muysken, P., di Sciullo, A., & R. Singh (1981). *Code-mixing and binding*. Unpublished manuscript, Université de Montreal.

Pfaff, C. (1979). Constraints on language mixing: Intrasentential code-switching and borrowing in Spanish/English. *Language 55*, 291–318.

Poplack, S. (1978). Syntactic structure and social function of code-switching. *Working Paper 2: Centro de Estudios Puertorriquenos*, the City University of New York.

Poplack, S. (1979). Sometimes I'll start a sentence in Spanish Y TERMINO EN ESPANOL. *Working Paper 4: Centro de Estudios Puertorriquenos*, the City University of New York.

Prince, E. (1981). Topicalization, focus-movement, and Yiddish-movement: A pragmatic differentiation. In D. Alford et al., (Eds.), *Proceedings of the Seventh Annual Meeting of the Berkeley Linguistic Society*, Berkeley, University of California.

Sankoff, G. (1971). Language use in multilingual societies: Alternate approaches. In J. B. Pride & J. Holmes (Eds.), *Sociolinguistics*. Sussex: Penguin.

Sankoff, D., & S. Poplack. (1980). Formal grammar of code-switching. *Working Paper 8: Centro de Estudios Puertorriquenos,* the City University of New York.

Smith, D. R. (1978). Mirror Image in Japanese and English. *Language 54,* 78–122.

Sridhar, S., & Sridhar, K. (1980). The syntax and psycholinguistics of bilingual code-mixing. *Canadian Journal of Psychology/Revue Canadienne de Psychologie 34,* 407–416.

Stubbs, M. (1984). *Discourse analysis.* Chicago: University of Chicago Press.

Timm, L. (1975). Spanish-English code-switching: El porque y how-not-to. *Romance Philology 28,* 473–482.

Weinreich, U. (1953). *Languages in contact.* The Hague: Mouton.

Woolford, E. (1980). *A formal model of bilingual code-switching.* Unpublished manuscript, Cambridge, MA: MIT.

Woolford, E. (1983). Bilingual code-switching and syntactic theory. *Linguistic Inquiry, 14,* 520–536.

# 7 Processing Mixed Language: Some Preliminary Findings

François Grosjean
*Northeastern University*

Carlos Soares
*Data General Corporation*

As psycholinguists working on the on-line processing of language in bilinguals, we are interested in obtaining a better understanding of how bilinguals produce, perceive, and comprehend their languages when they are using them separately, in a monolingual mode, and when they are using them together, in a bilingual mixed mode. In what follows we present some hypotheses concerning monolingual and mixed language processing and some preliminary findings from a research project aimed at studying language processing in the mixed language mode. We first describe the conceptual framework that underlies our work, and stress the differences that occur in the processing of language when the bilingual is in the monolingual and the bilingual mixed mode. We then discuss a number of studies aimed at exploring the production of code-switches, and more specifically, the phonetic and prosodic changes that take place when code-switches occur. We present next some preliminary data on the perception of code-switches and examine how soon and how well the listener can tell that a language switch has taken place. And finally, we discuss the lexical access (or word recognition) of code-switches and borrowings, and show why borrowings may be more complex to process than code-switches.

Several points need to be made from the outset. The first is that our work on bilingualism is based on a number of premises that are not always shared by other researchers. These concern how we define bilingualism, how we view the bilingual's language competence, how we judge the comparison that invariably takes place between monolinguals and bilinguals, and so on. These premises are presented in Appendix A and are discussed in greater detail in Grosjean (1982, in press). The second point is that the approach we use in our research is both descriptive and experimental. We use the techniques of acoustic phonetics to study the production of code-switches and we employ the paradigms of speech perception and word recognition to investigate the processing of mixed speech. We believe that code-switching and borrowing can indeed be studied in a laboratory situation (if certain precautions are taken) and that this research can complement the findings which have been obtained in more natural environments by linguists and sociolinguists. The third point is that most of the data we have obtained come from persons who share our bilingualism (French/English; Portuguese/English) and who feel comfortable code-switching and borrowing with us. Because mixing languages remains a phenomenon that is criticized by many monolinguals and bilinguals, we have only studied mixed language processing in members of our own bilingual communities. Finally, much of the data we present are still quite preliminary and pertain mainly to language perception and production in the mixed mode.

## THE CONCEPTUAL FRAMEWORK

In their everyday lives, bilinguals find themselves at various points along a situational continuum which induce a particular speech mode. At one end of the continuum, bilinguals are in a totally monolingual speech mode in that they are speaking to monolinguals of language A or language B. At the other end of the continuum, bilinguals find themselves in a bilingual speech mode in that they are speaking to bilinguals with whom they normally mix languages (more precisely, code-switch and borrow). For convenience, we refer to the two ends of the continuum when speaking of the monolingual or bilingual speech modes, but we should keep in mind that these are end points and that intermediary modes do exist between the two. This is the case, for example, when a bilingual is speaking to another bilingual who never mixes languages, or when a bilingual is interacting with a person who has limited knowledge of the second language.

In the monolingual speech mode, bilinguals adopt the language of the monolingual interlocutor. They also deactivate, as best they can, the other language. This deactivation has led to much theorizing and much controversy around the notion of a language switch or a monitor system (Grosjean, 1982; Macnamara, 1967; Paradis, 1980c). What is certain, however, is that bilinguals rarely deactivate the other language totally. This is seen in various types of production inteferences—the involuntary influence of one language on the other—as in the case of pronunciation "errors," accidental lexical borrowings, "odd" syntactic constructions, etc. In perception, researchers have also found evidence for this residual activation in cross-language Stroop tests (Obler & Albert, 1978; Preston & Lambert, 1969), word-nonword judgments (Altenberg & Cairns, 1983) and comprehension tasks using the phoneme monitoring paradigm (Blair & Harris, 1981). The question of interest is how the language processing of bilinguals in the monolingual speech mode differs from that of monolinguals given this residual activation of the other language.

In the bilingual speech mode both languages are activated. Here bilinguals employ various elements of one language when speaking the other. The actual choice of the language bilinguals will use with one another is an extremely complex question (see Chapter 3 in Grosjean, 1982) and is a function of factors such as the participants involved, the situation, the topic, and the function of the interaction. Once a particular language has been chosen (we call this the base language), bilinguals can bring in the other language in various ways. We should note that simply speaking to another bilingual does not automatically entail the use of the other language; again a number of factors are involved (Grosjean, 1982). One way of bringing in the other language is to code-switch, that is to shift *completely* to the other language. This can involve a word, a phrase, a clause, or a sentence. For example:

On n'est pas assez quick
(We're not quick enough)

Va chercher Marc and bribe him avec un chocolat chaud with cream on top
(Go get Marc and bribe him with a hot chocolate with cream on top)

(Note: code-switches are underlined in the text.) Code-switching is a domain that is now receiving increasing attention from researchers: Sociolinguists are studying the factors which lead to code-switching (see, for example, Gal, 1979; Gumperz, 1970; Scotton & Ury, 1977; Valdés Fallis, 1976); linguists are examining the constraints which govern code-switching and whether there is a code-switching grammar (see, for example, Joshi, 1985; Lipski, 1978, 1982; Pfaff, 1979; Poplack, 1978; Timm, 1975; Woolford, 1983) and developmental psycholinguists are studying the development of code-switching ability in children (McClure, 1977, for instance). The questions a psycholinguist can ask concerning code-switching are numerous. For example: How does the bilingual actually pass from one language to the other in the same utterance? How is this marked phonetically and prosodically? How and when does the bilingual listener realize that a code-switch has occurred? What are the underlying operations leading to the recognition and comprehension of code-switched elements? We will attempt to address these questions in the studies we present below.

The other way of bringing in the other language is by borrowing a word from that language and adapting it phonologically and morphologically into the base language. For example:

On a BRUNCHÉ avec eux
(We brunched with them)

Il faut SWITCHER les places
(We have to switch the seats)

(Borrowings are capitalized in the text.) Here the borrowings BRUNCHÉ and SWITCHER are pronounced in French (adapted phonologically) and are integrated morphologically in the sentence. Other types of borrowings involve taking a word in the base language and giving it the meaning of a word in the other language, or translating, word by word, an expression from one language to the other (Haugen, 1969). In our studies we are concerned with borrowings like BRUNCHÉ and SWITCHER which we call "speech borrowings" or simply "borrowings" to differentiate them from borrowings which have become an integral part of the base language (e.g., "weekend," "jazz," "transistor" in French; these we call "language borrowings"). Difficulties can exist in differentiating one word code-switches from borrowings, especially when the latter are said with a base language accent and are not integrated morphologically, but we will not discuss this here (see Grosjean, 1982, for an examination of this point as well as for a discussion of the difference between borrowings and lexical interferences). The questions a psycholinguist can ask about the processing of speech borrowings are quite similar to those asked about code-switching, but one that is important is how bilingual listeners access a borrowing in the appropriate lexicon. It could be argued that the acoustic-phonetic information leads them to search the base language lexicon when they should really be searching the other lexicon. Does accessing a borrowing, therefore, involve more steps than accessing a code-switch and, hence, take more time? This is a question that is posed in the last part of the chapter.

A psycholinguistic model of language processing in bilinguals will have to account for the perception and production of language in the bilingual's different speech modes: the monolingual and the bilingual modes. It will have to describe the ways in which bilinguals in the monolingual mode differ from monolinguals in terms of perception and production processes, and it will have to explain the actual interaction of the two languages during processing in the bilingual mode. In what follows, we leave aside processing in the monolingual speech mode (certainly the mode which has received the most attention from researchers; see, for example, among the more recent studies: Altenberg & Cairns, 1983; Blair & Harris, 1981; Mack, 1984; Obler, 1982; Soares & Grosjean, 1984; Williams, 1980) and we concentrate instead on spoken language processing in the bilingual mixed mode.

A question that can be asked from the outset is the following: What operations are involved during mixed language processing? We propose that during mixed language production, the bilingual's two language systems (and their various components: phonology, syntax, lexicon, etc.) are simultaneously active and interact to produce mixed language. One language system is involved in the production of the base language and the other language system interacts with it to help produce code-switches and borrowings. The interaction procedure is still unclear: There may be a control structure which permits shifting control from one grammar to the other by means of a general switching rule (Joshi, 1985); there may be an "assembly line" process where individual components of the "guest language'' are put together separately and inserted into appropriate slots in the syntactic frame of the base (host) language (Sridhar & Sridhar, 1980); or there may be a general assembly operation governed by the intersection of the phrase structure rules of the two languages (Woolford, 1983). We do not attempt to choose between these solutions but instead we study the phonetic and prosodic consequences of these operations (see the following section).

We may also ask how bilinguals perceive and comprehend mixed speech. Although a theory of attention may explain how the bilingual listener can ''switch'' from one language to another, we share (at least tentatively) Obler and Albert's (1978) view that a general language monitoring device helps the bilingual determine which language is being spoken at a particular point in time. We characterize the device in the following way: It is flexible, very rapid, and automatic in the sense that it usually functions without intent or conscious awareness (Posner & Snyder, 1975). Its function is to direct the information obtained from a preliminary analysis of the acoustic signal to the processors of the appropriate language. It is these processors that do higher level processing such as accessing the internal lexicon, parsing the sentence, analyzing it semantically, etc., so as to allow the listener to obtain an interpretative representation of the sentence. The monitoring device uses all the information it can to indicate as quickly as possible which language is being spoken: prosodic information (fundamental frequency, duration, rate, amplitude, stress pattern, etc.), segmental information (phoneme and syllable characteristics), syntactic and semantic rules, knowledge of the speaker and of the topic, pragmatic factors, as well as the constraints imposed on code-switching and borrowing by the two languages in question. This means, of course, that the device is constantly receiving feedback from the higher level processors. The device is always active, but especially so when the speaker is in a bilingual speech mode and the probability of language mixing is high. Like all devices which base their decision on multiple cues, situations of ambiguity will arise. This may be the case, for example, with speech borrowings where the phonetics and morphology indicate one language, but the actual word belongs to the lexicon of the other language. In this case, some delay may occur in the language decision and hence in lexical access. (Note that we have adopted Paradis' (1978; 1980a, 1980b) theory of two language lexicons each of which is connected to one conceptual store.) The language monitoring device does not itself process the language input; it leaves that to the processors of the two languages which share a number of basic cognitive and language processing operations but which also have language specific operations and strategies. These processors are, of course, in constant interaction when processing bilingual speech.

We are not able to provide direct evidence for the monitoring device or for its use in the on-line processing of mixed speech. Instead, we assume, for the time being at least, the existence and the use of such a device and examine questions about its operation: how much information it needs to identify the language in question, how early it can make a language decision and how categorical this decision is. We also investigate the impact that a particular language decision will have on a later processing stage: the lexical access (or word recognition) of code-switched words and speech borrowings.

## EXPLORING THE CODE-SWITCHING BOUNDARY

When a French/English bilingual says in a rather matter of fact way to his bilingual friend, as they are watching a hockey game on television,

T'as vu son smash
(Did you see his smash)

some rather amazing operations take place in the articulation of the code-switch smash. This is because the speaker must change, in an incredibly short time, the whole of his planning and execution programs so as to articulate the English /smæʃ/ and not the French /smaʃ/. This raises a number of interesting questions which have rarely been asked in the code-switching literature. Among these we find:

—At what point in the acoustic-phonetic stream does the speaker start switching from one language to the other? Is it grosso modo, prior to the code-switch boundary (during the "son" in the example above), at the code-switch boundary (during the frication of the /s/), or after the boundary during the /m/ or /æ/)?

—Which acoustic-phonetic traits are modified first? Which take more time?

—Are these changes dependent on the phonetic and syntactic environment?

—Does a complete switch actually take place or does it only sound that way?

—What happens to the prosody during a code-switch? Does it change whenever there is a code-switch or must the code-switch be of a certain length?

We have started a research project aimed at answering these questions and we discuss below some of the data obtained so far.

### Segmental Changes at the Code-switch Boundary

In Fig. 7.1 we present the spectrograms of a pair of English and French sentences. Each sentence pair is composed of a monolingual version

I saw the dack $/dæk/_E$ J'ai vu le daque $/dak/_F$

and a code-switched version, where the nonsense word "daque/dack" is code-switched after the initial monolingual part

J'ai vu le dack $/dæk/_E$ I saw the daque $/dak/_F$

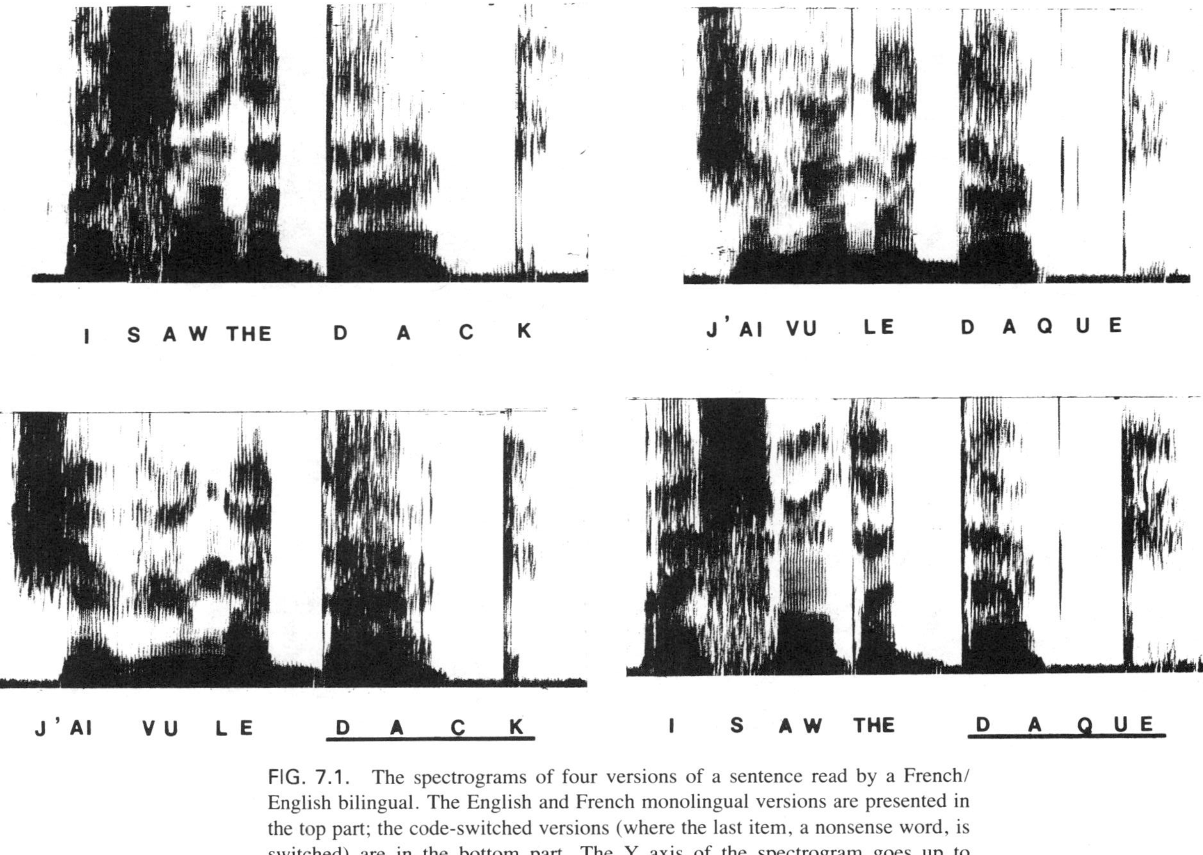


FIG. 7.1. The spectrograms of four versions of a sentence read by a French/English bilingual. The English and French monolingual versions are presented in the top part; the code-switched versions (where the last item, a nonsense word, is switched) are in the bottom part. The Y axis of the spectrogram goes up to 5000Hz.

These four sentences were read separately by a French/English bilingual and analyzed with a spectrograph. A comparison of the words "daque" and "dack" in the English and French monolingual versions (top spectrograms) clearly reflect the many differences which exist between the two languages (see Delattre, 1965). We note in particular a halt in vocal fold vibration during the closure in English but a continuation in French, a clear burst bar in English but an absence of one in French, quite distinct F2 and F3 vowel formant configurations in the two languages (beginning and end transitions, steady state portions), different vowel durations (about 46% of the duration of "dack" but only 37% of the duration of "daque"), different /k/ closure durations, as well as differences in vowel and /k/ intensity.

By comparing the top and bottom spectograms, either those on the left or those on the right, we can observe what happens when a word is code-switched. For example, if we compare code-switched "dack" (bottom left) with monolingual "dack" (top left), we note several striking differences in the code-switch caused by cross-language coarticulation. First, vocal fold vibration continues throughout the closure of code-switched "dack" as it does in the French "daque" (top right). Second, there is no visible burst bar in the code-switch (again as in the French version), and, third, there is a slightly falling F2 vowel transition. However, once the beginning of the code-switch is over, all other characteristics resemble the English "dack": vowel formant configuration, duration of the /k/ closure, intensity, etc. A similar pattern emerges when one compares code-switched "daque" (bottom right) with monolingual "daque" (top right). The two differ on the cessation or continuation of vocal fold vibration during the /d/ closure and on the absence or presence of a burst bar. From then on, the acoustic characteristics are quite comparable.

These pilot data, confirmed with a "dock/doque" pair, would seem to suggest that in an environment of this kind, the code-switch boundary at the acoustic level occurs not so much during the preceding vowel or the closure of the code-switched consonant, but during the consonant itself and the early part of the vowel which follows it. These data show that cross-language coarticulation "tinges" the beginnings (and probably the ends) of code-switches. This carry-over of the base language into the code-switch will have interesting consequences on its perception by the bilingual listener (see Part 3 of this chapter).

## The Prosody of Code-Switches

Delattre (1965, 1966), among others, has stressed the many and important differences that exist between English and French prosody. Using extracts of interviews of Margaret Mead for American English and Simone de Beauvoir for French he noted: (1) the prevalence of falling intonation in English and of rising intonation in French; (2) the falling or fall-rise patterns at the end of English phrases and sentences, and the rising continuation contours in French, and (c) the reversed S shape of the final sentence fall in English and the convex shape of the fall in French (a fall which starts on the first syllable of the final phrase). With such vastly differing prosodic patterns, to which we should add the basically stress timed characteristics of English and primarily syllable timed aspects of French, it is natural that we should ask ourselves how prosody is modified when a bilingual code-switches.

Pilot data, obtained by means of a Visi-Pitch recorder, and presented in Figs. 7.2 and 7.3, give some indication of the characteristics of code-switching pros-

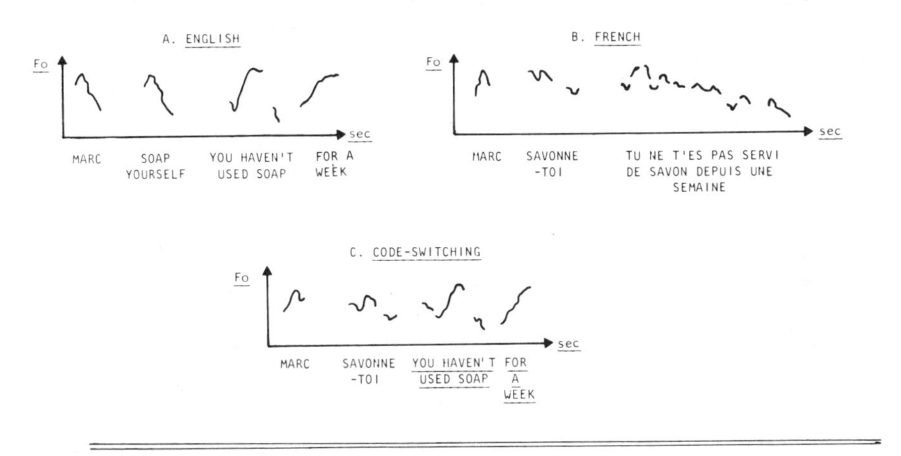


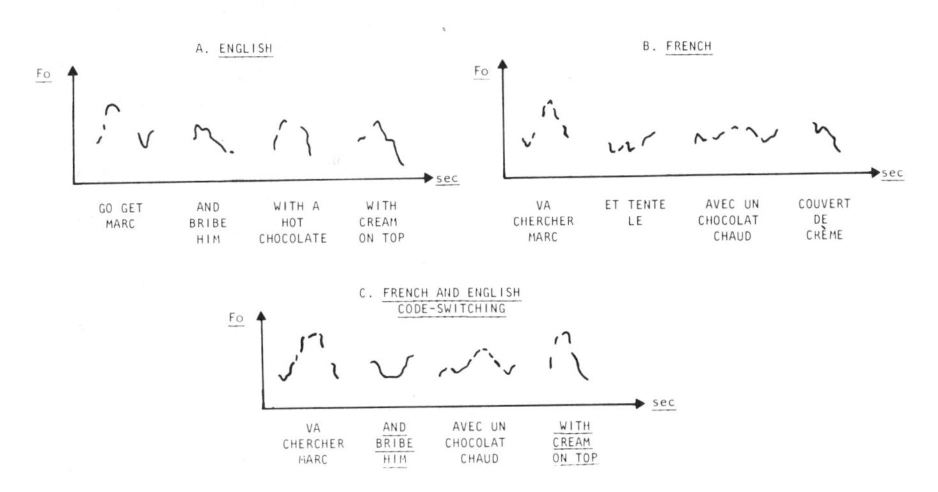


FIG. 7.2. The fundamental frequency (Fo) contours of the English, French and code-switched versions of two sentences read by a French/English bilingual. In the top part, the code-switched element is an independent clause; in the bottom part the code-switched elements are a conjoined clause and a phrase.

ody. In Fig. 7.2 (top half), we present the fundamental frequency (Fo) contour of an English version, a French version, and a code-switched version of a sentence read by a French-English bilingual with no apparent accent in either language. The English version (top left) shows the characteristic high fall contours of the commands (''Marc'' and ''soap yourself'') and the final rise at the end of the surprised comment (''you haven't used soap for a week''). The French version (top right) is quite different. The commands are less marked, and the comment has a long falling contour. As for the code-switched version (bottom representation), the commands in French respect the monolingual French contours, whereas the comment in English is identical to that in the English monolingual version. Thus, it would appear that when a code-switch occurs at an independent clause break, the prosody changes along with the segmental aspects. Is this also the case when a code-switched clause is coordinated to the preceding clause? The bottom half of Fig. 7.2 would seem to indicate that it is not. The top left and top right contours show the characteristic intonation patterns of English and French respectively: the falling pattern on each clause or phrase in English, the rising pattern in French when there is a continuation, and the final fall on the last phrase. In the code-switched version, the interesting clause is ''and bribe him'' because it is surrounded by French and is not in a sentence final position. A comparison of this code-switch with the two monolingual versions (''and bribe him'' and ''et tente le'') shows that the prosody of the code-switch does not take on the English contour—as one might have expected—but remains characteristically French (note in particular the rise on ''him'').

It seems, therefore, that the prosody of a code-switch does not always follow the segmental changes that occur at the switch boundary. This is confirmed in Fig. 7.3 where we present the prosodic contour of a one-word code-switch. Once again, the English and French monolingual versions are quite characteristic: a falling contour on ''soap'' and a rising contour on ''savonner.'' As for the code-switch soap in ''Il faut soap Marc,'' we note that it has a rising French contour instead of an English falling contour. The bottom pattern shows that integrating soap both morphologically and phonetically into the sentence (thus making it the borrowing SOAPER) only confirms the pattern—its contour is practically identical to ''savonner'' in the French version.

These pilot data need to be confirmed, but they are already extremely intriguing in that they indicate, along with the segmental pilot data presented earlier, that code-switches do not always involve a complete switch from one language to the other, even though such a switch may be heard as complete by the bilingual listener. The definition of a code-switch given earlier (the complete shift from one language to another) may therefore have to be modified in the future.

We are currently pursuing this line of research and studying the prosody of code-switching as a function of the syntactic status of the switch (sentence, clause, phrase, word), its language environment (which language precedes and

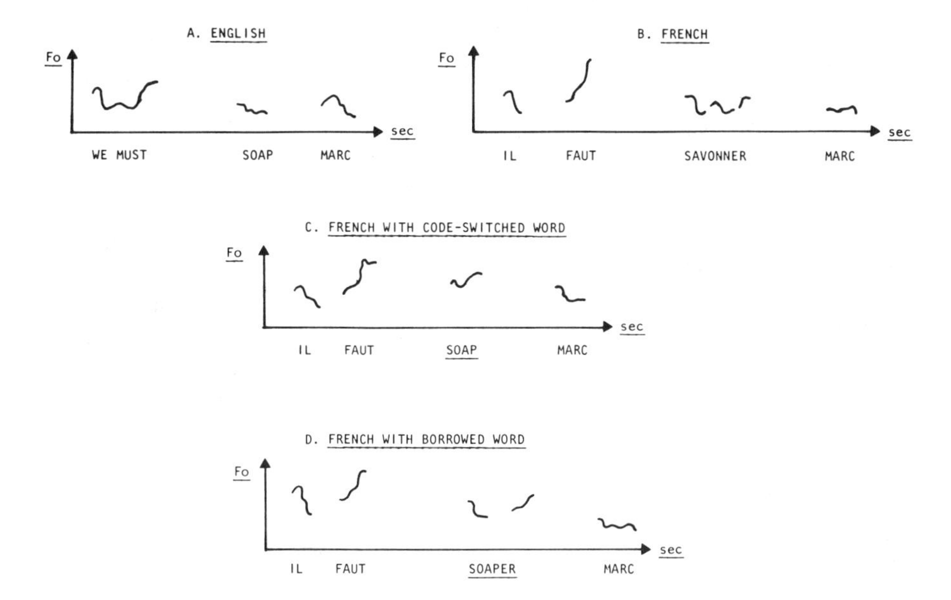


FIG. 7.3. The fundamental frequency contours of the English, French and code-switched versions of a sentence where the code-switched element is a word. The French version is also represented with a speech borrowing in contour D.

follows it) and its length. Based on the pilot data we have obtained, we expect that all of these factors will affect the prosody of code-switching.

These studies on the phonetic and prosodic characteristics of code-switches are of interest in their own right, but they also take on added importance when they are related to studies on the perception of code-switches. In what follows, we examine the impact that the phonetic change from one language to the other has on the perception and recognition of code-switches. We are especially interested in those cases where the changeover is delayed, incomplete or nonexistent, as is sometimes the case for some prosodic variables. The question that can be asked is how the bilingual listener processes a code-switch on-line and how he or she does so quickly enough to keep up with the speaker when the switch itself is delayed or incomplete. We examine this question in the next two sections.

## THE PERCEPTION OF CODE-SWITCHES

We hypothesized above that, when processing a code-switch in real time, a bilingual has to decide on the language status of the item: Does it belong to the base language or to the other language? This decision will help him or her identify the phonetic segments, access the lexical item in the appropriate lexicon and integrate its meaning in the interpretative representation that is being built.

We should note that researchers are not in agreement on whether a language decision does indeed need to be made. Proponents of a switch or a monitor mechanism (Obler & Albert, 1978; Macnamara & Kushnir, 1971) would probably defend such a decision, whereas proponents of direct access (Paradis, 1980c, for example) would not. We need to obtain experimental evidence for a language monitoring device (by using a speeded classification procedure, for instance) and show that it is not simply an artefactual outcome of the experimental tasks we use (Paradis, personal communication), but we also need more information on the nature of the device and on the underlying operations which allow a bilingual to decide whether a particular item being heard belongs to one language or the other. It is important to know, for example, how early on he or she can make this decision (before the code-switch boundary, at the boundary or after it), which factors influence language identification and how proficient the bilingual is in this task.

In order to study these questions further, we have been using two different approaches. First, we have been employing a language identification task in which the acoustic-phonetic information of a code-switch is presented in segments of increasing duration and where the bilingual listener has to identify the language of the item being presented as well as give a confidence rating. Second, we have been using categorical perception tasks in which stimuli taken from a synthesized French to English acoustic-phonetic continuum are identified and discriminated by bilingual listeners. Thus, the first approach examines how soon and how well a bilingual can perceive a change in language, while the second explores the nature of language categorization for complete items.

We should note at this point that even though the pilot data we present below pertain to language categorization and hence speak to the nature of the language monitor, they are also relevant to a view that defends direct mapping between the acoustic signal and the percept, and this without passing through a language monitor. As we will see, the factors which can speed up or delay language categorization will probably be those that can also speed up or delay direct phoneme and syllable identification.

## Identifying the Language of the Code-Switch

We have been using the gating paradigm (Grosjean, 1980) to determine how soon and how well the bilingual can determine the language of the item he or she is hearing. The approach entails presenting a word in segments, or gates, of increasing duration so that at the first gate little or no information concerning the word is given, whereas at the last gate, the entire word is presented. For example, if we were interested in testing ''dack'' in the context

J'ai vu le dack

the first gate would present the sentence up to the end of the "le" but no information about the following word, the second gate would present "J'ai vu le" plus 30 msec of dack, the third gate would present "J'ai vu le" plus 60 msecs of dack and so on, until at the very last gate, all of dack would be presented. In such a task the subject has to decide, after each presentation, whether the item is in French or English, and how confident he or she is. The answers are used to construct language identification curves which indicate the amount of information needed to choose the appropriate language.

Among the many factors which can affect the shape of these curves (psychosocial variables such as speaker, situation, listener; linguistic variables such as topic, preceding patterns of code-switches, the phonetic and phonotactic configuration of the code-switched item, etc.), we have so far concentrated on two. The first is the language specificity of the sounds or sound sequences in the code-switch. Some sounds belong specifically to one language or the other: /ð, θ, ŋ/ are found in English but not in French while /ɥ, õ, ɛ̃/ are only found in French; other sounds are relatively similar in the two languages (/b, d, g, s, z, i, e/ for instance). This is also true of sound sequences, consonant clusters and syllable types (see Delattre, 1965, 1966, for a discussion of this). We reasoned that the more language specific a particular sound or sound sequence in a code-switch, the more proficient the bilingual listener would be in identifying the appropriate language of the item. The second factor we examined was the impact of the language of the carrier sentence on the language identification of the item presented. We had no definite expectations here, although we felt that the language of the carrier sentence preceding a code-switch might perhaps bias the listener, at least in the first gates, towards that language.

To study these two factors, we gated a series of nonsense words (nonwords) embedded in a sentence context and read by a French-English bilingual with no apparent accent in either language. For example:

J'ai vu une bive (where "bive" is a French nonsense word)
I saw a bive (where the nonsense word "bive" is a French code-switch)
J'ai vu un chock (where the nonsense word "chock" is an English code-switch)

These readings were used to construct two presentation sets: the isolation and context sets. In the isolation sets, the nonsense words were excised from the sentence and presented in isolation. Thus, in each set, the first gate corresponded to the first 30 msec of the word, the second gate to the first 60 msec of the word, and so on, until the whole word was presented. In the context set, the same word fragments were preceded by their carrier sentence. Here, the first presentation of each set corresponded to the sentence up to the word but, apart from some coarticulatory information, contained little other acoustic-phonetic information pertaining to the word itself (we called this the 0 msec gate). The second presentation contained the carrier sentence and the first 30 msec of the word, the third presentation contained 60 msec of the word, and so on, until the whole word was presented.

The sets were randomized and presented in two separate sessions: In the first, subjects heard the isolation sets only and in the second they heard the context sets. Six French/English late bilingual adults served as subjects in both sessions. These bilinguals were all of French origin and had lived in the United States for at least 5 years; they used both French and English in their everyday lives. The subjects were told in French that they would be hearing segments of nonwords in isolation, or preceded by a short sentence, and they were asked to indicate after each segment the language of the nonword being presented (they were to circle "Ang" or "Fr" on the answer sheets); they were also to assess their level of confidence on a scale of 1 to 10. In the case of the context sets, they were told very clearly that the nonwords could be in the same language as the carrier sentence or in the other language. And throughout the experiment, the subjects were repeatedly reminded that the words could be in one or the other language.

The results were converted to language identification ratings in the following way. Each confidence rating at each presentation in a particular set was preceded by a "+" or "−" depending on whether the language identification of the nonword was correct (+) or incorrect (−). Thus, if a particular French fragment was circled "Ang" and was accompanied by a confidence rating of 6, the converted rating was −6. Ratings obtained in this way were averaged across subjects and were used to construct language identification curves.

In Fig. 7.4 (top part) we present the curves obtained for French "bive" (/biv/) and English "beeve" (/biv/) presented in isolation. Each nonword was read in a monolingual context and excised from the speech stream. These nonwords are phonetically very similar in the two languages although, as expected, "beeve" is longer than "bive" (480 msec as compared to 387 msec). Because of their phonetic similarity, we note that subjects have difficulties at first in identifying the language of the items. Both nonwords go through a period in which they are heard as belonging to the other language: note, for example, the minus ratings of "beeve" up to 210 msec and those of "bive" between 210 and 300 msecs. At the last gate, however, the two nonwords receive positive ratings, although these are not very high (+2.0 for "bive" and +4.83 for "beeve").

It is interesting to compare these identification curves with those presented in the bottom part of Fig. 7.4 where "bive" is a code-switch in the sentence "I saw a <u>bive</u>." (Note again that code-switches are underlined in the text and in the figures.) The top curve corresponds to "<u>bive</u>" presented in isolation and the bottom curve to the very same "<u>bive</u>" presented in context (for technical reasons, the full duration of "<u>bive</u>" (435 msec) could not be presented at the last gate in the context condition). We note, first of all, that the identification curve of the isolated "<u>bive</u>" never departs very far from the language border (the dotted line) and the last two points are in fact located precisely on that border.

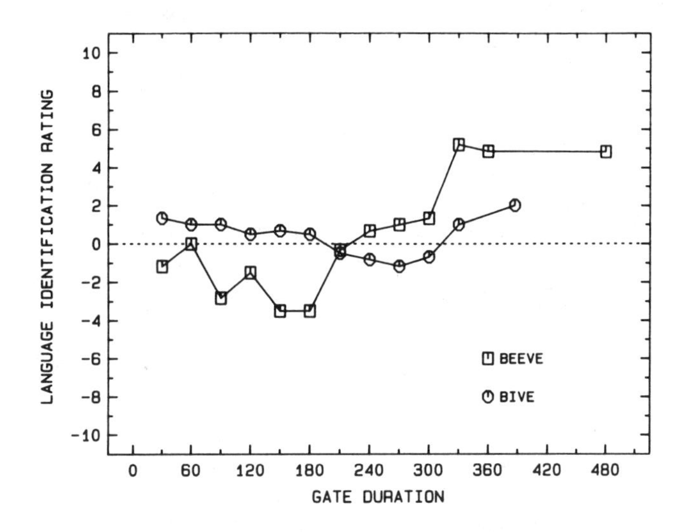


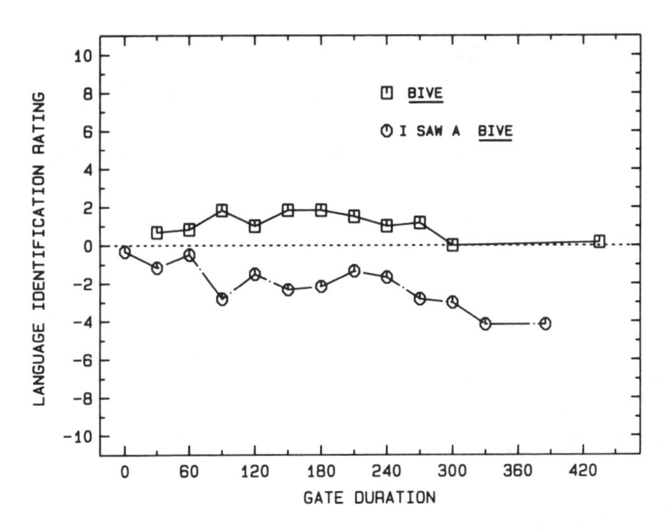


FIG. 7.4. The language identification curves of a number of English and French nonsense words. The top curves are those of English "beeve" and French "bive" presented in isolation. The bottom curves are those of code-switched French "bive" presented in isolation (squares) and preceded by the English carrier sentence "I saw a" (circles). Each point (square or circle) is the mean of six ratings, one by each of six subjects.

Subjects therefore had great difficulties identifying the language of "bive," and at the last presentation, three of the six subjects actually thought they heard the English "beeve." The reason for this must be that "bive," as a code-switch, has been tinged by English phonetics (there is cross-language coarticulation as there was with the dack/daque pair in Fig. 7.1), and this makes the language identification all the more difficult. Note that the monolingual "bive" in the top part of Fig. 7.4 receives higher French identification ratings, at the end at least. What is especially interesting in the bottom part of Fig. 7.4 is the identification curve of "bive" when presented in context. This is the very same phonetic sequence as the "bive" presented in isolation and yet the resulting identification curve is quite different. From the very first gate, the ratings are negative (that is, "bive" is identified as being an English item) and the ratings become progressively stronger as more of the item is heard. At the very last gate, 5 of the 6 subjects feel that the item is English and the final mean rating is −4.17.

Several reasons may explain these results. The first is that subjects may be expecting the next item to be in the same language as the sentence just heard; and this despite the repeated warnings given by the experimenter. The effect of this "base language expectation" (mentioned in a very different context by Macnamara & Kushnir, 1971) can best be seen in the results obtained at the first gates (0 and 30 msec) where almost no phonetic information about the word has been heard but where the ratings are already negative. A second reason is that the English traits at the beginning of "bive" (those that come from cross-language coarticulation) are made more salient by the English context and therefore the early gates are heard as being more English than they actually are. And the third reason is that the English carrier sentence "assimilates" the border-line "bive" so that it is now heard as a rather clear "beeve." As we saw above, "bive" in isolation is an ambiguous item, and it is this very ambiguity that allows the carrier sentence to pull it towards English. Only further investigation will allow us to assess whether these reasons are indeed correct, but already we can see that identifying the language of a code-switch is not always straightforward. When there is ambiguity at this level, we can hypothesize that later processing operations such as lexical access (for real words) may well be affected. We will return to this point in the last part of the chapter.

We now turn to the identification curves of nonsense words containing a sound that is specific to just one language. In Fig. 7.5 (top part) we present the curves obtained for the French nonword "bainve" (/bɛ̃v/) when presented in isolation and in context. Below these curves we have placed the spectrogram of the sentence in which it was produced: "J'ai vu une bainve" (the Y axis goes up to 4000 Hz). We should note here that "bainve" is strictly a French nonword and this because of the nasal vowel /ɛ̃/ it contains. An examination of the identification curve for "bainve" excised from the sentence and presented in isolation, reveals that for the first few gates the subjects are undecided as to the language of the word (English/b/ and French/b/ share a number of common

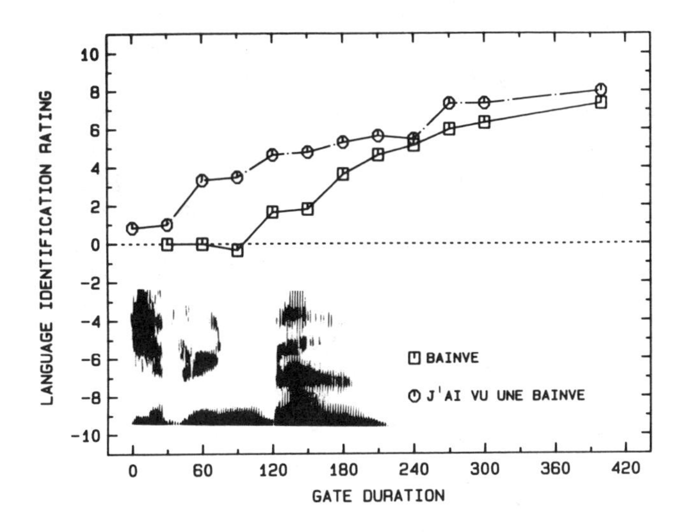


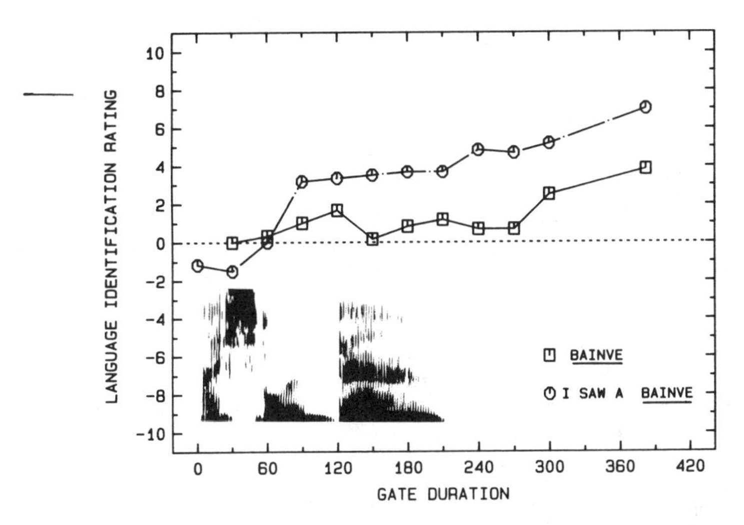


FIG. 7.5. The language identification curves of the monolingual and code-switched versions of the French nonsense word "bainve." The top curves are those of monolingual "bainve" presented in isolation (squares) and preceded by the French carrier sentence "J'ai vu une" (circles). The bottom curves are those of code-switched French "bainve" presented in isolation (squares) and preceded by the English carrier sentence "I saw a" (circles). Each point (square or circle) is the mean of six ratings, one by each of six subjects. The spectograms of the complete monolingual and code-switched sentences are presented below the respective curves (the Y axis goes up to 4000 Hz).

characteristics) but as soon as the nasal /ɛ̃/ starts being heard, the ratings increase substantially, and at the end of the nonword, all of the subjects are quite confident that they are listening to a French nonword. The curve for "bainve" presented in context is very similar except that subjects need to hear less of the item before giving relatively high ratings. We see the base language expectation effect at work at the early gates, as well as a language context effect. In this case, the language information provided by the carrier sentence brings converging evidence to the phonetic information of the item and thus strengthens the French ratings in the first eight gates. As expected, both in isolation and in context, the final ratings obtained for "bainve" are very high.

It is interesting to compare these results with those obtained when "bainve" is a code-switch in the sentence "I saw a bainve" (see the bottom part of Fig. 7.5 for the two curves and the spectrogram). When presented in isolation, "bainve" receives lower French ratings than did its monolingual counterpart. This is because, as a code-switch, the initial part of the item is tinged by English. As can be seen in the spectrogram, there is a cessation of vocal fold vibration before the burst and a very clear burst bar, neither of which occur in the monolingual version. Although the /ɛ̃/ counters this English information, it cannot do so completely, and the final "bainve" rating is +3.83 as compared to +7.33 for the monolingual item.

An interesting pattern emerges from the ratings obtained for "bainve" in context. We note, first of all, the presence of negative ratings at the first two gates. These are probably due to the base language expectation effect noted in the "bive" example above and to a saliency effect where the English context strengthens the English traits at the beginning of the word. We then note a sudden change of sign in the ratings and a rather steep rise of the language identification curve which culminates in a final rating that is very similar to the one obtained in the monolingual version (+7.00 as compared to +8.00). What is happening here is that the carrier sentence is serving as a contrast for the phonetic information carried by "bainve" and is helping the subjects choose the correct language. Unlike "bive" which was ambiguous and which could be assimilated into the language of the carrier sentence, "bainve" is a typically French item, and the language of the carrier sentence helps to make this even more clear. It is interesting to note, therefore, the two possible roles that the base language can have on the language identification of a code-switch (in addition to the expectation and the saliency effects already mentioned): it can either help to assimilate an ambiguous item into the base language or it can help set up a contrast with the code-switched item so that the language of this item becomes even more clear.

In Fig. 7.6, we offer converging evidence for the results obtained so far by presenting the identification curves for two code-switched English words: "zock" /zɔk/ and "chock" /čɔk/. What differentiates these two nonwords is that the initial consonant of the first has a closely resembling French counterpart (French /z/) whereas the initial consonant of the second nonword does not; /č/ is

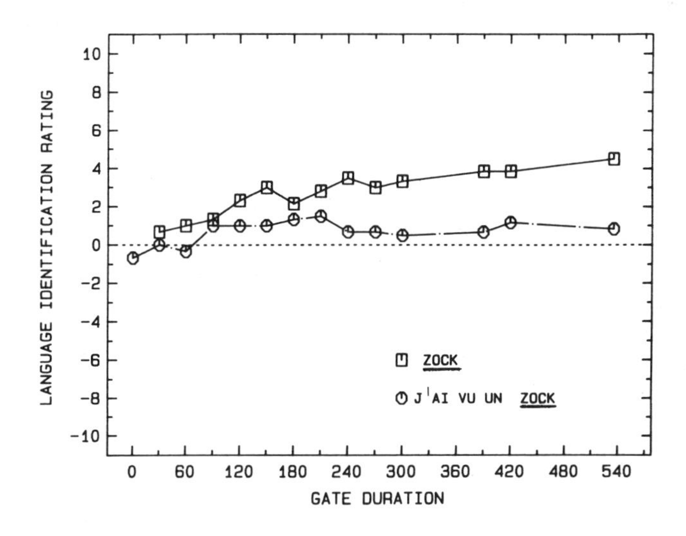


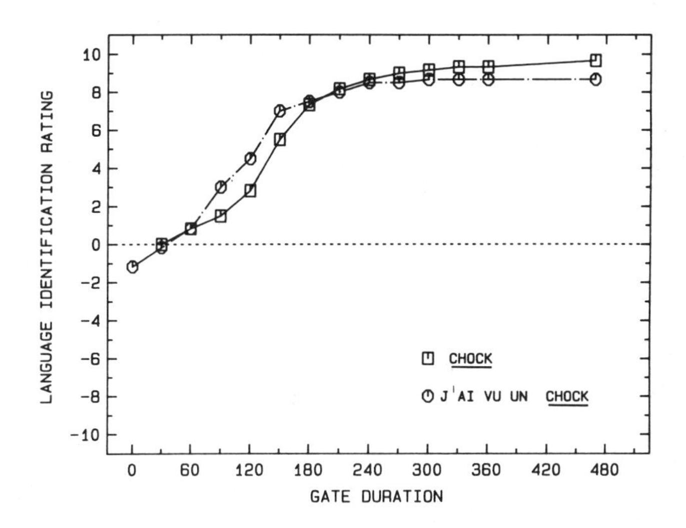


FIG. 7.6. The language identification curves of two English code-switched nonsense words: ''zock'' (top part) and ''chock'' (bottom part). Each word was presented in isolation (squares) and preceded by the French carrier sentence (J'ai vu un). Each point is the mean of six ratings, one by each of six subjects.

a phoneme that is specifically English. Given this difference, we expect the identification curves to be quite distinct and resemble in certain ways the bive, bainve examples discussed above.

In the top part of the figure we note that "zock" in isolation is identified progressively as English, but because we are dealing with a code-switch, the final rating is not as high as might be found with a monolingual nonword. In the context condition, the identification ratings are much lower than the ones obtained for the word presented in isolation. The factors that affected "bive" in context are also at work here (base language expectation, saliency effect, assimilation factor) but this time the English characteristics of "zock" are strong enough to avoid a cross-over into French.

In the bottom part of the figure, we note a very different pattern for "chock." The initial sound /č/ is so English that, both in isolation and in context, subjects identify the correct language of the nonword very quickly. It is interesting to note once again the base language expectation effect at the 0 msec gate in the context condition and the slight contrast effect at gates 4, 5 and 6 in the same condition.

It would appear, therefore, that a number of factors may affect the bilingual's ability to identify the language of a code-switch or, for those who defend direct access, his or her ability to identify the phonemes and syllables of the item. We have shown that the language specificity of the sounds or sound sequences contained in a switch will be a factor in how well and how soon the appropriate language is identified. We have also shown that the listener's base language expectation, the saliency effect created by the preceding language on the phonetic traits of the boundary, as well as the assimilation and contrast characteristics of the preceding language context, all appear to affect language identification. We are presently examining these and other factors in more depth, as well as studying how they interact with one another when a language decision is made.

## The Categorization of Language

In our attempt to investigate the nature of the language categorization process (assuming, as we have all along, that such a process exists and is vital in mixed language processing), we have also been employing traditional speech perception paradigms, namely the identification and discrimination tasks. Unlike the gating task which presents a stimulus from left to right in segments of increasing duration, identification and discrimination tasks use a series of complete syllables which range from one prototypical syllable to another with "hybrid" stimuli in between.

A number of categorical perception studies employing identification and discrimination have been reported in the bilingualism literature (Caramazza, Yeni-Komshian, Zurif & Carbone, 1973; Elman, Diehl & Buchwald, 1977; Williams, 1980; Obler, 1982, among others). The aim of these studies was to determine whether, in the appropriate language set, bilinguals would reflect the identification cross-over points and the discrimination peaks obtained with respective monolingual groups listening to stimuli ranging from one prototypical syllable to another.

Rather than confirming that bilinguals can indeed categorize speech stimuli within a language, we are interested here in examining the nature of the categorization of items which range across two languages. We are especially curious in seeing how syllables and words are categorized as belonging to one or the other language when these items are phonetically similar or different in the two languages, or when they have been brought into the base language by means of code-switching.

Before investigating these aspects, however, we first need to determine whether between-language categorization shares the same properties as within-language categorization. The specific questions we ask, therefore, are: if presented with stimuli taken from a computer generated English-French continuum, (English /ebe/ to French /ebe/, for example), do bilinguals perceive these stimuli as belonging to one language or the other with an abrupt perceptual break of the type that is found with a within-language continuum? Will their responses divide the acoustic-phonetic continuum into two sharply defined categories? Can bilinguals discriminate better between stimuli which lie on opposite sides of the language boundary than they can between stimuli which fall within the same boundary? Does the discrimination function have a sharp inflection which corresponds in position to the abrupt shift in the identification (labeling) responses?

In order to answer these questions, Grosjean and Miller (in progress) have been experimenting with a French/re/-English /re/ continuum. A French/English bilingual with no noticeable accent in his two languages produced the two prototypical endpoints. A continuum was then constructed by replacing segments of the French /re/ with segments of the English /re/. The first stimulus was the unaltered French /re/ (duration 463 msec). The second stimulus began with 20 msec of the English /re/ and continued with 443 msec of the French /re/. This hybrid stimulus was made by digitizing the prototypical /re/'s, splicing them into parts and then joining these parts by means of a computer waveform editing program. (Care was taken not to create any spectral discontinuity.) The third stimulus contained 40 msec of the English /re/ and 423 msec of French /re/, and so on until the twelfth (and last) stimulus contained 220 msec of English /re/ and 243 msec of French /re/. The identification test tape contained five blocks of the twelve stimuli presented randomly. For the discrimination experiment, a standard ABX task was used and the discrimination tape contained 10 two-step triads. Thus, for example, in the first triad, stimulus 1 was paired with stimulus 3, the third item of the pair being either stimulus 1 or 3. In the second triad, stimulus 2 was paired with stimulus 4, the third item being 2 or 4, etc. These triads were recorded in two permutations (ABA or BAB), six times in all.

Five French/English bilingual subjects whose first language was French and who had lived in the United States for at least 5 years, served as subjects. In the identification experiment they were asked in French to listen to each stimulus and to indicate whether they heard "re" or "ré" (they circled the appropriate item on a response sheet). In the discrimination experiment, the same subjects were asked to listen to each triad and to indicate, by writing down a 1 or a 2, whether the third stimulus was the same as the first or the second.

The results obtained in the two experiments are presented in Fig. 7.7. In the top graph, the percent French /re/ responses are plotted as a function of the 12 stimuli presented. The resulting identification function clearly shows that the subjects did not perceive the French /re/ as gradually becoming English. Instead, they divided the acoustic-phonetic continuum into two sharply defined categories: French /re/'s and English /re/'ș. The first six stimuli were perceived as French (the first five at or close to the 100% level) whereas the remaining stimuli were perceived as English, even though they contained large amounts of the French /re/ (as much as 343 msec in the 7th stimulus, for example). What is interesting is that the cross-over point corresponds to the moment at which the laryngeal frication that is so characteristic of the French /r/ finally disappears.

Converging evidence for the perceptual break obtained in the identification experiment is provided by the results of the discrimination task presented in the bottom part of Fig. 7.7. As can be seen, subjects show very poor discrimination between stimuli which fell to one side of the perceptual boundary, but very good discrimination between stimuli from opposite sides of the boundary. This is shown by the inflection in the discrimination function at the point where there is an abrupt shift in the identification responses. Indeed, the highest discrimination score was obtained with the triad that contained stimuli 5 and 7, precisely those stimuli closest to, but on either side of, the perceptual boundary.

Similar identification and discrimination results were obtained with a continuum whose end points are far more similar to one another: French /de/ and English /de/. A 16-step continuum was constructed by first cutting back the prevoicing of the French /de/ in steps of 35 msec (first 4 stimuli) and thus shortening the /de/. Then, as in the /re/-/re/ study, the French /de/ was gradually replaced with the English /de/ (stimuli 5 to 12; steps of 35 msec) and finally, when the replacement was complete, the English /de/ was lenthened to its original length. (The hybrid stimuli were thus shorter than either the French or English endpoints.) Three bilingual subjects were asked to identify the 16 stimuli presented randomly in five presentation blocks and to discriminate 4 pairs of stimuli in an ABX task with two-step comparisons. Three pairs were made up of stimuli from within a perceptual category (stimuli 1-3, 8-10, 14-16) and one pair was constructed with stimuli from either side of the boundary (stimuli 7 and 9).

As can be seen in Fig. 7.8, a clear perceptual boundary was obtained from the identification data, and this despite the close similarity of English /de/ and French /de/. This perceptual break was confirmed by the discrimination data (represented by circles in the figure): there was poor discrimination between stimuli that fell within the same boundary but excellent discrimination between stimuli from opposite sides of the language boundary (pair 7-9).

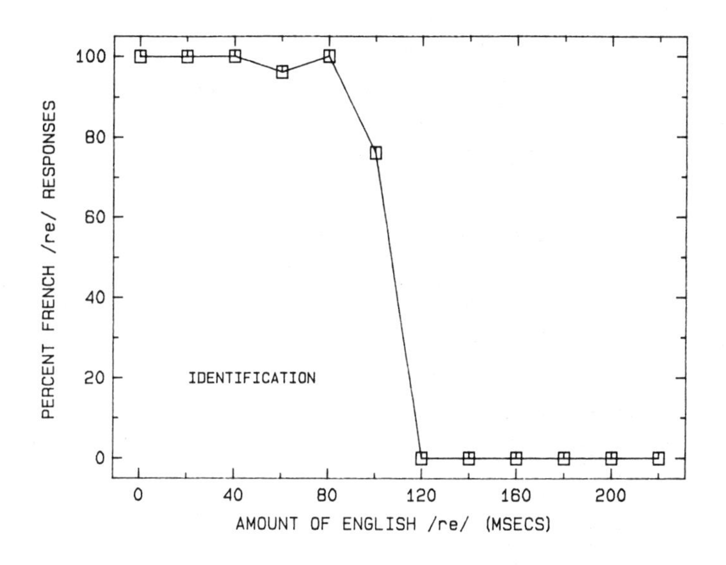


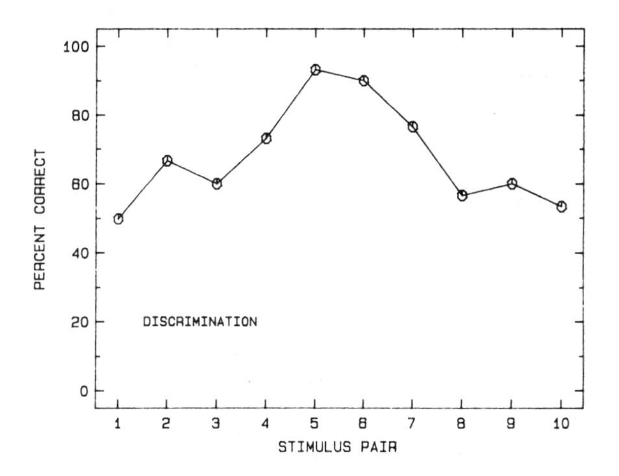


FIG. 7.7. Group identification and discrimination performance on the French /re/-English/re/ continuum. The top graph presents the percent French /re/ responses as a function of the amount of English /re/ in the stimuli. Each point is based on 25 responses, five by each of five subjects. The bottom graph presents the percent correct discrimination responses as a function of the stimulus pair presented. Each point is based on 30 responses, six by each of five subjects.

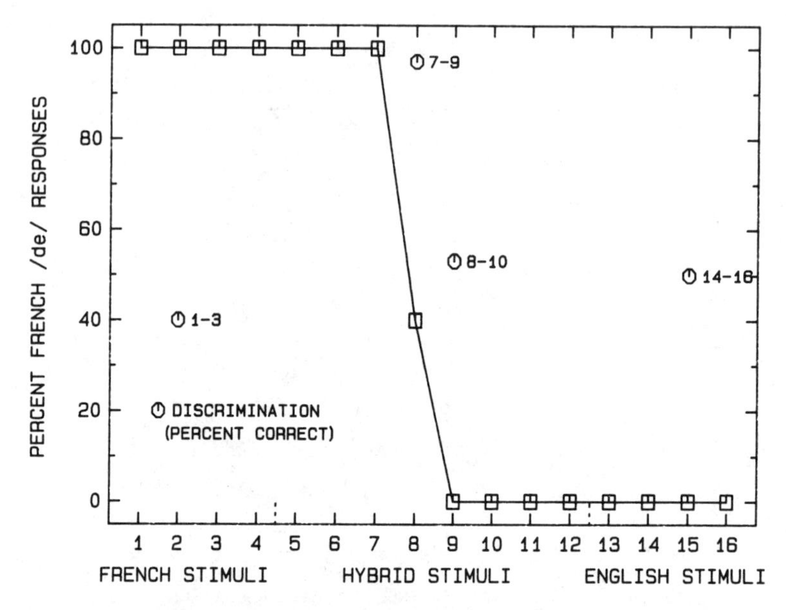


FIG. 7.8 Group identification on the French /de/-English/de/ continuum: percent French/de/ responses as a function of the 16 stimuli presented. Each square is based on 15 responses, five by each of three subjects. The discrimination performance obtained for 4 pairs of stimuli are also given (circles marked with the pair in question). For these, the Y axis represents percent correct. Each discrimination point is based on 30 responses, ten by each of three subjects.

Both sets of results show that between-language categorization is very similar in nature to within-language categorization. Just as a monolingual listener quickly loses the precise acoustic characteristics of a particular phoneme and retains its phonetic label, so too the bilingual listener quickly loses the acoustic characteristics of the particular sound and retains, we hypothesize, its language and phonetic labels. Our results are consistent with—but do not yet prove—the hypothesis that bilinguals categorize the speech input as belonging to one language or the other. Nor do they indicate at what point in the speech perception process language categorization takes place: prior to phoneme and syllable identification, along with this identification, or after it. As we suggested above, other tasks will have to be used to investigate this particular point.

Having shown that between language categorization shares many similarities with within language categorization, we can now investigate the identification and discrimination of code-switched syllables and words in and out of context. We wish to answer questions such as: Will the code-switched English /re/ spliced out of the sentence ''J'ai entendu un re'' be perceived as clearly as the monolingual /re/ in ''I heard a re''? Will the perceptual boundary obtained from a continuum where the two end points (English /re/ and French /re/) are code-switched be similar to that obtained with monolingual end-points? More interestingly, will the perceptual boundary shift when the code-switched stimuli are presented in context (''J'ai entendu un re; I heard a ré) instead of in isolation? Based on our gating results, we expect rather large boundary shifts when code-switched items are presented in context: more stimuli will be categorized as French when the carrier sentence is French and more will be perceived as English when the preceding sentence is English, although the phonetic characteristics of the stimuli themselves will also affect the final outcome (see the assimilation and contrast effects in the preceding section).

To conclude, we expect that a speech perception approach to mixed language processing will not only help us better understand the process by which the acoustic signal is mapped onto the appropriate phonetic percepts, but will also contribute valuable information to how this first stage of mixed language decoding is integrated into the word recognition process. It is this latter process that we will examine now.

## THE LEXICAL ACCESS OF CODE-SWITCHES AND BORROWINGS

An important aspect of language processing and one that has received considerable attention in recent years, is lexical access or word recognition. Researchers have sought to study the factors which affect word recognition, the importance of bottom-up and top-down information, and the role played by lexical access during speech perception and comprehension (see for example, Forster, 1976; Foss & Blank, 1980; Grosjean, 1980; Marslen-Wilson & Welsh, 1978). Word recognition in bilinguals has received much less attention, especially when it concerns the access of code-switches and borrowings. The literature most closely related to this question dates back a number of years and investigates the perception and production of often ungrammatical language mixtures, not code-switches. For example, Kolers (1966) haphazardly mixed English and French passages and found that bilinguals read them more slowly than monolingual passages. Macnamara and Kushnir (1971) asked bilinguals to judge the truth value of randomly mixed-language sentences and found that the reaction times to these sentences were slower than to monolingual sentences. But these and other studies have been criticized on at least two counts: many of the language mixtures were ungrammatical in that they violated both monolingual rules and code-switching constraints (no bilingual would ever have uttered them) and the bilingual subjects were never put in a bilingual speech mode (the experimenters and the experimental settings were usually monolingual). Since then a number of studies (Neufeld, 1973; Pandi, 1975; Wakefield, Bradley, Yom, & Doughtie, 1975) have controlled these factors, at least in part.

In a recent study (Soares & Grosjean, 1984), we investigated the lexical access of base language words and code-switched words by using the Phoneme Triggered Lexical Decision (PTLD) task (Blank, 1980). English/Portuguese bilingual subjects were presented with sentences and were asked to listen for a word or a nonword in them which began with a prespecified phoneme. Once this word (or nonword) was found, the subjects had to indicate as quickly as possible whether the item was a real word or not. Examples of the English, Portuguese, and code-switched sentences presented are as follows (note that target words are capitalized and code-switched words are underlined):

| | |
|---|---|
| English: | After lunch, the children asked for a piece of CAKE for dessert |
| Portuguese: | Depois do almoço os miudos pediram uma fatia de BOLO para sobremesa |
| Code-switched: | Depois do lunch os miudos pediram uma fatia de CAKE para dessert |

English monolingual subjects were run on the English sentences only, whereas the bilingual subjects were tested on three separate sets of sentences (English, Portuguese and code-switched). Before each set, every effort was made to induce the appropriate speech mode: English, Portuguese or bilingual.

Two interesting results emerged from this study. The first was that although bilinguals accessed real words in English as quickly as English monolinguals, they were substantially slower at responding to nonwords. This finding provides additional evidence for the residual activation of the other language when the bilingual is in a monolingual speech mode (Altenberg & Cairns, 1983; Obler & Albert, 1978; Preston & Lambert, 1969). We hypothesized that a nonword triggers a complete search of the base language lexicon which is then immediately followed by a (partial?) search of the other lexicon, and this before the stimulus is classified as a nonword. Hence the longer reaction times.

The second finding of interest was that bilinguals took longer to access code-switched words in the bilingual speech mode than they did base language words in the monolingual speech mode. To account for this, we suggested that bilinguals always search the base language lexicon first, whatever the speech mode they are in, monolingual or bilingual. This base language strategy causes delay in the access of code-switched words because these words belong to the other lexicon and are, therefore, only accessed after the base lexicon has been searched.

We proposed this account before undertaking the language identification studies of the previous section and we are now in a position to suggest another explanation. The longer reaction times to code-switched words may not be due, after all, to a preliminary search of the wrong lexicon but rather to a delay in the decision as to which lexicon to search. This delay itself could be caused either by the language monitoring device having problems deciding on the appropriate language (see some reasons for this in the previous section) or, if one defends direct processing, by the problems encountered in the mapping between the acoustic wave and the appropriate percepts (phonemes, syllables). Such aspects as cross-language coarticulation, delay or absence of certain segmental and supra-segmental switches in the speaker's production, and factors such as the listener's base language expectation and his or her tendency to assimilate ambiguous items during the perception of code-switches, make us prefer an explanation that involves delay rather than one that requires a search of the base language lexicon first.

In the remaining part of this section we discuss some of the factors which may affect the recognition of code-switches and borrowings. Before doing so, however, we need to make a number of basic assumptions. The first is that the bilingual has two lexicons, each of which is linked to one conceptual store (Paradis, 1978, 1980a, and 1980b). The second is that code-switched words are stored, and therefore have to be accessed, in their respective lexicons (English words in the English lexicon, French words in the French lexicon, etc). The third is that some partial phoneme or syllable specification must take place before word recognition can occur. And the fourth is that if there is delay in the processing of a code-switched or borrowed word at a particular point in time (as there may sometimes be) there will be recuperation at a later point in time. This must be the case if one acknowledges that many bilinguals communicate with one another by code-switching and borrowing and appear to do so at a normal rate of speech. The challenge for the psycholinguist is to isolate those strategies and heuristics used by bilinguals to process mixed speech and to explain how momentary delays are caught up so that the bilingual listener can stay with the speaker who is code-switching and borrowing.

## Factors Involved in the Recognition of Code-Switches

In Table 7.1 we present a nonexhaustive list of factors which may affect the recognition of code-switched words. Any one factor may account for the correct or incorrect, rapid or delayed, recognition of a code-switch but it is usually the combination of several factors which explains how a code-switch is perceived. These factors will also have quite different weightings attached to them depending on the linguistic and sociolinguistic context of the code-switch, but we have as yet no information concerning this point.

We have broken down the factors into two groups: those which pertain to words in general, whether they are code-switched or not (the general factors) and those which pertain to the actual code-switching situation (code-switching factors). General factors have been studied in great detail by psycholinguists interested in monolingual word recognition (see for example, Cole & Jakimik, 1978; Forster, 1976; Grosjean, 1980; Grosjean & Gee, in press; Marslen-Wilson & Welsh, 1978; Morton, 1969) and so we will not discuss them here. As for code-switching factors, little research has been conducted on them, although some pilot data point to the importance of a number of these. For example, our studies of language identification presented in the previous section showed the

TABLE 7.1
Factors that May Affect the Recognition of Code-Switched Words

A. General Factors

1. Properties of the word:
   a. frequency of occurrence: Does the word occur frequently or infrequently?
   b. separation point: How much of the word is needed to distinguish it from other words?
   c. prosodic saliency: Is the word stressed?

2. Preceding context:
   a. syntax: Can the word or its form class be predicted by the preceding syntax?
   b. semantics: Is the topic very constraining?
   c. prosody: Does the prosodic structure cue the listener to a particular type of word?

3. Listener's pragmatic and cognitive knowledge:
   a. how much does the listener know about the topic, the situation, the speaker, etc.

B. Code-Switching Factors

1. Psychosocial factors:
   a. speaker: Does the speaker often code-switch? What is his or her attitude towards code-switching?
   b. situation: Is the situation conducive to code-switching?
   c. listener: What is the listener's attitude towards code-switching? How strong is his or her base language expectation?

2. Linguistic variables:
   a. Semantics/Pragmatics: Is the topic conducive to code-switching?
   b. Syntax: Is a code-switch grammatically possible at this point or is a code-switch constraint being violated? Does the code-switch fit the subcategorization frame set up by the preceding context?
   c. Density of code-switching: Have there been many code-switches in the utterance so far?
   d. Language status of the word: Is the word specific to the code-switch language or does it have a near homophone in the base language?
   e. Phonotactic and phonetic characteristics of the word: Does the word contain phonemes or groups of phonemes that can only be part of the other language? Is the phonotactic configuration also possible in the base language? If not, how different is it? Where, in the word, is the critical phonetic evidence that signals a code-switch? How clear cut (complete) is the switch in terms of segmental and suprasegmental traits?

importance of the listener's base language expectation (factor B1c); some delay seemed to occur when the code-switched item was presented in its base language context. The consequence of this will be slower recognition of the code-switched word. We have also found some very indirect evidence that the listener's attitude to code-switching affects his or her recognition of code-switched words.

Among the questions relating to syntax, one that is of interest concerns the subcategorization frame set up by the preceding context (factor B2b). Using the gating paradigm, we presented the code-switch "bet" in the context "Il m'a demandé de bet pour lui'' (He asked me to bet for him) and asked bilinguals to guess the word (rather than the language) they heard. The results showed that 5 of the 6 subjects only needed the first 40% of the word to guess it correctly. This is because the structural context requires a verb in the infinitive form, there are very few verbs in French that start with /be/ (e.g., ''berner'' and ''bercer'') and the phonetic information at the early gates point towards an English word. Thus the combination of subcategorization information with bottom-up (acoustic-phonetic) information and the lack of possible candidates in French all contribute to speed up the recognition process of the code-switch.

As concerns the density of code-switching (factor B2c), we found in our lexical decision experiment (Soares & Grosjean, 1984) a −0.45 correlation between the density of code-switches before the target word and the time it took to access the code-switched word. From this we deduced that if a bilingual is in an environment where the frequency of code-switching is quite high, he or she will expect code-switches. This in turn will speed up the identification of the appropriate language and phonetic segments and hence the lexical access of the word.

The language status of the word itself will be a factor in how easily it will be recognized (factor B2d). If the word is specific to the code-switching language, then irrespective of the way it is pronounced, it will be accessed more rapidly than if it comes into conflict with a near homophone in the base language. Thus, all else being equal and in the appropriate context, we expect ''dime'' and ''dye'' to be accessed more rapidly in a French sentence than ''back'' or ''buck.'' The former have no close homophones in French whereas the latter do: ''bac,'' ''bock,'' etc.

The phonotactic and phonetic characteristics of the word itself will also be vital in speeding up or slowing down its recognition (factor B2e). If the word contains certain phonemes or groups of phonemes which can only be part of the other language, then segment identification and word recognition will be accelerated. For example, using the gating paradigm, we asked subjects to recognize ''check'' in the sentence ''Il m'a demandé de check pour lui'' (He asked me to check for him). Because /č/ is specifically an English phoneme, the subjects quickly identified the language of the word, and 5 of the 6 subjects guessed the word before its offset (something that is not always the case when monosyllabic words are recognized, be it by monolinguals or bilinguals). There will, of course, often be cases of code-switches that do not involve language specific sounds or groups of sounds, and then the question will be how different the total phonotactic configuration is from a possible base language configuration and how clear cut (or complete) the switch actually is (how strong the tinge from the base language). One can imagine, for example, the case of monosyllabic code-switches that are tinged by the base language at their onsets and offsets and where there is therefore little time for the phonetics of the other language to take hold, or the case of longer words that are pronounced with a base language "accent." In both cases, the recognition of the words will probably be delayed as the system strives to identify the language and the segments involved before initiating a lexical search.

## A Word About the Recognition of Borrowings

A major difference between code-switches and speech borrowings is that the latter are integrated phonologically and morphologically into the base language. Thus, in the sentence "Il faut MIXER cela" (We have to mix that), the borrowing "MIXER" that comes from the English "mix" is pronounced in French and is given the French infinitive ending (-er). The question which immediately comes to mind is the following: Are the underlying operations leading to the lexical access of a borrowing the same as those which permit the recognition of a code-switch?

We hypothesize that code-switched words will be easier to process because they usually retain phonetic cues which can be used by the language monitoring device to direct the signal to the appropriate processors and lexicon. Borrowings, on the other hand, will take longer to access because they do not have these cues and the search operations will be more complex. Those which come to mind are: search the base language lexicon; if no success, transform the phonetic configuration of the word to that of the other language; search the other lexicon, and finally access the word. Of course, this hypothesis rests on the assumption that unlike language borrowings, speech borrowings are not part of the base language lexicon and thus have to be accessed in the other lexicon.

Many of the factors which affect the access of code-switches (see Table 7.1) will probably also play a role in accessing borrowings (general factors, psychosocial factors, and many of the linguistic factors), and one can even imagine cases where some of these factors may render the access of a particular borrowing easier. We can hypothesize, for example, that if the borrowing has a phonotactic configuration specific to the other language, then listeners will recognize it quite easily despite the fact that the phonetics and the morphology of the word are those of the base language. To illustrate this point, we gated the borrowing "SCRATCHÉ" in the context "Il m'a SCRATCHÉ tout le dos" (He scratched my whole back), and asked six bilinguals to guess the word being presented after "Il m'a." As can be seen in the top part of Fig. 7.9, the subjects only needed a bit more than half of the world to isolate (guess) it and all except one felt perfectly confident about the word before its acoustic offset. At least two factors account for these results: first, "SCRATCHÉ" does not have a near homophone in French and second, it has an initial consonant cluster that is very rare in French (only 10 words in the Micro Robert dictionary start with /skr/ and only one is a verb: "scruter").

Thus, borrowings may at times be recognized as rapidly as code-switches, but we believe that in general this will not be the case as the acoustic-phonetic traits

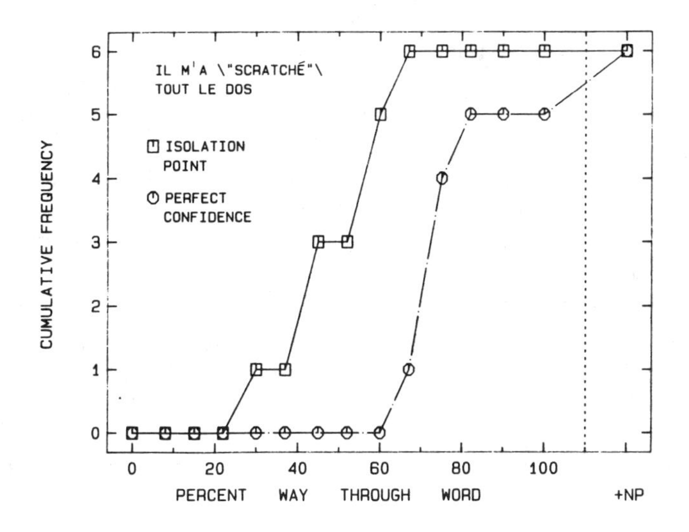


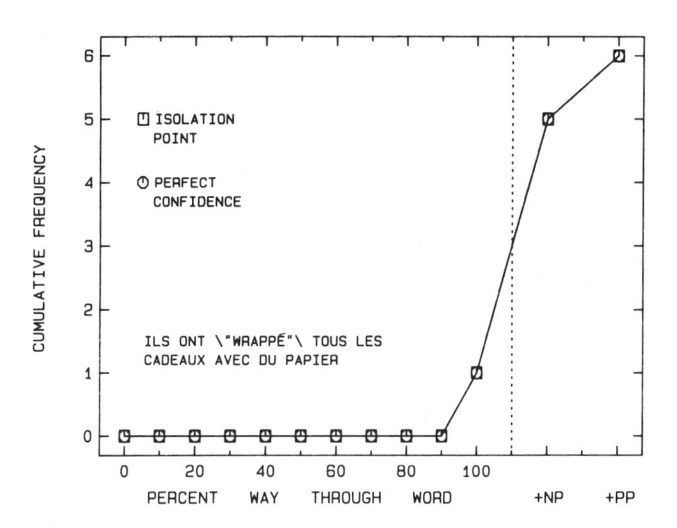


FIG. 7.9. Cumulative frequency of subjects isolating a word (squares) and giving their guess a perfect confidence rating (circles) as a function of the amount of the word presented (percent way through the word). Each point is the mean of six responses, one per subject. The top graph presents the functions for the borrowing "SCRATCHÉ." The last point was obtained by adding the NP "tout le dos" to the full version of the word. The bottom graph presents the functions for the borrowing "WRAPPÉ." The second to last point was obtained by adding the NP "tous les cadeaux" to the full version of the word; the last point by adding "tous les cadeaux avec du papier" to the same segment.

and the morphological information all point to the base language. An interesting additional problem arises when a borrowed word comes into conflict with a word which already exists in the base language, as for example: ''TIER'' (to tie) vs ''tailler'' (to sharpen); ''PEEKER'' (to peek) vs ''piquer'' (to prick, puncture, steal); etc. Unless the context is very constraining, the listener will go down a garden path and access the base language word instead of the borrowed word. An example of this is given in the bottom part of Figure 9. We presented bilingual subjects with the gated word ''WRAPPÉ'' (to wrap) preceded by the context ''Ils ont'' (they have). Only one subject out of six proposed ''wrappé'' instead of ''râpé'' (grated) before the word's offest. All the others needed the context after (''tous les cadeaux avec du papier'' = all the presents with paper) to change their guess and access ''wrappé.''

In conclusion, we can state that the lexical access of code-switched words and borrowings will be both variable and complex. Only further research involving the use of different paradigms, materials and procedures will allow us to better understand the operations which underlie the lexical access of these words. And in general, the challenge for the psycholinguist interested in studying mixed language processing will be to explain how communication in mixed language takes place so rapidly and so efficiently despite, as we have seen, some rather intricate operations and strategies.

## ACKNOWLEDGMENT

The preparation of this chapter was supported in part by grants from the National Science Foundation (BNS-8404565), the Department of Health and Human Services (RR 07143) and Northeastern University (RSDF). The authors would like to thank James Flege, Harlan Lane, Joanne Miller, Michel Paradis, Loraine Obler and Jyotsna Vaid for their insightful comments on a first draft of this chapter.

## REFERENCES

Altenberg, E., & Cairns, H. (1983). The effects of phonotactic constraints on lexical processing in bilingual and monolingual subjects. *Journal of Verbal Learning and Verbal Behavior 22,* 174–188.

Blair, D., & Harris, R. (1981). A test of interlingual interaction in comprehension by bilinguals. *Journal of Psycholinguistic Research 10,* 457–467.

Blank, M. (1980). Measuring lexical access during sentence processing. *Perception and Psychophysics 28,* 1–8.

Caramazza, A., Yeni-Komshian, G., Zurif, E., & Carbone, E. (1973). The acquisition of a new phonological contrast: The case of stop consonants in French-English bilinguals. *Journal of the Acoustical Society of America 54,* 421–428.

Cole, R., & Jakimik, J. (1978). A model of speech perception. In R. Cole (Ed.), *Perception and production of fluent speech.* Hillsdale, NJ: Lawrence Erlbaum Associates.

Delattre, P. (1965). *Comparing the phonetic features of English, French, German, and Spanish.* Heidelberg: Julius Groos Verlag.

Delattre, P. (1966). *Studies in French and comparative phonetics.* The Hague: Mouton.

Elman, J., Diehl, R., & Buchwald, S. (1977). Perceptual switching in bilinguals. *Journal of the Acoustical Society of America, 62,* 971–974.

Forster, K. (1976). Accessing the mental lexicon. In R. Wales & E. Walker (Eds.), *New approaches to language mechanism.* Amsterdam: North-Holland.

Foss, D., & Blank, M. (1980). Identifying the speech codes. *Cognitive Psychology 12,* 1–31.

Gal, S. (1979). *Language shift: Social determinants of linguistic change in bilingual Austria.* New York: Academic Press.

Grosjean, F. (1980). Spoken word recognition processes and the gating paradigm. *Perception and Psychophysics 28,* 267–283.

Grosjean, F. (1982). *Life with two languages: An introduction to bilingualism.* Cambridge, MA: Harvard University Press.

Grosjean, F. (in press). The bilingual as a competent but specific speaker-hearer. *The Journal of Multilingual and Multicultural Development.*

Grosjean, F., & Gee, J. (in press). Another view of spoken word recognition. *Cognition.*

Grosjean, F., & Miller, J. (in progress). *Language categorization in bilinguals.* Northeastern University, Boston, MA.

Gumperz, J. (1970). Verbal strategies in multilingual communication. In J. Alatis (Ed.), *Bilingualism and language contact.* Washington, DC: Georgetown University Press.

Haugen, E. (1969). *The Norwegian language in America: A study in bilingual behavior.* Bloomington: Indiana University Press.

Joshi, A. (1985). Processing of sentences with intra-sentential code-switching. In D. Dowty, L. Karttunen, & A. Zwicky (Eds.), *Natural language processing: Psychological, computational, and theoretical perspectives.* Cambridge: Cambridge University Press.

Kolers, P. (1966). Reading and talking bilingually. *American Journal of Psychology 3,* 357–376.

Lipski, J. (1978). Code-switching and the problem of bilingual competence. In M. Paradis (Ed.), *Aspects of bilingualism.* Columbia, SC: Hornbeam Press.

Lipski, J. (1982). Spanish-English language switching in speech and literature: Theories and models. *Bilingual Review/Revista Bilingüe 9,* 191–212.

Mack, M. (1984). Early bilinguals: How monolingual-like are they? In M. Paradis & Y. Lebrun (Eds.), *Early bilingualism and child development* (pp. 161–173). Lisse: Swets and Zeitlinger.

Macnamara, J. (1967). The bilingual's linguistic performance: A psychological overview. *Journal of Social Issues 23,* 59–77.

Macnamara, J., & Kushnir, S. (1971). Linguistic independence of bilinguals: the input switch. *Journal of Verbal Learning and Verbal Behavior 10,* 480–487.

Marslen-Wilson, W., & Welsh, A. (1978). Processing interactions and lexical access during word recognition in continuous speech. *Cognitive Psychology 10,* 29–63.

McClure, E. (1977). *Aspects of code-switching in the discourse of bilingual Mexican-American children* (Tech. Report No. 44). Urbana-Champaign: University of Illinois, Center for the Study of Reading.

Morton, J. (1969). Interaction of information in word recognition. *Psychological Review, 76,* 165–178.

Neufeld, G. (1973). The bilingual's lexical store. *Working Papers on Bilingualism, 1,* 35–65.

Obler, L. (1982). The parsimonious bilingual. In L. Obler & L. Menn (Eds.), *Exceptional language and linguistics.* New York: Academic Press.

Obler, L., & Albert, M. (1978). A monitor system for bilingual language processing. In M. Paradis (Ed.), *Aspects of bilingualism.* Columbia, SC: Hornbeam Press.

Pandi, G. (1975). *Understanding bilingual messages: The concept of the language switch.* Unpublished doctoral dissertation, University of California, San Francisco.

Paradis, M. (1978, December). *Bilingual linguistic memory: Neurolinguistic considerations*. Paper presented to the Linguistic Society of America, Boston.

Paradis, M. (1980a). Language and thought in bilinguals. In *The sixth LACUS forum*. Columbia, SC: Hornbeam Press.

Paradis, M. (1980b). Contributions of neurolinguistics to the theory of bilingualism. In *Applications of linguistic theory in the human sciences*. Department of Linguistics, Michigan State University.

Paradis, M. (1980c). The language switch in bilinguals: Psycholinguistic and neurolinguistic perspectives. In P. Nelde (Ed.), *Languages in contact and conflict*. Weisbaden: Franz Steiner Verlag.

Pfaff, C. (1979). Constraints on language mixing: intrasentential code-switching and borrowing in Spanish/English. *Language 55*, 291–318.

Poplack, S. (1978). Syntactic structure and social function of code-switching. *Working Papers: Centro de Estudios Puertorriqueños 2*, 1–32.

Posner, M., & Snyder, C. (1975). Attention and cognitive control. In Solso, R. (Ed.), *Information processing and cognition*. Hillsdale, NJ: Erlbaum Associates.

Preston, M., & Lambert, W. (1969). Interlingual interference in a bilingual version of the Stroop color word task. *Journal of Verbal Learning and Verbal Behavior 8*, 295–301.

Scotton, C., & Ury, W. (1977). Bilingual strategies: The social functions of code-switching. *Linguistics 193*, 5–20.

Soares, C., & Grosjean, F. (1984). Bilinguals in a monolingual and a bilingual speech mode: The effect on lexical access. *Memory & Cognition 12*, 380–386.

Sridhar, S., & Sridhar, K. (1980). The syntax and psycholinguistics of bilingual code-mixing. *Canadian Journal of Psychology/Revue Canadienne de Psychologie 34*, 407–416.

Timm, L. (1975). Spanish-English code-switching: el porque y how-not-to. *Romance Philology 28*, 473–482.

Valdés Fallis, G. (1976). Social interaction and code-switching patterns: a case study of Spanish/English alternation. In G. Keller, R. Teschner, & S. Viera (Eds.), *Bilingualism in the bicentennial and beyond*. New York: Bilingual Press/Editorial Bilingue.

Wakefield, J., Bradley, P., Yom, B., & Doughtie, E. (1975). Language switching and constituent structure. *Language and Speech 18*, 14–19.

Williams, L. (1980). Phonetic variation as a function of second-language learning. In G. Yeni-Komshian, J. Kavanaugh, & C. Ferguson (Eds.), *Child Phonology: Perception* (*vol. 2*). New York: Academic Press.

Woolford, E. (1983). Bilingual code-switching and syntactic theory. *Linguistic Inquiry 14*, 520–536.

# APPENDIX A

Premises that underlie our work on bilingualism:

1. Bilingualism is the regular use of two (or more) languages, and bilinguals are those people who need and use two (or more) languages in their everyday lives.

2. Bilinguals use their languages for different purposes and hence rarely have the same level of proficiency in the two languages.

3. Bilinguals develop skills in their languages to the extent needed by the environment. As the environment changes and the needs for particular skills also change, so will the bilingual's competence in these various language skills.

4. Bilinguals keep their two languages separate when speaking to monolinguals (at least attempt to do so), but may let them interact or mix them when speaking to other bilinguals who code-mix like them. This change of speech mode will have profound effects on the language processing mechanisms involved in production and perception.

5. Bilinguals who regularly mix their languages (code-switch or borrow) do so as naturally and as easily as bilinguals who stay within a monolingual mode. But they also do so differently, as two languages are involved simultaneously instead of one. The challenge for the psycholinguist is to isolate those operations, strategies and heuristics used by bilinguals to process language in the monolingual and in the bilingual speech modes.

6. Bilinguals should be studied as such and not always in comparison with monolinguals. Instead of being the sum of two monolinguals, bilinguals are competent "native speaker-hearers" of a different type; their knowledge of two languages makes up an integrated whole that cannot easily be decomposed into two separate parts. In addition, bilingual language processing will often be different from that of the monolingual: one language is rarely totally deactivated when speaking or listening to the other (even in completely monolingual situations) and in a mixed language mode, where the two languages interact simultaneously, bilinguals have to use specific operations and strategies rarely, if ever, needed by the monolingual.

If bilinguals must be compared to monolinguals, it should be at the level of communicative competence. The question that should be asked is the following: Can bilinguals, by means of one language, the other language, or the two languages together (depending on the situation, the topic, the listener, etc.) communicate as efficiently as monolinguals? It is our belief that because bilinguals, like monolinguals, are human communicators, they will develop a communicative competence that is equivalent to that of monolinguals, even if the linguistic form of that communication is often very different (as in the case of language mixing, for instance).

# II NEUROPSYCHOLOGICAL PERSPECTIVES

# 8 Aphasia in a Multilingual Society: A Preliminary Study

Prithika Chary
*Apollo Hospital, Madras*

Published cases of aphasia in speakers of two or more languages (see Albert & Obler, 1978; Paradis, 1977, 1983 for reviews) date back to the 19th century. One aspect of this literature that has attracted interest is the phenomenon of differential language impairment and/or language restitution of the bilingual or polyglot aphasic's languages.[1] Indeed, a major thrust of the early clinical literature was to determine which language recovered first in a polyglot aphasic and why. Various principles governing language recovery patterns, some of which were accorded the status of "laws," were put forth by neurologists studying polyglot aphasia in the 19th and early 20th century (see Pitres, 1895, Ribot, 1881). Unfortunately, no one principle appeared to be able to account for all of the recovery patterns observed.

Another aspect of the polyglot aphasia literature has recently been highlighted. Galloway (1981) examined published cases of polyglot aphasia for which information on handedness and side of lesion was reported. Her survey revealed a higher incidence of crossed aphasia, i.e., aphasia following right-hemisphere damage in right-handed polyglots (13%) than the corresponding estimate for right-handed unilinguals (2%); crossed aphasia in left-handers was 58% and 32% for polyglots and unilinguals, respectively (Galloway, 1981). The inference here is that the right hemisphere plays a greater role in normal language processing in bilinguals or polyglots than it does in unilinguals.

[1]The terms "polyglot" and "multilingual" are used interchangeably in this chapter.

At this point a number of caveats must be introduced. Although numerous cases of bilingual or polyglot aphasia have been documented, the number seen by any individual researcher is small. Vaid (1984) has pointed out that the ratio of single case studies to unselected group studies of aphasia in bilinguals or polyglots in the literature is on the order of 5 to 1. In view of the preponderance of selected case studies, it may be misleading to regard the phenomenon of crossed aphasia or the findings of selective language impairment or recovery as being representative of polyglot aphasics at large, for individual cases may well have been selected for publication because they were unusual and thereby interesting, rather than for their representativeness (see also Vaid & Genesee, 1980). Thus, it is difficult to arrive at generalizations about language organization and brain functioning in bilinguals on the basis of single, selected cases of polyglot aphasia. Studies based on unselected cases of bilingual or polyglot aphasics (see Gloning & Gloning, 1965; Nair & Virmani, 1973) suggest that differential recovery may be the exception rather than the rule.

Apart from the problem of a sampling bias, other problems have plagued the polyglot aphasia literature, including the lack of systematic neuropsychological and neurolinguistic testing of the patients, and inadequate information about the patients' premorbid language use. In several of the European cases, the languages used premorbidly by the patients belonged to the same language family, making it difficult to generalize to other language combinations. Furthermore, information about the functional domains in which each of the patient's languages had been used premorbidly was generally not reported or even solicited. Finally, nonaphasic bilingual or multilingual controls were rarely included in the language testing.

The present study sought to explore aphasia in bilinguals and multilinguals taking the above methodological issues into consideration. The population chosen for study namely, speakers of the Dravidian languages—Tamil, Telegu, Kannada, and Malayalam—in the four states of southern India, is one that has not previously received much attention in the aphasia literature (but see Rangamani, in preparation). It is not uncommon to find bi- and trilinguals in this region. A native speaker of one of these languages is likely to be proficient in at least one other Dravidian language, and, in one or both of the two official languages of India, Hindi, and English, both of which belong to the Indo-European family. Among literate individuals, in fact, English is often the language primarily used at school and at work. The type of multilingual language experience found in south India, then, may involve languages that differ widely in their structure, as well as in their domains of acquisition and use.

The present study presents some preliminary observations on aphasia in this multilingual setting. Instead of using a case study approach, patterns of language impairment and recovery were investigated in a random sample of patients with acquired speech disorders seen by the author at a neurology clinic in Madras.

## METHOD

*Subjects.* A group of 100 patients with acquired speech disorders and 40 healthy controls were tested. The control group consisted of medical student volunteers and patients with spinal lesions or neuromuscular disorders. The brain-damaged group were randomly selected from a neurology outpatient clinic of the Government General Hospital in Madras, using the following criteria: (1) all patients had developed normal speech prior to the onset of their illness producing the speech disorder. (2) No restrictions were imposed with regard to the patients' lesion etiology, sex, language experience, or age, although children below the age of 7 years were excluded as their language abilities were considered to be unstable. (3) Individuals with dementia, primary visual or hearing defects, developmental speech disorders or a history of epileptic seizures or speech problems due to drug therapy were excluded from the study.

*Incidence of Aphasia.* On the basis of an aphasia test battery developed by Chary (1980), 88 of the 100 patients were diagnosed as being aphasic and 12 had nonaphasic speech deficits, ranging from dysphonia (in four cases), dysarthria (in another four), stuttering (in one case), and three cases of deafness developing in childhood affecting speech following various neurological illnesses.

The aphasics ranged in age from 7 to 70 years and included 60 males and 28 females. Aetiology of the lesion was cerebrovascular in 46 of the 88 aphasics, head injury in 25, and space-occupying lesion in 17.

*Incidence of Multilingualism.* Both aphasic and control subjects were further classified as being unilingual or multilingual. The criterion adopted for multilinguality was production and comprehension of more than one language with near equivalent fluency. The ability to read and write in more than one language was not considered essential for classifying an individual as multilingual.

By this criterion, 31 (or 35.23%) of the 88 aphasics were multilingual; of these, 21 were men and 10 were women. (Of the 57 unilingual aphasics, 39 were

TABLE 8.1
Aetiology of Lesion and Language Experience

| | Multilingual Aphasics | | Monolingual Aphasics | |
|---|---|---|---|---|
| Type of Injury | #Ss | % Total | #Ss | % Total |
| Cerebrovascular | 15 | 48.39 | 31 | 54.38 |
| Head injury | 12 | 38.71 | 13 | 22.81 |
| Tumor | 4 | 12.90 | 13 | 22.81 |

TABLE 8.2
Age Range of Patients and Language Experience

| Age Range (Years) | Multilingual Aphasics No. Ss | Monolingual Aphasics No. Ss |
|---|---|---|
| 0 - 20 | 4 | 8 |
| 21 - 40 | 10 | 11 |
| 41 - 60 | 16 | 29 |
| 61 - 80 | 1 | 9 |

men and 18 were women.) Of the 40 healthy controls, 40% were multilingual, while 50% of the patients with a nonaphasic disorder were multilingual.

Table 8.1 presents a breakdown of lesion aetiology of the aphasics by language experience.

Table 8.2 provides a breakdown of the aphasics' age range by language experience.

*Range of Languages Known and Context of Language Acquisition.* With the exception of one Telegu-speaking monolingual, the remaining monolinguals were all Tamil speakers. Languages known by the bilingual controls, in decreasing order, were Tamil/English, English/Tamil, and English/Telegu.

In 22 of the 31 multilingual aphasics, either all or the first two languages were acquired in a common environment (or what has been referred to as compound bilingualism, see Ervin & Osgood, 1954) and in the remaining 9 patients they were acquired under different environmental conditions (or coordinate bilingualism). The language pairs spoken by individuals in the compound bilingual category were, in decreasing order, Tamil/English, Tamil/Telegu, and Telegu/English. Trilingual combinations were also seen, including Tamil/English/Hindustani, Tamil/Telegu/English, Kannada/English/Tamil, and Malayalam/English/Tamil; for some of the trilinguals, the first two languages were acquired in a compound manner and the third in a coordinate manner.

Among the coordinate bilinguals, language combinations in which patients were most proficient, in decreasing order, were Tamil/English, followed by Tamil/Telegu, and then Telegu/English.[2]

[2]Only the languages in which the patients considered themselves to be proficient prior to their brain injury have been mentioned above. Several patients had learned other languages as well, ranging from Sanskrit, Hindustani, Kannada, Malayalam, Urdu, Marathi, and, in two patients, French. These languages were acquired in a coordinate manner. As the patients and their relatives felt diffident about the patients' speaking ability in these languages, these languages were not included in the testing.

*Language of the Environment.* Languages used in the patients' larger environment (e.g., languages spoken by neighbors, servants, shopkeepers, etc.) are listed in Table 8.3, for the patients belonging to the compound bilingual subgroup.

*Incidence of Literacy.* The majority of the monolingual aphasics, 37 of the 57 patients (64.9%), were illiterate; an additional 3 were semi-literate, and 17 (29.8%) were literate. Among the multilingual aphasics, the incidence of literacy was much higher, being 61.3%; there were 5 semiliterates and 7 illiterates (22.5%). With two exceptions, fluency in reading and writing in multilinguals was greater in one of the patients' languages, although not necessarily in their mother tongue.

## Characteristics of Language Use

*Task-Related Use of Language.* Language use among the multilinguals was categorized into five functional domains: daily conversation, language used at work, language used for routine thinking, language used for prayer, and language used for mental arithmetic. See Table 8.4.

Information about the multilingual patients' premorbid language use was obtained either from the patients themselves, or from their relatives.

*Occurrence of Language Mixing.* The high incidence of code-switching and code-mixing characterizing bilingual communities such as those found in India (see Sridhar, 1978) makes it difficult to segregate the languages completely according to functional domain. Intrasentential language mixing is particularly prevalent among Tamil, Telegu, and English, and forms part of the day-to-day speech of this population. As such, instances of language mixing among aphasic

TABLE 8.3
Language of Environment as a Function of Language Background

| Language Background | No. of Ss | Language of Environment |
|---|---|---|
| Tamil/English; Telegu/English | 10 | Tamil/English; Telegu/English |
| Tamil/Telegu | 4 | Tamil |
| Telegu/Tamil/English | 4 | Telegu |
| Tamil/English/Hindustani | 1 | Tamil |
| Kannada/English/Tamil | 1 | Kannada |
| Malayalam/Tamil/English | 2 | Malayalam |

TABLE 8.4
Language Used for Various Functions by the 31 Multilingual Dysphasics as Elecited From the Patients, Their Relatives and on Recovery From Dysphasia

| Nature of Language Acquisition and Languages Known | No. of Patients | Mother Tongue | Languages Used | | | | |
|---|---|---|---|---|---|---|---|
| | | | Daily Conversation | At Work | To Think | To Pray | To Calculate |
| Compound Language Group (22) | | | | | | | |
| Tamil/English, English/Tamil and Telugu/English | 10 | Tamil or Telugu | Tamil or Telugu & English | English & Tamil | Tamil-6 English-4 | Tamil-8 English-2 | Tamil-9 English-1 |
| Tamil/Telugu | 4 | Tamil | Tamil | English & Tamil | Tamil | Tamil | Tamil |
| Telugu/Tamil/ English | 4 | Telugu | Telugu | English Tamil & Telugu | Telugu-3 Telugu & English-1 | Telugu | Telugu |
| Tamil/English/ Hindustani | 1 | Tamil | Tamil | English & Tamil | Tamil & English | Tamil | Tamil |
| Kannada/English/ Tamil | 1 | Kannada | Kannada | English & Tamil | Kannada | Kannada | Kannada |
| Malayalam/Tamil/ English | 2 | Malayalam | Malayalam | English & Tamil | Malayalam & English | Malayalam | Malayalam |
| Coordinate Language Group (9) | | | | | | | |
| Tamil/English & English/Tamil | 5 | Tamil | Tamil | English & Tamil | Tamil | Tamil | Tamil |
| Tamil/Telugu | 2 | Tamil | Tamil | English & Tamil | Tamil | Tamil | Tamil |
| Telugu/English | 1 | Telugu | Telugu | English | Telugu | Telugu | Telugu |
| Hindustani/Tamil/ English | 1 | Tamil | Hindustani | English & Tamil | Hindustani | Hindustani | Hindustani |

polyglots should not be regarded as abnormal, although certain forms of mixing may nevertheless signal disorders of language (see Perecman, 1984).

## NEUROPSYCHOLOGICAL ASSESSMENT

All subjects were administered a core aphasia test battery (Chary, 1980), adapted by the author from preexisting neuropsychological assessment measures (e.g., Benton & DeHamsher, 1976; Hécaen & Albert, 1978; Kaplan & Goodglass, 1975) with some additional tests devised to accommodate the particular characteristics (e.g., illiteracy, bi- and multilingualism) of the population under study. Stimulus cues were simple and easy to understand and were arranged as a base structure over which additional tests for literacy and multilingualism could be added.

### Initial Neurological Examination

At their initial visit, patients were tested for their mental state, hearing, vision and motor functions. Their stereognosis, touch localization, and two-point discrimination thresholds were assessed for both halves of the body, using identical and dissimilar objects.

### Measures of Handedness

Questionnaire and behavioral measures of overt and latent handedness, familial sinistrality, footedness, and eyedness were obtained.

### Evaluation of Language and Other Cognitive Functions

1. *Free conversation.* As a way of eliciting spontaneous conversation, patients were asked to give their name, occupation, age, address, and a short history of their illness. A four-point severity rating scale was used to assess their speech fluency, rhythm and melody, articulation, content, and occurrence of paraphasias or word-finding difficulty.
2. *Contextual conversation.* Subjects were asked questions pertaining to their orientation in time, place, and space.
3. *Auditory perception.* Subjects were first presented with nonverbal common sounds which they were to identify. They were then given pairs of nonsense words for repetition, and for same/different judgments. Similar sounds using different consonants (or vowels, or diphthongs) were repeated after every five or so nonsense words, e.g., Nan-lan, nen-mie, bac-thil, chok-jep, *nan*-tan. In the next phase of the test, the examiner spoke sentences varying in volume, tone,

inflection, rhythm, syntax and meaning. Subjects were to detect the changes. Multilinguals were tested in all their languages on this test.

4. *Repetition.* This test assessed the subjects' ability to repeat speech sounds, as in Item 3, as well as phonemes, morphemes, sentences, and short automatized material, such as prayers, nursery rhymes, and poems.

5. *Series recitation.* This subtest assessed the subjects' ability to recite the days of the week, the months of the year, the numbers of 1 to 10, and the alphabet (in the appropriate language).

6. *Simple speech formulation.* This subtest assessed the subjects' ability for abstract thought and expression. Patients were asked to provide synonyms and antonyms of target words, to form sentences, and to complete sentences.

7. *Complex speech formulation.* The first portion of this subtest was an extension of the preceding subtest. Subjects were first given pairs of sentences which differed only in one word, one phrase, or one idea and were asked to decide whether the sentences were same or different in their meaning. The next portion tested the patients' ability to comprehend a short passage.

Articulation, speech fluency, auditory comprehension, ability to formulate ideational concepts, understanding and use of grammar, and word finding difficulty were examined.

8. *Visual comprehension and perception.* This subtest measured object, picture, color, and form perception. Tests involving objects included naming objects, denoting their use, grouping them according to category, identifying named objects, and handling the objects meaningfully (e.g., demonstrating how to use a comb).

During picture description, special note was made of the following: mention of location, items, colors, shapes, depth and spatial relations; speech fluency, articulation, formulation and grammar; naming and paraphasia; visual inattention, unilateral neglect and affective response to the picture.

9. *Serial and sequential integration.* The inability to serially organize and shift from one motor activity to another was tested by giving subjects serially differing motor acts, e.g., put the watch on the table, take away the pencil, and turn over the card. Sequential integration was tested by asking subjects to identify and reproduce orally or tactually a set of varying rhythms tapped out by the examiner.

10. *Somatic orientation.* Somatic orientation was examined by asking the patients to identify various parts of their body, those of the examiner, and those in a picture. Right/left orientation, finger naming and identification, and questions regarding body image were included. The subjects' gestural behavior (praxis) was also observed.

11. *Spatial orientation and integration.* Subjects' orientation in space was tested by giving them instructions such as, "Place your hand above the table. Place your left hand to the right of the book."

12. *Numerical and topographical relationships.* Subjects were asked to draw a clock face, tell the time on it, read off the time on a clock face model presented by the examiner, and set the specified times requested on the model. Map relations were examined by showing the patient a map of the world and one of India and asking him/her to identify certain countries, states, etc. The ability to perform oral calculations was tested using objects, pictures, and coins and paper money. Problems of addition, subtraction, multiplication and division were also given.

13. *Drawing and copying.* Praxis for hand movements and for construction of geometrical figures by drawing, copying and matchstick construction was examined.

14. *Reading and writing.* Those subjects who, premorbidly, could read and write were tested in their reading of letters, words, numbers, sentences and narratives and in their written responses to the comprehension tests. The mechanics of writing, the ability for spontaneous writing, writing to dictation, written formulation, written confrontation naming, recall of written words, spelling and grammatical content were also examined.

### *Nonverbal Disorders*

Many tests were incorporated into the test battery described above to detect apraxia, agnosia and their influence on the speech disorder.

## Procedure

A short, screening format of the aphasia test battery was administered to all 100 patients at their first visit. When their neurological condition stabilized, the aphasics and the controls were given the longer version of the test. Follow-up was 6 and 12 weeks later, after the first detailed testing and included administration of the long version of the test in specific areas of deficit after first administration of the shortened version.

## Linguistic Analysis

At the phonological level, a distinction was made between articulatory and phonemic errors. Syntactic measures included examination of the patient's spontaneous and elicited speech for syntactic errors of omission or paragrammatic errors. The semantic content was examined for conceptual or denotative meaning and for perceptual or connotative meaning. An overall evaluation was then made in terms of whether the deficits were primarily in comprehension or in pro duction.

TABLE 8.5
Summary of Follow-up in Multilingual Disphasics

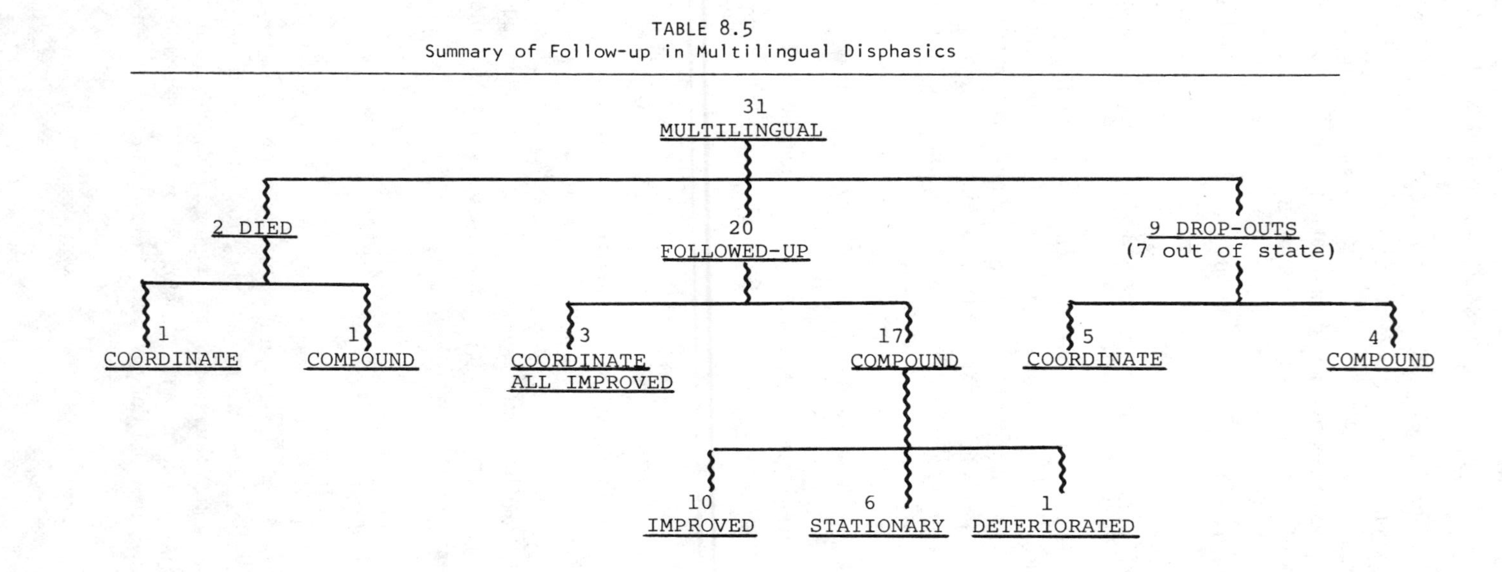

### Clinical Diagnosis

Final diagnosis of the nature of aphasia was undertaken after subjects had been tested on the long form of the aphasia battery. Diagnosis was done using a detailed coding scheme devised by the author (see Chary, 1980, for details). The diagnosis based on the neuropsychological assessment measures was then validated against other measures of lesion localization, including angiograms, CT scans, and exploratory surgery.

### Follow-up of Patients

Fifty-two of the aphasics (including 20 of the multilinguals) were followed up satisfactorily, 28 aphasics dropped out of the study (including 9 multilinguals), and 8 patients (including 2 multilinguals) died in the course of the study. (See Table 8.5.)

Although the figures were too small to permit statistical analysis, it was generally the case that literate individuals recovered better from aphasia than did illiterate individuals.

Of the 20 multilingual aphasics who were followed up, second language acquisition was of the compound type in 17 and of the coordinate type in 3. All 3 of the coordinate bilinguals improved, while only 10 of the 17 in the compound group improved. In view of the small sample sizes, it was not possible to test the notion that differential patterns of language recovery characterize coordinate bilinguals more so than compound bilinguals (Lambert & Fillenbaum, 1959).

## RESULTS

### Aphasia in Bilinguals: An Illustrative Case

Mr. S.R., 21 years old, doing his first year of a Master's degree in Zoology in an English medium of instruction college, was premorbidly equally fluent in Telegu and English. He could use the two languages interchangeably for all speech functions, although he was more fluent in written English than in written Telegu. His mother tongue was Telegu.

S.R. developed aphasia due to a fronto-parietal space-occupying lesion. On initial examination, his Telegu was restricted to occasional utterances, while his speech in English showed gross aphasic disturbances. He showed perseveration in speech and writing, poor speech content, paraphasia, a severe nominal aphasia, disordered spatial orientation, and numbness of the right half of the body, with no demonstrable sensory loss. On drawing a clock face, he showed unilateral neglect and perseveration even in number writing.

On follow-up 6 weeks later, after surgical removal of the left fronto-parietal tumor, there was no change in his speech abilities in English, but he acquired and used Telegu to express his needs. At the 12 week follow-up, however, there seemed to be no further improvement in Telegu, but his English had improved to a remarkable degree and he could manage moderately complex ideational materials and speech formulation tasks in English, while he showed no change from the initial level in his written language. He failed to perform the same tasks in Telegu, the use of which was limited to simple, need oriented sentences.

## Patterns of Language Impairment and/or Recovery

When considering the overall performance of the multilingual aphasics who were followed up, the following generalizations were supported.

1. The pattern of language recovery was dispersed widely in time, rate, level, degree and between languages known.

2. When task-oriented languages were considered, the following consistent patterns were noted.

(a) In the patients who improved, the language which recovered first and/or best was that used for routine thinking and calculations. This language was not necessarily the patient's mother tongue.

(b) Among patients who reported thinking mainly in one language (e.g., English) but who performed mental arithmetic in another language (e.g., Tamil) the language used for mental calculations was the one that recovered first.

(c) Among patients whose languages deteriorated over time, the language used for praying was retained the longest.

## Incidence of Crossed Aphasia

Seventy-nine (89.77%) of the 88 aphasics were right-handed, 9 (10.23%) were left-handed. The incidence of right and left-handedness for unilinguals and multilinguals in relation to the side of lesion (right, left, or bilateral) is summarized in Table 8.6.

TABLE 8.6
Incidence of Crossed Aphasia

| Number of Patients | Handedness | Side of Lesion: Left | Right | Diffuse/ Bilateral |
|---|---|---|---|---|
| 57 Monolinguals | Right | 34 | 5 | 13 |
| | Left | 2 | 1 | 2 |
| 31 Multilinguals | Right | 19 | 3 | 5 |
| | Left | 2 | 2 | 0 |

The incidence of crossed aphasia was fairly high, in both unilinguals and multilinguals, with the multilinguals showing a slightly higher incidence. Thus, the percentage of right-handed multilingual aphasics with a right-sided lesion was 13.63%, relative to 12.82% in unilingual right-handed aphasics; the corresponding figures for left-handed multilingual and unilingual aphasics were 50% and 33.3%.

## DISCUSSION

There are two noteworthy findings from the present study. The first concerns patterns of language impairment and/or recovery in polyglot aphasia. The second concerns the role of the right hemisphere in normal language processing.

With regard to the issue of differential impairment and/or recovery, no support was obtained for the notion that, in cases of selective recovery, it is the patient's mother tongue that recovers first, or that is least impaired (Ribot, 1881), nor was support found for the importance of language proficiency, viewed globally, (cf. Pitres, 1895). Rather, what seemed to be important was the domain in which the subjects were proficient in each language. Specifically, evidence was found that the languages in which routine thinking, mental calculations, and praying occur were the ones that were most resistant to the debilitating effects of brain injury. It is interesting that these functions are all highly overlearned, acquired fairly early in life, and used frequently over the course of many years. It is also perhaps not coincidental that these types of functions, among others, have been suggested to involve the right hemisphere. Indeed, one may speculate that the reason these functions were the most resistant to impairment in the present study was because they called on the processing of the non-lesioned right hemisphere.

The other interesting finding of the present study revolves around the incidence of aphasia produced by damage to the right hemisphere. Crossed aphasia was found among a sizable percentage of the aphasics, both in unilinguals and multilinguals. This could not be attributed to an overrepresentation of females in the sample, as there were about the same number of males and females. Greater right hemisphere involvement in (premorbid) language functioning in polyglots than in monolinguals has previously been claimed (see Galloway, 1981) on the basis of predominantly single case reports gleaned from the published literature. The nearly equivalent incidence of crossed aphasia among polyglots found in the present study, which was based on an unselected population, lends credence to Galloway's finding. However, the present study also found a remarkably high percentage of crossed aphasia among unilinguals (see Table 8.6). This finding suggests that the language capacities of the right hemisphere in unilinguals may have been underestimated in the literature at large, whether because right hemisphere-damaged patients are usually not tested for aphasia, or whether the range of measures used to assess language abilities in right-hemisphere damaged patients has not been sensitive enough (see Foldi, Ciconi, & Gardner, 1983; Ross & Mesulam, 1979).

The present work represents only the initial findings of a project that is currently in progress and which, in its final form, should provide much more detailed information about the role of language background, code-mixing, literacy, age, sex, and other parameters that are likely to influence brain organization of language among bi- and multilingual users in the Indian context. When considered with the results of ongoing work on bilingual aphasia in other language combinations (see Paradis, forthcoming) we should have a better understanding of what has been referred to as the "bilingual brain."

## ACKNOWLEDGMENTS

Portions of the research reported here are based on a doctoral dissertation submitted by the author to the University of Madras. The assistance of Jyotsna Vaid in the preparation of this chapter is gratefully acknowledged.

## REFERENCES

Albert, M., & Obler, L. (1978). *The bilingual brain.* New York: Academic Press.

Benton, A., & DeHamsher, K. (1976). *Multilingual aphasia examination.* Department of Neurology, University of Iowa Hospitals, Iowa City.

Chary, P. (1980). *Speech disorders in South Indians: Influence of multilingualism on dysphasias and a new dysphasia diagnosia and coding card system.* Unpublished doctoral dissertation, University of Madras.

Ervin, S., & Osgood, C. (1954). Second language learning and bilingualism. *Journal of Abnormal and Social Psychology, 49,* 139–146.

Foldi, N., Cicone, M., & Gardner, H. (1983). Pragmatic aspects of communication in brain-damaged patients. In S. Segalowitz (Ed.), *Language functions and brain organization* (pp. 51–86). New York: Academic Press.

Galloway, L. (1981). *Contribution of the right cerebral hemisphere to language and communication.* Unpublished doctoral dissertation, University of California, Los Angeles.

Gloning, I., & Gloning, K. (1965). Aphasien bei Polyglotten. Beitrag zur dynamik des sprachabbaus sowie zur Lokalisationsfrage dieser Storungen. *Wiener Zeitschrift fur Nervenheilkunde, 22,* 362–397.

Hécaen, H., & Albert, M. (1978). *Human neuropsychology.* New York: Wiley.

Kaplan, E., & Goodglass, H. (1975). *The assessment of aphasia and related disorders.* Philadelphia: Lea & Febiger.

Lambert, W. E., & Fillenbaum, S. (1959). A pilot study of aphasia among bilinguals. *Canadian Journal of Psychology, 13,* 28–34.

Nair, K., & Virmani, V. (1973). Speech and language disturbances in hemiplegics. *Indian Journal of Medical Research, 61,* 1395–1403.

Paradis, M. (1977). Bilingualism and aphasia. In H. Whitaker & H. A. Whitaker (Eds.), *Studies in neurolinguistics, 3.* New York: Academic Press.

Paradis, M. (1983). *Readings on aphasia in bilinguals and polyglots.* Montreal: Didier.

Paradis, M. (forthcoming). *Assessment of bilingual aphasia.* Hillsdale, NJ: Lawrence Erlbaum Associates.

Perecman, E. (1984). Spontaneous translation and language mixing in a polyglot aphasic. *Brain and Language, 23,* 43–63.

Pitres, A. (1895). Etude sur l'aphasie chez les polyglottes. *Revue de Medecine, 15,* 873–899.

Rangamani, G. (in preparation). *Aphasia and multilingualism.* Doctoral dissertation, All India Institute of Speech and Hearing, Mysore.

Ribot, T. (1881). *Diseases of memory: An essay in the positive psychology.* London: Paul.

Ross, E., & Mesulam, M. (1979). Dominant language functions of the right hemisphere? Prosody and emotional gesturing. *Archives of Neurology, 36,* 144–148.

Sridhar, S. N. (1978). On the functions of code-mixing in Kannada. *International Journal of the Sociology of Language, 16,* 109–118.

Vaid, J. (1984). Review of M. Paradis' *Readings on aphasia in bilinguals and polyglots. Journal of the History of the Behavioral Sciences.*

Vaid, J., & Genesee, F. (1980). Neuropsychological approaches to bilingualism: A critical review. *Canadian Journal of Psychology, 34,* 417–445.

# 9 Sentence Interpretation Strategies in Healthy and Aphasic Bilingual Adults

Beverly B. Wulfeck
Larry Juarez
Elizabeth A. Bates
Kerry Kilborn
*University of California, San Diego*

## Introduction

To anyone who has acquired a second language, and to anyone who moves at irregular intervals from one language to another, it is clear that bilingualism is a matter of degree. And it is just as clear, from research on polyglot aphasia, that languages break down in a ragged and uneven fashion, with recovery proceeding at different rates in each language, depending on a host of poorly understood circumstances. A psycholinguistic theory of bilingualism must account not only for the *presence* or *absence* of a given linguistic rule, but for the statistical nature of bilingual language processing under normal and abnormal conditions.

A large body of bilingual research has been directed at describing the nature of the bilingual's lexicon(s) (see Kolers, 1966; Lambert, 1978; Lopez, 1977; Macnamara, 1967; Paradis, 1978; Weinreich, 1968). Until recently (see Hummel, this volume; McDonald, 1984), research on sentence or text level processing in bilinguals has been relatively scarce.

This chapter focuses on the issue of modes of sentence processing in bilingual individuals. We will consider some preliminary findings from a sentence interpretation task carried out with bilingual Spanish-English speaking adults and one bilingual Spanish-English agrammatic aphasic. Because the sample size is small, our conclusions about bilingual processing are tentative at best. Nevertheless, this new work is grounded on a large body of crosslinguistic research by Elizabeth Bates and Brian MacWhinney and their colleagues, with normal adults and children, and several groups of aphasic patients, in a variety of structurally distinct language groups. This crosslinguistic research has led to the development of a probabilistic theory of grammatical processing called the "competition model" (see Bates & MacWhinney, 1982; MacWhinney, Bates, & Kliegl, 1984; and MacWhinney, Pleh, & Bates, 1985, for a complete description). Although this research has been carried out almost exclusively with monolinguals, some of the "design features" of the competition model are relevant here. For purposes of this chapter, the major features of the model are briefly described below.

### *The "Competition Model"*

The competition model is a theory of grammatical performance that seeks to account for the real-time processing involved at every level of discourse. It is a functionalist theory in the sense that the relationship between linguistic form and underlying meanings or intentions is stated as directly as possible. As such, the model postulates no *a priori* division of the language processor into separate modules, e.g., grammar versus semantics (Forster, 1979). Instead, the statistical relations that are observed between surface forms and underlying functions are stated directly in terms of a set of form-function mappings.

The competition model is a probabilistic theory in that the difference between statistical tendencies and obligatory rules is treated quantitatively rather than qualitatively. This means that particular relations between a surface form and associated functions can be expressed in terms of the strength or degree to which these form-function mappings interact. These form-function relations are not limited to one-to-one mappings since it is argued that a given form may map onto several functions and vice versa (Bates & MacWhinney, 1982; MacWhinney et al., 1984).

### *Crosslinguistic Research and the Competition Model*

Bates and MacWhinney (1982) consider the probabilistic aspect of the competition model to be an important element in their crosslinguistic research. Two languages may both employ a set of rules that are equally obligatory from the point of view of a competence model, yet the strength of the mappings implied by those rules may differ significantly between languages. Language differences emerge most clearly when rules are set into competition with one another (e.g., word order versus agreement), or when grammatical rules compete with semantic-pragmatic factors that are typically excluded from competence theories of grammar (e.g., word order versus animacy). Such competitions can reveal language-specific differences in the "strength" of cues to sentence meaning.

The concept of "cue strength" is closely related to the concept of "cue validity," which MacWhinney et al. (1984) define as the degree to which a given aspect of grammar can be relied upon to furnish useful information. For example, Spanish and English are both languages in which the default or unmarked order of sentence constituents is Subject-Verb-Object (SVO). However, in informal Spanish every logically possible combination of subject-verb-object ordering can be found. Insofar as SVO word order is an unreliable cue to sentence meaning, we would say that it is low in *cue validity* in Spanish. Compensatory sources of information (i.e., semantic and/or morphological cues) must be available in Spanish for adequate communication to take place. By contrast, in English we find very few violations of SVO order even in informal conversation. Hence, in English, SVO ordering is high in cue validity, and there is less need to attend to other sources of information. This notion of cue validity is based upon observations of how the language works in actual conversation. The corresponding notion of "cue strength" refers to the way that cue validity is represented in the mind of an individual listener. Cue strength is the mechanism that MacWhinney and Bates use to model the probabilistic nature of grammatical performance within and between languages.

Sentence interpretation studies based on the competition model have been conducted with both children and adults in languages including English, Italian, German, Hungarian, Serbo-Croatian, Dutch, and Chinese (Bates, McNew, MacWhinney, Devescovi, & Smith, 1982; Bates, MacWhinney, Caselli, Devescovi, Natale, & Venza, 1984; MacWhinney et al., 1984; MacWhinney et al., 1985; McDonald, 1984; Smith & Mimica, 1984). Comparisons have also been undertaken between the performance of normal and brain-damaged adults on this task (Bates, Friederici, Miceli, Smith, Wulfeck, & Zurif, 1984). The comprehension experiments involve the same basic format: Subjects are asked to interpret simple grammatical or semi-grammatical sentences, each containing two concrete nouns and a transitive action verb. Listeners are asked to indicate which of the two nouns refer to the agent, that is, the one who does the action; alternatively, they may be asked to act out each sentence using toys or small objects provided for this purpose.

Studies using the sentence interpretation paradigm are designed in such a way that competing and converging combinations of surface cues, which normally co-occur in natural discourse to indicate agent-object assignment, are incorporated into sentence stimuli. In English sentences, for example, the agent of a sentence is usually the first noun phrase (in preverbal position); the noun here agrees with the main verb in person and number, and is the most human and/or animate semantic element in the sentence. In the sentence *The dog is hitting the ball,* all three cues *converge* to indicate that the first noun is the agent. However, when both nouns agree with the verb and are both animate (e.g., *The dog is hitting the cow*), the only cue to role assignment is the canonical SVO (Subject-Verb-Object) word order. An example of a sentence in which the various cues are in competition with one another is *The pencils is hitting the dog*. Here, word order suggests that the first noun is subject, while animacy and agreement *conspire* to suggest that the second noun is subject.

By examining the degree to which specific cues contribute to sentence interpretation, in particular, which cues *win* in cases where there is a competition among the cues, a hierarchy of importance of cues to sentence meaning can be derived for each language. For example, in one sentence interpretation study

(MacWhinney et al., 1984), monolingual adult speakers of English, Italian, and German were asked to interpret sentences which were constructed by manipulating word order, agreement, stress, and animacy cues in all possible orthogonal combinations. Results indicated that word order cues are the most salient for speakers of English. In noncanonical word orders, they tend to choose the second noun as agent, indicating a marked bias for OSV and VOS interpretations. Italians demonstrate a different processing strategy: They rely primarily on agreement and then on animacy cues. When sentences are ambiguous with respect to both morphology and semantics, Italians still show a much smaller bias toward SVO than their English counterparts with no sign whatsoever of an OSV or VOS pattern. Finally, native German speakers rely on animacy and then on agreement cues in interpreting sentences, followed by a slight preference for the first noun on any sentence type. The point to note from this study is that performance on the sentence interpretation task reveals striking differences in sentence processing patterns among monolingual speakers of different languages.

These processing differences among monolingual adults are reflected in patterns of language acquisition by children, and language breakdown in adults. For example, there does not appear to be a single universal sequence by which children acquire grammatical cues. Rather, children tend to pick up cues to sentence meaning in order of their importance (i.e., cue validity) in adult language (Bates et al., 1982; MacWhinney et al., 1985). Similarly, there is no universal pattern of grammatical breakdown in brain-damaged adults. The strength of cues to meaning in aphasic listeners is at least partially determined by the strength of those cues in the language spoken prior to illness. In particular, Italian aphasics make more use of subject-verb agreement than English aphasics with a similar etiology; and English aphasics have a correspondingly greater control over the use of word order (Bates et al., 1984).

### *Sentence Interpretation and Bilingualism*

With the preceding as background, we now turn to issues of bilingualism. Because processing strategies differ for monolingual speakers of different languages, we wondered how bilingual individuals would perform in each of their languages. A pilot study by Bates and MacWhinney (1981) examined English sentence interpretation strategies of a small group of nonnative users of English. The single Italian subject and four of five German-English bilinguals in their study tended to apply their first language strategies while interpreting sentences in English, despite extensive exposure to English. Only one of the German-English bilinguals demonstrated processing strategies which resembled those of monolingual English speakers.

This pilot study suggests that at least two outcomes are possible in bilingual sentence interpretation tasks: transfer of first language strategies in the interpretation of sentences in the second language, or adoption of different strategies for the two languages corresponding to the strategies used by monolingual speakers of those languages. A third outcome is possible, though not found by Bates and MacWhinney (1981): namely, the use of a particular strategy by bilinguals for both their languages that is distinct from the strategies characterizing either group of monolinguals. In the present study, we sought to assess each of these possibilities in a larger and more homogeneous sample of brain-intact bilinguals and in brain-damaged bilinguals.

With aphasic bilinguals, the number of possible modes of performing the sentence interpretation task is much greater. We already alluded to data suggesting that language-specific patterns of sentence interpretation are preserved (although degraded) for aphasic monolingual speakers of English, Italian, and German (Bates et al., 1984). But in fact the situation is more complex. Some aspects of sentence processing (i.e., word order and semantics) seem to be preserved in a form that is much more similar to the processing strategies of a normal listener; while other aspects (i.e., morphology) seem to be more vulnerable to brain damage even though language-specific differences do remain. How would language-specific patterns in bilinguals interact with different clinical syndromes of aphasia?

One may find that whatever language deficits are present in the first language (L1) will be observed for the second language (L2). Conversely, if language differences can "hold their own" against brain damage, then we might expect that whatever differences are seen in the processing strategies for L1 and L2 with healthy bilinguals should be similar but less pronounced for aphasic bilinguals. In the former case the clinical syndrome dominates language, while in the latter, language processing patterns remain qualitatively similar to those patterns which were in operation before neurological insult.

In what follows, we first report findings from a sentence interpretation study with normal Spanish-English bilingual adults. Then, data from an aphasic bilingual adult are discussed.

## I. SENTENCE INTERPRETATION IN NORMAL BILINGUALS

### Method

*Subjects.* Subjects were 6 male and 6 female middle-class, right-handed, bilingual adults ranging in age from 20 to 42 years of age. All were native speakers of Spanish who were speaking English by 11-years-of-age. Half of the subjects were first exposed to English before 6-years-of-age and all subjects reported receiving formal training in English from the elementary school level. All subjects were either undergraduate or graduate level students attending college in the United States. At the time of testing, they reported using English and

Spanish to about the same degree. Ten of the bilinguals were of Mexican descent, the other two were from Ecuador and Uruguay.

*Stimuli.* The stimuli consisted of three sets of 54 test sentences in English and Spanish, constructed from a pool of six animate (animals) and 4 inanimate (common objects) nouns and nine transitive action verbs. The four variables manipulated were language (whether a sentence was presented in English or Spanish), word order sequences (NVN: noun-verb-noun, VNN: verb-noun-noun, or NNV: noun-noun-verb), animacy (animate first noun with animate second noun = AA, animate first noun with inanimate second noun = AI, or inanimate first noun with animate second noun = IA), and agreement between noun(s) and verb (ambiguous agreement = Ag0, first noun agrees with the verb = Ag1, or second noun agrees with the verb = Ag2). Each set of 54 test sentences (2 for each of the 27 Animacy × Agreement × Word-order combinations) was generated by randomly assigning two nouns and a verb from the pool. The sentences used the present progressive form of the verb for comparability with earlier studies (see MacWhinney, Bates, & Kliegl, 1984, for issues surrounding processing of different verb forms). Exact Spanish translations of the three sentence sets were then prepared by bilingual research assistants. Nouns, verbs, and sample sentences are given in Table 9.1.

*Procedure.* Each subject was tested individually by a bilingual research assistant in two sessions, one for each language. Half the subjects were tested in Spanish first and half in English. During a session only the tested language was

TABLE 9.1
Nouns and Verbs Used in Experimental Sentences

| Animate Nouns | | Inanimate Nouns | | Verbs | |
|---|---|---|---|---|---|
| Spanish | English | Spanish | English | Spanish | English |
| cebra | zebra | lapiz | pencil | comiendo | eating |
| puerco | pig | piedra | rock | acariciando | patting |
| vaca | cow | bloque | block | besando | kissing |
| oso | bear | pelota | ball | lambiendo | licking |
| burro | donkey | | | mordiendo | biting |
| elefante | elephant | | | pegando | hitting |
| | | | | empujando | pushing |
| | | | | agarrando | grabbing |
| | | | | oliendo | smelling |

Sample Sentences

The pencil is eating the donkey.
El lapiz esta comiendo el burro.

Is hitting the rock the elephants.
Esta pegando la piedra los elefantes.

The cow the blocks is kissing.
La vaca los bloques esta besando.

spoken by the research assistant and the subject was requested to do the same. Both sessions were conducted on the same day, separated by at least one hour.

A set of miniature toy animals (for animate nouns) and objects (for inanimate nouns), 5 cm high, accompanied the test sentences. The instructions and test sentences were read aloud to the subjects. For each test sentence, the experimenter selected the appropriate models, named them, and placed them on a table in front of the subject. Naming order and left-right orientation of the models were varied randomly. The experimenter then read the test sentence, and the subject indicated interpretation of the test sentence by picking up one of the models and moving it against the other. While healthy adults do not need the models to perform this task, we used them to allow for comparison with aphasics, for whom these models facilitate performance.

*Data Analysis.* Scoring of the dependent variable was based on the choice of one of the two nouns as the agent. For each test sentence, subjects were given a score of 1 for choosing an object corresponding to the first noun in the test sentence, a 0 for choosing the second noun, and on rare occasions, 0.5 for an ambiguous response or refusal. The values were summed for the two sentences belonging to each sentence type, and the resulting frequencies of first noun selection were entered as the raw data for subsequent statistical analysis. For purposes of discussion and comparison with other studies, we also translate these frequencies into a "percent choice of first noun" measure by multiplying the value by 50. This percent-first-choice measure can thus range from 0 (never selected first noun) to 100 (always selected first noun), with 50% indicating "chance performance."

## Results

As a first step, individual subjects' scores were examined for evidence of processing strategy differences; two very different patterns seemed to be present. One critical data point clearly differentiated the subjects: English NVN sentences in which the verb agreed with the *second* noun (Ag2) (collapsed across animacy). These NVN Ag2 sentences are, of course, the crucial "competition items" where canonical word-order points to the first noun as actor, while the agreement cue points to the second. In one group (N = 7), one subject chose the first noun 66% of the time, another 80%, and the rest more than 95% of the time. In the second group (N = 5), four subjects never chose the first noun, and a fifth chose the first noun only 8.3% of the time. Thus, subjects in the second group preferred the second noun. These differences were not related to any obvious subject variables such as language fluency, current patterns of language use, language or educational history, or to any particular properties of the experiment such as differences in sentence lists, language session orders, or experimenters. Nevertheless, it appears to be the case that the bilingual subjects were using different strategies for sentence interpretation. We examined this possibility further by using the group difference as a blocking variable in our statistical analyses.

The frequencies of first noun selection were entered in a 2 × 2 × 3 × 3 × 3 analysis of variance (Group × Language × Word Order × Animacy × Verb Agreement), with the Group factor as the between subject variable, and the remaining four factors as within subject variables. The analysis revealed significant two-way interactions of group by word order and group by verb agreement, as well as significant higher-order interactions involving group. These results show that the difference between groups that emerged from our examination of individual scores is statistically reliable. To simplify the remaining discussion, we will report separate analyses of variance for each of the two groups.

Table 9.2 summarizes the Language × Word Order × Animacy × Verb Agreement ANOVA for Group 1, the seven subjects who chose the first noun in English NVN Ag2 sentences. Table 9.3 gives the summary table for the corresponding ANOVA for Group 2, the five subjects who preferred the second noun. Following MacWhinney et al. (1984), these tables also show amounts of variance accounted for by significant effects using the $\omega^2$ statistic. This statistic indicates the magnitude as well as the reliability of the effects.

### *Word Order*

The mean percent choice of first noun for NVN, VNN, and NNV word orders is plotted for both groups in Fig. 9.1. There is clearly a strong tendency for Group 1 subjects to select the first noun on NVN sentences. There is also a slight tendency to choose the second noun on noncanonical VNN and NNV sentences, a "shadow" version of the robust VOS and OSV strategies that are repeatedly found for monolingual English listeners. However, this pattern holds for both

TABLE 9.2
ANOVA Summary for Group 1

| Effect | df | $MS_{error}$ | $F$ | $p$ | $\omega^2$ |
|---|---|---|---|---|---|
| Language (L) | 1,6 | 0.2809 | 1.038 | 0.347 | - |
| Animacy (AN) | 2,12 | 0.3032 | 28.901 | 0.000 | 5.62 |
| Agreement (AG) | 2,12 | 1.2569 | 10.486 | 0.002 | 7.90 |
| Word Order (WO) | 2,12 | 2.1908 | 25.368 | 0.000 | 35.27 |
| L x AN | 2,12 | 0.2329 | 1.951 | 0.185 | - |
| L x AG | 2,12 | 0.2812 | 3.055 | 0.085 | - |
| L x WO | 2,12 | 0.8176 | 2.890 | 0.094 | - |
| AN x WO | 4,24 | 0.1756 | 6.537 | 0.001 | 1.29 |
| AN x AG | 4,24 | 0.2760 | 1.826 | 0.157 | - |
| AG x WO | 4,24 | 0.1596 | 6.839 | 0.001 | 1.24 |
| L x AN x AG | 4,24 | 0.2070 | 1.774 | 0.167 | - |
| L x AN x WO | 4,24 | 0.1565 | 1.705 | 0.182 | - |
| L x AG x WO | 4,24 | 0.2122 | 1.187 | 0.342 | - |
| AN x AG x WO | 8,48 | 0.1925 | 1.992 | 0.068 | - |
| L x AG x AN x WO | 8,48 | 0.1975 | 0.932 | 0.499 | - |

TABLE 9.3
ANOVA Summary for Group 2

| Effect | df | $MS_{error}$ | $F$ | $p$ | $\omega^2$ |
|---|---|---|---|---|---|
| Language (L) | 1,4 | 0.1884 | 10.398 | 0.032 | 0.84 |
| Animacy (AN) | 2,8 | 0.1762 | 27.537 | 0.000 | 4.45 |
| Agreement (AG) | 2,8 | 0.3512 | 169.711 | 0.000 | 56.47 |
| Word Order (WO) | 2,8 | 0.4824 | 5.069 | 0.038 | 1.87 |
| L x AN | 2,8 | 0.2530 | 0.465 | 0.644 | - |
| L x AG | 2,8 | 0.3697 | 1.761 | 0.232 | - |
| L x WO | 2,8 | 0.0537 | 6.431 | 0.022 | 0.50 |
| AN x WO | 4,16 | 0.2984 | 1.679 | 0.204 | - |
| AN x AG | 4,16 | 0.2369 | 8.604 | 0.001 | 3.44 |
| AG x WO | 4,16 | 0.2796 | 3.649 | 0.027 | 1.47 |
| L x AN x AG | 4,16 | 0.1082 | 1.433 | 0.268 | - |
| L x AN x WO | 4,16 | 0.1558 | 0.933 | 0.470 | - |
| L x AG x WO | 4,16 | 0.3162 | 0.802 | 0.541 | - |
| AN x AG x WO | 8,32 | 0.1987 | 1.032 | 0.433 | - |
| L x AG x AN x WO | 8,32 | 0.2922 | 0.341 | 0.943 | - |

Spanish and English, since there were no significant main or interaction effects of language. From Table 9.2, the significant main effect for word order was substantial, accounting for 35% of the variance.

For Group 2, the word order effect was also significant, but accounted for only 1.87% of the variance. As shown in Fig. 9.1, there was some preference for first nouns in canonical NVN sentences. However, in general, word order only weakly influenced the performance of subjects in Group 2, and there is no sign at all of the noncanonical word order strategies reported for monolingual English speakers.

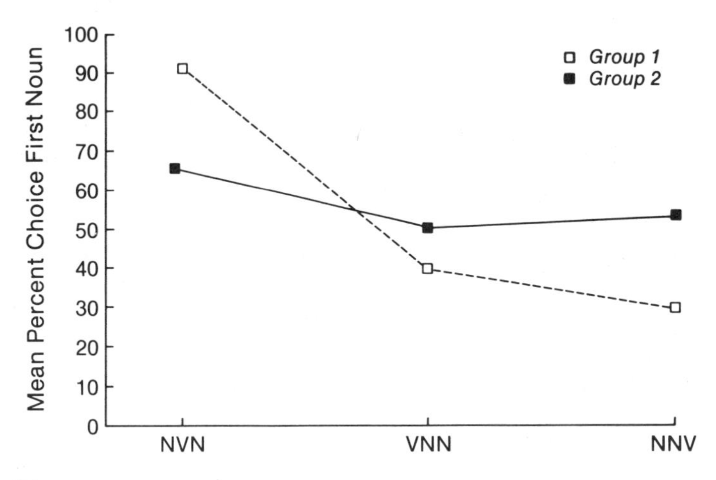


FIG. 9.1. Mean percent choice of first noun across word orders for Groups 1 and 2.

### *Agreement*

Figure 9.2 shows the mean percent choice of first noun for the three agreement conditions for the two groups. In Group 1, there was a moderate preference for the first noun when the verb agreed with it (Ag1), and similarly for the second noun (Ag2). When agreement was ambiguous (Ag0), there was no bias either way. From Table 9.2, this effect was significant, and accounted for a moderate 7.9% of the variance.

In Group 2, the situation is much more extreme. When the verb agreed with the first noun (Ag1), subjects chose the first noun 93% of the time. When it agreed with the second noun (Ag2), they chose the first noun only 12% of the time. When agreement was ambiguous (Ag0), there was some preference for the first noun. Table 9.3 shows the dramatic effect of agreement for Group 2; it accounted for over 56% of the variance.

As can be seen from Tables 9.2 and 9.3, there was a significant word order by agreement interaction in each group (accounting for just over 1% of the variance in both analyses). However, the interpretation of this interaction effect is different in the two groups (see Fig. 9.3). In Group 1, with noncanonical VNN and NNV constructions, agreement with the first noun weakens the second-noun bias. In Group 2, when agreement is ambiguous, there is a preference for the first noun in the canonical NVN word order.

### *Animacy*

The two groups also differed in the way that semantic cues are used. Figure 9.4 shows the percent choice of first noun for the three animacy conditions; both nouns animate (AA), first noun animate (AI), and second noun animate (IA). For

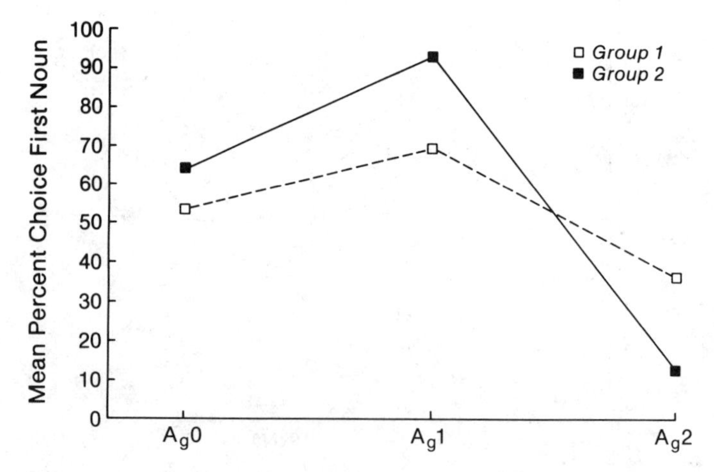


FIG. 9.2. Mean percent choice of first noun across agreement conditions for Groups 1 and 2.

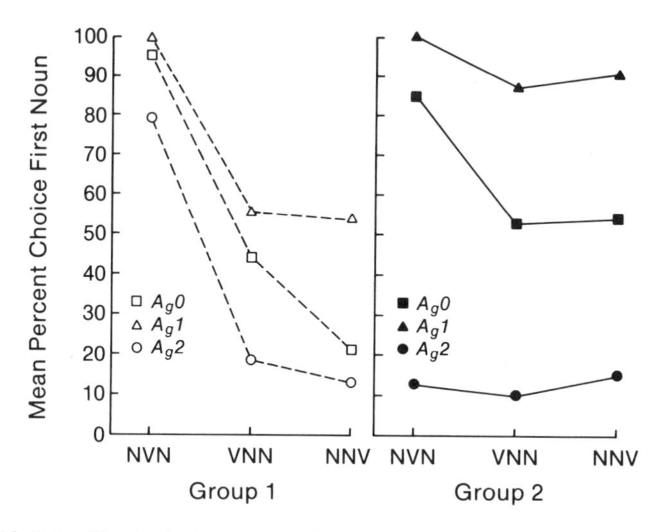


FIG. 9.3. Word order by agreement interaction for Groups 1 and 2.

both groups, there is a moderate preference for the first noun for the AI condition, and a slight preference for the second noun in the IA condition. When animacy is ambiguous (AA), there is essentially no preference. In Tables 9.2 and 9.3, the animacy variable accounted for around 5% of the variance for both groups.

However, in other respects the two groups handle animacy information quite differently. Figure 9.5 illustrates a significant word order × animacy interaction that occurred for Group 1. Briefly summarized, in this group animacy had its

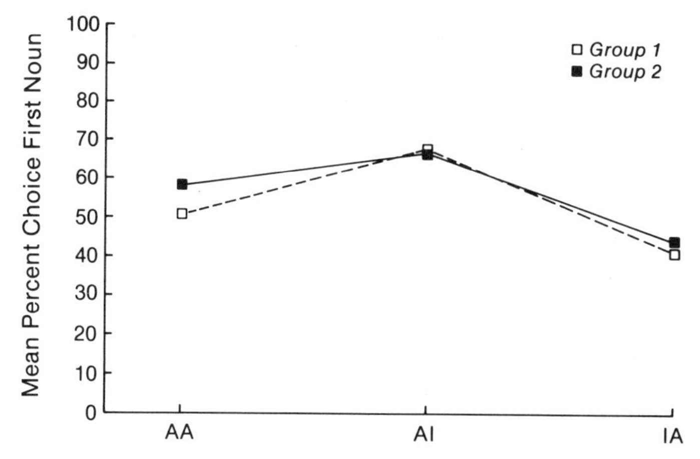


FIG. 9.4. Mean percent choice of first noun across animacy conditions for Groups 1 and 2.

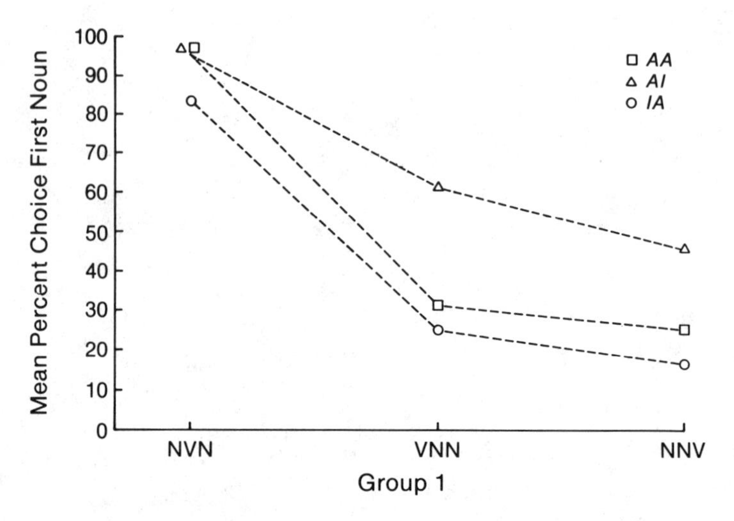


FIG. 9.5. Word order by animacy interaction for Group 1.

greatest effect in the two "weak" word order types (i.e., in competition and convergences with their VOS and OSV strategies). The semantic manipulation had very little impact on the "strong" SVO word order type for these listeners. For Group 2 subjects, animacy interacted with agreement rather than with word order (illustrated in Fig. 9.6). Specifically, animacy effects were seen primarily in sentences where agreement cues were ambiguous. In other words, for each of the two bilingual groups, animacy effects showed up when the respective "preferred cue" was missing.

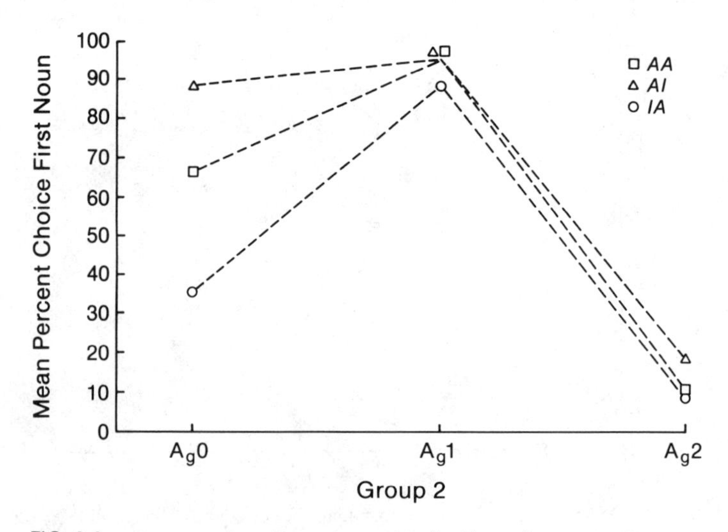


FIG. 9.6. Agreement by animacy interaction for Group 2.

### *Language*

As shown in Table 9.2, Group 1 showed no discernible language differences since neither the language effect nor interactions involving language reached significance.

In Group 2, there was a significant but very minor language effect: Subjects chose the first noun 60.7% of the time for Spanish sentences, versus 52.2% for English. This effect accounted for less than 0.8% of the variance. There was also a significant but very small interaction with word order: first nouns were chosen slightly more often for Spanish than English NNV constructions. This interaction accounted for less than 0.5% of the variance. It seems that when agreement and animacy are ambiguous, subjects showed a small bias toward first nouns in Spanish VNN and NNV constructions while remaining essentially random in English. It is at least *possible* that Group 2 bilinguals have a low level sensitivity to the English OSV and VOS strategies, sufficient to neutralize the small SOV and VSO biases that hold in Spanish.

## Discussion

A number of generalizations can be drawn from the findings of our study. First, there were individual differences in performance, suggesting differences in processing styles. One group (Group 1) of subjects used word order as their primary cue, with agreement as a secondary cue, followed by animacy, for both languages. Another group (Group 2) used agreement as their primary cue, then animacy, and then word order. The former group applied a richer set of cues for sentence interpretation, that is, they seemed to have adopted the strongest cue (word order) from their second language (English) and coordinated this with agreement, and to a lesser extent, animacy cues from Spanish. The latter group, while showing some sensitivity to word order cues, were most reliant on agreement followed by animacy cues.

A second generalization is that, within groups, subjects did *not* use different strategies for their two languages. This is evidenced by the absence of any language effects at all in Group 1. Moreover, while there was a slight language interaction in Group 2, it was with word order—the weakest cue for that group.

### *Comparisons with Monolingual Studies*

Our results reveal two distinct patterns of sentence processing, one or the other of which a bilingual seems to apply consistently to both languages. Also, as stated earlier, previous investigations show strong sentence processing differences across languages for monolingual subjects. The next question is whether the patterns observed here are similar to strategies monolingual speakers use in either English or Spanish, or whether they represent strategy amalgams unique to bilingual individuals.

Substantial information on monolingual English speakers is available. However, we have not yet obtained sufficient comparison data on this sentence processing task with monolingual Spanish speakers. This is due to the difficulty of locating such subjects in our highly bilingual United States/Mexico border community. Bilingual education, easy access to English-language radio, television, movies, and general reading materials, as well as the importance of "functional" English in the job market on both sides of the border, have contributed to our difficulties in finding Spanish monolinguals.

Italian and Spanish are structurally similar particularly along the relevant parameters present in our sentence processing task. For example, both languages have similar morphological systems, and both allow for greater word order variation than English. Fortunately, we have a substantial body of data from monolingual Italian speakers. We feel that the hierarchy of importance of processing cues in Italian might be comparable to that in Spanish.

Figure 9.7 shows word-order data and Fig. 9.8 shows agreement data obtained from monolingual English and Italian speakers (Bates et al., 1984). These data are similar to previous findings reported by Bates et al. (1982) and MacWhinney et al. (1984). The word order and agreement results from our bilingual groups are overlaid on the two figures.

In Fig. 9.7, our Group 1 subjects show in both their languages the same strong first-noun preference for NVN sentences observed in monolingual English speakers. However, they do not show as strong a second-noun bias on noncanonical word orders as has been observed for monolingual English speakers in several experiments (Bates et al., 1984; MacWhinney et al., 1984). It appears that English OSV and VOS biases are tempered by attention to agreement and animacy cues. This hypothesis is supported by the agreement results in Fig. 9.8. Here, our subjects show the same low level agreement sensitivity as do mono-

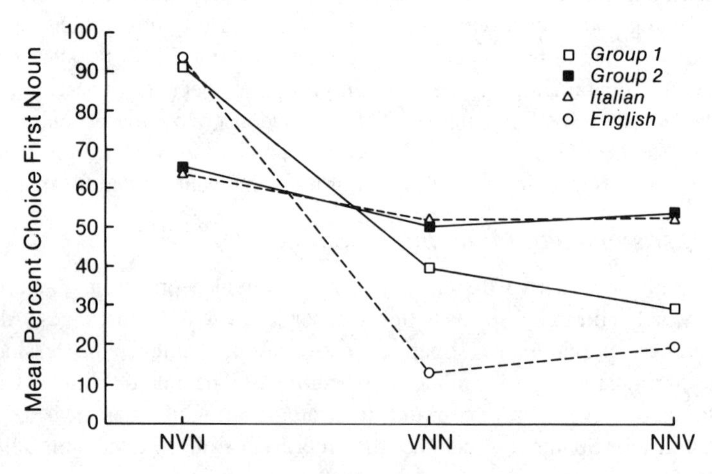


FIG. 9.7. Word order results for Groups 1 and 2 overlaid on results for monolingual speakers of English and Italian.

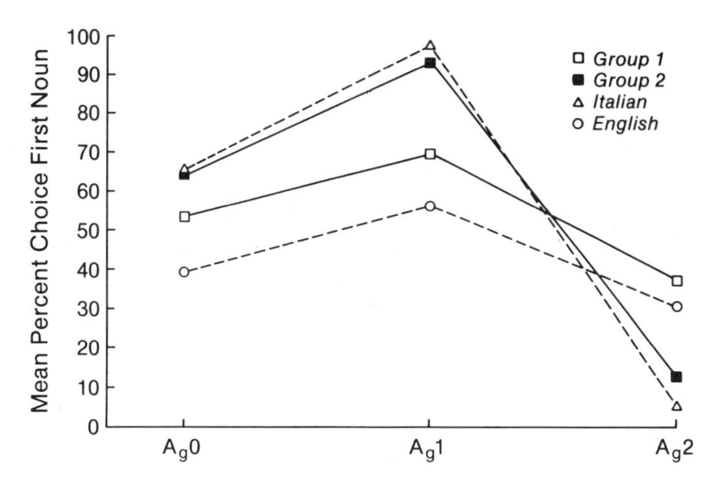


FIG. 9.8. Agreement results for Groups 1 and 2 overlaid on results for monolingual speakers of English and Italian.

lingual English speakers, but with a less pronounced second noun bias. The result is further supported by the percentage of variance accounted for in Group 1 (Table 9.2). While Bates et al. (1984) and MacWhinney et al. (1984, see their Table 2) observed that agreement and animacy accounted for 1% and 0.9% respectively of the variance for monolingual English speakers; agreement and animacy accounted for 7.9% and 5.6% here.

In summary, Group 1 subjects seem to have adopted an SVO word-order strategy typical of monolingual English speakers, but they have adopted agreement and animacy strategies from Spanish as well. The resulting amalgam is applied in the same way to *both their languages* for sentence interpretation.

The Group 2 subjects, as shown in Figs. 9.7 and 9.8, are virtually indistinguishable from monolingual speakers of *Italian.* Their performance (Table 9.3) is as close as that of another monolingual Italian sample (MacWhinney et al., 1984). Our subjects are also indistinguishable when we compare the percentages of variance accounted for in our Table 9.3, and those observed by MacWhinney et al. (1984, their Table 3). In MacWhinney et al.'s (1984) study, agreement accounted for 54% of the variance, animacy, 4.2%; word order, 1.4%; and animacy × agreement, 5.3%. Our Group 2 bilingual subjects applied this "Agreement > Animacy > Word Order" strategy for sentence interpretation in *both* English and Spanish.

## II. SENTENCE INTERPRETATION IN APHASIA

In this section we discuss the performance of a bilingual Spanish-English speaking adult aphasic on the sentence interpretation task.

### Case History

C.N. is a 70-year-old right-handed male who immigrated to the United States from Puerto Rico at 20-years-of-age. He learned Spanish as his first language from his monolingual Spanish speaking parents. He studied English in school starting in the first grade and continued formally until immigrating to the United States. After coming to the U.S., he enlisted in the army and worked as a cook in the Pacific during World War II. After the war he retired from the army and worked in food services for various schools in California.

C.N. is married and the father of four grown children. His wife and children are bilingual Spanish/English speakers. C.N. also has three bilingual siblings living in California. Information from interviews with C.N. and his wife and from a detailed language history questionnaire indicate that before his illness, Spanish and English were spoken equally in the home.

In 1984, C.N. suffered a cerebrovascular accident resulting in a lesion in the region of the left inferior frontal gyrus. He developed a moderate right hemiparesis and a moderate nonfluent aphasia with some motor speech involvement. While hospitalized, he was enrolled in a rehabilitation program with physical and speech therapy services. He continues to attend group speech therapy sessions as an outpatient.

Speech pathology reports and interview information indicate that immediately after his stroke C.N. could produce only fragments of Spanish although he seemed to understand simple commands in both Spanish and English. After a few weeks English fragments began to appear and Spanish continued to improve. When C.N. was neurologically stable, he was given a battery of speech and language tests, mostly in English. Testing results revealed a moderate nonfluent, agrammatic aphasia with mild-to-moderate auditory comprehension deficits. Such a language deficit profile (Goodglass & Kaplan, 1972) is consistent with anterior damage in the region surrounding Broca's area.

### Clinical Observations

We saw C.N. 6 months after his illness. We collected both Spanish and English data using our behavioral battery which includes free speech, picture naming and comprehension, constrained production, and sentence interpretation tasks. Detailed analysis of C.N.'s spontaneous and constrained production has not been completed, however, certain characteristics are emerging. While C.N.'s expressive utterances in both languages are classified as nonfluent and telegraphic, fluency is slightly better for Spanish than for English. Also, Spanish-language intrusions during English testing are more frequent than English intrusions during Spanish testing. Finally, when C.N. was tested in English, he left out articles almost all the time, even if a Spanish lexical intrusion occurred; for example, "Cat to *perro* to cat" (*perro* = dog). This is, of course, a common characteristic of agrammatism. However, when tested in Spanish, C.N. included articles with many of his lexicalization attempts, even if an English noun was inserted (e.g., "el *boy*"). In short, C.N.'s expressive language suggests that Spanish is still dominant, although some competence is preserved in English as well.

### Performance on Sentence Interpretation Test

We now turn to C.N.'s performance in Spanish and English with our sentence interpretation task. Administration procedures were similar to those used with our healthy bilingual adults except that C.N. was tested in Spanish one week after testing in English.

The most important feature of C.N.'s results is that his sentence interpretation patterns seem to reflect sensitivity *both* to word order and agreement cues in *both* languages. They resemble the patterns reported for Group 1, although C.N.'s results show more variability than our healthy bilinguals, perhaps because of the effects of brain damage. The similarity is clearest in the word order by agreement results for both languages as shown in Fig. 9.9.

The strongest evidence for word order cues dominating agreement cues can be seen with the NVN constructions for English and Spanish. With the English sentences, a first noun bias is observed across all three agreement conditions. For Spanish, there is a clear preference for the first noun when it is in greatest competition with agreement cues (Ag2). (Recall that NVN Ag2 performance clearly differentiated our groups.) However, agreement cues also have an influence in both languages, at least with the noncanonical sequences. With the VNN and NNV constructions in either language, there is a moderate to strong bias of noun selection based on agreement cues.

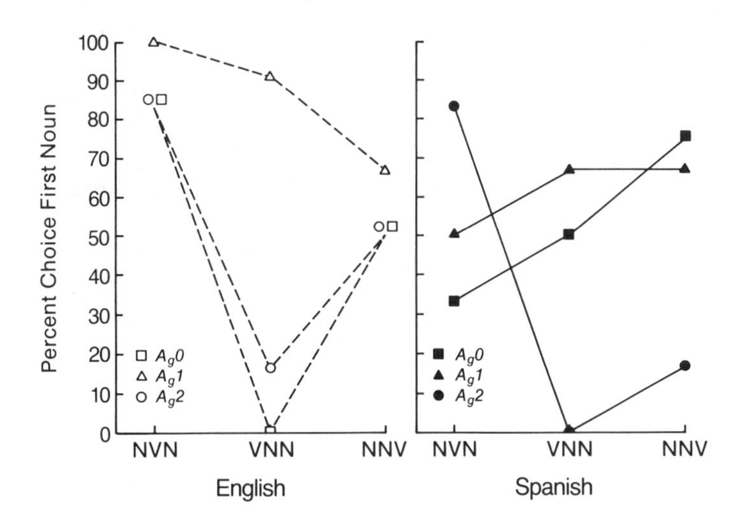


FIG. 9.9. English and Spanish word order by agreement results for bilingual aphasic subject C.N.

While we hesitate to draw firm conclusions based on only one subject, it seems that C.N. is sensitive to word order as well as agreement cues; however, he seems to apply these somewhat haphazardly. This inconsistency was also observed in C.N.'s sensitivity to animacy cues. In general, he showed no particular preference for first or second nouns across animacy conditions, except in certain circumstances. For example, for NVN AI items in Spanish, C.N. chose the *second* noun which was *inanimate* on five of the six sentences. This suggests a sensitivity to the animacy contrast in the face of strong word order competition, but confusion about how to *use* animacy information.

## Conclusion

We hope to have demonstrated that the competition model, and the methods used in studies based on it, provide a useful basis for examining language processing in both healthy and aphasic bilinguals. The methodology used in the study reported here, which examined the salience of semantic, syntactic, and morphological cues placed in competing or converging configurations, yielded important information with respect to the processing strategies employed by bilinguals during sentence interpretation in each of their languages.

Our data indicate that bilinguals do not engage in separate modes of processing in their two languages. On the contrary, they appear to possess a unitary system which operates in the same fashion for both languages. Thus, we found no evidence for any sort of "input switching mechanism" (Macnamara & Kushnir, 1971), at least at the level of sentence interpretation.

However, not all bilinguals in our study processed sentences in the same way; indeed, two distinct patterns of response were observed. One group of bilinguals (Group 1) showed a combination of cue sensitivity reflecting the adopting of processing strategies from both their languages. This result indicates that processing strategies from more than one language can sometimes combine to form a strategy "amalgam." This finding is not inconsistent with that of McDonald (1984) who studied sentence interpretation in different groups of bilingual adults (Dutch-English, English-Dutch, and German-Dutch). Her findings revealed that with increasing exposure to a second language, bilinguals tend to rely less on their first language strategies and shift to the second language strategies when processing sentences in that second language. The findings are also consistent with the notion of a continuum of bilingualism (see Grosjean & Soares, this volume).

Our other group of subjects (Group 2) failed to show sensitivity to word order, which is the strongest cue for monolingual English speakers. This indicates that, under some circumstances, highly salient processing cues from one of a bilingual's languages need not be adopted as primary, even for that language.

One may well ask what determines which sentence interpretation cues will be more salient for bilinguals. In the present study, performance was not related in any obvious way to age of second language acquisition or fluency in either language, although, given the small sample size, further work should be directed at establishing the possible contribution of these and other language variables. A sentence interpretation study involving Dutch-English bilinguals (Kilborn & Cooreman, 1985) found language differences in interpretation patterns for the two languages. Word order was the strongest cue for English while agreement and animacy cues were strongest for Dutch. These Dutch-English bilinguals reportedly code-switch or mix their two languages infrequently. In contrast, code-switching and borrowing are common among Spanish-English bilinguals; it is possible, then, that this sociolinguistic factor may have contributed to the development of mixed strategies for some of our bilinguals.

Our results with normal bilingual adults provide evidence for two of the three outcomes outlined in the introduction. Subjects in Group 1 deviated from monolingual patterns in either language, and appear to have developed amalgamated strategies. Group 2 subjects look very much like the subjects described by Bates and MacWhinney (1981), with L1 subject-verb agreement strategies imposed upon L2. While research with monolinguals has suggested that there is enormous flexibility in language processing across natural languages, the research reported here suggests that even more flexibility is present in bilinguals.

Our bilingual aphasic behaved in a manner similar to our Group 1 bilinguals, showing evidence of sensitivity to both word order and agreement cues. This behavior is not inconsistent with the patterns of performance of monolingual aphasics, discussed earlier. Recall that Bates et al. (1984) found that sentence interpretation patterns were preserved for monolingual English, German, and Italian aphasics, but that their performance was "noisier" than that of monolingual controls. The performance of aphasics on the sentence interpretation task suggests that aphasics retain *sensitivity* to the same cues as their language-matched healthy controls, but that *utilization* of these cues in assigning interpretations to sentences is disturbed.

With aphasics, there is always a potential danger in drawing conclusions about performance deficits since there is rarely information on their communicative competence before their brain injury. The problem is obviously more complicated for bilingual aphasics, since a number of possible strategies might have been in use premorbidly (see Albert & Obler, 1978; Paradis, 1983, for a detailed discussion of polyglot aphasia). Lack of sensitivity to word order, for example, might be because it was not a primary cue in the first place, or because the strength of this cue was lowered as a result of brain damage. Our finding of different sentence processing strategies among brain-intact bilinguals complicates the interpretation of aphasics' performance on this task. Further studies are needed involving other subgroups of bilinguals (both normal and aphasic) so that one can distinguish language-specific differences in the strength of cues from qualitative changes in the organization of form-function mappings as a result of focal brain damage.

## ACKNOWLEDGMENT

This work was supported in part by a grant from NINCDS to Elizabeth Bates and by a USPHS Predoctoral Traineeship to Beverly Wulfeck.

## REFERENCES

Albert, M., & Obler, L. (1978). *The bilingual brain*. New York: Academic Press.

Bates, E., Friederici, A., Miceli, G., Smith, S., Wulfeck, B., & Zurif, E. (1984, October). *Cross-linguistic studies of aphasia*. Symposium conducted at the annual meeting of the American Academy of Aphasia, Santa Monica.

Bates, E., & MacWhinney, B. (1981). Second language acquisition from a functionalist perspective: Pragmatic, semantic and perceptual strategies. In H. Winitz (Ed.), *Annals of the New York Academy of Sciences Conferences on Native and Foreign Language Acquistion* (pp. 190–214). New York: New York Academy of Sciences.

Bates, E., & MacWhinney, B. (1982). Functionalist approaches to grammar. In E. Wanner & L. R. Gleitman (Eds.), *Language acquisition: The state of the art* (pp. 173–218). Cambridge: Cambridge University Press.

Bates, E., MacWhinney, B., Caselli, C., Devescovi, A., Natale, F., & Venza, V. (1984). A cross-linguistic study of the development of sentence interpretation strategies. *Child Development, 55*, 341–354.

Bates, E., McNew, S., MacWhinney, B., Devescovi, A., & Smith, S. (1982). Functional constraints on sentence processing: A cross-linguistic study. *Cognition, 11*, 245–299.

Forster, K. I. (1979). Levels of processing and the structure of the language processor. In W. T. Cooper & C. T. Walker (Eds.), *Sentence processing: Psycholinguistic studies presented to Merrill Garrett* (pp. 27–85). Hillsdale, NJ: Lawrence Erlbaum Associates.

Goodglass, H., & Kaplan, E. (1972). *The assessment of aphasia and related disorders*. Philadelphia: Lea and Febiger.

Kilborn, K., & Cooreman, A. (1985). *Sentence interpretation strategies in adult Dutch-English bilinguals*. Unpublished manuscript.

Kolers, P. (1966). Reading and talking bilingually. *American Journal of Psychology, 3*, 357–376.

Lambert, W. (1978). Psychological approaches to bilingualism, translation and interpretation. In D. Gerver & H. Sinaiko (Eds.), *Language interpretation and communication*. New York: Plenum Press.

Lopez, M. (1977). Bilingual memory research: Implications for bilingual education. In J. Martinez (Ed.), *Chicano psychology*. New York: Academic Press.

Macnamara, J. (1967). The linguistic independence of bilinguals. *Journal of Verbal Learning and Verbal Behavior, 6*, 729–736.

Macnamara, J., & Kushnir, S. (1971). Linguistic independence of bilinguals: The input switch. *Journal of Verbal Learning and Verbal Behavior, 10*, 480–487.

MacWhinney, B., Bates, E., & Kliegl, R. (1984). Cue validity and sentence interpretation in English, German, and Italian. *Journal of Verbal Learning and Verbal Behavior, 23*, 127–150.

MacWhinney, B., Pleh, C., & Bates, E. (1985). The development of sentence interpretation in Hungarian. *Cognitive Psychology, 17*, 178–209.

McDonald, J. (1984). *The mapping of semantic and syntactic processing cues by first and second language learners of English, Dutch, and German*. Unpublished doctoral dissertation, Carnegie-Mellon University.

Paradis, M. (1978). The stratification of bilingualism. In M. Paradis (Ed.), *Aspects of Bilingualism* (pp. 165–175). Columbia, SC: Hornbeam Press.
Paradis, M. (Ed.). (1983). *Readings on aphasia in bilinguals and polyglots*. Quebec: Didier.
Smith, S., & Mimica, I. (1984). Agrammatism in a case-inflected language. *Brain and Language, 13*, 274–290.
Weinreich, U. (1968). *Languages in contact*. The Hague: Mouton.

# 10 The Aging Bilingual

Loraine Obler
Martin Albert
Sandra Lozowick
*Aphasia Research Center*
*Boston V.A. Medical Center*

Although in the last century we have gained insights into the bilingual brain, and in the past decade we have begun to explore aging as it relates to language and the brain, our knowledge of bilingualism as it interacts with the aging brain is still minimal. The approach that we and others have taken with regard to the issue of language and aging is that the neural substrate for language changes throughout the lifespan and is subject to a variety of influences. Among these are the impact of education, selective cortical atrophy accompanying aging in the normal person, and selective neuropathological changes in the different varieties of dementia (Albert, 1980).

Research on bilingualism suggests that the context of second language acquisition may be a relevant index of differences in language processing and, possibly, in patterns of brain lateralization for language both between bilingual subgroups, and between bilinguals and monolinguals (see Vaid, 1983). It would be interesting to study whether these differences extend throughout the lifespan, or whether they are reduced (or possibly even exaggerated). Another question of interest with regard to language in the elderly bilingual concerns intraindividual differences in the processing of the first and second language as a function of time. In the course of an individual's life, the patterns of usage of two languages are likely to vary, given variations in the language environment (situations, interlocutors, etc.). The repercussions of these variations on language ability of the aging bilingual, and their interaction with neurological alterations accompanying aging, are questions of pragmatic as well as theoretical interest.

If one surveys the literature on aging, or on bilingualism, there is hardly any study of language in the aging bilingual. We were able to find only three studies bearing on this topic. One (Clyne, 1977) was a case report of an elderly German/English bilingual woman whose proficiency in her second language declined in later age, her English showing increasing traces of first language accent and words. Clyne provides little information about the woman's health status, in particular, whether she was of normal health or in the early stages of dementia.

The second study was conducted by two of us (Albert & Obler, 1978) as part of a larger project on the neuropsychology of bilingualism. We examined numerous parameters linked to differential recovery from aphasia in a sample of 107 cases of bilingual aphasia culled from the neurological literature. The most striking finding was that, for aphasics under the age of 65 years, the language in use at the time of brain injury (whether or not it was the patient's mother tongue) was significantly more likely to recover than any other language known to the patient prior to the injury (Obler & Albert, 1977). In contrast, for bilingual aphasics over the age of 65 years, we found no systematic language recovery pattern. However, when we considered the thirty-eight cases of bilingual aphasia (cited in Paradis, 1977, 1983) reported since our study, this differential effect of aging on recovery from aphasia was not substantiated (Obler, unpublished).

The only other study of language in elderly bilinguals that we could find was that of Bergman (1980). Bergman reported that bilinguals who otherwise appeared quite fluent in their second language, having acquired it in childhood or early adulthood, were more impaired than elderly monolinguals on comprehension tasks involving temporally distorted materials.

To pursue further the issue of language skills in elderly bilinguals and monolinguals, we undertook a preliminary study, described below. This study emerged from an ongoing longitudinal project in our laboratory initiated in 1976 on language in healthy aging and dementia. By healthy aging we mean changes in ability among those who continue to function successfully. In contrast, dementia refers to changes in ability that prevent normal cognitive functioning. In the course of selecting 160 men and women aged 30–79 years for this larger study, we selected a modest sample of subjects with some history of bilingualism. We administered a series of language tests and two nonlanguage tests to these bilinguals, and to monolingual controls. (Some of these tests are routinely administered to aphasics as well.) Our general expectation was that there would be no group differences between monolinguals and bilinguals on the nonlanguage measures, but that the groups might differ on some of the language measures.

## METHOD

*Subjects.* Eleven bilinguals (mean age of 73.6 years) and 32 monolinguals (mean age of 73.8 years) were tested. All subjects were right-handed with no history of neurologic or psychiatric illness nor of substance abuse. Alcohol consumption across the lifespan of these individuals was minimal—no more than three drinks per week. Subjects who were on medication for such conditions as hypertension or arthritis were not excluded. Vision and hearing were screened such that all subjects had 20/40 corrected vision and hearing loss no greater than 35db.

Monolinguals and bilinguals did not significantly differ in their educational background; years of education for the bilinguals ranged from 9 to 15 (with a mean of 12.5) and, for the monolinguals, from 8 to 25 (with a mean of 14.3).

The bilinguals were all born in the United States to immigrant families. Their home language for the first several years was the native language of their parents which in most cases was Yiddish, and they had acquired English by the age of 3 or 4 years (and, in one case, by 5 years). Most of these bilinguals had learned to read and write in both their languages and continued to use both languages throughout their lifespan, although English has been the language they use predominantly in their daily activities.

*Materials and Procedures.* Ten language and two visuospatial measures were administered to each subject in a single testing session. The language tests were selected to tap a broad range of language capabilities which are thought to remain stable over age. The visuospatial tests were included to provide information about possible nonlanguage changes in cognitive functioning associated with bilingualism.

## Language Tests

*1. Naming.* Three naming tests were employed. In the Boston Naming Test (Kaplan, Goodglass, & Weintraub, 1978) the subject is shown a series of 85 line drawn objects graded in difficulty and asked to name them. In the Action Naming Test (Obler & Albert, 1979), the subject is required to name 63 pictured activities, also graded in difficulty. A third naming test, the Famous Faces Test (Albert, Butters, & Levin, 1979) was included since a common complaint of aging people is a problem recalling proper names. This test required naming 17 photographs of people who were famous over the past several decades.

*2. Word Fluency.* Word fluency was measured by various word list generation tasks. Subjects were asked to name as many words as they could beginning with a certain letter (e.g., "f," "a," "s"), excluding proper nouns, numbers, and words differing only in their suffixes. Subjects were also asked to generate as many words as they could think of in a particular semantic category (animal names). The score in these tasks was the number of words produced in the first 60 seconds of a 90-second time period.

*3. Morphological Antonyms.* On this task, the subject was asked to form the opposite of a word by adding a prefix to it; for example, for the word "comfortable'' they were to say ''uncomfortable, for ''legal,'' ''illegal,'' etc. There were a total of twenty-five words.

*4. Automatic Speech.* Here, subjects were instructed to recite the alphabet, to count from 1 to 21, and to recite the months of the year. Response time and accuracy were noted.

*5. Reciting Months Backward.* This task was included as a contrast to the months forward recitation task.

*6. Facts about Numbers.* This was a control task for the Boston Naming Test (Kaplan et al., 1978) included to tap long-term memory for facts of a type that does not involve linguistic retrieval. In this test, questions about 24 simple number facts were posed to subjects, e.g., ''How many days are there in a week,'' or ''How many feet are there in a mile.''

*7. Semantic Interference.* The Stroop Color Word test (Stroop, 1935) was used to provide a measure of semantic interference generated by automaticity in reading. In the first part of this test, subjects are given a card with an array of five different colors (10 columns of 10 color bars each) and are asked to name the colors as quickly as possible. They are then shown a card containing words that are names of colors, e.g., ''red,'' ''blue,'' but there is always a mismatch between the color designated by the word and the ink color in which the word is written (e.g., the word ''red'' might be written in blue ink). Here again, subjects are to name the color of the ink as quickly as possible, ignoring the word's meaning. Speed of color naming and accuracy were noted.

*8. Sentence Comprehension.* The Speech Perception in Noise test was used as a measure of semantic/syntactic comprehension (Kalikow, Stevens, & Elliott, 1977). Subjects were required to listen to sentences containing final words that had either a high or a low probability, and had to write down the final word of each sentence. The sentences were presented in low or high noise conditions. An example of a sentence containing a high probability final word is ''The rose bush has thorns''; a sentence containing a low probability final word is ''The boy was discussing thorns.'' In both cases, the subject would have had to write down the word, ''thorns.''

*9. Idiom Interpretation.* In this task, subjects were given seven idioms in English to interpret (e.g., ''loud tie,'' or ''put it down in black and white''). The number of correct responses was noted, each correct response being assigned a score of 2. An abstractness score, ranging from 0 to 2 (where 0 refers to a literal interpretation) was also assigned to each response. A vagueness score was computed by summing the number of vague terms used in each response. A measure of literalness was also computed by counting the number of words in the response that were taken directly from the idiom. Finally, subjects' use of circumlocutions was noted.

*10. Proverb Interpretation.* Four common proverbs in English (e.g., ''Too many cooks spoil the broth,'' or ''Rome wasn't built in a day'') were presented to the subjects for interpretation. Responses were scored by the same criteria as were used in the idiom interpretation task.

## Visuospatial Tasks

*1. Visual Memory.* The Rey-Osterreith Complex Figure Test (Osterreith, 1944) was used as a measure of memory for a complex visuospatial form. The test was presented under three conditions: subjects first had to copy it; immediately thereafter, the figure was to be reproduced from memory, then after a 20-minute delay it was to be reproduced once more from memory. The standard scoring system, as described in Lezak (1983, p. 400) was used.

*2. Visual Closure.* In the visual closure task subjects were shown twenty-four incomplete pictures and asked to identify them. This test taps the ability to deduce a form given minimal or fragmentary information.

# RESULTS

The performance of bilinguals and monolinguals on each of the above tasks was assessed by means of separate one-way analyses of variance, the results of which are summarized below.

## Language Tasks

*Naming Tests.* No significant group differences were found on any of the three naming tests, although on the Boston Naming Test there was a trend for the bilinguals to name more items than the monolinguals (71.1 vs. 66.8 mean words named, respectively; $p = .06$). On the Action Naming Test, bilinguals and monolinguals performed at a comparable level (55.6 vs. 56.4, respectively). Women performed better on the Action Naming Test than did men (mean words named were 57.6 and 55.1, respectively; $F = 8.18$, $df = 1$, $p = .007$). Mean performance for bilinguals and monolinguals on the Famous Faces Test was 15.3 and 15.4, respectively.

*Word Fluency.* The only significant group difference on this task emerged for the animal word list generation; bilinguals generated more animal names than did monolinguals (21.4 vs. 19.2, respectively; $F = 6.36$, $df = 1$, $p < .01$). There was a trend towards superior performance of the bilinguals on the word generation task for words beginning with certain letters, (49.0 vs. 42.8; $p = .1$).

*Morphological Antonyms.* Monolinguals and bilinguals performed equally well on this task (23.2 vs. 22.8, respectively).

*Automatic Speech.* Monolinguals were significantly faster than bilinguals in reciting the alphabet and in counting from 1 to 21 ($t = 4.77$, $df = 41$, $p < .001$).

*Reciting Months Forward and Backward.* For reciting the months forwards or backwards there was no significant group difference.

*Number Facts.* When amount of education was entered as a covariate, there were no significant group differences in performance on this task.

*Stroop Color Word Interference Test.* Bilinguals were faster than monolinguals (74.9 vs. 80.1 seconds; $t = 3.16$, $df = 35$, $p < .01$) and made fewer errors than monolinguals in naming color bars (2.2 vs. 2.6; $t = 2.25$, $df = 35$, $p < .05$). However, monolinguals and bilinguals were equally susceptible to semantic interference when incongruent information was available from the word name and color of ink (155 and 137 seconds, respectively). There was a tendency for the monolinguals to make more errors than the bilinguals on the incongruent part of the test (6.3 vs. 2.2) but this effect failed to reach significance ($p < .1$).

*Speech Perception in Noise Test.* There was no group differences in overall reaction time on this test, and monolinguals and bilinguals made an equal number of errors (47.8 and 36.4).

*Idiom Interpretation.* Monolinguals and bilinguals interpreted about the same number of idioms correctly (.89 and .93). No significant difference was seen in the literalness of response between the monolinguals (.09) and the bilinguals (.26). monolinguals and bilinguals used an equal number of vague terms (.05 and .09) and circumlocutions (.04 and .07). Thus, no significant group differences were obtained on any of the scoring dimensions of this test.

*Proverb Interpretation.* No significant difference was seen in the abstractness of response of monolinguals and bilinguals (7.2 vs. 6.7). However, bilinguals used significantly more vague terms than monolinguals (2.1 vs. 1.1; $t = 6.99$, $df = 36$, $p < .001$) and gave more circumlocutions (1 vs. 0.4, respectively; $t = 11.7$, $df = 36$, $p < .001$).

## Visuospatial Tasks

*Rey Osterreith Figure.* The Rey Osterreith Figure test data were available only for the males. There was no difference between bilinguals and monolinguals in the copying (33 vs. 29.4) or delayed recall conditions (11.5 vs. 13.3, respectively). However, in the immediate recall condition, monolinguals performed better than bilinguals (13.9 vs. 10.6; $t = 2.3$, $df = 13$; $p < .05$).

*Visual Closure.* On this test, subjects' performance was scored in three ways. No difference was seen between bilinguals and monolinguals on the first score, in which subjects received an unlimited amount of time and partial credit (18.1 vs. 17.9, respectively). Bilinguals were significantly better than monolinguals on the second score in which a 3-minute time limit was imposed (15.4 vs. 8.4, respectively; $t = 3.24$, $df = 33$; $p < .01$), and on the third score, where the 3-minute time limit was imposed without partial credit (14.4 vs. 6.4; $t = 3.64$, $df = 33$; $p < .01$).

## DISCUSSION

Table 10.1 provides a summary of the relative performance of bilinguals and monolinguals on each of the tests. Perhaps the most striking generalization that emerges is how few differences there were in the performance of the two groups. This finding stands in sharp contrast to that of Bergman (1980), whose results suggested that bilinguals never fully master a second language. We were therefore surprised to find that on a number of measures the bilinguals in our study were not only as good as monolinguals, but, in some cases, they were even better than monolinguals.

*Superior Performance by Monolinguals.* Indeed, there were only three instances in which the monolinguals were significantly superior: (1) They were faster at reciting the alphabet and counting from 1 to 21; (2) They gave fewer vague interpretations and circumlocutions on the proverbs test, and (3) Male monolinguals were better than male bilinguals in the immediate recall of a complex visual form. The tendency for the monolinguals to perform better than the bilinguals on the proverb task may be explained by environmental factors; proverbs even more than idioms are learned in childhood through cultural experience. Had we used English translations of proverbs from Yiddish-speaking cultures, we might well have seen performance by our bilinguals to be equal to or better than that of our monolinguals. As for the significantly faster performance of the monolinguals on the automatic speech tasks, our results suggest that learning to recite a series such as the alphabet or numbers in one's second

TABLE 10.1
Performance of Bilinguals (N=11) and Monolinguals (N=32) on Test Battery[a]

| No Group Differences | Bilinguals Better | Monolinguals Better |
|---|---|---|
| Boston naming test | Word fluency (animal list generation) | Automatic speech (reciting alphabet; counting) |
| Action naming test | | |
| Famous faces test | Stroop color word (congruent condition) | Proverbs test |
| Word fluency (words beginning with certain letters) | Visual closure (timed condition) | Rey Osterreith figure (immediate recall) |
| Morphological antonyms | | |
| Reciting months forward or backward | | |
| Number facts test | | |
| Stroop color word test (incongruent condition) | | |
| Speech perception in noise test | | |
| Idiom interpretation | | |

[a]Group differences, where obtained, were significant at or beyond the .05 level.

language after, presumably, having already mastered the series in one's native language, results in a slightly slower performance, even decades later.

*Superior Performance by Bilinguals.* The performance of bilinguals, in turn, was superior on three measures as well: (1) Bilinguals generated significantly more items than monolinguals on the animal list generation test; (2) They were faster and made fewer errors than monolinguals in naming colors in the congruent condition of the Stroop color word interference test, and (3) They scored higher than monolinguals on the time-constrained condition of the visual closure test. Finally, bilinguals tended to outperform monolinguals on the Boston Naming Test and on the remaining word fluency subtests, and tended to make fewer errors than monolinguals on the incongruent part of the Stroop Color Word test, but these effects did not reach significance. Taken together, these results suggest that, by virtue of being bilingual, one actually develops exceptional language production skills, especially labeling skills. The superiority of the bilinguals on the visual closure test was an unexpected finding since this task does not have any ostensible linguistic basis. The fact that bilinguals were significantly faster than monolinguals in the timed condition of the test suggests that greater efficiency at making guesses about meaning on the basis of limited information is a byproduct of mastery of two languages (see Ben-Zeev, 1977, for a similar conclusion with bilingual children).

*Similar Performance by Bilinguals and Monolinguals.* Except for the above significant group differences, and some nonsignificant trends, the tasks were generally performed at the same level by bilinguals and monolinguals. The groups were equivalent in their comprehension of high- and low-probability sentences presented under high- or low-noise conditions. They also performed similarly in the generation of morphological opposites, in their accuracy of recitation of automatized series, in their numerical knowledge, in their susceptibility to semantic interference, and in their accuracy of idiom and proverb interpretation. On the nonlanguage measures, the groups were equivalent in their accuracy in copying a complex visual form from a model and from memory after a 20-minute delay, and in their accuracy of visual closure (in an unlimited time condition).

*Methodological Issues.* Two sets of caveats are in order for the researcher who would undertake future work in this field. One set is pertinent to bilingualism and the other is pertinent to aging. Methodological factors to be considered in research on bilingualism have been detailed in Obler, Zatorre, Galloway, and Vaid (1982). Crucial to any study of bilingualism is how bilingualism is defined: what proficiency need be achieved, and what measures can document its achievement. Such definition is particularly important in a study which may show differences in language performance between the elderly bilingual and the elderly monolingual. In addition, the age of acquisition of a second language and the manner of acquisition must be considered. Moreover, the individual's usage history of the two languages must be recorded in as great detail as possible.

As to issues in the study of healthy aging, a similar problem of definition must be addressed. What do we define as healthy aging? If we attempt to include only older people with hearing equivalent to that of younger adults, or older people who have no naming problems, we restrict our sample unduly. If we insist on excluding individuals on medication for any ailment, we would have virtually no subjects. Do we consider alcohol intake over the course of the lifespan to constitute healthy aging?

Educational equivalencies will cause problems for studies both of aging and of bilingualism. If we match a younger and older group on years of education, we may not be assured of the same quality of education in the two groups. And for the bilingual who is bicultural, years of education provide only a shallow indication of actual knowledge.

## CONCLUSION

The present findings suggest that, for the most part, the performance of elderly fluent bilinguals in their second learned language is comparable to that of their monolingual counterparts in that language. Where differences occur, these point to certain domains in which monolinguals show a superiority, and others in which bilinguals show a superior level of performance.

This domain-specificity in the relative performance of bilinguals and monolinguals suggests that further research in this area, investigating other domains of language and nonlanguage functioning, might uncover additional differences in patterns of language ability (see also Mägiste, this volume).

Further research on language in the aging bilingual should also probe the phenomenon described by Clyne (1977) of an apparent disinhibition in switching between the two languages, or a selective deterioration of one of the bilingual's languages. A number of questions can be raised with respect to the issue of language attrition in the normal or dementing bilingual (see Obler, 1983). Might it be that production and perception deteriorate differentially? Do certain word-classes or semantic features disappear more rapidly than others? How does accent deteriorate and why? What features of the individuals' language history (e.g., age and manner of second language acquisition, early acquisition of more than two languages, etc.) interact with the rate or pattern of language attrition? How do such factors as gender and handedness interact with language performance in later life? What factors affect language performance in later life? What factors of the languages in question exacerbate language attrition and what factors hinder it? Do these factors include structural or cognate closeness to the first language; do they include a shared phonology or morphology or lexicon or syntax? Does practice in reading hinder attrition of speaking or of aural comprehension skills? Finally, is there a critical proficiency in a second language that protects against subsequent loss of that language?

An obvious limitation of the present study was that we only tested bilinguals in their nonnative language. Future work should investigate performance in both languages of the bilingual (see, for example, Paradis, forthcoming, on aphasics), and should, ideally, do so using a longitudinal paradigm. Only then can more definitive statements be made about which aspects of language (or nonlanguage) behavior remain stable and which are modified by increasing language experience and the neurological changes that accompany the aging process.

## ACKNOWLEDGMENTS

Thanks are due to Ingrid Allard for her work on the polyglot aphasia study, and to Marj Nicholas for her contribution of computer analysis for both studies and statistical expertise. Jyotsna Vaid and Jane Litter provided substantial editorial assistance. These studies were supported in part by the Medical Research Service of the Veterans Administration and by grants No. R23AG01243 and PHS2POINSO6209-16 of the National Institutes of Health.

## REFERENCES

Albert, M. (1980). Language in normal and dementing elderly. In L. Obler & M. Albert (Eds.), *Language and communication in the elderly* (pp. 145–150). Lexington, MA: D. C. Heath.

Albert, M., & Obler, L. (1978). *The bilingual brain: Neuropsychological and neurolinguistic aspects of bilingualism.* New York: Academic Press.

Albert, M., Butters, N., & Levin, H. (1979). *Famous Faces Test.* Boston: Experimental Edition.

Ben-Zeev, S. (1977). The influence of bilingualism on cognitive strategy and cognitive development. *Child Development, 48,* 1009–1018.

Bergman, M. (1980). *Aging and the perception of speech.* Baltimore: University Park Press.

Clyne, M. (1977). Bilingualism of the elderly. *Talanya, 4,* 45–56.

Kalikow, D., Stevens, K., & Elliott, L. (1977). Development of a test of speech intelligibility in noise using sentence materials with controlled word predictability. *JASA, 61,* 1337–1351.

Kaplan, E., Goodglass, H., & Weintraub, S. (1978). *The Boston Naming Test.* Unpublished manuscript, Aphasia Research Center, V. A. Medical Center, Boston.

Lezak, M. (1983). *Neuropsychological assessment* (Second edition). New York: Oxford University Press.

Obler, L. (1983). La neuropsychologie du bilinguisme. In M. Paradis & Y. Lebrun (Eds.), *La neurolinguistique du bilinguisme,* (special issue of *Langages*), *vol. 72,* 33–44.

Obler, L., & Albert, M. (1977). Influence of aging on recovery from aphasia in polyglots. *Brain and Language, 4,* 460–463.

Obler, L., & Albert, M. (1979). *Action Naming Test.* Unpublished manuscript, Aphasia Research Center, V.A. Medical Center, Boston.

Obler, L., Zatorre, R., Galloway, L., & Vaid, J. (1982). Cerebral lateralization in bilinguals: Methodological issues. *Brain and Language, 15,* 40–54.

Osterreith, P. (1944). Le test de copie d'une figure complexe. *Archives de Psychologie, 19,* 87–95.
Paradis, M. (1977). Bilingualism and aphasia. In H. Whitaker & H. A. Whitaker (Eds.), *Studies in Neurolinguistics,* (*Vol. 3,* pp. 65–121). New York: Academic Press.
Paradis, M. (Ed.). (1983). *Readings on aphasia in bilinguals and polyglots.* Montreal: Didier.
Paradis, M. (forthcoming). *Assessment of bilingual aphasia.* Hillsdale, NJ: Lawrence Erlbaum Associates.
Stroop, J. (1935). Studies of interference in serial verbal reactions. *Journal of Experimental Psychology, 18,* 643–662.
Vaid, J. (1983). Bilingualism and brain lateralization. In S. Segalowitz (Ed.), *Language functions and brain organization* (pp. 315–339). New York: Academic Press.

# 11 Leaning to the Right: Some Thoughts on Hemisphere Involvement in Language Acquisition

Eta I. Schneiderman
*University of Ottawa*

## INTRODUCTION

Overwhelming evidence in the clinical and experimental literature supports the view that, in normal, right-handed adults, the majority of language functions are governed by the left cerebral hemisphere (see Lecours & L'Hermitte, 1979, Chapter 2). There are, however, data from a number of sources to suggest that although the right hemisphere is probably much less essential than the left hemisphere for mature language processing, it may play an important role during the acquisition of both first and second languages. The goal of this paper is to characterize the right hemisphere's role in language acquisition, with reference to relevant (although admittedly controversial) data from the fields of language acquisition and neuroscience.

The first two sections of the paper review evidence for right hemisphere participation in first- and second-language acquisition. In a subsequent section, evidence from child and adult acquirers is shown to be compatible with the processing mode typical of the right hemisphere. This compatibility provides a basis for the depiction of the right hemisphere's role in acquisition. Evidence of language processing capacities in the adult right hemisphere is also cited in support of this model. It is further suggested that such a role for the right hemisphere is not limited to language acquisition but may also be extended to the learning process in other cognitive domains.

It should be noted here that the terms right and left hemisphere, as they are used in the present paper, are meant to imply the processing mode typically associated with each hemisphere. This assumed link between greater right- and left-hemisphere activity measured during the performance of a particular task and the manner in which the stimuli are actually being processed appears tenable in the light of current knowledge in the field of neuroscience, especially with respect to language.

Evidence for the existence of these distinct processing modes is by now extremely well documented, although not undisputed (see Bogen, 1969; Bradshaw & Nettleton, 1981; Corballis, 1983; Kinsbourne & Smith, 1974; Lecours & L'Hermitte, 1979; Witelson, 1977). Although a number of different labels have been used to describe the two modes, the most well-known and widely cited are "analytic-sequential" for the left hemisphere and "holistic-parallel" for the right.[1] At the same time, it is recognized that hemispheric specialization may not be exclusive and that each hemisphere may, to a certain extent, be capable of processing information in the other's primary mode (Witelson, 1977).

## Evidence for Right Hemisphere Participation in First Language Acquisition

In spite of the left hemisphere's dominance for most language processing tasks, recent experimental and clinical findings have prompted researchers to posit a role for the right hemisphere in the acquisition of a first language. Interestingly, there are two separate lines of argumentation which lead to this view. The first is based on studies of the development of lateralization which have found that although children show left hemisphere dominance for language stimuli, they appear to be relatively less lateralized than adults. Witelson (1977) interprets this as implying greater right hemisphere involvement for language in children than in adults. However, there are also studies that indicate no developmental change in children's degree of lateralization for language (see Segalowitz, 1979; Witelson, 1977).

These latter studies do not necessarily refute Witelson's arguments in favor of right hemisphere participation in first language acquisition. They provide instead an alternative framework for viewing such participation, one in which lateralization in infants and adults is seen to differ more in kind than in degree, since a baby's responses may be more governed than an adult's by inborn reflexive asymmetries. In this view, a lack of increase in left lateralization with age could be an indication of the adult's greater freedom to selectively engage the two hemispheres in processing given stimuli (Segalowitz, 1979, 1983).

The "difference in kind" argument proposed by Segalowitz (1979, 1983) is further supported by Levy's (in press) proposal that collaboration between the two hemispheres is made increasingly more efficient as the fibres of the corpus

---

[1]Among the other labels attached to the contrasting processing modes typical of the two hemispheres are sequential successive/simultaneous synthesis (Das, 1973), serialist/holist (Pask & Scott, 1972), and verbal/imaginal (Paivio, 1971).

callosum undergo the process of mylenization in early childhood. As the speed of transmission increases with age throughout early childhood, the child in the first stages of language acquisition would have greater access than the neonate to both right- and left-hemisphere strategies in dealing with as yet unanalyzed language data. Taken together with evidence that the acallosal brain demonstrates very little syntactic competence (Dennis, 1981), Levy's and Segalowitz's proposals lend support to the position that the right hemisphere plays a definite and important role in first language acquistion, rather than an accidental one resulting from incomplete hemispheric specialization.

One well-established clinical finding which appears to support these views of right hemisphere involvement in first language acquisition is that, in children under 5 years, the right hemisphere can successfully take over most language functions after left hemispherectomy (Basser, 1962; Dennis, 1980; Dennis & Kohn, 1975; Dennis & Whitaker, 1976; Milner, 1974; Rasmussen & Milner, 1977; White, 1961). This, of course, could be attributed entirely to early interhemisphere plasticity without any need to postulate initial right hemisphere involvement for language. However, other findings support the position that the right hemisphere is involved in normal children's early language processing. For example, based on verbal IQ scores of early right-brain damaged children, Woods (1980) concludes that right hemisphere lesions sustained by children in their first year ". . . could somehow interfere with the normal development of left hemisphere [verbal] functions, but similarly localized lesions later in childhood could not" (1980, p. 155). One of two possible explanations offered for these latter findings is that they are due to ". . . the lack of some critical early facilitatory role of the right hemisphere" (Woods, 1980, p. 155). Furthermore, some researchers report that the incidence of language deficits caused by right hemisphere lesions is far more likely in children under age 5 than in older children or adults (Basser, 1962; see Krashen, 1973, 1975; McFie, 1961). This last claim is, however, disputed by Woods (1980) whose own data do not fit this pattern.

Lastly, in support of right hemisphere involvement in first language acquisition, is the generally held view that the right hemisphere takes over language very quickly in children with left hemisphere damage (Lenneberg, 1967). But other evidence suggests that the time required for recovery from early onset aphasia varies considerably from patient to patient (Woods, 1980). Also, Dennis and Whitaker's (1976) results indicate that early left hemisphere damage may result in delayed language acquisition. One possible explanation for these contradictory findings is that such delays in recovery and onset of language could be due to other complications, given the unique nature of each case. In any event, these counterclaims are not necessarily incompatible with a proposed role for the right hemisphere in language acquisition. Rather, they suggest that whatever the right hemisphere's role, it cannot fully compensate for a damaged left hemisphere.

## Evidence for Right Hemisphere Participation in Adult Second Language Acquisition[2]

In spite of its controversial nature, the evidence for right hemisphere involvement during first language acquisition had led a number of scholars to speculate on both the nature of this involvement and whether there may be analogous involvement of the right hemisphere in adult second language acquisition. One characterization of right hemisphere involvement in adult acquisition, known as the stage hypothesis (Obler, 1981; Obler, Albert & Gordon, 1975),[3] is based on a rationale similar to the one to be presented in the following section of this paper. It assumes an interaction between the processing mode typical of the right hemisphere and the processing requirements of the acquirer.

*The Stage Hypothesis—Experimental Studies.* The stage hypothesis predicts that in right-handed individuals, right hemisphere involvement is greater for the language being acquired than for the first language. It also predicts that right hemisphere participation should be especially apparent in the early stages of second language acquisition. The stage hypothesis thus implies that laterality differences between the bilingual's two languages will decrease as second language proficiency increases.

Support for the stage hypothesis comes primarily from studies which found bilinguals to be more left lateralized in their first language than in their second (Gaziel, Obler, Bentin, & Albert, 1977; Maitre, 1974; Obler et al., 1975; Schneiderman & Wesche, 1983; Sewell & Panou, 1983; Silverberg, Bentin, Gaziel, Obler, & Albert, 1979; Sussman, Franklin, & Simon, 1982). A few studies also found proficient bilinguals to be more left lateralized in their second language than were nonproficient bilinguals. The stimuli in most of these latter studies were presented tachistoscopically (Gaziel et al., 1977; Obler et al., 1975; Silverberg et al., 1979), although one study employed a dichotic listening paradigm (Wesche & Schneiderman, 1982).

---

[2]Although the discussion of hemisphere involvement in second language acquisition which follows is focussed on adults, it is recognized that many, if not all, the claims made about adult second language acquisition apply to children as well. However, children acquiring a second language may have not yet completed acquisition of their first language, and there is still some controversy over whether hemispheric specialization and lateralization for language is present at birth or whether it develops gradually as a first language is acquired (see Krashen, 1973; 1975; Witelson, 1977; Segalowitz, 1979, 1983 for discussion of this issue). Thus it would be difficult, if not impossible, to derive a clear interpretation of data regarding hemisphere involvement in child second language acquisition when the basis for comparison is first language acquisition.

[3]Galloway & Krashen (1980) have proposed a modification to the stage hypothesis which makes a distinction between hemisphere involvement in conscious language *learning* (involving use of the Monitor) and unconscious language *acquisition*. However, the version of the stage hypothesis referred to in this article is the one proposed by Obler et al. (1975) and Obler (1981).

In contrast to the studies just cited, several others bearing on the issue of right hemisphere participation in second language acquisition do not support the stage hypothesis. Some studies report no significant differences in lateralization patterns for first and second languages (Barton, Goodglass, & Shai, 1965; Carroll, 1978a; Galloway & Scarcella, 1982; Gordon, 1980; Hamers & Lambert, 1977; Rapport, Tan, & Whitaker, 1983; Soares & Grosjean, 1980; Walters & Zatorre, 1978) and a few report greater left lateralization for the second language (Carroll, 1978b; Kotik, 1975; Rogers, Ten Houten, Kaplan, & Gardiner, 1977). Included among the alternative explanations offered for these results are age of second language acquisition (Genesee et al., 1978; Sussman et al., 1982) and context of language acquisition (Galloway & Krashen, 1980; Kotik, 1975). Artifacts of the experimental design such as choice of the subject or stimulus sample and of the measure of lateralization, as well as the appropriateness of testing procedures and the presence of individual differences in strategies have also been proposed to account for the disparate results of these studies. (For further discussion of these variables, see Bryden, 1978, 1980; Obler, Zatorre, Galloway, & Vaid, 1982; Segalowitz & Orr, 1981; Vaid, 1983.)

However, it is not within the scope of this paper to debate either the methodological issues surrounding these studies or their interpretations, both of which are discussed elsewhere (see Obler et al., 1982; Vaid, 1983; Vaid & Genesee, 1980). With such a variety of findings and explanations, it seems reasonable to rely on those which, together with other evidence, can lead to a coherent characterization of right hemisphere participation in language acquisition. In this case, such an organizing principle is provided by evidence supporting the stage hypothesis (Obler, 1981; Obler et al., 1975).

*The Stage Hypothesis—Clinical Studies.* Clinical evidence can be cited in partial support of the stage hypothesis. This comes from two surveys of aphasia in adult polyglots which found that these individuals were somewhat more likely than monolinguals to suffer aphasic symptoms as a result of right hemisphere lesions (Albert & Obler, 1978; Galloway, 1980). For example, of 70 cases where lesion site was known or could be inferred from a hemiplegia, Albert and Obler (1978) report 7 cases of crossed aphasia. Of these 7 cases, 3 (or 4% of the 70 cases) were known right-handers and an equal number were known left-handers. This equivalent incidence of crossed aphasia in right- and left-handed polyglots contrasts with findings from Zangwill's (1967) extensive review of reported cases of brain damage in which the incidence of crossed aphasia was much higher for left-handers than for right-handers.

Albert and Obler (1978) also note that a greater proportion of right-sided than left-sided lesions resulted in nonparallel recovery in bilinguals. Of 5 aphasic patients with right hemisphere lesions, 4 (or 80%) showed nonparallel recovery of their language abilities. This contrasts with 26 aphasic cases resulting from left hemisphere lesions, where only 11 (or 42%) evidenced nonparallel recovery

(Albert & Obler, 1978). Despite the small sample sizes, these results do support the view that the bilingual's two languages may be differentially organized and that the right hemisphere may play a more significant role in language processing for bilinguals than for monolinguals.

Again, there is some controversy regarding the conclusions of these surveys of polyglot aphasia. Vaid (1983) cautions that the cases of selective recovery reported in the literature may not be typical, having been published because they were unusual and therefore interesting. Furthermore, as Paradis (1977) points out, it is difficult to judge whether such case studies support or refute any of the hypotheses concerning lateralization in adult bilinguals, since crucial information about the representativeness of the sample, as well as on stage, context and age of second language acquisition is not consistently available. It is clear, however, that the polyglot aphasia literature represents individuals who varied greatly in their second, third, or even first language proficiency premorbidly. Thus, if right hemisphere participation indeed has an inverse relationship with degree of second language proficiency, there is little reason to expect the polyglot aphasia literature to be at all consistent as regards right hemisphere-linked aphasias.

There is one final piece of evidence supporting an integral role for the right hemisphere in second language acquisition. Critchley (1962, cited in Searleman, 1977) reports that individuals who have suffered right hemisphere damage experience difficulty in learning novel linguistic materials. This finding is apparently corroborated in the cases of some individuals with intact first language skills and high verbal IQ's who suffered severe damage restricted to the right hemisphere in childhood and who later reported considerable difficulty in acquiring a second language (Teuber & Rudel as cited in Obler, 1981). Unfortunately, the possibility that these subjects had also suffered some left hemisphere damage could not be entirely ruled out (Rudel, personal communication, 1984).

## THE RIGHT HEMISPHERE'S ROLE IN ACQUISITION

Consideration of a possible role for the right hemisphere in first or second language acquisition follows naturally from the evidence cited above. What might be the nature of such a role? Is it, as some would claim, merely to provide additional computational capacity of essentially the same sort as that for which the left hemisphere seems better suited? And, if this is the case, is the right hemisphere's main function in language processing to help the left hemisphere with difficult tasks in a kind of work-sharing arrangement (Hardyck, 1980)? Given the volume of research which has characterized the typical and distinct processing modes of the two hemispheres, it seems reasonable to propose that the right hemisphere's role in language acquisition is probably something more than the mere performance of a subset of left-hemisphere functions. This is not to insist that the right hemisphere's role falls within boundaries delineated by a standard view of linguistic competence (Chomsky, 1965) or of core grammar (Chomsky, 1981). Rather, it may play a crucial, but essentially nonlinguistic part in developing such competence.

The left-hemisphere advantage for the majority of language tasks is probably an indication that linguistic stimuli are normally processed most efficiently in the analytical-sequential mode characteristic of that hemisphere.[4] However, it is argued here that the efficient processing of linguistic stimuli in the left hemisphere is probably as much dependent on the speaker's knowledge of the linguistic system as it is on the characteristics of language. The language learner, lacking such knowledge, must presumably approach the processing of the target language at a more fundamental level. Put another way, it seems plausible to suppose that the processing of a given linguistic unit by a linguistically mature native speaker who recognizes it as an element of complex syntactic and semantic systems in which it can have multiple meanings is probably quite different from the processing of that same word as a novel stimulus by an acquirer who lacks such systems in the target language and who may simply perceive the stimulus as an undifferentiated string of sounds.

In order to develop native-like processing capacity in a language, the learner must first identify and decode or attach meaning to the relevant language stimuli. This is a complex task which involves the simultaneous integration of incoming language stimuli with previously encountered language data and with knowledge from a number of different cognitive domains. The learner would likely draw on all relevant linguistic cues, as well as on extralinguistic information from the situational/emotional context of the incoming stimuli. The right hemisphere, with its holistic-parallel mode of functioning, would appear to be ideally suited to such a task. In this section of the paper, we review evidence supporting an essential role for the right hemisphere both in identifying or recognizing relevant second language stimuli and in attaching meaning to them.

To begin with, a number of studies suggest that both first- and second-language acquirers go through similar early stages in which they attempt to organize novel target language stimuli into perceptual patterns which ultimately take on meaning and serve as the basis for speech production. Indirect evidence for such a stage comes from research on second language teaching methodology. Studies in which various forms of delayed speaking are employed provide evidence that adults benefit from an initial "active listening period" before they begin to speak the second language (Asher, 1977; Gary, 1978; Krashen, 1981; Neufeld, 1977; Neufeld & Schneiderman, 1980; Nord, 1980; Postovsky, 1974). During this silent period adults can focus almost exclusively on comprehension of the target language. This appears to correspond to the natural strategy adopted

[4]It is important to note here that a distinction is made between this type of left hemisphere dominance for language and the possibly reflexive-type left hemisphere bias for speech sounds found in neonates and very young children discussed earlier.

by most child acquirers (see Dulay, Burt, & Krashen, 1982) and to the almost universal observation that learners' comprehension exceeds their production ability (see Tarone, 1974).

It has also been noted that both first- and second-language acquirers produce unsegmented routines and patterns in the early stages of acquisition (Burling, 1959; Fillmore, 1979; Hakuta, 1976; Huang, 1971, Itoh & Hatch, 1978; Keller-Cohen, 1979; Krashen & Scarcella, 1978; Peters, 1977; Vihman, 1982). Based on data obtained from four children acquiring English as a second language, Fillmore (1979) states that

> the strategy of acquiring formulaic speech is central to the learning of language: indeed, it is this step that puts the learner in a position to perform the analysis which is necessary for language learning . . . the formulas the children learned and used constituted the linguistic material on which a large part of the analytical activities involved in language learning could be carried out. (p. 212)

Fillmore describes the child acquirer's use of formulas as data for analysis in the following way: Children notice recurring parts of such an utterance and figure out that these recurring parts can be substituted for or varied. They then begin using the substitutable parts as constituents of other utterances. When all the constituents of a formulaic utterance have been freed from the original construction, children end up with an abstract structure consisting of a pattern of rules by which they can construct like utterances. One compelling type of evidence from Fillmore's data in support of this view is that, as they began to play with constituents, the children she studied often proceeded from well-formed formulaic utterances learned as wholes to less well-formed ones (Fillmore, 1979). Peters (1983) puts forth a similar argument based on an extensive review of the acquisition literature.

Although the above evidence is circumstantial, it nonetheless raises the possibility that the early acquirer applies a right hemisphere type holistic or "chunking" strategy to novel data in the target language. These chunks of data must then be linguistically processed, presumably by the left hemisphere in its characteristic analytical-sequential mode. Variability in degree of right hemisphere participation could also be accounted for within this model, since acquirers apparently may rely on such chunking strategies to greater or lesser degrees (Peters, 1977).

A similar picture of the role of the right hemisphere in a related area is provided by work on the early perception of novel typescripts by literate adults and preliterate children (Bakker, 1981; Bentin, 1980; Endo, Shimizu, & Nakamura, 1981; Gordon & Carmon, 1976; Lamm, 1978; Silverberg, Gordon, Pollock, & Bentin, 1980; Vaid, 1981). In all of these studies, subjects exhibit a left visual field/right hemisphere advantage for such stimuli. By contrast, familiar typescripts yield a left hemisphere advantage. These results suggest that novel typescripts could be handled by holistic-parallel right hemisphere type processing in much the same manner as that proposed for novel phonetic strings. Once familiar, typescripts as well as phonetic strings appear to be processed in the more analytic mode characteristic of the left hemisphere. It is also worth emphasizing here that these results with typescripts have been found with both children and adults, suggesting that this effect is not limited to immature subjects.

Two characterizations of the difference between right- and left-hemisphere processing of the acoustic speech signal lend additional credence to such a view of the right hemisphere's role in language acquisition (Levy & Trevarthen, 1977; Studdert-Kennedy & Shankweiler, 1970). In both studies, the authors conclude that the right hemisphere is unable to carry out phonetic analysis. Only the left hemisphere is capable of complex linguistic tasks that go beyond a gross "auditory analysis of the stimuli." Thus the "rudimentary comprehension" by the right hemisphere must be based on ". . . auditory analysis which, by repeated association with the outcome of subsequent linguistic processing, had come to control simple discriminative responses" (Studdert-Kennedy & Shankweiler, 1970, pp. 590–591). By contrast, the left hemisphere is assigned ". . . that portion of the perceptual process which is truly linguistic: the sorting out of a complex of auditory parameters into phonological features" (Studdert-Kennedy & Shankweiler, 1970, p. 590). Levy and Trevarthen also suggest that right hemisphere-initiated formulaic utterances reported in a number of clinical studies (see below) ". . . are probably formed as motor Gestalts, and are not constructed analytically from phoneme-elicited articulemes as many linguists would claim to be necessary for speaking" (Levy & Trevarthen, 1977, p. 116). Similar findings have been reported regarding the right hemisphere's ability to read. Zaidel and Peters (1981) suggest that the disconnected right hemispheres of two commissurotomy patients ". . . read "ideographically," recognizing words directly as visual gestalts without intermediate phonetic recoding or grapheme-to-phoneme translation." (Zaidel & Peters, 1981, p. 205).

As was noted earlier, the right hemisphere may also play a semantic role in language acquisition. In order to guess at the referential meaning of recurring linguistic units, the learner must establish some real world reference, some interface between linguistic and pragmatic knowledge. It is here that the right hemisphere may make its contribution in the initial use of "heuristic" strategies which rely on pragmatic knowledge to determine reference.[5] This notion appears consonant with the semantic capabilities of the right hemisphere demonstrated in a study of hemidecorticate children (Dennis, 1980). Dennis suggests that "the process by which words become attached to visual arrays is mediated . . . perhaps more efficiently by the right hemisphere" (p. 170).

Findings from several sources demonstrate some first language processing capacities in the adult right hemisphere that appear to correspond with its pro-

---

[5]This notion is derived (indirectly) from Woods (1980).

posed role in language acquisition. These apparently residual right hemisphere capacities may be accessible to adult second language acquirers as well as to those who have suffered severe impairments of the left hemisphere. For example, a number of clinical studies provide evidence that the adult right hemisphere may be capable of receptively processing concrete nouns (Gazzaniga & Hillyard, 1971; Levy & Trevarthen, 1977; Zaidel, 1973, 1978). In addition, left-hemispherectomized adults and those who have suffered damage to the speech centers of the left hemisphere have been reported to produce certain types of *automatic* or *routine* speech, such as greetings or swear words, presumably from the intact right hemisphere (Gott, 1973; Jackson, 1958; Smith, 1966).

Other studies suggest that the right hemisphere plays a role in intact language processing as well. For example, right hemisphere involvement in processing the prosodic aspects of the first language has been demonstrated in healthy, left lateralized adults (Blumstein & Cooper, 1974;[6] Borod & Goodglass, 1980; Kimura, 1964). There have also been reports of language disturbances in adults who have suffered damage to the right hemisphere. These include articulation difficulties, word finding problems (Brodel, 1973; Critchley, 1970), naming problems (Joanette, Lecours, Lepage, & Lamoureux, 1983), prosodic disturbances (Botez & Wertheim, 1959; Ettlinger, Jackson, & Zangwill, 1955; Joanette et al., 1983; Tucker, Watson, & Heilman, 1977), and difficulty with certain abstract concepts (Eisenson, 1962). In addition, right hemisphere patients have been characterized as being extremely literal, lacking in the ability to appreciate subtleties and nuances in a message, and insensitive to the communicative situation (Brownell, Michel, Powelson, & Gardner, 1983; Foldi, Cicone, & Gardner, 1983; Gardner, Brownell, Wapner, & Michelow, 1983; Gardner, Ling, Flamm, & Silverman, 1975; Wapner, Hamby, & Gardner, 1981; Weinstein, 1964; Weinstein & Kahn, 1955; Winner & Gardner, 1977). The right hemisphere may also mediate in the interpretation and expression of emotion (Moscovitch, 1983). In contrast to the performance of right hemisphere patients, left hemisphere damaged patients appear able to draw on contextual and paralinguistic cues to make inferences about communicative intent (Foldi et al., 1983; Gardner et al., 1983). Severely aphasic, left hemisphere damaged patients have also been observed to use intonation and a variety of pragmatic devices in an effort to communicate (Foldi et al., 1983).

Such findings prompt further speculation on the right hemisphere's role in determining the real-world reference of linguistic units. Based partially on the

[6]In discussing Blumstein and Cooper's results, Zurif (1974) suggests that, due to their methodology, the right hemisphere processing of prosody in their study was essentially nonlinguistic. This alternative interpretation is, however, still consistent with the claim made here concerning the right hemisphere's role in the holistic perception of prosodic strings. Whether or not such processing as that demonstrated in the Blumstein and Cooper study is linguistic in a standard, theoretical sense does not bear on the nature of its relationship to the early stages of language acquisition.

work of Neisser (1967, 1969), Tarone (1974) posits a preliminary, nonlinguistic stage in learners' speech perception. Decoding in this preliminary stage is not based on syntactic rules, but rather on the ". . . context of situation, such as facial expression, suprasegmental features, and various "props" from the physical setting" (p. 231). To illustrate the operation of this process, Tarone describes how the rhythmic structure of English, with its fairly predictable pattern of stressed, content carrying syllables, interspersed with unstressed syllables, may help learners to segment speech into chunks or "Gestalts" from which meaningful constituents can be extracted. Based on the findings cited above concerning right hemisphere involvement in language functioning, we can reasonably conclude that the segmentation and extraction of meaning described by Tarone may rely on the right hemisphere's abilities to deal with the prosodic components of the speech signal and to integrate pragmatic, contextual and emotive features of a situation in the interpretation of target language utterances.

Tarone's (1974) suggestion of a preliminary stage of perception is supported by other research on speech perception (see Lehtonen & Sajavaara, 1980; Sajavaara, 1981; Sanders, 1977), as well as by data from the early stages of both first and second language acquisition in which learners' utterances consist primarily of content words. The normally unstressed grammatical functors, such as inflections and prepositions, are initially left out of learners' production and then added in a gradual progression of stages (Brown, 1973; Dulay et al., 1982). Additional evidence for the importance of pragmatics in learners' interpretation of language comes from research indicating that young children initially rely more on contextual, rather than on syntactic cues, in their comprehension of sentences in their first language (de Villiers & de Villiers, 1973).

The above findings also suggest that the right hemisphere's role in language processing ties in with the social and expressive functions of language, which are undoubtedly the learner's primary concern in first language acquisition. It is interesting to note that such concerns represent the most successful motivating force behind second language acquisition as well (Gardner & Lambert, 1972; Gardner, Smythe, Clément, & Gliksman, 1976; Schumann, 1976).

Although right hemisphere processing may play an important role in normal language acquisition, the evidence to date suggests that it has only a limited role in mature processing of the core linguistic system. Once language is acquired, the left hemisphere appears capable of performing all core language-related functions, including those for which the right hemisphere has a demonstrated capacity. Research on later abilities of early left hemidecorticate children (Dennis & Kohn, 1975) and on children with early left hemisphere damage (Woods, 1980) in fact indicates that in spite of early interhemispheric plasticity, there are certain core linguistic functions, such as the comprehension of complex syntactic constructions, that can only be performed by the left hemisphere. Thus, the most plausible characterization of right hemisphere participation in normal language acquisition is that of a limited, specialized, perhaps essential role in the initial perception, retention, and rudimentary comprehension of novel language stimuli. The evidence presented above also supports a continuing role for the right hemisphere in facilitating the use of grammatical knowledge in real-world situations. In this view, it is a role which complements the clearly linguistic role of the left hemisphere.

A related perspective to the one presented here is that of Goldberg and Costa (1981), who have outlined a crucial role for the right hemisphere in the apprehension of novel stimuli. They claim that structural differences between the two hemispheres underly the right hemisphere's advantage for the processing of novel stimuli across various modalities. The process of learning is very much dependent on the right hemisphere's preponderance of interareal connections and the greater proportion of associative cortex on the right than in the left hemisphere. The left hemisphere plays the major role in storing and operating the descriptive systems such as language, reading, and musical ability, formed during the learning process.

In support of this position, Goldberg and Costa (1981) cite several studies where subjects showed right hemisphere dominance during early exposure to novel stimuli and where increasing familiarity with those stimuli resulted in a shift to left hemisphere dominance. These include verbal naming of unfamiliar visual symbols (Gordon & Carmon, 1976), a face recognition task (Reynolds & Jeeves, 1978), and dichotically presented musical sounds (Kallman & Corballis, 1975) and musical patterns (Spellacy, 1970). There are also studies in which a right hemisphere advantage for subjects who were musically naive contrasted with a left hemisphere advantage for trained musicians (Bever & Chiarello, 1974; Johnson, 1977). Similarly, a weaker right ear advantage for Morse code has been reported for naive subjects than for experienced Morse code operators (Papcun, Krashen, Terbeek, Remington, & Harshman, 1974).

## CONCLUSION

This paper has attempted to draw together those data from the fields of neuroscience and first- and second-language acquisition which can be used to formulate a coherent characterization of the right hemisphere's role in language acquisition. Although it is recognized that a great deal of controversy surrounds many of the claims upon which the above arguments are based, the counterclaims are no less subject to challenge. Clearly, much further research into the nature of the both right and left hemisphere participation in the acquisition process is needed before these issues can be sorted out. Future research techniques will hopefully overcome some of the methodological issues which cloud the interpretation of the findings to date. Such research should focus on the role of the right hemisphere in mature language processing as well as on patterns of laterality in stable bilinguals and in those who are in the process of becoming bilingual. In addition to contributing to our understanding of the role of the right hemisphere in the acquisition of the various descriptive subsystems of human cognition (Goldberg & Costa, 1981), the results of such research would also add to the growing body of work which focusses on similarities between language acquisition in children and adults (see Dulay et al., 1982).

## ACKNOWLEDGMENT

I would like to express my thanks to Marjorie Wesche, Stephen Krashen, P. G. Patel, and Christian Adjemian for their helpful comments on an earlier draft of this paper. (However, the views expressed here do not necessarily reflect their own views on this topic). I am also grateful to Chantal Desmarais for her careful typing and editing of the manuscript.

## REFERENCES

Albert, M., & Obler, L. (1978). *The bilingual brain: Neuropsychological and neurolinguistic aspects of bilingualism.* New York: Academic Press.

Asher, J. J. (1977). *Learning another language through actions.* Los Gatos, CA: Sky Oaks Productions.

Bakker, D. J. (1981). A set of brains for learning to read. In K. Diller (Ed.), *Individual differences and universals in language learning aptitude* (pp. 65–71). Rowley, MA: Newbury House.

Barton, M., Goodglass, H., & Shai, A. (1965). Differential recognition of tachistoscopically presented English and Hebrew words in right and left visual fields. *Perception and Motor Skills, 21,* 431–437.

Basser, L. S. (1962). Hemiplegia of early onset and the faculty of speech with special reference to the effects of hemispherectomy. *Brain, 85,* 427–460.

Bentin, S. (1980, March). *Right hemisphere role in reading a second language.* Paper read at the Symposium on Cerebral Lateralization in Bilingualism, BABBLE Conference, Niagara Falls, New York.

Bever, T. G., & Chiarello, K. (1974). Cerebral dominance in musicians and non-musicians. *Science, 185,* 537–539.

Blumstein, S., & Cooper, W. E. (1974). Hemispheric processing of intonation contours. *Cortex, 10,* 146–158.

Bogen, J. E. (1969). The other side of the brain II: An appositional mind. *Bulletin of the Los Angeles Neurological Societies, 34,* 135–161.

Borod, J. C., & Goodglass, H. (1980). Lateralization of linguistic and melodic processing with age. *Neuropsychologia, 18,* 79–83.

Botez, M. I., & Wertheim, N. (1959). Expressive aphasia and amusia following right frontal lesion in a right handed man. *Brain, 82,* 186–202.

Bradshaw, J. L., & Nettleton, N. C. (1981). The nature of hemisphere specialization in man. *Behavioral and Brain Sciences, 4,* 51–63.

Brodel, A. (1973). Self-observations and neuro-anatomical considerations after a stroke (in the right hemisphere). *Brain, 96,* 675–694.

Brown, R. (1973). *A first language.* Cambridge, MA: Harvard University Press.

Brownell, H. H., Michel, D., Powelson, J., & Gardner, H. (1983). Surprise but not coherence: Sensitivity to verbal humor in right-hemisphere patients. *Brain and Language, 18*(1), 20–27.

Bryden, M. P. (1978). Strategy effects in the assessment of hemispheric asymmetry. In G. Underwood (Ed.), *Strategies of information processing.* (pp. 117–149). New York: Academic Press.

Bryden, M. P. (1980, February). Strategy and attentional influences on dichotic listening and tachistoscopic lateralization assessments. Paper presented at the Annual Meeting of the International Neuropsychology Society, San Francisco.

Burling, R. (1959). Language development of a Garo and English-speaking child. *Word, 15,* 45–68.

Carroll, F. W. (1978a). Cerebral dominance for language: A dichotic listening study of Navajo-English bilinguals. In H. Key, S. McCullough, & J. Sawyer (Eds.), *The bilingual in a pluralistic society: Proceedings of the Sixth Southwest Area Language and Linguistics Workshop* (pp. 11–17). Long Beach: California State University.

Carroll, F. W. (1978b, April). *The other side of the brain and foreign language learning.* Paper presented at the TESOL Conference, Mexico City, Mexico.

Chomsky, N. (1965). *Aspects of the theory of syntax.* Cambridge, MA: MIT Press.

Chomsky, N. (1981). *Lectures on Government and Binding.* Dordrecht: Foris Publications.

Corballis, M. C. (1983). *Human laterality.* New York: Academic Press.

Critchley, M. (1962). Speech and speech loss in relation to the duality of the brain. In V. B. Mountcastle (Ed.), *Interhemispheric relations and cerebral dominance,* Baltimore, MD: John Hopkins University Press.

Critchley, M. (1970). *Aphasiology and other aspects of language.* London: Arnold.

Das, J. P. (1973). Structure of cognitive abilities: Evidence for simultaneous and successive processing. *Journal of Educational Psychology, 65*(1), 103–108.

Dennis, M. (1980). Language acquisition in a single hemisphere: Semantic organization. In D. Caplan (Ed.), *Biological studies of mental processes* (pp. 159–186). Cambridge, MA: MIT Press.

Dennis, M. (1981). Language in a congenitally acallosal brain. *Brain and language, 12,* 33–53.

Dennis, M., & Kohn, B. (1975). Comprehension of syntax in infantile hemiplegics after cerebral hemidecortication: Left hemisphere superiority. *Brain and Language, 2,* 472–482.

Dennis, M., & Whitaker, H. A. (1976). Language acquisition following hemidecortication: Linguistic superiority of the left over the right hemisphere. *Brain and Language, 3,* 404–433.

DeVilliers, P., & DeVilliers, J. (1973). Development of the use of word order in comprehension. *Journal of Psychological Research, 2,* 331–341.

Dulay, H., Burt, M. K., & Krashen, S. (1982). *Language Two.* New York: Oxford University Press.

Eisenson, J. (1962). Language and intellectual modifications associated with right cerebral damage. *Language and Speech, 5,* 49–53.

Endo, M., Shimizu, A., & Nakamura, I. (1981). The influence of Hangul learning upon laterality differences in Hangul word recognition. *Brain and Language, 14,* 114–119.

Ettlinger, G., Jackson, C. V., & Zangwill, O. L. (1955). Dysphasia following right temporal lobectomy in a right-handed man. *Journal of Neurology, Neurosurgery, and Psychiatry, 18,* 214–217.

Fillmore, L. W. (1979). Individual differences in second language acquisition. In C. J. Fillmore, D. Kempler, W. S-Y. Wang (Eds.), *Individual differences in language ability and language behavior* (pp. 203–228). New York: Academic Press.

Foldi, N. S., Cicone, M., & Gardner, H. (1983). Pragmatic aspects of communication in brain-damaged patients. In S. J. Segalowitz (Ed.), *Language functions and brain organization* (pp. 51–86). New York: Academic Press.

Galloway, L. (1980, March). *Clinical evidence: Polyglot aphasia.* Paper read at the symposium on Cerebral Lateralization in Bilingualism, BABBLE Conference, Niagara Falls, New York.

Galloway, L., & Krashen, S. (1980). Cerebral organization in bilingualism and second language acquisition. In R. Scarcella & S. Krashen (Eds.), *Research in second language acquisition* (pp. 74–80). Rowley, MA: Newbury House.

Galloway, L., & Scarcella, R. (1982). Cerebral organization in adult second language acquisition: Is the right hemisphere more involved? *Brain and Language, 16,* 56–60.

Gardner, H., Brownell, H. H., Wapner, W., & Michelow, D. (1983). Missing the point: The role of the right hemisphere in the processing of complex linguistic materials. In E. Perecman (Ed.), *Cognitive processing in the right hemisphere* (pp. 169–191). New York: Academic Press.

Gardner, R., & Lambert, W. (1972). *Attitudes and motivation in second-language learning.* Rowley, MA: Newbury House.

Gardner, H., Ling, P. K., Flamm, L., & Silverman, J. (1975). Comprehension and appreciation of humorous material following brain damage. *Brain, 98,* 399–412.

Gardner, R., Smythe, P., Clément, R., & Gliksman, L. (1976). Second language learning: A social-psychological perspective. *Canadian Modern Language Review, 32,* 198–213.

Gary, H. O. (1978). Why speak if you don't need to? The case for a listening approach to beginning foreign language learning. In W. C. Ritchie (Ed.), *Second language acquisition research: Issues and implications* (pp. 189–199). New York: Academic Press.

Gaziel, T., Obler, L., Bentin, S., & Albert, M. (1977, October). *The dynamics of lateralization in second language learning: Sex and proficiency effects.* Paper read at Boston University Conference on Language Development, Boston, MA.

Gazzaniga, M. S., & Hillyard, S. A. (1971). Language and speech capacity of the right hemisphere. *Neuropsychologia, 9,* 271–280.

Genesee, F., Hamers, J., Lambert, W. E., Mononen, L., Seitz, M., & Starck, R. (1978). Language processing in bilinguals. *Brain and Language 5,* 1–12.

Goldberg, E., & Costa, L. D. (1981). Hemisphere differences in the acquisition and use of descriptive systems. *Brain and Language, 14,* 144–173.

Gordon, H. (1980). Cerebral organization in bilinguals. *Brain and Language, 9,* 255–268.

Gordon, H., & Carmon, A. (1976). Transfer of dominance in speed of verbal response to visually presented stimuli from right to left hemisphere. *Perception and Motor Skills, 42,* 1091–1100.

Gott, P. S. (1973). Language after dominant hemispherectomy. *Journal of Neurology, Neurosurgery, & Psychiatry, 36,* 1082–1088.

Hakuta, K. A. (1976). A case study of a Japanese child learning English as a second language. *Language Learning, 26,* 321–351.

Hamers, J., & Lambert, W. (1977). Visual field and cerebral preferences in bilinguals. In S. Segalowitz & F. Gruber (Eds.), *Language development and neurological theory* (pp. 57–62). New York: Academic Press.

Hardyck, C. (1980, August). *Hemisphere differences and language ability.* Paper read at the Symposium on Bilingualism and Brain Function, Summer Linguistics Institute, Albuquerque, New Mexico.

Huang, J. A. (1971). *A Chinese child's acquisition of English syntax.* Master's thesis, University of California, Los Angeles.

Itoh, H., & Hatch, E. (1978). Second language acquisition: A case study. In E. Hatch (Ed.), *Second language acquisition: A book of readings* (pp. 76–90). Rowley, MA: Newbury House.

Jackson, J. H. (1958). *Selected writings of John Hughlings Jackson.* J. Taylor (Ed.), New York: Basic Books.

Joanette, Y., Lecours, A. R., Lepage, Y., & Lamoureux, M.(1983). Language in right-handers with right hemisphere lesions: A preliminary study including anatomical genetic, and social factors. *Brain and Language, 20*(2), 217–248.

Johnson, P. R. (1977). Dichotically-stimulated ear differences in musicians and non-musicians. *Cortex, 13,* 385–389.

Kallman, H. W., & Corballis, M. C. (1975). Ear asymmetry in reaction time to musical sounds. *Perception and Psychophysics, 17*(4), 368–370.

Keller-Cohen, D. (1979). Systematicity and variation in the non-native child's acquisition of conversational skills. *Language Learning, 29,* 27–44.

Kimura, D. (1964). Left-right differences in the perception of melodies. *Quarterly Journal of Experimental Psychology, 26,* 111–116.

Kinsbourne, M., & Smith, W. L. (Eds.), (1974). *Hemispheric disconnection and cerebral function.* Springfield, IL: CC Thomas.

Kotik, B. (1975). *Lateralization in bilinguals.* Unpublished thesis, Moscow State University.

Krashen, S. (1973). Lateralization, language learning, and the critical period: Some new evidence. *Language Learning, 23*(1), 63–74.

Krashen, S. (1975). The development of cerebral dominance and language learning: More new evidence. In D. Dato (Ed.), *Developmental psycholinguistics, Georgetown Round Table on Languages and Linguistics* (pp. 209–233). Washington, DC: Georgetown University Press.

Krashen, S. (1981). *Language acquisition and second language learning.* Oxford: Pergamon Press.

Krashen, S., & Scarcella, R. (1978). On routines and patterns in language acquisition and performance. *Language Learning, 28*(2), 283–300.

Lamm, O. (1978). *Interhemispheric differences in operating formal symbolic systems.* Master's Thesis, Technion School, Haifa, Israel.

Lecours, A. R., & L'Hermitte, F. (1979). *L'aphasie.* Paris: Flammarion.

Lehtonen, J., & Sajavaara, K. (1980). Phonology and speech processing in cross-language communication. In S. Eliasson (Ed.), *Theoretical issues in contrastive phonology.* Heidelberg: Julius Groos.

Lenneberg, E. (1967). *Biological foundations of language.* New York: Wiley.

Levy, J. (1985). Interhemispheric collaboration: Single-mindedness in the asymmetric brain. In C. T. Best (Ed.), *Hemispheric function and collaboration in the child: Theoretical, developmental and educational perspectives.* Orlando, FL: Academic Press.

Levy, J., & Trevarthen, C. (1977). Perceptual, semantic and phonetic aspects of elementary language processes. *Brain, 100,* 105–118.

Maitre, S. (1974). *On the representation of second language in the brain.* Master's thesis, University of California, Los Angeles.

McFie, J. (1961). The effects of hemispherectomy on intellectual functioning in cases of infantile hemiplegia. *Journal of Neurology, Neurosurgery, and Psychiatry, 24,* 240–249.

Milner, B. (1974). Functional recovery after lesions of the nervous system, 3. Developmental processes in neural plasticity. Sparing of language functions after early unilateral brain damage. *Neuroscience Research Program Bulletin, 12,* 213–217.

Moscovitch, M. (1983). The linguistic and emotional functions of the normal right hemisphere. In E. Perecman (Ed.), *Cognitive processing in the right hemisphere* (pp. 57–82). New York: Academic Press.

Neisser, U. (1967). *Cognitive psychology.* New York: Appleton-Century-Crofts.

Neisser, U. (1969). The role of rhythm in active verbal memory: Serial intrusions. *American Journal of Psychology, 82*(4), 540–546.

Neufeld, G. G. (1977). Language learning ability in adults: A study on the acquisition of prosodic and articulatory features. *Working Papers on Bilingualism, 12,* 45–60.

Neufeld, G. G., & Schneiderman, E. I. (1980). Prosodic and articulatory features in adult language learning. In R. C. Scarcella & S. Krashen (Eds.), *Research in second language acquisition: Selected papers of the Los Angeles Second Language Research Forum.* (pp. 105–109). Rowley, MA: Newbury House.

Nord, J. R. (1980). Developing listening fluency before speaking: An alternative paradigm. *System, 8,* 1–22.

Obler, L. K. (1981). Right hemisphere participation in second language acquisition. In K. Diller (Ed.), *Individual differences and universals in language learning aptitude* (pp. 53–64). Rowley, MA: Newbury House.

Obler, L. K., Albert, M., & Gordon, H. (1975, October). *Asymmetry of cerebral dominance in Hebrew-English bilinguals.* Paper read at Thirteenth Annual Meeting of the Academy of Aphasia, Victoria, Canada.

Obler, L., Zatorre, R., Galloway, L., & Vaid, J. (1982). Cerebral lateralization in bilinguals: methodological issues. *Brain and Language, 15,* 40–54.

Paivio, A. (1971). *Imagery and verbal processes.* New York: Holt, Rinehart and Winston.

Papcun, G., Krashen, S., Terbeek, D., Remington, R., & Harshman, R. (1974). Is the left hemisphere specialized for speech, language and/or something else? *Journal of the Acoustical Society of America, 55,* 319–327.

Paradis, M. (1977). Bilingualism and aphasia. In H. A. Whitaker & H. A. Whitaker (Eds.), *Studies in neurolinguistics,* (pp. 65–121). New York: Academic Press.

Pask, G., & Scott, B. (1972). Learning strategies and individual competence. *International Journal of Man-machine Studies, 4,* 217–253.

Peters, A. (1977). Language learning strategies: Does the whole equal the sum of the parts? *Language, 53,* 560–573.

Peters, A. (1983). *The units of language acquisition.* Cambridge, Eng.: Cambridge University Press.

Postovsky, V. A. (1974). Effects of delay in oral practice at the beginning of second language learning. *Modern Language Journal, LVIII 5–6,* 229–239.

Rapport, R. L., Tan, C. T., & Whitaker, H. A. (1983). Language function and dysfunction among Chinese and English-speaking polyglots: Cortical stimulation, Wada testing, and clinical studies. *Brain and Language, 18*(2), 315–341.

Rasmussen, T., & Milner, B. (1977). The role of early left-brain injury in determining lateralization of cerebral speech functions. In S. J. Diamond & D. A. Blizard (Eds.), *Evolution and lateralization of the brain. Annals of the New York Academy of Sciences, 229,* 355–369.

Reynolds, D. M., & Jeeves, M. A. (1978). A developmental study of hemisphere specialization for recognition of faces in normal subjects. *Cortex, 14,* 511–520.

Rogers, L., Ten Houten, W., Kaplan, C. D., & Gardiner, M. (1977). Hemispheric specialization of language: An EEG study of bilingual Hopi Indian children. *International Journal of Neuroscience, 17,* 89–92.

Sajavaara, K. (1981). Psycholinguistic models, second language acquisition and contrastive analysis. In J. Fisiak (Ed.), *Contrastive linguistics and the language teacher.* (pp. 87–120). Oxford: Pergamon Press.

Sanders, D. A. (1977). *Auditory perception of speech: An introduction to principles and problems.* Englewood Cliffs, NJ: Prentice-Hall.

Schneiderman, E. I., & Wesche, M. B. (1983). The role of the right hemisphere in second language acquisition. In K. M. Bailey, M. H. Long, & S. Peck (Eds.), *Second language acquisition studies.* (pp. 162–174). Rowley, MA: Newbury House.

Schumann, J. (1976). Social distance as a factor in second language acquisition. *Language Learning, 26,* 135–143.

Searleman, A. (1977). A review of right hemisphere linguistic capabilities. *Psychological Bulletin, 84*(3), 503–528.

Segalowitz, S., & Orr, C. (1981, February). *How to measure individual differences in brain lateralization: Demonstration of a paradigm.* Presented at the International Neuropsychological Society meeting in Atlanta, Georgia.

Segalowitz, S. J. (1979, June). *Infant cerebral asymmetries and developmental models of brain lateralization.* Paper read at the 40th Annual Meeting of the Canadian Psychological Association, Quebec, Canada.

Segalowitz, S. J. (1983). Cerebral asymmetries for speech in infancy. In S. J. Segalowitz (Ed.), *Language functions and brain organization* (pp. 221–229). New York: Academic Press.

Sewell, D. F., & Panou. L. (1983). Visual field asymmetries for verbal and dot localization tasks in monolingual and bilingual subjects. *Brain and Language, 18*(1), 28–34.

Silverberg, R., Bentin, S., Gaziel, T., Obler, L. K., & Albert, M. L. (1979). Shift of visual field preference for English words in native Hebrew speakers. *Brain and Language, 8,* 184–190.

Silverberg, R., Gordon, H., Pollock, S., & Bentin, S. (1980). Shift of visual field preference for Hebrew words in native speakers learning to read. *Brain and Language, 11,* 99–105.

Smith, A. (1966). Speech and other functions after left (dominant) hemispherectomy. *Journal of Neurology, Neurosurgery, and Psychiatry, 29,* 467–471.

Soares, C., & Grosjean, F. (1980). Left-hemisphere language lateralization in bilinguals and monolinguals. *Perception and Psychophysics, 29*(6), 599–604.

Spellacy, F. (1970). Lateral preferences in the identification of patterned stimuli. *Journal of the Acoustical Society of America, 47*(2), 574–578.

Studdert-Kennedy, M., & Shankweiler, D. (1970). Hemispheric specialization for speech perception. *Journal of the Acoustical Society of America, 48:2*(2), 579–594.

Sussman, H., Franklin, P., Simon, T. (1982). Bilingual speech: Bilateral control? *Brain and Language, 15,* 125–142.

Tarone, E. (1974). Speech perception in second language acquisition: A suggested model. *Language Learning, 24* (2), 223–233.

Tucker, D. M., Watson, R. T., & Heilman, K. M. (1977). Discrimination and evocation of affectively intoned speech in patients with right parietal disease. *Neurology, 27,* 947–950.

Vaid, J. (1981, May). *Cerebral lateralization of Hindi and Urdu: A pilot tachistoscopic Stroop study.* Paper read at the South Asian Languages Association, Stonybrook, New York.

Vaid, J. (1983). Bilingualism and brain lateralization. In S. J. Segalowitz (Ed.), *Language functions and brain organization* (pp. 315–339). New York: Academic Press.

Vaid, J., & Genesee, F. (1980). Neuropsychological approaches to bilingualism: a critical review. *Canadian Journal of Psychology, 34,* 417–445.

Vihman, M. M. (1982). Formulas in first and second language acquisition. In L. K. Obler & L. Menn (Eds.), *Exceptional language and linguistics.* (pp. 261–284). New York: Academic Press.

Walters, J., & Zatorre, R. (1978). Laterality differences for word identification in bilinguals. *Brain and Language, 2,* 158–167.

Wapner, W., Hamby, S., & Gardner, H. (1981). The role of the right hemisphere in the apprehension of complex linguistic materials. *Brain and Language, 14,* 15–33.

Weinstein, E. A. (1964). Affections of speech with lesions of the non-dominant hemisphere. *Research in Nervous and Mental Disease, 42,* 220–225.

Weinstein, E. A., & Kahn, R. L. (1955). *Denial of illness.* Springfield, IL: C C Thomas.

Wesche, M. B., & Schneiderman, E. I. (1982). Language lateralization in adult bilinguals. *Studies in Second Language Acquisition, 4*(2), 153–169.

White, H. (1961). Cerebral hemispherectomy in the treatment of infantile hemiplegia. *Confinia Neurologica, 21,* 1–50.

Winner, E., & Gardner, H. (1977). The comprehension of metaphor in brain-damaged patients. *Brain, 100,* 717.

Witelson, S. F. (1977). Early hemisphere specialization and interhemispheric plasticity: An empirical and theoretical review. In S. J. Segalowitz & F. A. Gruber (Eds.), *Language development and neurological theory* (pp. 149–158). New York: Academic Press.

Woods, B. T. (1980). Observations on the neurological basis for initial language. In D. Caplan (Ed.), *Biological studies for mental processes* (pp. 149–158). Cambridge, MA: MIT Press.

Zaidel, E. (1973). *Linguistic competence and related functions in the right hemisphere of man following commissurotomy and hemispherectomy*. Doctoral dissertation, California Institute of Technology.

Zaidel, E. (1978). Lexical organization in the right hemisphere. In P. Buser & A. Rougeuil-Buser (Eds.), *Cerebral correlates of conscious experience* (pp. 177–197). Amsterdam: Elsevier.

Zaidel, E., & Peters, A. (1981). Phonological encoding and ideographic reading by the disconnected right hemisphere: Two case studies. *Brain and Language, 14*, 205–234.

Zangwill, O. (1967). Speech and the minor hemisphere. *Acta Neurologica et Psychiatrica Belgica, 67*, 1013–1020.

Zurif, E. (1974). Auditory lateralization. *Brain and Language, 1*, 391–404.

# 12 Bilingualism in a Visuo-Gestural Mode

Catherine Kettrick
Nancy Hatfield
*University of Washington*

The overwhelming majority of research on bilingualism has involved spoken languages, that is, languages which make use of the auditory/oral modality. Interest in signed languages, which make use of the visual/gestural modality, is more recent, dating from the pioneering work of William Stokoe (1960) and his colleagues (Stokoe, Casterline, & Croneberg, 1965). Stokoe et al. (1965) showed that American Sign Language (ASL), the signed language used by the majority of Deaf[1] adults in North America, could be analyzed on the same basis as spoken languages such as English. Numerous studies have since investigated the structural properties of ASL (see Klima & Bellugi, 1979; Liddell, 1980; Siple, 1978b, and Wilbur, 1976 for reviews). Linguistic research is also being conducted on signed languages used by Deaf Communities[2] in other countries.[3]

---

[1]Deaf is written with a capital D to distinguish people who are culturally Deaf. When written with a lower case d, deaf refers only to hearing loss.

[2]The Deaf Community consists of people who in some way identify with or share the values of Deaf people. Perceived hearing loss, ASL language skills, or political or social involvement are all routes by which one can become a member. Attitude is of prime importance in determining membership: a person who is totally deaf might reject ASL as a language, not associate with Deaf people or support their goals and values. On the other hand, a hearing person who can communicate with Deaf people and works for and accepts the goals of the Deaf Community could become a member. Only people who are deaf can truly be members of the core Deaf Community, however. For a more thorough discussion of Deaf Culture and the Deaf Community see Baker and Cokely, 1980, and Padden, 1980.

[3]See, for example, research in French Canada (Mayberry, 1978), France (Woodward, 1980), Hong Kong (Fok, Bellugi, & Lillo-Martin, 1985), Brazil (Ferreira-Brito, 1984; Hoemann & Hoemann, 1981), Great Britain (Brennan, 1983; Deuchar, 1984; Lawson, 1983; Woll, 1983), Sweden (Bergman, 1983; Wallin, 1983), Russia (Zaitseva, 1983), and Norway (Vogt-Svendsen, 1983; Von Tetzchner, 1984).

This research strongly suggests that signed and spoken languages share common linguistic features. However, it is possible that the modality difference (i.e., visual/gestural vs. the auditory/oral) differentially influences the processing of each type of language. This issue has been explored at both psycholinguistic and neuropsychological levels (see Poizner & Battison, 1980, and Siple, 1982 for reviews).

Although studies of signed language processing offer a unique perspective on the question of how modality differences might affect language organization, another perspective afforded by this research has largely been ignored, namely the bilingual background of the subjects used in this research. A signed language, while it may be the primary language used by Deaf people, is unlikely to be the sole language they know. In order to communicate with the hearing world, Deaf signers must be able to use, at least to some extent, the language of the majority culture in which they live (see Grosjean, 1982). It is therefore curious that research on deafness and signed languages has for the most part neglected to consider the varying linguistic experiences of Deaf people. Yet, as we argue in this chapter, a consideration of this factor should influence research on signed languages as well as the interpretation of research findings already available.

We begin by considering the varieties of bilingualism possible among deaf and hearing signers, and will isolate factors that are likely to influence their acquisition of ASL and English. We then review relevant psycholinguistic and neuropsychological research, including experimental studies with deaf and hearing signers and clinical studies of brain-damaged signers. Finally, we raise certain methodological issues and suggest directions for further research on bilingual users of signed and spoken languages.

## VARIETIES OF BILINGUALISM WITHIN SIGNING COMMUNITIES

It is often assumed that all deaf people can sign, or that all deaf signers are fluent in ASL. In reality, deaf peoples' signing skills vary considerably. This wide variation is possible because English, a spoken language, can be represented in a signed form. For example, "Pidgin Sign English" (PSE), a naturally evolved variety of signing, serves as an interface between ASL and English and is used with people who sign, but who are not fluent in ASL. It is characterized by ASL signs used in English word order, with relatively more fingerspelling than used in ASL and fewer ASL grammatical mechanisms such as inflections on verbs, nonmanual grammatical signals and the grammatical use of space. Another form of signing in English involves artificially contrived signed codes developed for use in the educational setting. These systems, known as Manually Coded English (MCE), supplement ASL signs with invented signs to manually represent every English morpheme. In addition, communication in English is possible through writing or speechreading. Here, too, individuals vary considerably in their degree of proficiency and context for language learning.

Many varieties of bilingualism, involving different languages and different modalities, are possible within signing communities. A few of the more common varieties are described below.

*Signed Language—Signed Language Bilingualism.* This type of bilingualism involves skill in two different signed languages, for example, American Sign Language and Chinese Sign Language (CSL). Although such bilinguals do exist, they are relatively uncommon and little research has been done on them (see Jordan & Battison, 1976; Mayberry, 1978).

*Signed Language—Signed Code Bilingualism.* Many Deaf people fluent in ASL are also competent in a variety that more closely approximates English, namely, Pidgin Sign English (PSE). Hatfield, Caccamise, and Siple (1978) and Hatfield (1982) found that deaf college students' ability to comprehend ASL and PSE varied systematically according to language background variables such as age of acquisition, parental hearing status, and attendance at a residential school. Hatfield et al. (1978) assessed the comprehension of ASL and PSE stories by 219 college students judged to be skilled signers. Students with deaf parents who had learned ASL as a native language made significantly fewer errors on both the ASL and PSE stories than did the other students, and as such were the most "balanced" bilinguals. Those with hearing parents who attended residential schools and learned to sign from peers before age 12 comprehended both ASL and PSE better than the remaining students, who had attended day classes and learned to sign in later adolescence in more formal contexts. This latter group of students had better comprehension in PSE than in ASL.

*Signed Language-Spoken Language Bilingualism.* Nearly all Deaf people fluent in ASL have at least minimal competency in some form of English, the majority language, since they are educated in it and, as adults, are regularly required to communicate in English by speechreading, speaking, reading, or writing. However, their English skills vary greatly depending on factors such as amount of residual hearing, overall language aptitude, and context for language acquisition.

ASL-English bilingualism is perhaps most established in hearing individuals of Deaf parents who were fluent in ASL and who used it to communicate with their children. A number of researchers have looked at the acquisition of English in this group (e.g., Murphy & Slorach, 1983; Sachs, Bard, & Johnson, 1981; Todd & Aitchison, 1980), while others have studied their ASL and English acquisition (e.g., Mayberry, 1976; Prinz & Prinz, 1981; Wilbur & Jones, 1974). Recently, a few studies have begun to investigate the processing of ASL and English in members of this group as well as in hearing adults who learned ASL later in life (see Corina & Vaid, 1985; Kettrick, 1985; Neville, & Lawson, in press(b);

Vaid & Corina, 1985, and Corina & Vaid, 1985). Members of this latter group are often professional interpreters, who should provide a unique perspective on bilingual processing.

*Spoken Language—Signed Code.* Hearing people who learn to sign as adults (for example with the intent of working in the field of deaf education) or orally educated deaf people who first learn to sign as adults in a formal setting are more apt to learn a form of signed English. In addition, deaf children who have hearing parents, attend a day school program which uses Manually Coded English as the major form of communication, and have little or no contact with Deaf people from whom they could learn ASL, will also learn to sign in English. These situations may lead to little competence in ASL, except to the extent that the lexicons of ASL and forms of signed English are shared. As such, these individuals may more accurately be described as "bimodal" (knowing English in signed and spoken/written forms) rather than as bilingual. For example, Hatfield (1982) found that hearing teachers of college deaf students judged to be skilled at producing simultaneously signed and spoken English were not necessarily proficient at understanding English in signed form, and were even less proficient at understanding ASL. Clearly, these individuals can not be called bilingual. Indeed as Bernstein, Maxwell, and Matthews (1985) suggest, the whole question of bimodalism versus bilingualism is a very complex one. They propose a continuum of bimodality dependent on the spoken form of the message, ranging from " 'only speech' through 'dominant use of speech accompanied by sign' to 'dominant use of sign and some speech' to 'sign only' " (p. 138).

It should be obvious from the above that the deaf signing population is characterized by linguistic diversity. As Meadow (1978) noted, variations in performance are often greater within groups of deaf people than between deaf and hearing people. It is therefore critical that studies involving deaf people and signed languages consider variables that contribute to differences in their language skills, such as the degree and age of onset of hearing loss, parental hearing status, age of acquisition of each language, and the context for language acquisition. In what follows, we will consider how some of these variables may affect the results of studies with deaf and hearing signers.

## Influence of Diversity in Language Experience

*Parental Hearing Status.* The hearing status of an individual's parents is often used as the major criterion for establishing ASL fluency in research studies, the assumption being that deaf people with deaf parents are "native" users of ASL. Although valid for the most part, this assumption is sometimes erroneous. Some deaf parents are not themselves fluent in ASL; others may be fluent but choose to use speech or signed English to communicate with their children (see Brasel & Quigley, 1977; Corson, 1973). Therefore, parental hearing status is not necessarily an indicator of an individual's fluency in ASL.

*Age of Language Acquisition.* Age of language acquisition (which is to a large degree confounded with parental hearing status) also appears to be related to fluency in both ASL and English. Children exposed to ASL from birth are likely to acquire ASL as a native language. Deaf children of hearing parents may also attain native-like fluency in ASL, especially if they acquire it before a certain age. Some researchers have posited 5 or 6 years as the critical age for language acquisition (Fischer, 1984; Hatfield, 1982; Mayberry, Fischer, & Hatfield, 1983; Woodward, 1973). However, Mayberry et al. (1983) noted that, in studies using college-age students, age of acquisition is confounded with years of experience in ASL. That is, a person who acquired ASL in adolescence might function as a nonnative signer at the time of the study, but might attain native-like fluency as an older adult. To investigate this question, Mayberry and Tuchman (1978, cited in Fischer, 1984) tested older deaf people on a recall task. These individuals had learned to sign at different ages, but had all been signing for at least 20 to 30 years. Results showed that early acquisition of ASL (by age 5) had a larger effect on subjects' performance on the recall task than did years of experience in ASL.

In a recent study involving cerebral lateralization for ASL and English, Kettrick (1985) administered a receptive ASL proficiency test to four groups of subjects: Deaf and hearing native signers, and Deaf and hearing nonnative signers. Most of the hearing subjects (native and nonnative signers) were professional interpreters. All of the nonnative signers learned ASL after age 13. Results showed that the native signers, as well as the nonnative hearing signers, significantly outperformed the nonnative Deaf signers on the ASL proficiency test, even though the latter group had an average of almost 28 years experience in signing ASL. These findings are even more striking when one considers that the Deaf nonnative signers use ASL as their primary mode of communication, whereas the hearing signers do not. Kettrick's data corroborate those of Mayberry and Tuchman (1978) and provide evidence that normal acquisition of a first language, regardless of whether it is signed or spoken, is a key to acquiring a second language with native-like fluency.

*Other Variables.* Other factors, such as individual language-learning ability, motivation, and context for language learning, may interact with age of acquisition to result in near-native fluency even when the language is learned later in life (see Fischer, 1984; Hatfield et al., 1978). Hatfield (1982) examined the contributions of language background variables on receptive ASL and PSE proficiency and found that age of acquisition and residential school attendance were the best predictors of ASL and PSE performance, respectively. Interestingly, students who learned to sign after age 12 from peers did nearly as well at comprehending ASL as did students who learned earlier, but they were relatively worse at comprehending PSE, and as such, were less "balanced" bilinguals than their peers, who were equally proficient at comprehending both ASL and PSE.

From the above, it should be apparent that nearly all deaf people are bilingual to some extent, and that their skill in ASL, in spoken and written English, and in signed varieties of English varies greatly as a function of parental hearing status, age of language acquisition and other factors.

In what follows, we will review psycholinguistic and neuropsychological research on signers, with a view to probing the influence, acknowledged or potential, of bilingualism on the results obtained.

## PSYCHOLINGUISTIC STUDIES WITH DEAF AND HEARING SIGNERS

Much of the psycholinguistic research involving deaf subjects, ASL, or English has focused on memory for signs or words. Errors in recall of signs are based primarily on the sublexical, phonological features of the language (e.g., Fok, Bellugi, & Lillo-Martin, 1985; Klima & Bellugi, 1979; Poizner, Bellugi, & Tweney, 1981; Poizner, Newkirk, Bellugi, & Klima, 1981), and provide evidence for the importance of these features in lexical encoding for spoken and signed languages.

Studies of memory for English letters or words (e.g., Conlin & Paivio, 1975; Locke & Locke, 1971; Odom, Blanton, & McIntyre, 1970) suggest that deaf people employ not only visual and manual-based codes but also strategies based on English phonology (e.g., Conrad, 1970; Hanson, 1982). Effects of subjects' bilingual skills, however, were not considered in these studies.

Studies of long-term memory (e.g., Hanson & Bellugi, 1982; Siple, Caccamise, & Brewer, 1984) have shown that deaf signers store information in an abstract form of representation that is independent of phonological or syntactic surface structure. In one of the few studies to look at deaf subjects' long-term memory from a bilingual perspective, Siple, Fischer, and Bellugi (1977) presented lists of ASL handshapes and printed English words to students fluent in both languages. The patterns of recall for the two types of stimuli were different, suggesting that ASL and English were encoded separately. These results are similar to findings with hearing bilinguals, who may differentially store the lexicons of their two languages (see discussion in Hummel, this volume).

Thus far we have shown that users of signed languages, in particular ASL, call on processes similar to those employed by users of spoken languages. This similarity in processing at the psycholinguistic level might lead one to expect a similarity in processing at the neuropsychological level as well. In addition, since a signed language is a linguistic system it might be expected to involve the left hemisphere; however, given its reliance on visuospatial mechanisms, one might expect greater involvement of the right hemisphere. Thus, neuropsychological research on signed languages provides an opportunity to probe the underlying nature of hemispheric differences.

## NEUROPSYCHOLOGICAL STUDIES WITH HEARING BILINGUALS

A traditional assumption when comparing bilingual and monolingual populations is that their differing language experiences may have an effect on their subsequent cerebral lateralization. Two main areas of research that provide evidence are clinical cases of aphasia in bilinguals and experimental procedures with brain-intact bilinguals.

### *Clinical Studies*

Reviews of early case studies of aphasia in bilinguals found a number of cases involving selective language recovery (see Albert & Obler, 1978; Paradis, 1977, 1983). Because of the case study approach and the lack of systematic assessment of language proficiency and other potentially relevant variables, the early clinical literature may not be particularly informative, and its value may be largely heuristic (see Vaid & Genesee, 1980).

One characteristic of this literature that is of interest is an unusually high incidence of crossed aphasia among bilinguals and polyglots, relative to that reported in monolinguals (Galloway, 1982; see also Chary, this volume). Galloway (personal communication, 1984) reports that the incidence of aphasia following right-sided lesions is even greater the more the individual relies on nonverbal, pragmatic skills for communication. However, the issue of greater right hemispheric involvement in bilingual language organization cannot entirely be resolved on the basis of the early clinical literature for, as Galloway herself has noted (1982), overinclusion of interesting rather than more representative cases may have given rise to a spuriously high estimate of crossed aphasia in bilinguals compared to that in monolinguals.

Nonetheless, the bilingual aphasia literature is useful in that it raises the possibility that variables in the context of language acquisition and use may differentially influence patterns of cerebral organization of language, a topic discussed more fully below.

### *Experimental Studies*

Three variables have been isolated in the experimental neuropsychological literature to account for differences among bilinguals in patterns of cerebral lateralization: age, stage, and manner of second language acquisition (see Vaid & Genesee, 1980; Vaid, 1983).

Age of language acquisition has been invoked to account for differences in patterns of cerebral lateralization between early and late bilinguals, that is, individuals who learned both languages in early childhood or in adolescence, respectively (see Vaid, 1983). The stage hypothesis, first proposed by Obler (1981), predicts a greater right hemisphere participation in the early rather than late stages of language acquisition (see also Schneiderman, this volume). Galloway and Krashen (1980) modified the stage hypothesis to specify greater right hemisphere involvement only during informal acquisition of a second language. Finally, manner of language acquisition was invoked to distinguish between the performance of individuals who had acquired a second language in a formal classroom setting with an emphasis on language form and structure, and those who had acquired it in a more naturalistic setting (see Krashen, 1977). More left hemisphere involvement would be predicted for more formal learning of a second language.

When one considers the body of research bearing on these models, it appears that the variables of age and manner of language acquisition have received the strongest support, while that of stage of language acquisition has only been supported for written language acquisition (see Galloway, 1982; Vaid & Genesee, 1980; and Vaid, 1983 for reviews). However, as Obler et al. (1982) and Vaid (1983) have pointed out, research on lateralization in bilinguals has generally neglected consideration of other variables that might influence patterns of lateralization, namely, parameters of the stimuli and tasks (see Fairweather, Brizzolara, Tabossi, & Umilta, 1982; Sergent & Bindra, 1981; and Vaid, 1984). Indeed, when one considers that any of these parameters might in turn interact with specific subject variables, one can appreciate the difficulty of interpreting neuropsychological research in the field of bilingualism.

## Neuropsychological Studies with Deaf and Hearing Signers

### *Clinical Studies*

A potentially rich source of information about cerebral organization of language in deaf individuals is case reports of brain-damaged signers. In her review of all such cases published in the literature as of 1981, numbering eleven, Kimura (1981) found only two cases that provided sufficient information on the patient's linguistic background to be useful (Chiarello, Knight, & Mandel, 1982; Leischner, 1943). Kimura summarized the clinical literature as suggesting a greater left hemisphere involvement in language functioning in deaf users of signed language.

In a recent set of papers, Bellugi and her colleagues reported on the linguistic and nonlinguistic performance of a group of left- or right-hemisphere damaged right-handed deaf patients (Bellugi, Poizner, & Klima, 1983; Poizner, Bellugi, & Iragui, 1984; Poizner, Bellugi, & Kaplan, 1985, and Poizner, Kaplan, Bellugi, & Padden, 1984). They were interested in the following critical question: Since it uses space as part of its grammatical organization, is ASL more represented in the left or in the right cerebral hemisphere? Bellugi's findings, in general, indicate that deaf stroke patients' pattern of deficits bears a striking resemblance to those of their hearing counterparts. Patients with unilateral left hemisphere damage showed various types of impairment in sign production and comprehension, while right hemisphere-damaged patients did not show comparable linguistic deficits, but were in turn impaired in various nonlanguage spatial tasks. In addition, evidence was obtained for differential impairment of linguistic functions among left-hemisphere-damaged signers (see Bellugi, Poizner, & Klima, in press). Deaf patients' English deficits were not reported as thoroughly as were their deficits in ASL. Because of deaf people's varying skill in English, and the necessity for determining pretrauma linguistic competence, this area is difficult to adequately study. Nonetheless, the question of differential impairment and recovery in deaf and hearing ASL/English bilinguals is an interesting one and deserves further attention.

The clinical data reported above suggest that neither speech nor auditory input is necessary for cerebral specialization. Furthermore, even though ASL uses spatial mechanisms for its grammatical structure, the evidence suggests that deaf signers' cerebral hemispheres can be specialized separately for linguistic and nonlinguistic uses of space. Taken as a whole, these data clearly indicate that the left cerebral hemisphere is specialized for language regardless of which sensory modality the language happens to use.

### *Experimental Studies*

Within the last 10 years, researchers have begun to explore lateralization of language and spatial functions in brain-intact signers. Given results obtained with similar research on hearing bilinguals, one might predict left hemisphere lateralization for ASL in native signers, and varying patterns of lateralization for nonnative signers, depending upon the conditions under which the language was learned. Unfortunately, results from early studies are ambiguous at best (see Poizner & Battison, 1980, and Ross, 1983, for reviews). In several studies, the linguistic background of the subjects varied unsystematically (see also Samar, 1983, for a discussion of subject heterogeneity), or the choice of stimuli and mode of response was either inappropriate or inadequate. We review this research below, organizing our discussion according to the type of experimental paradigm employed.

*1. Visual Hemifield Presentation.* Although most of the early tachistoscopic studies were flawed by methodological problems (see Poizner & Battison, 1980; Ross, 1983 for reviews), the combined results show for deaf signers a general pattern of a slight right visual field (RVF) superiority for English words and a left visual field (LVF) superiority for statically presented signs. Two exceptions to this latter trend have been reported. Neville and Bellugi (1978) presented static ASL signs both unilaterally and bilaterally to congenitally deaf signers whose major form of communication was ASL. Results showed no asymmetry for the bilaterally presented signs, but an RVF advantage for the unilateral presentation. In a more recent study, Panou and Sewell (1984) also found a significant RVF advantage for statically presented signs. Their congenitally deaf subjects had all learned a signed language (in this case British Sign Language) before the age of three.

Since movement is an integral part of ASL (Klima & Bellugi, 1979; Poizner, Bellugi, & Lutes-Driscoll, 1981), results from static presentation of signs may not truly reflect the cerebral organization of ASL. A few studies have used moving sign stimuli to assess cerebral lateralization. Poizner, Battison, and Lane (1979) found a smaller LVF superiority in deaf native signers for moving signs than for static signs. They interpreted their results as indicating a shift toward left hemisphere processing when moving signs are used. In a study by Vargha-Khadem (in press), moving signs were presented to deaf signers and to subgroups of hearing signers and nonsigners. Vargha-Khadem (1983) found an RVF superiority for moving signs in hearing moderately proficient signers as well as in hearing nonsigners. Because the signs were meaningless for the nonsigners, Vargha-Khadem interpreted the left hemisphere superiority shown by this subgroup to reflect only temporal-sequential processing rather than linguistic processing of the stimuli. As a group the deaf signers, who had learned to sign in early childhood, showed no visual field asymmetries for any of the tasks, although individually they showed either a left or a right visual field preference.

The equivocal results from the studies discussed above may be due to the methods used to present ASL signs tachistoscopically, i.e., line drawings, photographs, and film. In an attempt to represent more directly the linguistic structure of signed languages, an analysis of ASL signs as abstract movements and points in space of the hands and arms has been translated into computer graphics at the Salk Institute (Bellugi et al., 1984). The resulting images lack the pictorial quality inherent in the other techniques, a quality which may have contributed to the generally observed right hemisphere advantage. Using this technique, Poizner & Bellugi (1984) presented moving signs tachistoscopically to right-handed congenitally deaf signers, all of whom had learned ASL from parents or deaf siblings. A significant right visual field superiority was found. These same subjects showed no asymmetry for English words, although a control group of hearing people showed the expected right visual field superiority.

Vaid and Corina (1985) used a Stroop-like task to explore patterns of cerebral lateralization in congenitally deaf and hearing native signers, and in hearing nonnative but proficient signers (working as interpreters). They presented pairs of numbers tachistoscopically in three conditions: in the form of digits, number words, and ASL number signs. The physical size of the second number was either larger or smaller than that of the first; however, these variations in physical size were to be ignored and subjects were to decide whether the second stimulus in each pair was larger or smaller in numerical size relative to the first. Interference from mismatches in physical and numerical size was expected, and was expected to be greater to the extent that physical size was encoded visually (as distinct from being recoded in some abstract form). Results were as follows:

There was a larger Stroop interference for digits and English number words than for ASL number signs in the deaf group. Moreover, greater interference was observed for left visual field presentation of digits in all groups, and for left visual field presentation of words in the deaf group only. The two hearing groups showed greater right visual field interference for English number words; a similar tendency was observed for ASL signs in the deaf group. Although complex, these results suggest that there may be some internal recoding for one's first acquired (or otherwise dominant) language.

In most visual laterality studies with signers, researchers have been constrained by the technical difficulties inherent in attempting to represent a signed language adequately through tachistoscopic presentation. With English or any other language that has a written form, one can present printed stimuli, and the average hearing person has daily exposure to that written form. However, the methods used to represent ASL, e.g., line drawings of signs, photographs, or film clips, do not seem wholly satisfactory. Signs do not look like line drawings, nor does the average deaf person often have an opportunity to see ASL in a pictorial form. Moreover, while printed words represent the underlying abstract phonological form of spoken language, pictures of signs, whether in the form of line drawings or photographs, are merely concrete, two-dimensional representations of a three-dimensional reality. What is needed, then, is either a deliberately abstract form of signed language representation that captures the information conveyed by hand and arm movement (as does the method used by Poizner & Bellugi, 1984), or a digitized representation of actual signers (a procedure currently being used by Neville & Lawson, in press, (a)). Both computer synthesized and digitized signs have the additional advantage of allowing a precise control of stimulus onset and duration.

2. *Dichaptic presentation.* Using a dichaptic paradigm, Cranney and Ashton (1980) and LaBreche, Manning, Goble, and Markham (1977) presented nonsense shapes to deaf and hearing children. Both studies failed to find a left tactual field advantage. Cranney and Ashton (1980) found instead a right tactual field advantage for both hearing and deaf children for recognizing nonsense shapes, although the difference between the two hemispheres for the deaf children was not significant. LaBreche et al. (1977) also found a right tactual field superiority for deaf and hearing children on both nonsense shapes and letters. However, as Vargha-Khadem (1982) points out, the tasks used in these studies may not have been sufficiently complex to access the processing system of any given hemisphere.

In an attempt to create a dichaptic measure sufficiently complex to differentially access the two hemispheres, Vargha-Khadem (1982) presented pairs of abstract three-letter words and nonsense shapes to deaf and hearing children. In the verbal task, the children felt with each hand simultaneously a sequence of letters which formed three-letter words; each hand felt a separate word. They then indicated which words they had felt by pointing to a choice board on which the target words and four distractor words appeared. The nonsense shapes task was similar, except that there were only two shapes presented simultaneously.

Results indicated that the hearing group did significantly better on the verbal than on the nonverbal task while the deaf group did not show a comparable difference. Moreover, there was an overall right tactual field superiority in both groups, for the verbal task only.

Vargha-Khadem (1982) suggests that the relatively poorer performance by the deaf subjects on the verbal task may reflect inadequate rehearsal strategies. Presumably, hearing people once they had identified the stimulus, could use a phonetic coding system of some kind to remember it. Deaf subjects who do not utilize this type of strategy would be slower at identifying a stimulus in the right tactual field, leaving little time to identify the one in the left tactual field. The fact that the deaf subjects were as accurate on the nonverbal task as on the verbal task (unlike the hearing subjects) lends support to this argument. The lack of asymmetry for both groups on the nonverbal tasks may have arisen because the task was too simple.

Gibson and Bryden (1984) also investigated cerebral lateralization using a dichaptic task with a sample of deaf and hearing school children. Most of the deaf children had hearing parents and were enrolled in a school which used "fingerspelling and sign language as well as audition" (p. 3). The children were presented with either two letters or two random shapes, and reported what they felt by pointing to the appropriate display on a choice board. The results showed a right hand superiority for accuracy of tactual letter recognition among the hearing children, and a left hand superiority for shape recognition. For the deaf children no significant differences in performance of the two hands were found for the nonverbal task; for the verbal task a left hand superiority was obtained, a finding which contrasts with that of Vargha-Khadem (1982).

Gibson and Bryden (1984) suggest two explanations for their results. One is that language may be lateralized differently in deaf and hearing people. If this is so, then lack of auditory input may indeed have an effect on lateralization, at least of English. The other explanation is that language (presumably both ASL and English) and reading are two different systems, and deaf people approach the task of reading (or in this case of tactually identifying letters) using a strategy that differs from that of hearing people. If, as some of the electrophysiological work by Neville and her colleagues would suggest, there is cerebral reorganization in individuals who lack auditory input from infancy, then it is plausible that congenitally deaf people may never show a left hemisphere advantage for printed English to the same degree as that found among hearing subjects.

*Electrophysiological Studies.* Event-related brain potentials (ERPs) (electrophysiological measures of brain wave activity recorded from the scalp) have provided an additional source of information about language and visuospatial processing in deaf and hearing signers.

Neville, Schmidt, and Kutas (1983) used a nonlanguage task to study brain organization in congenitally deaf signers and hearing nonsigners. ERPs were recorded over left and right occipital, parietal and temporal, anterior temporal and frontal regions of the brain. Hearing subjects showed a smaller neural response to peripherally than to foveally presented stimuli; in contrast, deaf subjects showed large responses to both types of input, particularly over the frontal, anterior temporal and occipital regions of both hemispheres. According to Neville et al. (1983), these data suggest that when cortical areas normally subserving audition are deprived of auditory experience, they may reorganize to subserve visual processing instead. Moreover, the enhanced response to peripheral stimuli among the deaf subjects is consistent with the claim (see Siple, 1978a) that peripheral vision is heavily utilized by deaf signers to perceive signs, most of which are made outside the domain of the signer's face, the area in which attention is usually focused in signed conversation.

In another study, Neville and Lawson (in press,a,b) examined the processing of nonlanguage information (perception of apparent motion) by congenitally deaf and hearing native signers, and hearing English-speaking monolinguals. The task was to attend to the right or left field to detect the motion of a small white square presented in the right or left visual field. Concurrently recorded ERPs showed considerable right hemisphere involvement for monolingual hearing subjects on this task. In contrast, for the deaf subjects both the behavioral and ERP data indicated left hemisphere involvement. In addition, the ERPs recorded over the occipital regions of the deaf subjects were several times larger than those found in the hearing subjects. Hearing individuals with deaf parents did not display the larger ERPs from the occipital regions, a result in line with the data from the other hearing subjects. However, like the deaf subjects, hearing subjects with deaf parents showed a left hemisphere superiority on both electrophysiological and behavioral measures. These findings suggest that early exposure to a signed language, rather than hearing status per se, affects the pattern of cerebral organization for certain nonlanguage material (see also Vaid & Corina, 1985).

An earlier electrophysiological study (Neville, 1977) provides evidence for the mediating effect of the context of signed language acquisition on brain functioning. Neville recorded ERPs from young deaf and hearing children during a picture matching task; all of the deaf children were in an oral program at the time. The hearing children all showed the expected right hemisphere advantage on the picture matching task. Responses from the deaf children varied depending on their language background. Those with hearing parents showed no asymmetries on this task, while deaf children who reported signing with their deaf parents showed a left hemisphere advantage, opposite to that obtained for the normally hearing nonsigning control group. Thus it seems clear that signed linguistic input affects cerebral organization for nonlanguage tasks, possibly in ways opposite to that of spoken language input. In addition, the data support the idea that lateral cerebral specialization itself is facilitated by normal first language acquisition.[4]

In another experiment, Neville, Kutas, and Schmidt (1982) recorded ERPs from congenitally deaf and hearing subjects in recall of unilaterally and bilaterally presented English words. Hearing subjects were found to show a left hemisphere superiority for this task, while deaf subjects were equally accurate at reporting words in both visual fields. The hearing subjects' ERPs for the more anterior left hemisphere showed a negative to positive shift which was not seen in the deaf subjects. Neville et al. (1982) suggest that the absence of such an asymmetry in deaf subjects may indicate that the left hemisphere's specialty is to encode or recode printed linguistic information into a phonological form. Alternately, it may indicate deaf subjects' lack of expertise with the grammar of English. If the former speculation is true, then one would not expect ERP asymmetries when presenting ASL signs to deaf subjects. On the other hand, as the authors point out, if the left hemisphere subserves formal linguistic structure regardless of modality, then one would expect asymmetries when presenting ASL linguistic information to congenitally deaf signers. As mentioned above, Neville and Bellugi (1978), Panou and Sewell (1984), and Poizner and Bellugi (1984) did find a left hemisphere advantage for ASL signs presented tachistoscopically to congenitally deaf signers. Currently, Neville and Lawson (in press, a,b) are examining visual field asymmetries for digitized ASL signs presented on a computer screen, while concurrently recording ERPs. Preliminary behavioral and electrophysiological results point to a right visual field superiority for ASL recognition among both hearing and deaf native signers. Variability in response characterizes hearing individuals who learned ASL later in life, but who are fluent signers. In summary, the findings by Neville and her colleagues indicate that early competence in a language, regardless of its sensory modality, results in greater left hemisphere involvement for that language. Deaf subjects' lack of left hemisphere involvement for English words may reflect their lack of expertise with English grammar, resulting from nonnative acquisition of the language.

---

[4]Phippard (1977) also tested oral deaf children as well as children attending a school which used Total Communication (a methodology which uses both speech and English signing to communicate with the children) on a spatial task. Her results indicated that the orally raised children (like her hearing control group) showed an RHA for the spatial task, whereas the children attending the Total Communication program showed no asymmetries. While these results might seem to argue against signed language input having an effect on cerebral organization, it must be remembered that the signing used in deaf education programs is not a language in its own right, but a code for a spoken language. It remains to be seen what effects early exposure to a signed code for a spoken language might have on cerebral organization.

## SUMMARY OF PSYCHOLINGUISTIC AND NEUROPSYCHOLOGICAL RESEARCH

In reviewing work that has been done on psycholinguistic processing by deaf and hearing signers, we find little conducted from a bilingual perspective, i.e., a perspective that would consider the context of acquisition and degree of proficiency of the subjects in the particular language being studied. Taken as a whole however, this research shows that ASL is processed in ways similar to spoken language by hearing people. However, most researchers failed to consider varying levels of proficiency in ASL, English, and various signed codes for English, or did not acknowledge effects of language background variables on results obtained.

Results from experimental and clinical neuropsychological work are varied and sometimes conflicting, often due to methodological issues. However, particularly when examining recent work, which has for the most part resolved these problems, the following conclusions may be drawn:

1. Although auditory experience has an effect on the neural organization of the brain, neither speech nor auditory input is necessary for the development of cerebral asymmetries.
2. In congenitally deaf native signers, the left hemisphere appears to be specialized for signed language just as it is for spoken language in the majority of hearing people.
3. In response to spatial stimuli, people who had early exposure to signed language, whether they were deaf or hearing, seem to show left hemisphere involvement.
4. The requirements of the task may differentially affect the results of any given experiment. For example, given the integral importance of movement in a signed language, it may be impossible to separate, in a tachistoscopic paradigm, a linguistic response from one which responds simply to the temporal sequential nature of the stimuli.

## CONCLUSION

Deaf people form an extremely heterogeneous group, with language backgrounds and other defining characteristics varying greatly. For the most part they must be considered as bilinguals with varying language skills; proficiency in signed languages, signed codes, and English must be addressed and assessed. People conducting research involving signed languages and deaf subjects must obtain and report background information regarding subjects' hearing loss, including age of its onset; parental hearing status and use of manual communication; age of signed language acquisition; from whom the signed language was learned and in what context; types of schools attended, and subjects' current competence in the languages being tested. In addition, they must also take care that the task of the experiment itself actually taps the subjects' linguistic competencies. Statically presented signs are an incomplete measure to use when testing for lateralization of ASL; unfortunately, Vargha-Khadem's (1982) work suggests that moving signs may access other than linguistic capabilities of the left hemisphere, making any results which show an LHA somewhat suspect. Event related potentials, being a more direct measure of cerebral activity, may offer a more sound method of measurement, particularly when used in tandem with a visual half field task (see Samar, 1983 for discussion).

Data from deaf and hearing native signers can provide insights into the normal acquisition and bilingual cerebral organization of signed and spoken languages. Hearing late learners of ASL or signed codes for English can provide insights into second language acquisition and bimodal processing of language. Hearing late learners of ASL who are working interpreters are a source of information regarding the processing task of simultaneously interpreting language in two different modalities. In addition, the formal nature of their training, which generally emphasizes analyzing linguistic discourse, may well have an effect on both the cerebral organization of their languages and on the results of any experimental task (see Kettrick, 1985). Hearing late learners of a signed code for English can provide information regarding another question that has largely been neglected, namely the bimodal task of simultaneously signing and speaking English. As Hatfield (1982) suggested, producing simultaneous communication and comprehending it are two very different tasks. In addition, Bernstein, Maxwell, and Matthews (1985) argue that much more information is needed about how deaf students comprehend different signed codes and how that comprehension relates to reading and writing skills.

In all of this research, Deaf late learners of ASL have generally been neglected (but see Kettrick, 1985; Mayberry & Tuchman, 1978, cited in Fischer, 1984). Although this group is extremely heterogeneous, making subject selection difficult, there are important questions regarding primary language acquisition as it relates to age of language acquisition that can only be studied with this group.[5]

Evidence is slowly beginning to emerge relating to deaf and hearing signers' psycholinguistic processing and functional cerebral organization. However, more research is needed utilizing a variety of signers that meet specific selection criteria and using tasks that are methodologically sound. Such research will prove invaluable in providing information on language organization in bilingual users of signed and spoken languages.

[5]What, for example, is the effect on cerebral lateralization of not having normal language input during the critical years for language acquisition? Is acquisition of ASL at a later age different or similar in deaf and hearing populations?

## ACKNOWLEDGMENTS

We would like to thank Jyotsna Vaid for her careful reading of previous drafts of this chapter.

## REFERENCES

Albert, M., & Obler, L. (1978). *The bilingual brain.* New York: Academic Press.

Baker, C., & Cokely, D. (1980). *American Sign Language: A teacher's resource text on grammar and culture.* Silver Springs, MD: TJ Publishers, Inc.

Bellugi, U. et al. (1984). *Laboratory for Language and Cognitive Studies: Annual Report.* The Salk Institute, La Jolla, CA.

Bellugi, U., Poizner, H., & Klima, E. (1983). Brain organization for language: Clues from sign aphasia. *Human Neurobiology, 2,* 155–170.

Bellugi, U., Poizner, H., & Klima, E. (in press). *What the hands reveal about the brain.* Cambridge, MA: Bradford Books.

Bergman, B. (1983). Verbs and adjectives: Morphological processes in Swedish Sign Language. In J. Kyle & B. Woll (Eds.), *Language in sign* (pp. 3–9). London: Croom Helm.

Bernstein, M., Maxwell, M., & Matthews, K. (1985). Bimodal or bilingual communication. *Sign Language Studies, 47,* 127–140.

Brasel, K., & Quigley, S. (1977). Influence of certain language and communication environments in early childhood on the development of language in deaf individuals. *Journal of Speech & Hearing Research, 20,* 95–107.

Brennan, M. (1983). Marking time in British Sign Language. In J. Kyle & B. Woll (Eds.), *Language in sign* (pp. 10–31). London: Croom Helm.

Chiarello, C., Knight, R., & Mandel, M. (1982). Aphasia in a prelingually deaf woman. *Brain, 105,* 29–51.

Conlin, D., & Paivio, A. (1975). The associative learning of the deaf: The effects of word imagery and signability. *Memory & Cognition, 3,* 335–340.

Conrad, R. (1970). Short-term memory processes in the deaf. *British Journal of Psychology, 61,* 179–195.

Corina, D. & Vaid, J. (1985). *Tapping into bilingualism: Cerebral lateralization for ASL and English.* Working paper, Laboratory for Language and Cognitive Studies, The Salk Institute, San Diego.

Corson, O. (1967). *Comparing deaf children of oral deaf parents and deaf parents using manual communication with deaf children of hearing parents on academic, social, and communicative functioning.* Unpublished doctoral dissertation, University of Cincinnati.

Cranney, J., & Ashton, R. (1980). Witelson's dichaptic task as a measure of hemispheric asymmetry in deaf and hearing populations. *Neuropsychologia, 18,* 95–98.

Deuchar, M. (1984). *British Sign Language.* Oxford: Routledge & Kegan Paul.

Fairweather, H., Brizzolara, D., Tabossi, P., & Umilta, C. (1982). Functional cerebral lateralization: dichotomy or plurality? *Cortex, 18,* 51–66.

Ferreira-Brito, L. (1984). Similarities and differences in two Brazilian sign languages. *Sign Language Studies, 42,* 45–56.

Fischer, S. (1984, August). *The effects of age on the acquisition of sign language: A critical period?* Paper presented at The Tenth Annual Meeting of the Japanese Association of Sign Language Studies, Nagoya, Japan.

Fok, A., Bellugi, U., & Lillo-Martin, D. (1985). Remembering in Chinese signs and characters. In H. Kao & R. Hoosain (Eds.), *Neuropsychological studies in processing Chinese languages.* Hong Kong: University of Hong Kong.

Galloway, L. (1982). Bilingualism: Neuropsychological considerations. In G. Hynd (Ed.), *Journal of Research & Development in Education, 15,* 12–28.

Galloway, L., & Krashen, S. (1980). Cerebral organization in bilingualism and second language acquisition. In R. Scarcella & S. Krashen (Eds.), *Research in second language acquisition.* Rowley, MA: Newbury House.

Gibson, C., & Bryden, M. (1984). Cerebral laterality in deaf and hearing children. *Brain and Language, 23,* 1–12.

Grosjean, F. (1982). *Life with two languages: An introduction to bilingualism.* Cambridge, MA: Harvard University Press.

Hanson, V. (1982). Short-term recall by deaf signers of American Sign Language: Implications of encoding strategy for order recall. *Journal of Experimental Psychology, 8,* 572–583.

Hanson, V., & Bellugi, U. (1982). On the role of sign order and morphological structure in memory for American Sign Language sentences. *Haskins Laboratories: Status Report on Speech Research SR-69.*

Hatfield, N. (1982). *An investigation of bilingualism in two signed languages: American Sign Language and manually-coded English.* Unpublished doctoral dissertation, University of Rochester, Rochester, NY.

Hatfield, N., Caccamise, F., & Siple, P. (1978). Deaf students' language competencies: A bilingual perspective. *American Annals of the Deaf, 123,* 847–851.

Hoemann, H., & Hoemann, S. (1981). *The sign language of Brazil.* Mill Neck, NY: Mill Neck Foundation.

Jordan, I. K., & Battison, R. (1976). A referential communication experiment with foreign sign languages. *Sign Language Studies, 8,* 69–101.

Kettrick, C. (1985). *Cerebral lateralization for ASL and English in deaf and hearing native and non-native signers.* Unpublished Doctoral Dissertation, University of Washington, Seattle, WA.

Kimura, D. (1981). Neural mechanisms in manual signing. *Sign Language Studies, 33,* 291–312.

Klima, E., & Bellugi, U. (1979). *The signs of language.* Cambridge, MA: Harvard University Press.

Krashen, S. (1977). The monitor model for adult second language performance. In M. Burt, H. Dulay, & M. Finocchiaro (Eds.), *Viewpoints on English as a second language.* New York: Regents.

LaBreche, T., Manning, A., Goble, W., & Markham, R. (1977). Hemispheric specialization for linguistic and non-linguistic tactual perception in a congenitally deaf population. *Cortex, 13,* 184–194.

Lawson, L. (1983). Multi-channel signs in British Sign Language. In J. Kyle & B. Woll (Eds.), *Language in sign* (pp. 97–105). London: Croom Helm.

Leischner, A. (1943). Die "Aphasie" der Taubstummen. Archir fur Psychiatry und Nervenkr, 115, 469–548.

Liddell, S. (1980). *American Sign Language syntax.* The Hague: Mouton.

Locke, J., & Locke, V. (1971). Deaf children's phonetic, visual, and dactylic coding in a grapheme recall task. *Journal of Experimental Psychology, 89,* 142–146.

Mayberry, R. (1976). An assessment of some oral and manual language skills of hearing children of deaf parents. *American Annals of the Deaf, 121,* 507–512.

Mayberry, R. (1978). French Canadian Sign Language: A study of inter-sign language comprehension. In P. Siple (Ed.), *Understanding language through sign language research* (pp. 349–372). New York: Academic Press.

Mayberry, R., Fischer, S., & Hatfield, N. (1983). Sentence repetition in American Sign Language. In J. Kyle & B. Woll (Eds.), *Language in sign* (pp. 206–214). London: Croom Helm.

Meadow, K. (1978). The "natural history" of a research project: An illustration of methodological issues in research with deaf children. In L. Liben (Ed.), *Deaf children: Developmental perspectives* (pp. 21–40). New York: Academic Press.

Murphy, J., & Slorach, N. (1983). The language development of pre-preschool hearing children of deaf parents. *British Journal of Disorders of Communication, 18,* 118–126.

Neville, H. (1977). Electroencephalographic testing of cerebral specialization in normal and congenitally deaf children: A preliminary report. In S. Segalowitz & F. Gouber (Eds.), *Language development and neurological theory* (pp. 121–132). NY: Academic Press.

Neville, H., & Lawson, D. (in press a). Attention to cerebral and peripheral visual space in a movement detection task: An event-related potential and behavioral study. II. Congenitally deaf adults. *Brain Research.*

Neville, H., & Lawson, D. (in press b). Attention to central and peripheral visual space in a movement detection task: separate effects of auditory deprivation and acquisition of a visual language. *Brain Research.*

Neville, H., & Bellugi, U. (1978). Patterns of cerebral specialization in congenitally deaf adults: A preliminary report. In P. Siple (Ed.), *Understanding language through sign language research* (pp. 239–257). New York: Academic Press.

Neville, H., Kutas, M., & Schmidt, A. (1982). Event-related potential studies of cerebral specialization during reading: Studies of congenitally deaf adults. *Brain and Language, 16,* 316–337.

Neville, H., Schmidt, A., & Kutas, M. (1983). Altered visual-evoked potentials in congenitally deaf adults. *Brain Research, 266,* 127–132.

Obler, L. (1981). Right hemisphere participation in second language acquisition. In K. Diller (Ed.), *Individual differences and universals in language learning aptitude* (pp. 53–64). Rowley, MA: Newbury House.

Obler, L., Zatorre, R., Galloway, L., & Vaid, J. (1982). Cerebral lateralization in bilingualism: Methodological issues. *Brain and Language, 15,* 40–54.

Odom, P., Blanton, R., & McIntyre, C. (1970). Coding medium and word recall by deaf and hearing subjects. *Journal of Speech and Hearing Research, 13,* 54–58.

Padden, C. (1980). The Deaf Community and the culture of deaf people. In C. Baker & R. Battison (Eds.), *Sign language and the Deaf Community: Essays in honor of William C. Stokoe* (pp. 89–103). Silver Springs, MD: National Association of the Deaf.

Panou, L., & Sewell, D. (1984). Cerebral asymmetry in congenitally deaf subjects. *Neuropsychologia, 22,* 381–383.

Paradis, M. (1977). Bilingualism and aphasia. In H. Whitaker & H. A. Whitaker (Eds.), *Studies in neurolinguistics* (Vol. 3., pp. 65–121), New York: Academic Press.

Paradis, M. (1983) (Ed.), *Readings on aphasia in bilinguals and polyglots.* Montreal: Didier.

Phippard, D. (1977). Hemifield differences in visual perception in deaf and hearing subjects. *Neuropsychologia, 15,* 555–561.

Poizner, H., & Battison, R. (1980). Cerebral asymmetry for sign language: Clinical and experimental evidence. In H. Lane & F. Grosjean (Eds.), *Recent perspectives on American Sign Language* (pp. 79–101). Hillsdale, NJ: Lawrence Erlbaum Associates.

Poizner, H., Battison, R., & Lane, H. (1979). Cerebral asymmetry for perception of American Sign Language: The effects of moving stimuli. *Brain and Language, 7,* 351–362.

Poizner, H., & Bellugi, U. (1984, February). *Hemispheric specialization for a visual-gestural language.* Paper presented at International Neuropsychological Society meeting, Houston, TX.

Poizner, H., Bellugi, U., & Iragui, V. (1984). Apraxia and aphasia for a visual-gestural language. *American Journal of Physiology, 246,* 868–883.

Poizner, H., Bellugi, U., & Kaplan, E. (1985, February). *Spatial capacities of brain damaged signers.* Paper presented at International Neuropsychology Society, San Diego.

Poizner, H., Bellugi, U., & Lutes-Driscoll, V. (1981). Perception of American Sign Language in dynamic point-light displays. *Journal of Experimental Psychology: Human Perception and Performance, 7,* 430–440.

Poizner, H., Bellugi, U., & Tweney, R. (1981). Processing of formational, semantic, and iconic information in American Sign Language. *Journal of Experimental Psychology: Human Perception and Performance, 7,* 1146–1159.

Poizner, H., Kaplan, E., Bellugi, U., & Padden, C. (1984). Visual-spatial processing in deaf brain-damaged signers. *Brain & Cognition, 3,* 281–306.

Poizner, H., Newkirk, D., Bellugi, U., & Klima, E. (1981). Representation of inflected signs from American Sign Language in short-term memory. *Memory & Cognition, 9,* 121–131.

Prinz, P., & Prinz, E. (1981). Acquisition of ASL and spoken English by a hearing child of a deaf parent mother and a hearing father: Phase II, early combinatory patterns. *Sign Language Studies, 30,* 78–86.

Ross, P. (1983). Cerebral specialization in deaf individuals. In S. Segalowitz (Ed.), *Language functions and brain organization* (pp. 287–313). New York: Academic Press.

Sachs, J., Bard, B., & Johnson, M. (1981). Language learning with restricted input: Case studies of two hearing children of deaf parents. *Applied Psycholinguistics, 2,* 33–54.

Samar, V. (1983). Evoked potentials and visual half-field evidence for task-dependent cerebral asymmetries in congenitally deaf adults. *Brain & Cognition, 2,* 383–403.

Sergent, J., & Bindra, D. (1981). Differential hemispheric processing of faces: Methodological considerations and reinterpretation. *Psychological Bulletin, 89,* 544–554.

Siple, P. (1978a). Visual constraints for sign language communication. *Sign Language Studies, 19,* 95–110.

Siple, P. (Ed.). (1978b). *Understanding language through sign language research.* New York: Academic Press.

Siple, P. (1982). Signed language and linguistic theory. In L. Obler & L. Menn (Eds.), *Exceptional language and linguistics.* New York: Academic Press.

Siple, P., Caccamise, F., & Brewer, L. (1984). Signs as pictures and signs as words: The effect of language knowledge on memory for new vocabulary. *Journal of experimental psychology: Learning, memory, and cognition, 8,* 619–625.

Siple, P., Fischer, S., & Bellugi, U. (1977). Memory for nonsemantic attributes of American Sign Language signs and English words. *Journal of Verbal Learning and Verbal Behavior, 16,* 561–574.

Stokoe, W. (1960). *Sign language structure: An outline of the visual communication system of the American Deaf* (Occasional Papers No. 8). Studies in linguistics. Silver Springs, MD: Linstok Press, (Rev. ed., 1978).

Stokoe, W., Casterline, D., & Croneberg, C. (1965). *A dictionary of American Sign Language on linguistic principles* (Rev. ed., 1976). Silver Springs, MD: Linstok Press.

Todd, P., & Aitchison, J. (1980). Learning language the hard way. *First Language, 1,* 122–140.

Vaid, J. (1983). Bilingualism and brain lateralization. In *Language functions and brain organization* (pp. 315–339). New York: Academic Press.

Vaid, J. (1984). Visual, phonetic, and semantic processing in early and late bilinguals. In M. Paradis & Y. Lebrun (Eds.), *Early bilingualism and child development.* Lisse: Swets & Zeitlinger.

Vaid, J., & Corina, D. (1985, June). *Visual field asymmetries in numerical size judgments for digits, words, and ASL.* Paper presented at International Neuropsychological Society, Copenhagen.

Vaid, J., & Genesee, F. (1980). Neuropsychological approaches to bilingualism: A critical review. *Canadian Journal of Psychology, 34,* 417–445.

Vargha-Khadem, F. (1982). Hemispheric specialization for the processing of tactual stimuli in congenitally deaf and hearing children. *Cortex, 18,* 277–286.

Vargha-Khadem, F. (1983). Visual field asymmetries in congenitally deaf and hearing children. *British Journal of Developmental Psychology 1,* 375–387.

Vogt-Svendsen, M. (1983). Positions and movements of the mouth in Norwegian Sign Language (NSL). In J. Kyle & B. Woll (Eds.), *Language in sign* (pp. 85–96). London: Croom Helm.

Von Tetzchner, S. (1984). First signs acquired by a Norwegian deaf child of deaf parents. *Sign Language Studies, 44,* 225–257.

Wallin, L. (1983). Compounds in Swedish Sign Language in historical perspective. In J. Kyle & B. Woll (Eds.), *Language in sign* (pp. 56–68). London: Croom Helm.

Wilbur, R. (1976). Linguistics of manual languages and manual systems. In L. Lloyd (Ed.), *Communication assessment and intervention strategies.* Baltimore, MD: University Park Press.

Wilbur, R., & Jones, M. (1974, April). *Some aspects of the acquisition of American Sign Language and English by three hearing children of deaf parents.* Paper presented at The Tenth Regional Meeting, Chicago Linguistic Society.

Woll, B. (1983). The semantics of British Sign Language. In J. Kyle & B. Woll (Eds.), *Language in sign* (pp. 41–55). London: Croom Helm.

Woodward, J. (1973). Some observations on sociolinguistic variation and American Sign Language. *Kansas Journal of Sociology, 9,* 191–200.

Woodward, J. (1980). Some sociolinguistic aspects of French and American sign languages. In H. Lane & F. Grosjean (Eds.), *Recent perspectives on American Sign Language* (pp. 103–118). Hillsdale, NJ: Lawrence Erlbaum Associates.

Zaitseva, G. (1983). The sign language of th deaf as a colloquial system. In J. Kyle & B. Woll (Eds.), *Language in sign* (pp. 77–84). London: Croom Helm.

# 13 Script Effects and Cerebral Lateralization: The Case of Chinese Characters

Reiko Hasuike
*Princeton University*
Ovid Tzeng
Daisy Hung
*University of California, Riverside*
*The Salk Institute, San Diego*

The invention of written symbols to represent speech must be regarded as one of the most important cultural developments in history. With these written symbols, language at last overcame the limitations of time and space. While all humans learn to speak effortlessly and naturally, learning to read has never been easy regardless of the type of orthography used. In fact, in most literate societies there are people who cannot master this skill.

For those who do learn to read, there remains the question of whether the information processing system is modified in such a way that it can meet the various cognitive demands imposed by the particular writing system. There is evidence that preliterate children cannot readily count the number of syllables in English words (Liberman & Shankweiler, 1979). Illiterate adults are much worse than literate adults at performing operations such as adding or deleting a consonant at the beginning of a nonword (Morais, Cary, Alegria, & Bertelson, 1979). Cole and Scribner (1981) found that adults literate in Vai, a syllabic script, performed better than illiterates on an auditory integration task involving comprehension and recall of Vai sentences parsed into syllables. Thus, an apparent consequence of learning to read a script is an enhancement of the implicit knowledge of the segmental structure of the corresponding spoken language.

Among the many writing systems existing in the world today, Chinese characters are unique in that their relationship with the spoken language they transcribe is rather opaque. The relationship can be described as morphosyllabic in nature. However, the characters and the syllables do not have a one-to-one correspondence. The same syllable may be represented by different characters which have different meanings.

There is another unique aspect of Chinese characters that needs mention. Centuries ago, these characters were adopted by the Koreans, the Japanese, and the Vietnamese to become their respective national writing systems. The sound systems of these languages are quite different from Chinese, and there were major problems in adopting the Chinese writing system to transcribe their spoken languages. Today, North Korea and Vietnam have dropped the use of Chinese characters altogether and opted for an alphabetic system. However, South Korea and Japan maintained Chinese characters and created sound-based systems (Hangul alphabet for Korean and kana syllabaries for Japanese) to overcome the problem of a mismatch between the writing and the sound system. This unique historical development provides an opportunity to study the effects of orthographic variations on visual information processing within and across languages (Hung & Tzeng, 1981; Morton & Sasanuma, 1984).

Chinese characters now number in the thousands, and their configurations are often quite complex (Hung & Tzeng, 1981; Wang, 1981). Indeed, there is evidence to suggest that expertise in reading Chinese characters may confer an advantage on certain nonverbal tasks requiring visuospatial processing. Mann (1984) observed that American good and poor grade school readers did not differ in their ability to memorize nonsense figures. However, Japanese good readers of the same age were significantly better than Japanese poor readers on this nonverbal task. Moreover, the performance of the Japanese readers on this task correlated with their ability to read kanji (Chinese characters) but not kana. Mann interpreted this finding as evidence for a special graphomotoric coding scheme in reading kanji. Studies with adults have reported that fluent readers of Chinese perform better in memory tasks under visual than auditory presentation, whereas American readers perform better under auditory presentation conditions (Fang, Tzeng, & Alva, 1981; Turnage & McGinnies, 1973).

Studies such as the above (see also Tsao, Wu, & Feustel, 1981) have prompted researchers to investigate whether the presumed enhancement of visuomotoric coding of Chinese characters is reflected at the neuropsychological level in greater right hemisphere activity in processing this type of script. A related question that has been raised is whether readers of Japanese or Korean (who possess two contrasting types of script mapped onto one spoken language) process Chinese characters in the same way as do native readers of Chinese (who have only one script).

Studies with Japanese and Chinese readers suggest positive answers to both these questions. Japanese aphasic patients are reported to be more likely to be impaired in reading kanji (Chinese characters) than kana. In brain-intact Japanese individuals, a right visual field (left hemisphere) advantage has been reported for processing kana and a left visual field (right hemisphere) advantage for processing kanji (Hatta, 1977a; Sasanuma, Itoh, Mori, & Kobayashi, 1977).

In contrast, native readers of Chinese tend to show a right visual field advantage for processing Chinese characters (Besner, Daniels, & Slade, 1982; Hardyck, Tzeng, & Wang, 1977).

In what follows, we provide a critical review of both the clinical and the normative literature on script variations and cerebral lateralization, with particular reference to the Japanese and Chinese literature. We argue that one must be extremely cautious about drawing conclusions about differential lateralization of kana and kanji from the studies to date.

## EVIDENCE FROM CLINICAL STUDIES

*Separate Brain Centers for Different Scripts.* The idea that brain functioning may be related to the type of script used is not new. Dejerine, cited in Hécaen and Kremin (1976), a 19th century investigator of dyslexia, had put forth a theory in which he distinguished the "center for visual images of letters" from the "center serving their interpretation." He speculated that separation of these two centers would result in a special type of neurological syndrome, which he called "pure alexia." Patients with this syndrome were expected to show an impairment in reading words while maintaining an ability to read numerals. Hinshelwood (1899) described five patients who could not name letters or words yet were able to read numerals quite successfully. His interpretation of this selective impairment was that these different types of reading were controlled by separate brain centers. In fact, in a later book, Hinshelwood (1917) claimed that the ideal therapy for patients with the syndrome of word-blindness was to teach them Chinese characters because, according to him, Chinese was a script in which each word was represented by a different symbol. Interestingly, almost 50 years later, a group of dyslexic children in Philadelphia were reported to have been successfully taught to read English represented in Chinese characters (Rozin, Poritsky, & Stotsky, 1971; but see Tzeng & Hung, 1980 for a critique of this study).

*Dual-Processing Account of Reading.* The notion of separate brain centers for different script representations was not without criticism (e.g., Lenneberg, 1967). After all, the failure of phrenology had not been forgotten. However, cases in which successful reading of numbers were coupled with a severe impairment in reading alphabetic materials continued to be seen (Benson & Geschwind, 1969; Hécaen & Kremin, 1976; Luria, 1970). These data demanded an interpretation. Rather than focusing on a strictly compartmental view, the new interpretation emphasized processing differences. Selective impairments in reading different types of written material were thought to substantiate the existence of two different neurolinguistic pathways in reading: a phonologically mediated mechanism, which was thought to underlie the reading of a sound-based script, and a holistic-configurational mechanism, thought to underlie the reading of so-called ideographic script. Clinical evidence that the isolated right hemisphere can read, even though it is unable to perform phonological operations, was used to support such a dual-process account (Marshall & Newcombe, 1973; Zaidel & Peters, 1981).

*Differential Intrahemispheric Representation of Script in Bilinguals.* The issue of the effects of script variations on hemispheric organization has also been discussed in relation to the brain organization of language in bilinguals (Vaid, 1983). It was hypothesized that in readers of two scripts that differed in their degree of sound-symbol correspondence, damage to a particular region of the brain would result in a differential pattern of reading and writing impairments of the two scripts. Luria (1960) described a French-Russian bilingual who, after a left inferior parietal lesion, showed a greater impairment in writing French than Russian (presumably due to the less direct sound-symbol correspondence in French). In a similar vein, the report of a Chinese-English bilingual who, following a left parieto-occipital injury, showed greater impairment in the recognition of written Chinese than English was also taken to support the notion of script-related differences in the brain organization of language in bilinguals (Lyman, Kwan, & Chao, 1938). A general principle seems to emerge from these and other studies, suggesting that lesions in the temporal cortex are associated with greater impairment of reading/writing of languages that are sound-based (see de Agostini, 1977; Peuser & Leischner, 1974), whereas lesions in the posterior, parieto-occipital cortical areas are associated with a greater impairment in reading and writing of scripts with a logographic or irregular phonetic base (see Newcombe, cited in Critchley, 1974).

Data from these bilingual case studies are illuminating, However, the studies are limited by a lack of appropriate control over the degree of impairment in the patient's spoken languages. In this respect, the studies of Sasanuma and colleagues with Japanese bi-scriptual readers may provide the most definitive evidence on the issue of script effects on cerebral lateralization, since patients in these studies used two types of scripts, but spoke only one language.

In the following section, we provide a brief overview of clinical and normative studies with Japanese and Chinese subjects (a comprehensive review of the Japanese literature is presented in Paradis, Hagiwara, & Hildebrandt, 1985). In particular, we examine the question of why Japanese readers seem to show a different pattern than Chinese readers in their patterns of hemispheric specialization for Chinese characters.

*Aphasia in Readers of Japanese.* As early as 1914, Asayama (cited in Lyman et al., 1938) described a single case in which the patient's comprehension as well as writing of kanji was much better than that in kana. This observation was consistent with a comment by Beasly (cited in Geschwind, 1971), who concluded that Japanese aphasics' comprehension of kana was usually more severely affected than their comprehension of kanji. This observation has subsequently been replicated. Among the 378 aphasics surveyed by Sasanuma (1975), a majority showed a selective impairment of kana reading. Cases of kanji sparing have also been reported by other investigators (Sugishita, Iwata, Toyokura, Yoshioka, & Yamada, 1978; Yamadori, 1975).

Both Asayama and Beasly attributed this difference to the fact that phonetic mediation is not required to read kanji. Sasanuma (1975) similarly argues that the primary difference between reading the kanji and kana scripts is the necessity of a phonological processor for the latter, needed to mediate the grapheme-sound-meaning correspondence. Sasanuma and colleagues (Sasanuma, 1975, 1980; Sasanuma & Fujimura, 1971; Tatsumi, Itoh, Konno, Sasanuma, & Fujisaku, 1982) interpreted their findings as reflecting a differential disruption of language following localized lesions within the left hemisphere. However, Beasly (in Geschwind, 1971) and others have claimed that the right hemisphere is specialized to process kanji and the left hemisphere for kana.

There are three problems with the claim that the right hemisphere is involved in the processing of kanji. The first is that some left hemisphere-damaged aphasics are reported to be selectively impaired in reading kanji. In fact, Tatsumi et al. (1982) showed that the majority of their seventeen patients (including Broca's aphasics) could identify kana symbols more easily than kanji ones. This pattern of results conflicts with their earlier study (Sasanuma & Fujimura, 1971). The authors claim that the discrepancy may be due to the difference in testing conditions. However, it would appear that the earlier findings of kanji sparing despite a severe impairment of kana cannot and should not be taken as definitive evidence for right hemisphere processing of kanji.

The second problem with the claim of right hemisphere mediation of kanji characters is the lack of strong evidence for a relationship between right hemisphere damage and impairment of kanji. Of the 60 cases, since 1901, of dyslexia in Japanese readers (reviewed by Paradis et al., 1985), five had right hemisphere damage. Of these five, only one patient performed better with kana than with kanji (Okamoto, 1948). Three cases showed better performance with kanji than with kana (Aoki, 1930; Imura, Asawaka, Hotta, & Nihonmatsu, 1959; Miura, 1934), and one showed no difference between the two (Hirose, Kin, & Murakami, 1977).

Finally, there are a few cases where there is a differential impairment of kanji and another type of "ideographic" script, namely, numerals. Yamadori (1975) described a patient who could not read numbers while his ability to read kanji was preserved. Sasanuma and Monoi (1975) described a patient who could name Arabic numerals but had great difficulty reading kanji characters. Similarly, Lyman et al.'s (1938) Chinese patient could not read Chinese but could recognize numbers. It would appear that the nature of ''ideographic processing'' needs to be more carefully delineated before it can be assigned to the right hemisphere.

In summary, the evidence for right hemisphere mediation of kanji characters based on clinical data is rather weak; there has been only one case of selective impairment in kanji recognition following right hemisphere damage.

## Evidence from Experimental Studies

Before the 1970s, there seemed to be no disagreement about the role of the left hemisphere for processing Chinese characters. The only exception was Beasley's review in which right hemisphere processing of kanji characters seemed to be implicated. However, as we have discussed above, the clinical data clearly point to the left hemisphere as the site for processing language, regardless of whether it is the spoken language or the written script. However, some papers published in the late 1970s attracted much attention because they pointed to right hemisphere involvement in reading kanji.

*Visual Half-Field Experiments with Readers of Japanese.* The first study was by Hatta (1977a), who showed that native readers of Japanese identified singly presented kanji characters better when they were presented in the left visual field than in the right visual field. In his previous study (Hatta, 1976; see also Hirata & Osaka, 1967), a reverse pattern had been observed for the identification of kana symbols. Hatta's new finding was in accord with results obtained by Sasanuma et al. (1977). These researchers presented nonsensical two-character kana and kanji words to native Japanese readers and found a significant right visual field superiority for the recognition of kana symbols and a nonsignificant left visual field superiority for kanji characters.

In a similar vein, Sugishita et al. (1978) reported three cases and Watanabe, Hojo, Sato, Sakurada, Tanaka, and Shimoyama (1979) described two cases of patients who had undergone surgical section of the splenium of the corpus callosum, thus partially isolating the two hemispheres. Careful examination of the performance of these five patients on a visual hemi-field paradigm to compare the recognition of kanji and kana characters presented directly to the right or left hemisphere revealed minimal recognition of kanji in the right hemisphere.

These findings were interpreted as evidence for right hemisphere involvement in processing kanji characters (Hatta, 1980).

*Visual Half-field Experiments with Readers of Chinese.* Using a standard tachistoscopic visual half-field presentation with Chinese brain-intact subjects, Hardyck, Tzeng, and Wang (1977, 1978) obtained a right visual field superiority for the recognition of Chinese characters. A similar effect was reported by Kershner and Jeng (1972) and by Besner et al. (1982).

## The Controversy

As reviewed above, laterality studies with Japanese subjects and those with Chinese subjects conflict in their patterns of asymmetry observed for Chinese character recognition. The discrepancy between the Japanese and the Chinese results could be attributed to the existence of two different scripts mapped onto one spoken language in the former case, resulting perhaps in a heightened contrast in the processing of the two scripts among Japanese readers. However, an alternative explanation must also be considered, in terms of methodological differences between the two sets of studies.

*Methodological Issues.* One variable that has been shown to influence patterns of visual field asymmetries in laterality studies with monolinguals is the angle of stimulus presentation (see Sergent, 1982a, 1982b). A larger angle of exposure is thought to magnify the left visual field (right hemisphere) advantage. However, this factor has not been considered as influencing the results in Japanese studies. Yet it is to be noted that Hatta's (1977a) study used a fairly large angle of exposure (4.01 degrees).

Exposure duration is also believed to influence the pattern of visual field asymmetries. Brief exposure durations result in an incomplete visual image with a very low spatial resolution. The right hemisphere may be particularly adept at perceiving the relationship between fragmentary components and the whole configuration (Hellige, 1980; Sergent, 1983). When the stimulus is presented for a longer exposure, spatial resolution is better. Under such conditions, the left hemisphere seems to take charge, especially when the task requires further linguistic analysis. When one considers the range of exposure durations in the Japanese laterality studies (see Fig. 13.1), it becomes clear that a left visual field superiority was found only in those studies in which the exposure duration was less than 50 msecs.

An additional variable that seems relevant was highlighted by Tzeng, Hung, Cotton, and Wang (1979), who noted that studies that obtained a left visual field superiority presented either a single character at a time (Hatta, 1977a) or two nonsense characters (Sasanuma et al., 1977). In contrast, those studies that obtained a right visual field superiority presented two-character meaningful words as their stimuli. Tzeng et al. (1979) manipulated the number of Chinese characters in two experiments with readers of Chinese and found a left visual field superiority for recognition of single characters and a right visual field superiority for two-character word recognition. Hatta (1978) similarly obtained a right visual field superiority for the recognition of two-character meaningful kanji words. Given such consistent findings of a right visual field superiority for processing two-character words across the two language populations, it is curious to note that Hatta (1981) and others still maintain that the right hemisphere is specialized for processing kanji or Chinese characters.

KEY TO STUDIES CITED IN FIGURE 13.1

| Study Number | Authors and Year of Publication |
|---|---|
| 1 | Besner, Daniel, & Slade (1982, Exp. 2) |
| 2 | Cheng & Fu (1984, Exp. 1) |
| 3 | Elman, Takahashi, & Tohsaku (1981a, Exp. 2) |
| 4 | Elman, Takahashi, & Tohsaku (1981b) |
| 5 | Hardyck, Tzeng, & Wang (1978) |
| 6 | Hatta (1977a) |
| 7 | Hatta (1977b) |
| 8 | Hatta (1978, Exp. 1) |
| 9 | Hatta (1979) |
| 10 | Hatta (1980) |
| 11 | Hatta (1981) |
| 12 | Hayashi & Hatta (1978) |
| 13 | Huang & Jones (1980) |
| 14 | Kershner & Jeng (1972) |
| 15 | Nguy, Allard, & Bryden (1980) |
| 16 | Sasanuma, Itoh, Kobayashi, & Mori (1980) |
| 17 | Sasanuma, Itoh, Mori, & Kobayashi (1977) |
| 18 | Tsao, Wu, & Feustel (1981) |
| 19 | Tzeng, Hung, Cotton, & Wang (1979, Exp. 1) |
| 20 | Tzeng, Hung, Cotton, & Wang (1979, Exp. 2) |

LVF Superiority
8
7
6
2 3 19 13 11[a]
No visual field differences
17
RVF Superiority
20
18
14
12
10
15 9
1 16 4 5
10 20 30 40 50 60 70 80 90 100 and up
STIMULUS EXPOSURE DURATION (in msecs)

[a]This experiment used a nonstandard measure of visual field asymmetries (a Stroop Color Word Interference Test).

FIG. 13.1. Visual field asymmetries as a function of stimulus exposure duration: A survey of twenty studies with Chinese characters as stimuli.

Japanese visual half-field studies which compare kana and kanji processing have a serious problem of keeping the number of symbols constant because kana transcription usually consists of more characters than its kanji counterpart. As discussed above, the use of single versus two or more kanji characters appears to have different consequences for lateralization patterns. Whether a similar effect occurs with two-character and single-character kana stimuli has not been studied, but it may be an interesting question for further research.

Other methodological problems related to the stimulus materials include stimulus familiarity, concreteness and the type of characters used. Hung and Tzeng (1981) discuss the arbitrary selection of characters which are termed "common" or "pictorial" characters. Paradis et al. (1985) note that familiarity cannot be easily defined because familiarity of a spoken word is not necessarily the same as that of the written symbols used to represent the word.

## Resolution

After Tzeng et al. (1979) argued against the claim that the right hemisphere is specialized for the linguistic analysis of Chinese characters, a number of studies found that a left visual field superiority in the processing of singly presented characters could only be obtained under very specific conditions (Elman, Takahashi, & Tohsaku, 1981a, 1981b; Nguy, Allard, & Bryden, 1980).

A particularly relevant study was conducted by Cheng and Fu (1984). In 1975, Krueger had demonstrated a right visual field advantage for the word superiority effect in readers of English. In Cheng and Fu's study, the analogue in Chinese to a word-superiority effect was also obtained only in the right visual field. This result suggests that Chinese characters are treated as meaningful words only in the left hemisphere. A character-superiority effect was demonstrated in the left visual field (Cheng & Fu, 1984). This latter effect may simply indicate that the perception of a single character is better in the left visual field than in the right visual field.

The above findings suggest that successful visuo-spatial transformation in the right hemisphere requires the presence of a preplanned organization of some familiar patterns. As long as there is some organization, fragmentary sensory data can be picked up by the right hemisphere under degraded visual presentation and become integrated into a meaningful whole. In this sense, the occasionally observed left visual field superiority in recognizing Chinese characters in visual half-field experiments does not show any script-specific property in higher cortical function.

## Conclusion

As we have seen above, research in the area of script variations and cerebral lateralization has produced conflicting data which are difficult to interpret. Dejerine and Hinshelwood in the 19th century (see Hécaen & Kremin, 1976) as well as Luria and others in this century have studied bilingual aphasic patients who showed selective impairment of one type of script while preserving the ability to read and write another type of script. More recently, some Japanese aphasic patients are reported to have selective impairment of kana symbols while preserving the use of kanji. These clinical data together with experimental data from visual half-field experiments have been taken to argue that a sound-based script is processed in the left hemisphere whereas Chinese/kanji characters are processed in the right hemisphere. In this chapter, we have pointed out how weak the clinical evidence for this claim is and how many of the experimental studies suffer from methodological problems. In the last few years, a critical evaluation of those past studies has begun to appear (Hung & Tzeng, 1981; Paradis et al., 1985), and new directions have been suggested for further research in this area.

At this point it may be in order to raise the issue of the properties of Chinese characters which distinguish them from sound-based scripts such as alphabets. In the past, the main difference between sound-based script and Chinese characters was considered to be the degree of grapheme-to-sound correspondence. The interpretation of selective impairment of kana rather than kanji has focused on the possibility of bypassing grapheme-to-sound conversion in the case of Chinese characters. Chinese characters are different from alphabets or syllabaries in that they do not have to undergo this conversion. Some investigators have attributed this difference to the iconicity of Chinese characters (Lecours, Basso, Moraschini, & Nespoulous, 1984). However, this view mistakenly assumes that Chinese characters are all pictographic. Hung and Tzeng (1981) and Wang (1981) present strong arguments against such a view. They point out that over 90% of Chinese characters are in fact phonograms rather than pictograms. This fact also argues against the view that Chinese characters can bypass grapheme-to-sound conversion.

It is true that the relationship between script and speech is not as clear with Chinese phonograms as it is with certain alphabetic scripts. It is also true that linguistic properties do not necessarily imply certain modes of psychological processing. There has been sufficient evidence (see Hung & Tzeng, 1981) to show that reading sentences written in Chinese characters involves the process of speech recoding as much as reading sentences written in alphabets does. Furthermore, recent studies by Fang and Horng (1984) and Hung, Tzeng, Salzman, and Dreher (1984) suggest that the activation-synthesis model of naming words, as proposed by Glushko (1979) for English, applies equally well to naming Chinese characters. Instead of grapheme-to-sound conversion, naming by analogy seems to be a better explanation for the results obtained in these studies. Thus, Chinese characters and other types of scripts appear to show more similarities than differences in terms of the way printed symbols are transformed into linguistic codes.

The selective impairment of different types of scripts reported in the studies of Japanese aphasic patients needs to be explained. Since we have argued that there is no strong evidence to support the claim that the kanji characters are processed in the right hemisphere, we have to look for other interpretations. At present, we do not have any plausible interpretations to account for this selective impairment. It may be due to the different degree of learning involved, as suggested by Hung and Tzeng (1981): Chinese characters are visually more complex, and the number of characters to be learned increases exponentially each year at the beginning reading stage. Beginning readers of Chinese spend much more time learning Chinese characters than do children who are learning alphabets. Moreover, the complexity and vast number of characters to be memorized may force them to search for various mnemonics such as the graphomotoric coding strategy mentioned by Mann (1984) in order not to overload the visual information processing system. Japanese children learn kana symbols first, and then they begin to learn kanji. They have to spend much more time learning kanji than kana, and the learning of kanji characters continues for at least 10 years or more. At this point, we do not know how such a difference in the learning process may affect the way different scripts are coded and represented in the brain.

In conclusion, we would like to suggest the need for more research in the following four areas. The first is in the area of orthography; there is a need for a comprehensive theory of script capable of explaining the relationship between script and speech. Turvey (1984), following the tradition of his associates at Haskins Laboratories, has employed the concept of "depth of orthography" to specify this relationship; similarly, Wang (1981) has used the concept of an "optimal orthography" based on the way in which the relationship between script and speech is captured in a two-dimensional array. The second area for future research is the process of perceptual learning. We need to understand the perceptual and cognitive capacity of beginning readers and how they learn to deal with the requirements which have been imposed upon them by the writing system. The third area is in the understanding of reading behavior. We need a comprehensive theory which specifies various components of reading and explains the way these components interact with other conditions such as the nature and presentation of the reading materials and the nature of the task. Finally, the neural basis of mechanisms of reading needs to be investigated in both normal and aphasic populations. Coltheart, Patterson, and Marshall (1980) wrote, "Brains may be similar from one culture to another but orthographies certainly are not" (p. viii). The relationship between writing systems and the brain cannot be studied without taking all these dimensions into consideration.

## ACKNOWLEDGMENTS

We would like to thank William Wang for useful comments on earlier drafts of this chapter, and Jyotsna Vaid for her editorial revisions.

## REFERENCES


Aoki, G. (1930). Shitsugoshoo ni kansuru chikenhoi. *Seishin Shinkeigaku Zasshi, 65,* 818.

Benson, D. F., & Geschwind, N. (1969). The alexias. In P. U. Vinkel & G. W. Bruyn (Eds.), *Handbook of clinical neurology* (Vol. 1). Amsterdam: North Holland.

Besner, D., Daniels, S., & Slade, C. (1982). Ideogram reading and right hemisphere language. *British Journal of Psychology, 73,* 21–28.

Cheng, C.-M., & Fu, G.-L. (1984, July). *The recognition of Chinese characters and words under divided visual field presentation.* Paper presented at the Third International Symposium on Psychological Aspects of the Chinese Language. Hong Kong.

Cole, M., & Scribner, S. (1981). *Psychology of literacy,* Cambridge, MA: Harvard University Press.

Coltheart, M., Patterson, K., & Marshall, J. C. (Eds.). (1980). *Deep dyslexia.* London: Routledge and Kegan Paul.

Critchley, M. (1974). Aphasia in polyglots and bilinguals. *Brain and Language, 1,* 15–27.

de Agostini, M. (1977). A propos de l'agraphie des aphasiques sensoriels: Etude comparative Italien–Francais. *Language, 47,* 120–130.

Elman, J. L., Takahashi, K., & Tohsaku, Y.-H. (1981a). Asymmetries for the categorization of kanji nouns, adjectives, and verbs presented to the left and right visual fields. *Brain and Language, 13,* 290–300.

Elman, J. L., Takahashi, K., & Tohsaku, Y.-H. (1981b). Lateral asymmetries for the identification of concrete and abstract kanji. *Neuropsychologia, 19,* 407–412.

Fang, S.-P., & Horng, R.-Y. (1984, July). *Consistency effects in naming real and pseudo Chinese characters.* Paper presented at the Third International Symposium on Psychological Aspects of the Chinese Language. Hong Kong.

Fang, S.-P., & Tzeng, O. J. L., & Alva, L. (1981). Intralanguage vs. interlanguage Stroop effects in two types of writing systems. *Memory and Cognition, 9,* 609–617.

Geschwind, N. (1971). Dyslexia. *Science, 173,* 190.

Glushko, R. J. (1979). The organization and activation of orthographic knowledge in reading aloud. *Journal of Experimental Psychology: Human Perception and Performance, 5,* 574–691.

Hardyck, C., Tzeng, O. J. L., & Wang, W. S-Y. (1977). Cerebral lateralization effects in visual half-field experiments. *Nature, 269,* 705–707.

Hardyck, C., Tzeng, O. J. L., & Wang, W. S-Y. (1978). Cerebral lateralization of function and bilingual decision processes: Is thinking lateralized? *Brain and Language, 5,* 56–71.

Hatta, T. (1976). Asynchrony of lateral onset as a factor in difference in visual field. *Perceptual and Motor Skills, 42,* 163–66.

Hatta, T. (1977a). Recognition of Japanese kanji in the left and right visual fields. *Neuropsychologia, 15,* 685–688.

Hatta, T. (1977b). Lateral recognition of abstract and concrete kanji in Japanese. *Perceptual and Motor Skills, 45,* 731–734.

Hatta, T. (1978). Recognition of Japanese kanji and hiragana in the left and right visual fields. *Japanese Psychological Research, 20,* 51–59.

Hatta, T. (1979). Hemispheric asymmetries for physical and semantic congruency matching of visually presented kanji stimuli *The Japanese Journal of Psychology, 50,* 273–278.

Hatta, T. (1980). Kanji processing levels and cerebral hemisphere differences. *Annals of Osaka University of Education IV.29.1,*7–14.

Hatta, T. (1981). Differential processing of kanji and kana stimuli in Japanese people: Some implications from Stroop-test results. *Neuropsychologia, 19,* 87–93.

Hayashi, R., & Hatta, T. (1978). Hemispheric differences in mental rotation task with kanji stimuli. *Psychologia, 21,* 210–215.

Hécaen, H., & Kremin, H. (1976). Neurolinguistic research on reading disorders resulting from left hemisphere lesions: Aphasia and "pure" alexia. In H. Whitaker & H. A. Whitaker (Eds.), *Studies in neurolinguistics* (Vol. 2). New York and London: Academic Press.

Hellige, J. B. (1980). Cerebral hemisphere asymmetry: Methods, issues, and implications. *Educational Communication and Technology, 28,* 83–98.

Hinshelwood, J. (1899). *Letter, word, and word-blindness.* London: Lewis.

Hinshelwood, J. (1917). *Congenital word-blindness.* London: Lewis.

Hirata, K., & Osaka, R. (1967). Tachistoscopic recognition of Japanese letter material in left and right visual fields. *Psychologia, 10,* 7–18.

Hirose, G., Kin, T., & Murakami, E. (1977). Alexia without agraphia associated with right occipital lesion. *Journal of Neurology, Neurosurgery, and Psychiatry, 40,* 225–227.

Huang, Y. L., & Jones, B. (1980). Naming and discrimination of Chinese ideograms presented in the right and left visual fields. *Neuropsychologia, 18,* 703–706.

Hung, D. L., & Tzeng, O. J. L. (1981). Orthographic variations and visual information processing. *Psychological Bulletin, 90,* 377–414.

Hung, D. L., Tzeng, O. J. L., Salzman, B., & Dreher, J. (1984). A united evaluation of the horse-racing model of skilled reading. In H. S. R. Kao & R. Hoosain (Eds.), *Psychological studies of the Chinese language.* Hong Kong: Language Society of Hong Kong.

Imura, T., Asakawa, K., Hotta, S., & Nihonmatsu, S. (1959). Koosasei shitsugo no ichirei. *Seishin Shinkeigaku Zasshi, 61.* (Reprinted in Imura, T. 1967. *Seishin igaku kenkyuu, Vol. 2.,* Tokyo: Misuzu Shoboo.)

Kershner, J. R., & Jeng, G.-R. (1972). Dual functional hemisphere asymmetry in visual perception: Effects of ocular dominance and post-exposural processes. *Neuropsychologia, 10,* 437·

Krueger, L. E. (1975). The word superiority effect: Is its locus visual-spatial or verbal? *Bulletin of the Psychonomic Society, 6,* 465–468.

Lecours, A. R., Basso, A., Moraschini, S., & Nespoulous, J-L. (1984). In D. Caplan, A. R. Lecours, & A. Smith (Eds.), *Biological perspectives on language.* Cambridge, MA: MIT Press.

Lenneberg, E. H. (1967). *Biological foundations of language.* New York: Wiley.

Liberman, I. Y., & Shankweiler, D. (1979). Speech, the alphabet, and teaching to read. In L. Resnick & P. Weaver (Eds.), *Theory and practice of early reading.* Hillsdale, NJ: Lawrence Erlbaum Associates.

Luria, A. R. (1960). Differences between disturbance of speech and writing in Russian and French. *International Journal of Slavic Linguistics and Poetics, 3,* 13–22.

Luria, A. R. (1970). *Traumatic aphasia.* The Hague: Mouton.

Lyman, R., Kwan, S. & Chao, W. (1938). Left occipito-parietal brain tumor with observations on alexia and agraphia in Chinese and English. *Chinese Medical Journal, 54,* 491–516.

Mann, V. A. (1984, July). *The relation between temporary phonetic memory and the acquisition of Japanese Kana and Kanji.* Paper presented at the third International Symposium on Psychological Aspects of the Chinese Language. Hong Kong.

Marshall, J. C., & Newcombe, F. (1973). Patterns of paralexia: A psycholinguistic approach. *Journal of Psycholinguistic Research, 2,* 175–199.

Miura, K. (1934). Choohihitsusei shitsugoshoo no chiken hoi. *Seishin Shinkeigaku Zasshi, 37,* 757–793.

Morais, J., Cary, L., Alegria, J., & Bertelson, P. (1979). Does awareness of speech as a sequence of phones arise spontaneously? *Cognition, 7,* 323–331.

Morton, J., & Sasanuma, S. (1984). Lexical access in Japanese. In L. Henderson (Ed.), *Orthographies and reading,* Hillsdale, NJ: Lawrence Erlbaum Associates.

Nguy, T., Allard, F., & Bryden, M. P. (1980). Laterality effects for Chinese characters: Differences between pictorial and nonpictorial characters. *Canadian Journal of Psychology, 34,* 270–273.

Okamoto, S. (1948). Shitsusho shitsudoku keisanshoogai o shushookoo to seru ichi shitsudokushoorei no bunseki. *shinri, 4,* 33–43.

Paradis, M., Hagiwara, H., & Hildebrandt, N. (1985). *Neurolinguistic aspects of the Japanese writing system.* New York and London: Academic Press.

Peuser, G., & Leischner, A. (1974). Impairments of phonetic script in an aphasic. *Neuropsychologia, 12,* 557–560.

Rozin, P., Poritsky, S., & Stotsky, R. (1971). American children with reading problems can easily learn to read English represented by Chinese characters. *Science, 171,* 1264–1267.

Sasanuma, S. (1975). Kana and Kanji processing in Japanese aphasics. *Brain and Language, 2,* 360–383.

Sasanuma, S. (1980). Acquired dyslexia in Japanese: Clinical features and underlying mechanisms. In M. Coltheart, K., Patterson, & J. C. Marshall (Eds.), *Deep dyslexia.* London: Routledge and Kegan Paul.

Sasanuma, S., & Fujimura, O. (1971). Selective impairment of phonetic and nonphonetic transcription of words in Japanese aphasic patients: Kana vs. Kanji in visual recognition and writing. *Cortex, 7,* 1–18.

Sasanuma, S., Itoh, M., Kobayashi, Y., & Mori, K. (1980). The nature of the task-stimulus interaction in the tachistoscopic recognition of kana and kanji words. *Brain and Language, 9,* 298–306.

Sasanuma, S., Itoh, M., Mori, K., & Kobayashi, Y. (1977). Tachistoscopic recognition of kana and kanji words. *Neuropsychologia, 15,* 547–553.

Sasanuma, S., & Monoi, H. (1975). The syndrome of Gogi (word-meaning) aphasia: Selective impairment of Kanji processing. *Neurology, 25,* 627–632.

Sergent, J. (1982a). Methodological and theoretical consequences of variations in exposure duration in visual laterality studies. *Perception & Psychophysics, 31,* 451–461.

Sergent, J. (1982b). Basic determinants in visual-field effects with special reference to the Hannay et al. (1981) study. *Brain and Language, 16,* 158–164.

Sergent, J. (1983). Role of the input in visual hemispheric asymmetries. *Psychological Bulletin, 93,* 481–512.

Sugishita, M., Iwata, M., Toyokura, Y., Yoshioka, M., & Yamada, R. (1978). Reading of ideograms and phonograms in Japanese patients after partial commissurotomy. *Neuropsychologia, 16,* 417–426.

Tatsumi, I. F., Itoh, M., Konno, K., Sasanuma, S., & Fujisaku, H. (1982). Identification of speech, kana, and kanji, and the span of short-term memory for auditorily and visually presented stimuli in aphasic patients. *Annual Bulletin of R. I. L. P., 16,* 205–218.

Tsao, Y.-C., Wu, W.-F., & Feustel, T. (1981). Stroop interference: Hemispheric dominance in Chinese speakers. *Brain and Language, 13,* 372–378.

Turnage, T. W., & McGinnies, E. (1973). A cross-cultural comparison of the effects of presentation mode and meaningfulness of short-term recall. *American Journal of Psychology, 86,* 369–382.

Turvey, M. T. (1984, July). *Investigations in a phonologically shallow orthography.* Paper presented at the Third International Symposium on Psychological Aspects of the Chinese Language. Hong Kong.

Tzeng, O. J. L., & Hung, D. L. (1980). Reading in the nonalphabet writing system: Some experimental studies. In J. F. Kavanaugh & R. L. Venezky (Eds.), *Orthography, reading, and dyslexia.* Baltimore, MD: University Park Press.

Tzeng, O. J. L., Hung, D. L., Cotton, B., & Wang, W. S-Y. (1979). Visual lateralization effect in reading Chinese characters. *Nature, 282,* 499–501.

Vaid, J. (1983). Bilingualism and brain lateralization. In S. Segalowitz (Ed.), *Language functions and brain organization.* New York and London: Academic Press.

Wang, W. S-Y. (1981). Language structure and optimal orthography. In O. J. L. Tzeng & H. Singer (Eds.), *Perception of print: Reading research in experimental psychology.* Hillsdale, NJ: Lawrence Erlbaum Associates.

Watanabe, S., Hojo, K., Sato, T., Sakurada, T., Tanaka, T., & Shimoyama, M. (1979). Neurological studies of two subjects after the intersection of splenium of the corpus callosum. *Nohshinkei, 31,* 837–842.

Yamadori, A. (1975). Ideogram reading in alexia. *Brain, 98,* 231–238.

Zaidel, F., & Peters, A. M. (1981). Phonological encoding and ideographic reading by the disconnected right hemisphere: Two case studies. *Brain and Language, 14,* 205–234.

# Author Index

## M



## N



## O

P



Q



R



S

## T



## U



## V

# Subject Index

## E



## H



## I



## L



## M